# Jiu Jiu

Vol. 2

Story & Art by
Touya Tobina

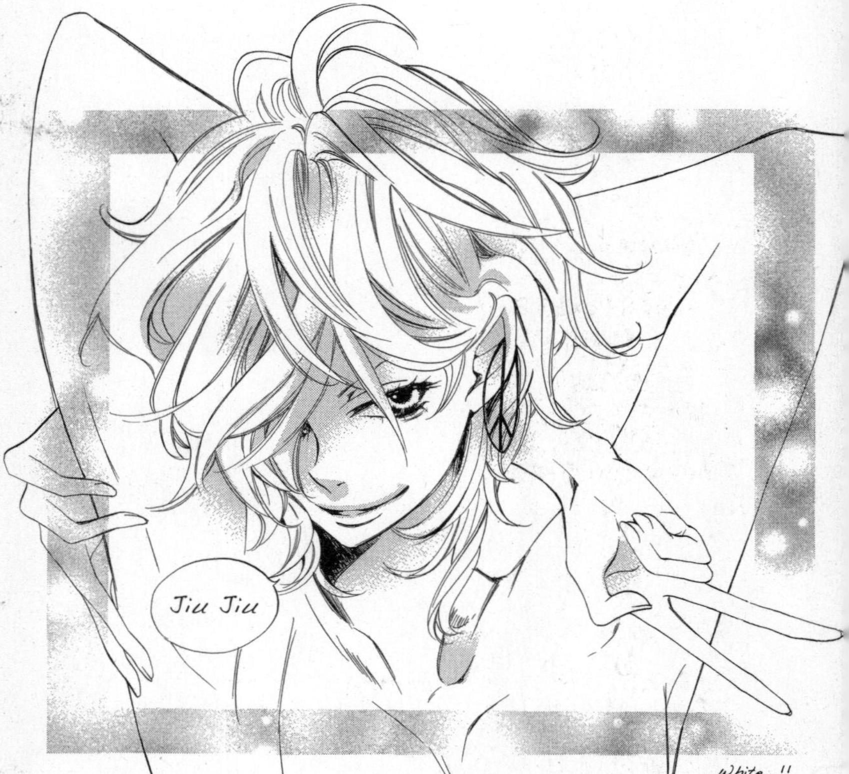
Jiu Jiu
White...!!

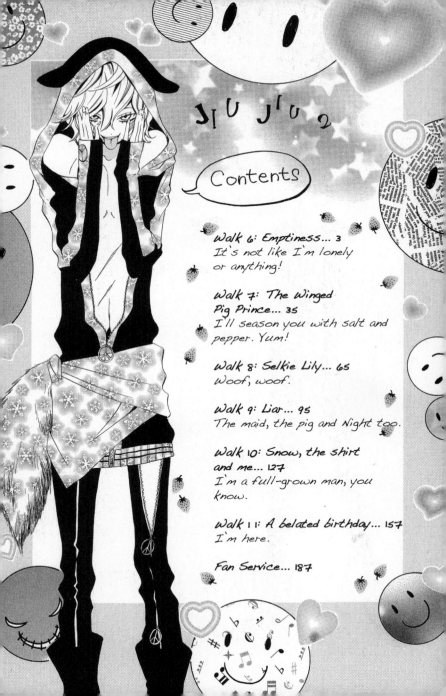

# JIU JIU 2

## Contents

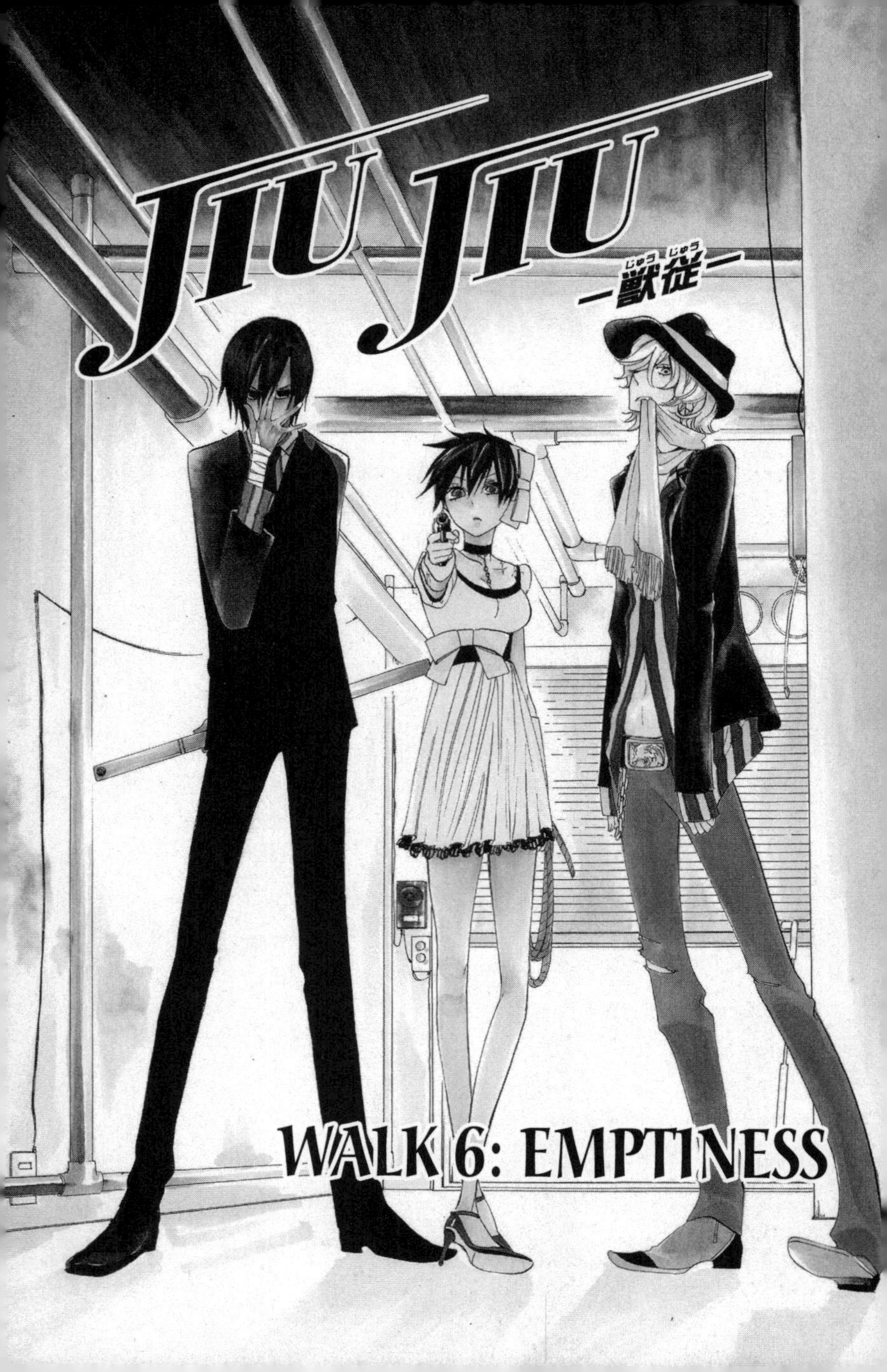
JIU JIU
—獣従—
じゅうじゅう
WALK 6: EMPTINESS

Nice to meet you! Or... glad to see you again! Here's *Jiu Jiu* volume 2...

I set a theme for every volume of *Jiu Jiu*...

By the way, the theme for vol. 1 was "bond."

I once heard a commentator declare, "An author shouldn't announce the theme of their work." Probably they meant it's better to give readers a chance to discover the theme for themselves.

But I think knowing the theme in advance helps you get into the story.

That doesn't mean you have to read it with my theme in mind though...

After all, everybody is different so everybody will have a different take on the story. I'm happy for readers to discover their own theme when reading my manga. That's right! We're all free thinkers!

All right then... *Jiu Jiu* volume 2, with the theme of "fun" begins...***now***!

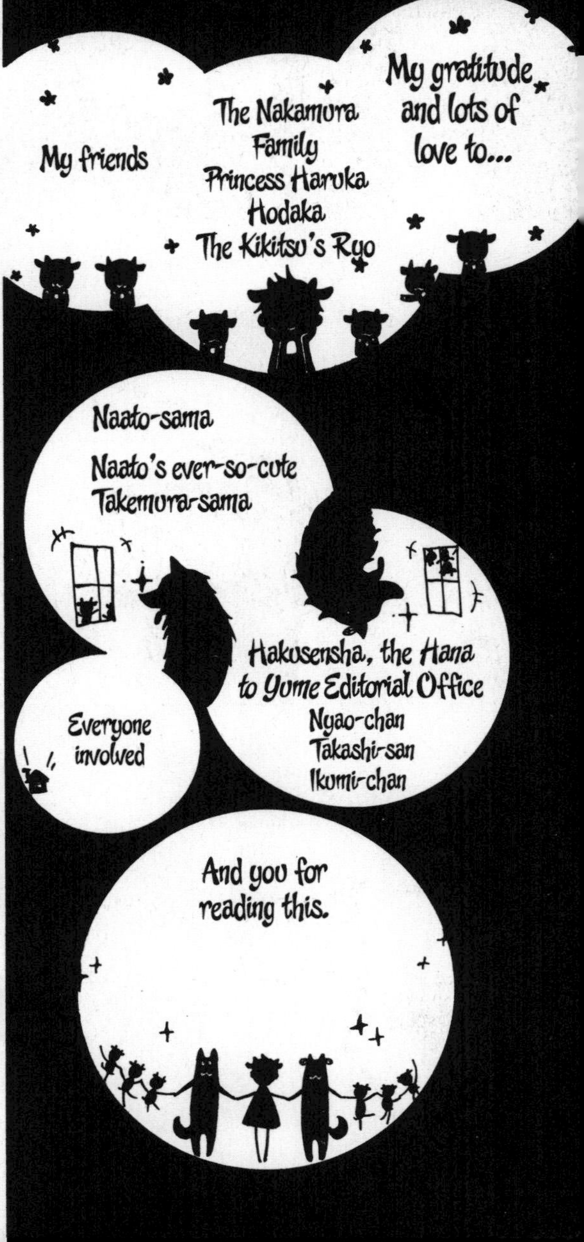
My gratitude and lots of love to...
The Nakamura Family
Princess Haruka
Hodaka
The Kikitsu's Ryo
My friends
Naato-sama
Naato's ever-so-cute Takemura-sama
Hakusensha, the Hana to Yume Editorial Office
Nyao-chan
Takashi-san
Ikumi-chan
Everyone involved
And you for reading this.

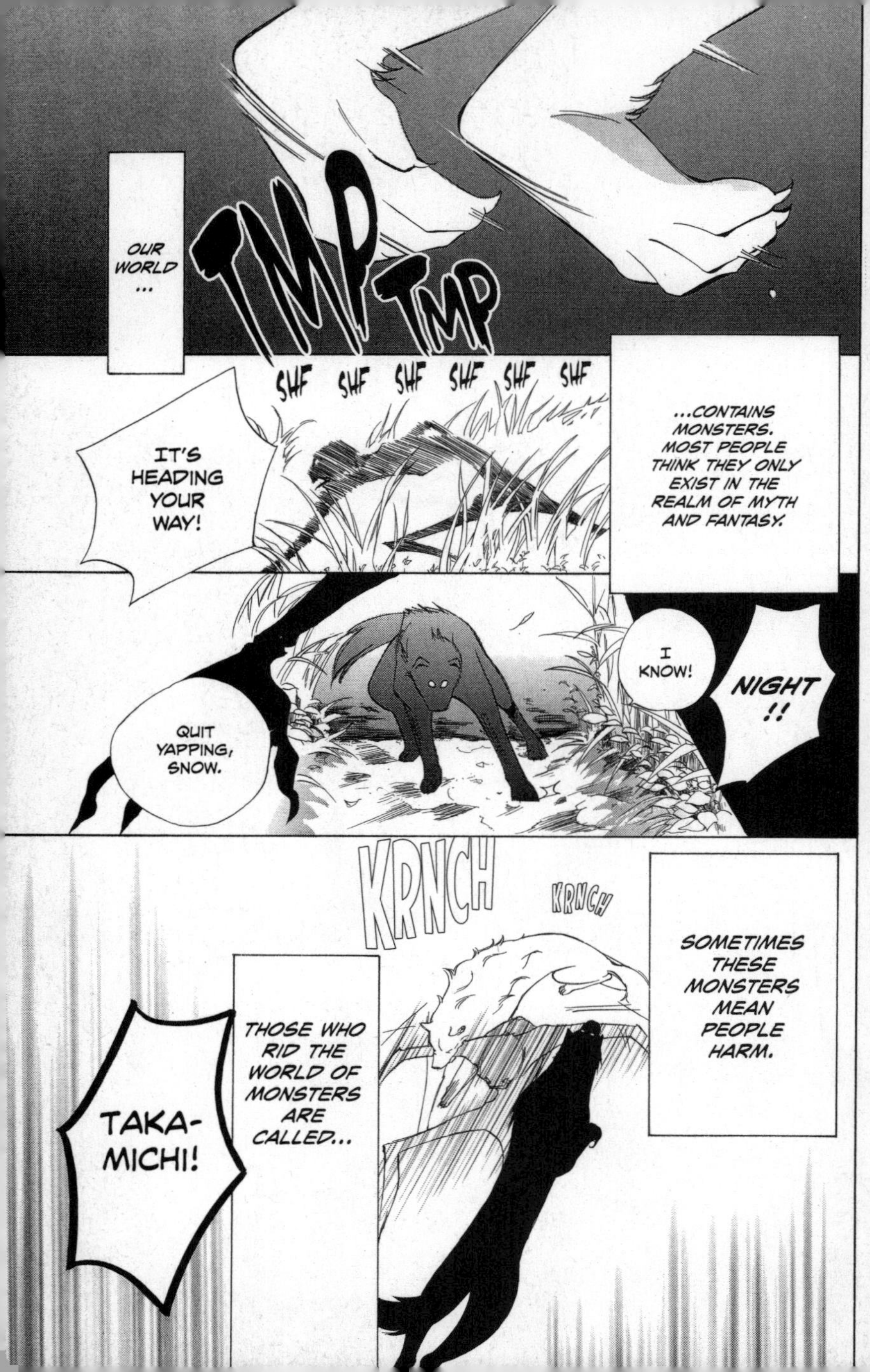
TMP
TMP
OUR WORLD ...
...CONTAINS MONSTERS. MOST PEOPLE THINK THEY ONLY EXIST IN THE REALM OF MYTH AND FANTASY.
SHF SHF SHF SHF SHF SHF
IT'S HEADING YOUR WAY!
NIGHT !!
I KNOW!
QUIT YAPPING, SNOW.
SOMETIMES THESE MONSTERS MEAN PEOPLE HARM.
KRNCH
KRNCH
THOSE WHO RID THE WORLD OF MONSTERS ARE CALLED...
TAKA-MICHI!

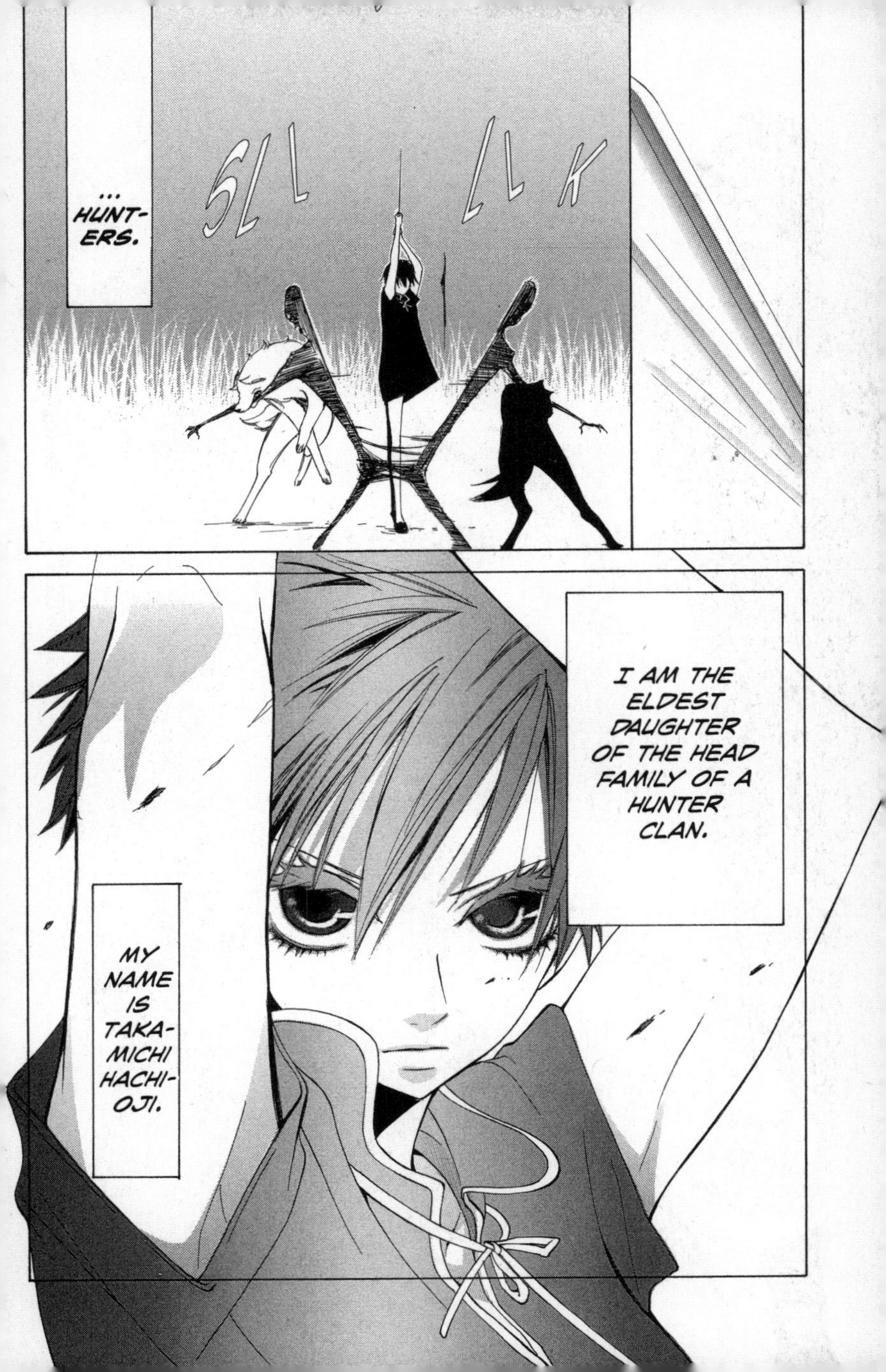
SLLLLK
...HUNTERS.
I AM THE ELDEST DAUGHTER OF THE HEAD FAMILY OF A HUNTER CLAN.
MY NAME IS TAKAMICHI HACHIOJI.

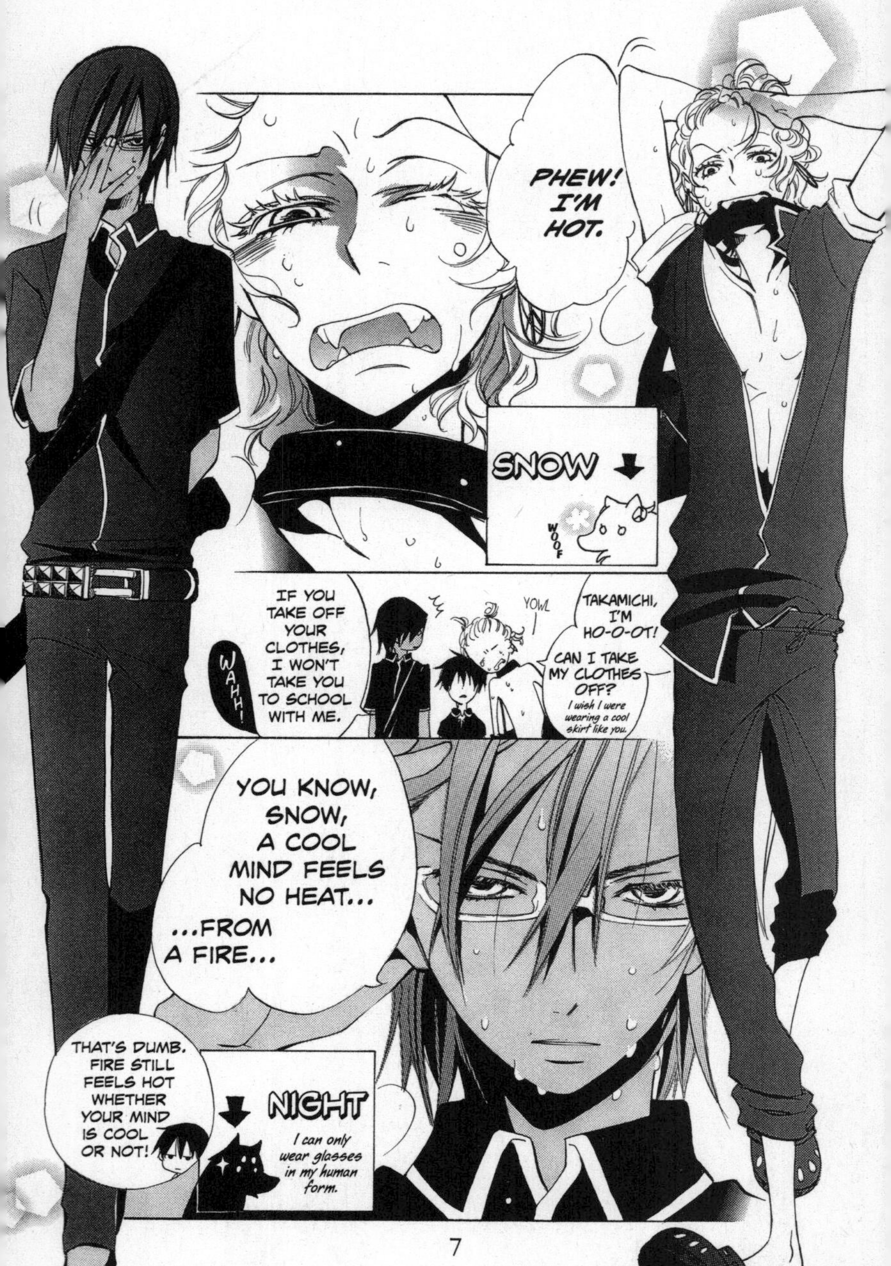
PHEW! I'M HOT.
SNOW
WOOF
TAKAMICHI, I'M HO-O-OT!
YOWL
CAN I TAKE MY CLOTHES OFF?
I wish I were wearing a cool skirt like you.
IF YOU TAKE OFF YOUR CLOTHES, I WON'T TAKE YOU TO SCHOOL WITH ME.
WAHH!
YOU KNOW, SNOW, A COOL MIND FEELS NO HEAT...
...FROM A FIRE...
NIGHT
I can only wear glasses in my human form.
THAT'S DUMB. FIRE STILL FEELS HOT WHETHER YOUR MIND IS COOL OR NOT!

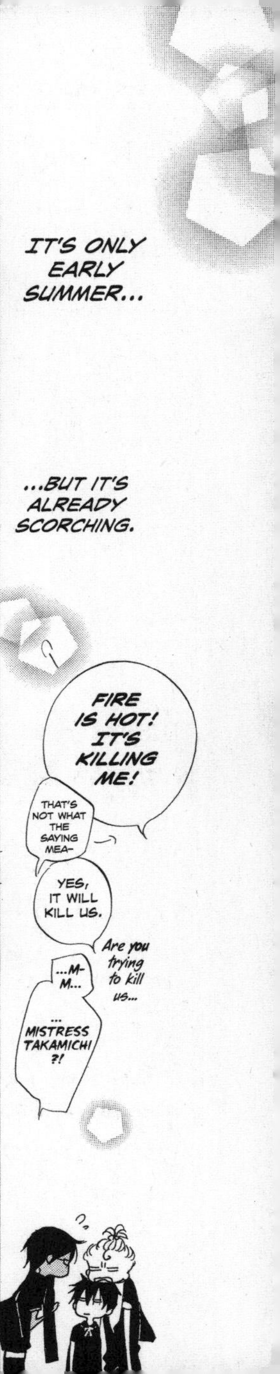
IT'S ONLY EARLY SUMMER...
...BUT IT'S ALREADY SCORCHING.
FIRE IS HOT! IT'S KILLING ME!
THAT'S NOT WHAT THE SAYING MEA-
YES, IT WILL KILL US.
Are you trying to kill us...
...M-M...
...MISTRESS TAKAMICHI?!

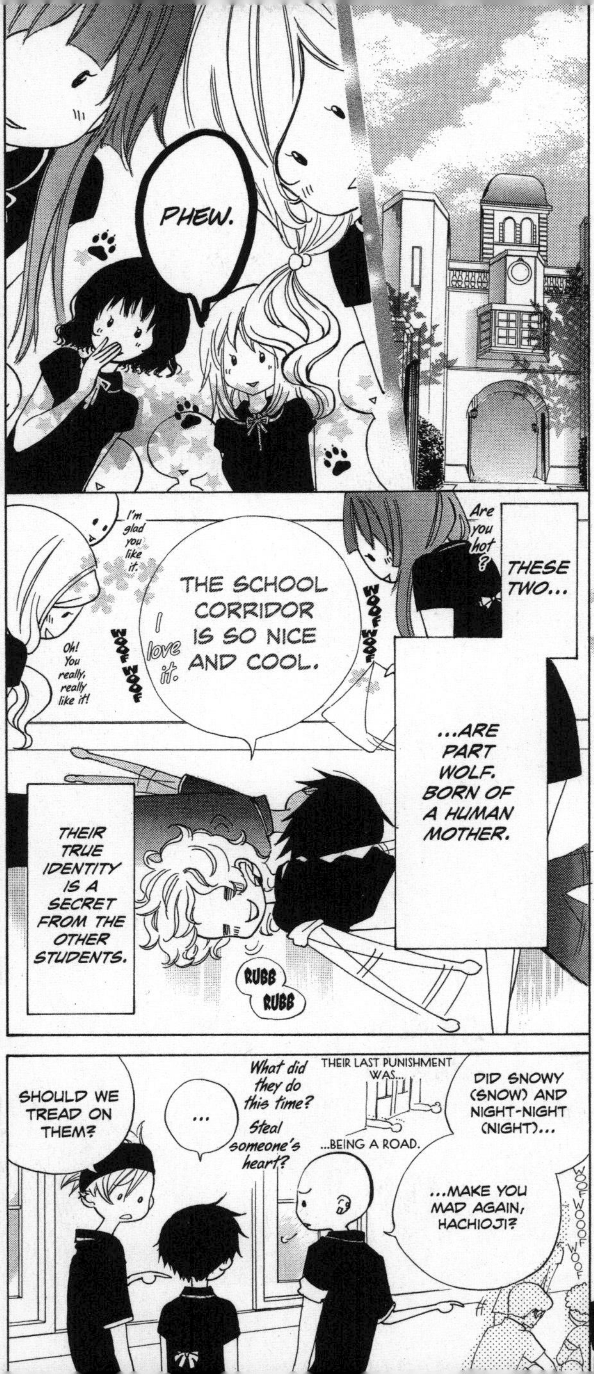
PHEW.
Are you hot?
THESE TWO...
I'm glad you like it.
THE SCHOOL CORRIDOR IS SO NICE AND COOL.
I love it.
WOOF WOOF
Oh! You really, really like it!
WOOF WOOF
...ARE PART WOLF. BORN OF A HUMAN MOTHER.
THEIR TRUE IDENTITY IS A SECRET FROM THE OTHER STUDENTS.
RUBB RUBB
DID SNOWY (SNOW) AND NIGHT-NIGHT (NIGHT)...
...MAKE YOU MAD AGAIN, HACHIOJI?
WOOF WOOOF WOOF
THEIR LAST PUNISHMENT WAS...
...BEING A ROAD.
What did they do this time?
Steal someone's heart?
...
SHOULD WE TREAD ON THEM?

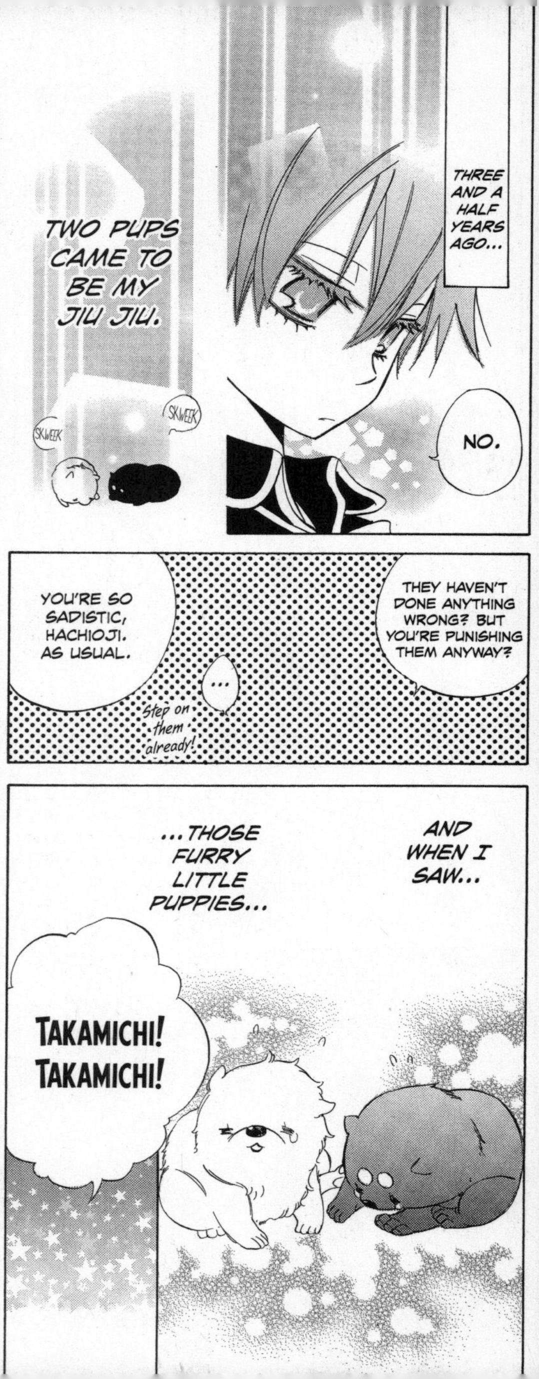
THREE AND A HALF YEARS AGO...
NO.
TWO PUPS CAME TO BE MY JIU JIU.
SKWEEK
SKWEEK
THEY HAVEN'T DONE ANYTHING WRONG? BUT YOU'RE PUNISHING THEM ANYWAY?
...
YOU'RE SO SADISTIC, HACHIOJI. AS USUAL.
Step on them already!
AND WHEN I SAW...
...THOSE FURRY LITTLE PUPPIES...
TAKAMICHI! TAKAMICHI!

## Thank you, heroes.

Nice to meet... Oh, I already said that, didn't I?
Hello, I'm Touya "I love the female figure" Tobina.

As I'm sure you've all noticed, the cover illustration for this volume has gone up several levels. Specifically, I'm talking about the level of the breasts (She's a growing girl!) and the level of your courage to take a manga with that image up to the cash register.

In other words, those of you who are reading Jiu Jiu vol. ② right now are true heroes.

**Thank you very much, hero!**

To tell the truth, I was going to make this the cover for vol. 3 since I'm working on the Family Head Meeting story arc now...
But I believe you should draw whatever you're inspired to draw whenever you want to!

**I'm so thrilled to get to draw the cover illustration for this volume!!!**

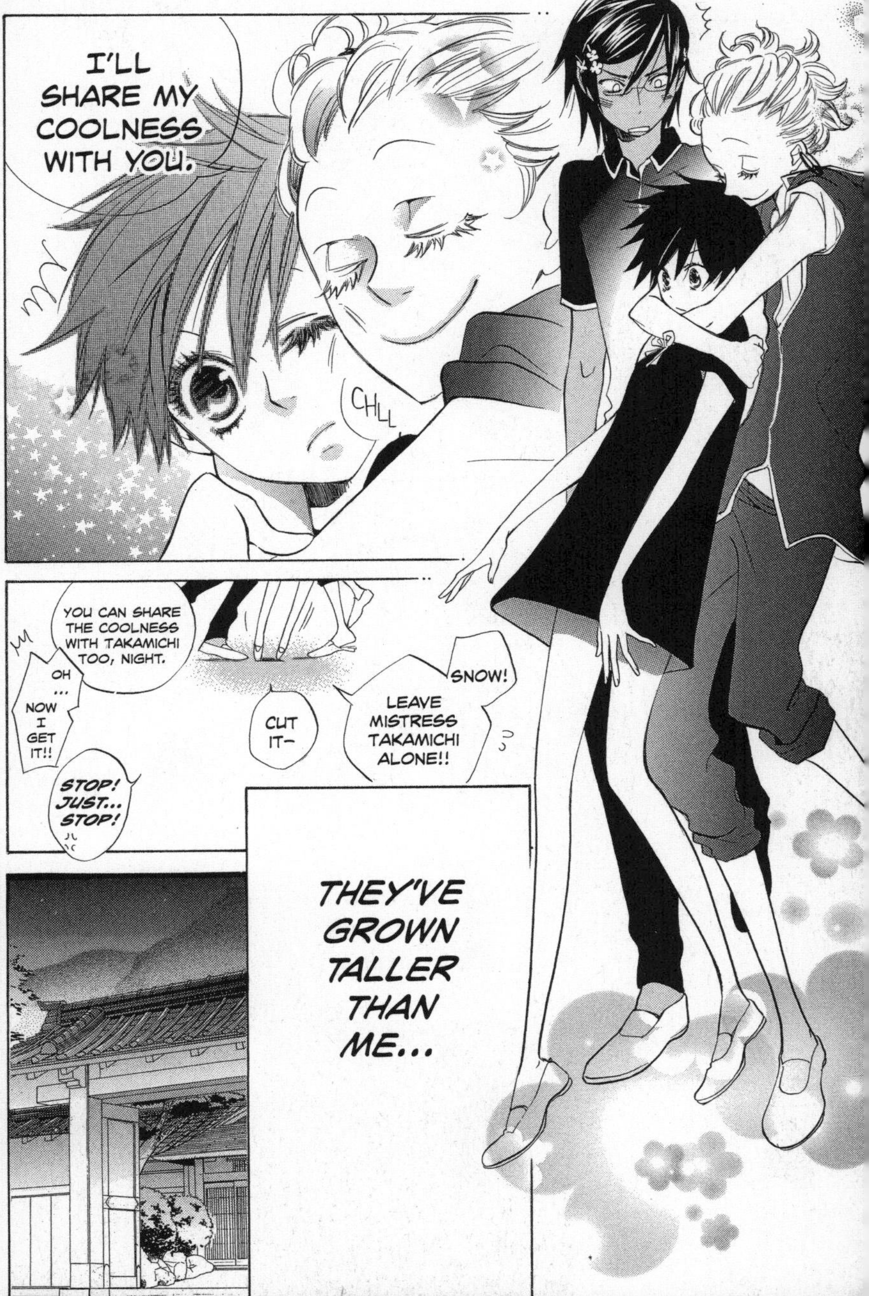
I'LL SHARE MY COOLNESS WITH YOU.
CHLL
YOU CAN SHARE THE COOLNESS WITH TAKAMICHI TOO, NIGHT.
OH ... NOW I GET IT!!
SNOW!
LEAVE MISTRESS TAKAMICHI ALONE!!
CUT IT-
STOP! JUST... STOP!
THEY'VE GROWN TALLER THAN ME...

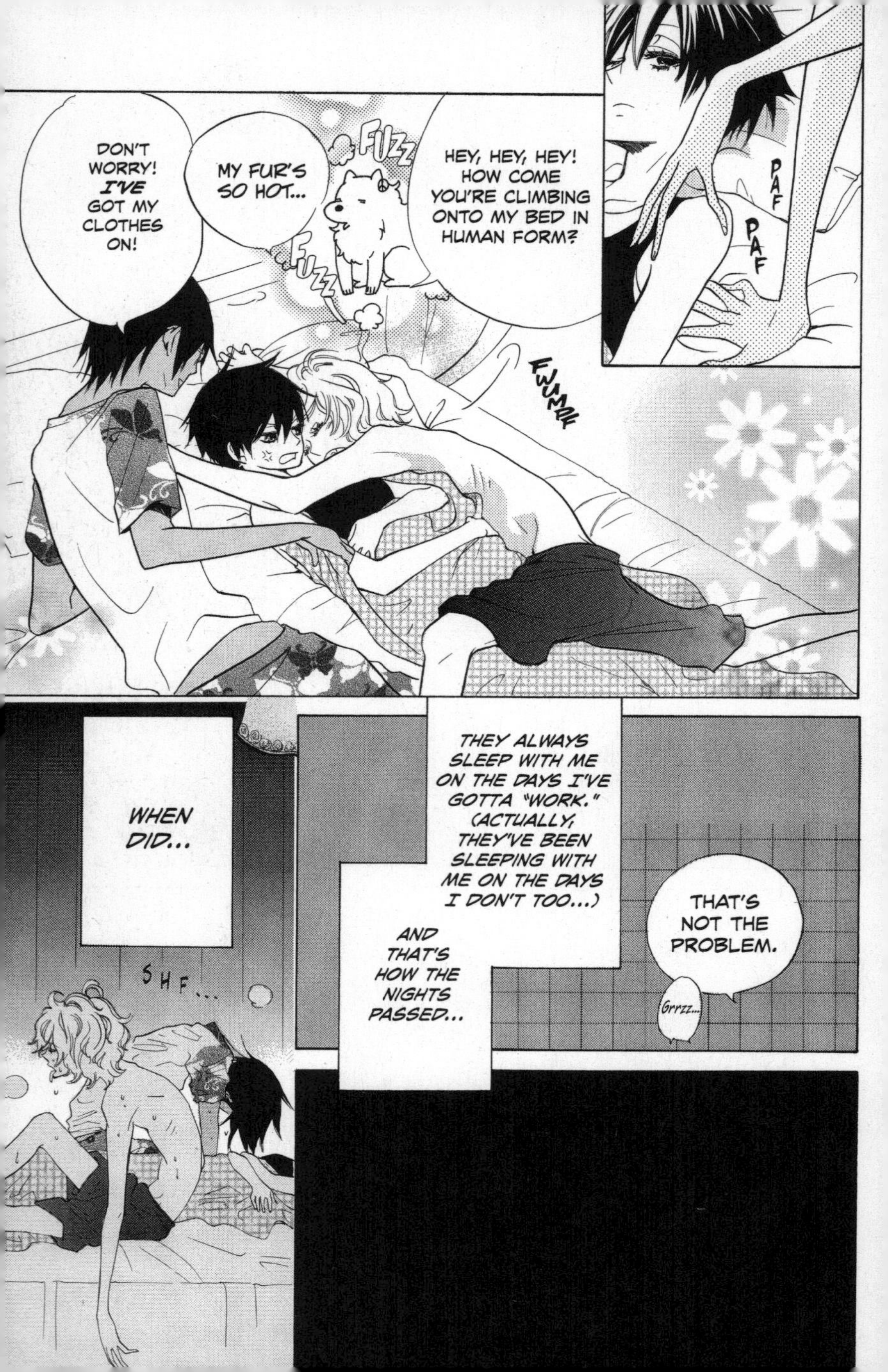

PAF
PAF
HEY, HEY, HEY! HOW COME YOU'RE CLIMBING ONTO MY BED IN HUMAN FORM?
FUZZ
MY FUR'S SO HOT...
DON'T WORRY! *I'VE* GOT MY CLOTHES ON!
FUZZ
FWUMP
THEY ALWAYS SLEEP WITH ME ON THE DAYS I'VE GOTTA "WORK." (ACTUALLY, THEY'VE BEEN SLEEPING WITH ME ON THE DAYS I DON'T TOO...)
THAT'S NOT THE PROBLEM.
Grrzz...
AND THAT'S HOW THE NIGHTS PASSED...
WHEN DID...
SHF...

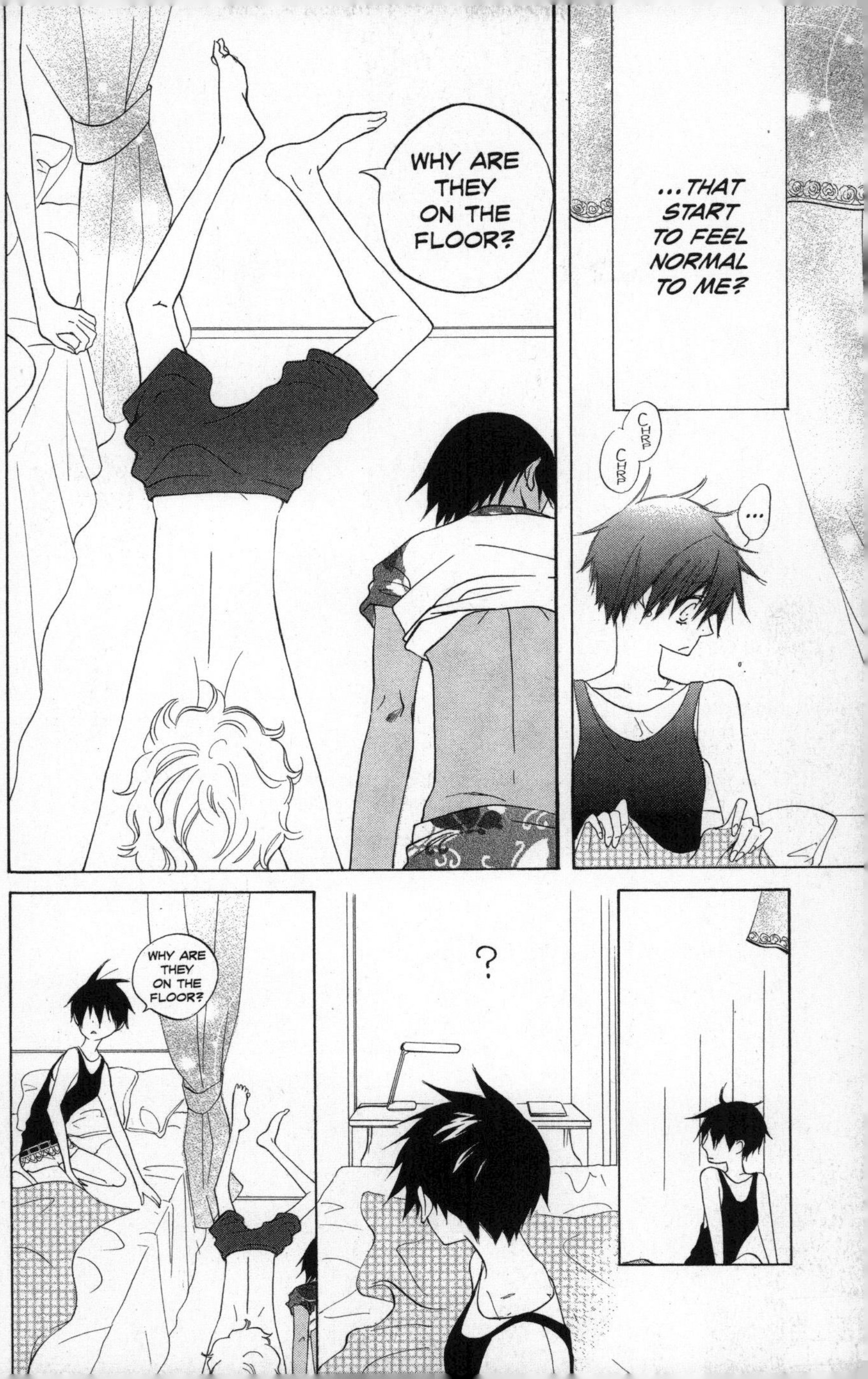
...THAT START TO FEEL NORMAL TO ME?
CHRP CHRP
...
WHY ARE THEY ON THE FLOOR?
?
WHY ARE THEY ON THE FLOOR?

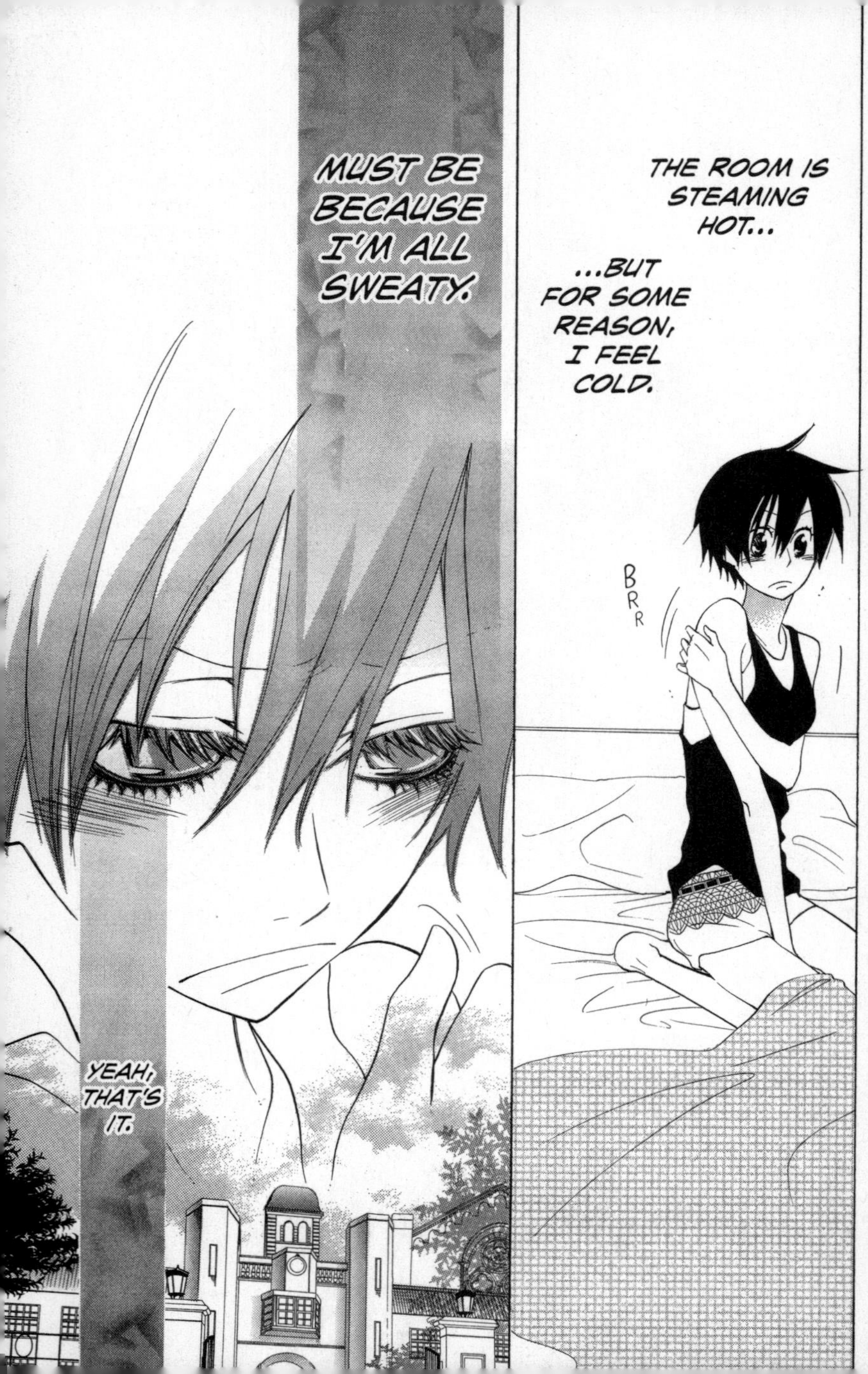
THE ROOM IS STEAMING HOT...
...BUT FOR SOME REASON, I FEEL COLD.
BRRR
MUST BE BECAUSE I'M ALL SWEATY.
YEAH, THAT'S IT.

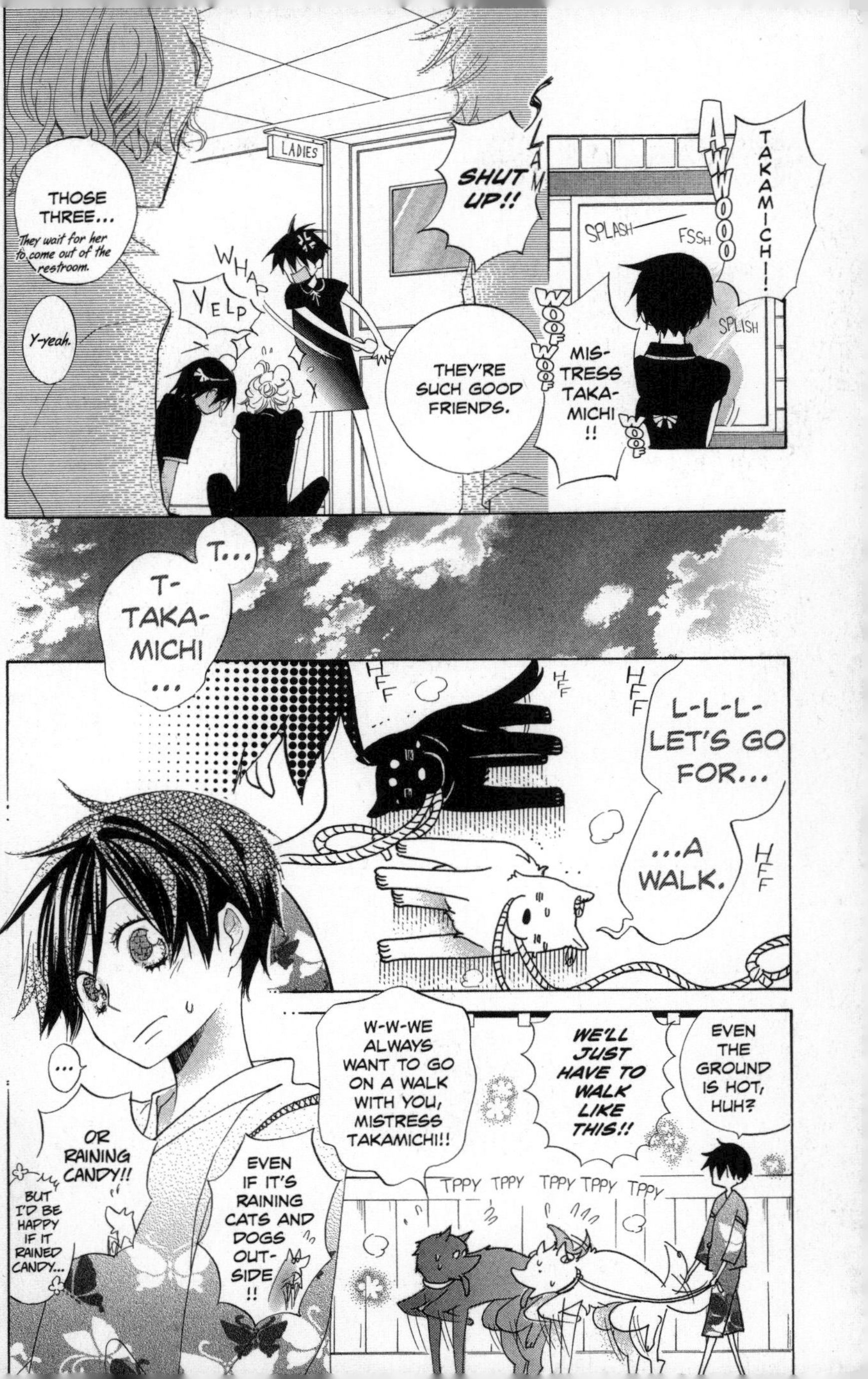
TAKAMICHI!!
AWWOOOO
SPLASH
FSSH
SPLISH
MISTRESS TAKAMICHI!!
WOOF WOOF WOOF
SLAM
SHUT UP!!
WHAP
YELP
THEY'RE SUCH GOOD FRIENDS.
THOSE THREE...
They wait for her to come out of the restroom.
Y-yeah.
T...
T-TAKAMICHI...
HFF HFF HFF
L-L-L-LET'S GO FOR...
...A WALK.
HFF
EVEN THE GROUND IS HOT, HUH?
WE'LL JUST HAVE TO WALK LIKE THIS!!
W-W-WE ALWAYS WANT TO GO ON A WALK WITH YOU, MISTRESS TAKAMICHI!!
TPPY TPPY TPPY TPPY TPPY
EVEN IF IT'S RAINING CATS AND DOGS OUTSIDE!!
OR RAINING CANDY!!
BUT I'D BE HAPPY IF IT RAINED CANDY...
...

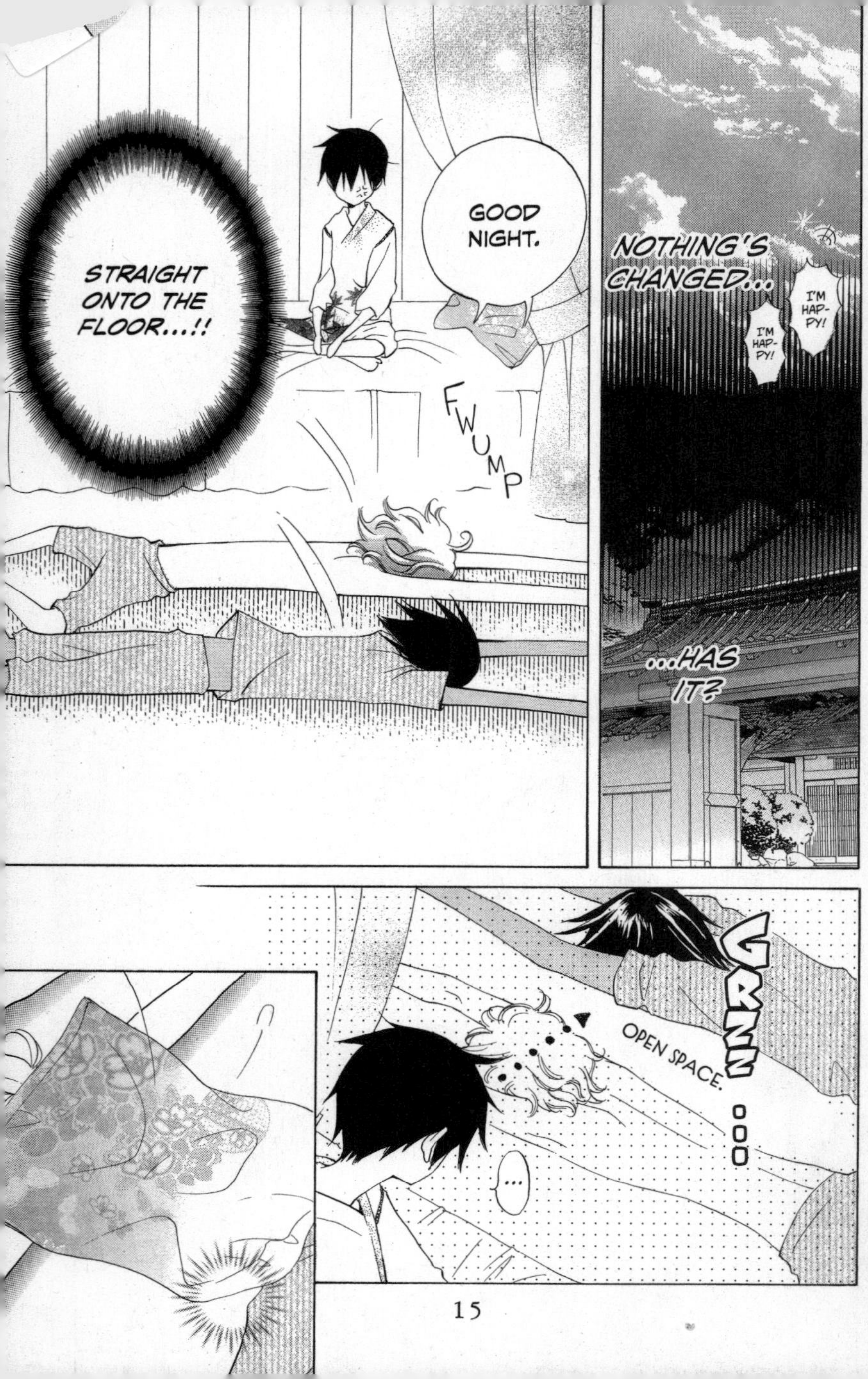
NOTHING'S CHANGED...
I'M HAPPY!
I'M HAPPY!
...HAS IT?
GOOD NIGHT.
STRAIGHT ONTO THE FLOOR...!!
FWUMP
GRNN
OPEN SPACE.
OOO
...

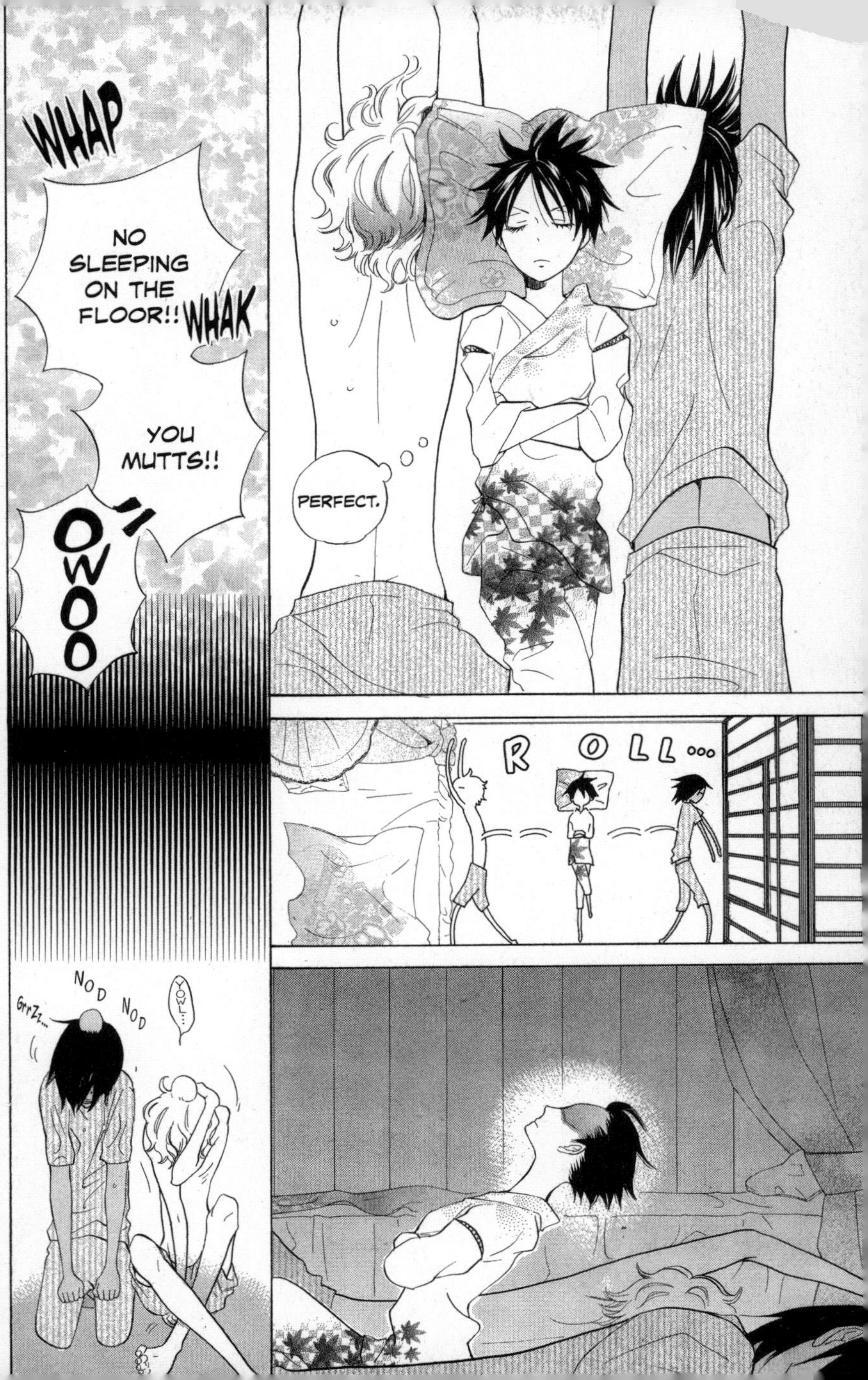
PERFECT.
ROLL...
WHAP
NO SLEEPING ON THE FLOOR!!
WHAK
YOU MUTTS!!
OWOO!!
NOD NOD
GrrZz...
YOWL...

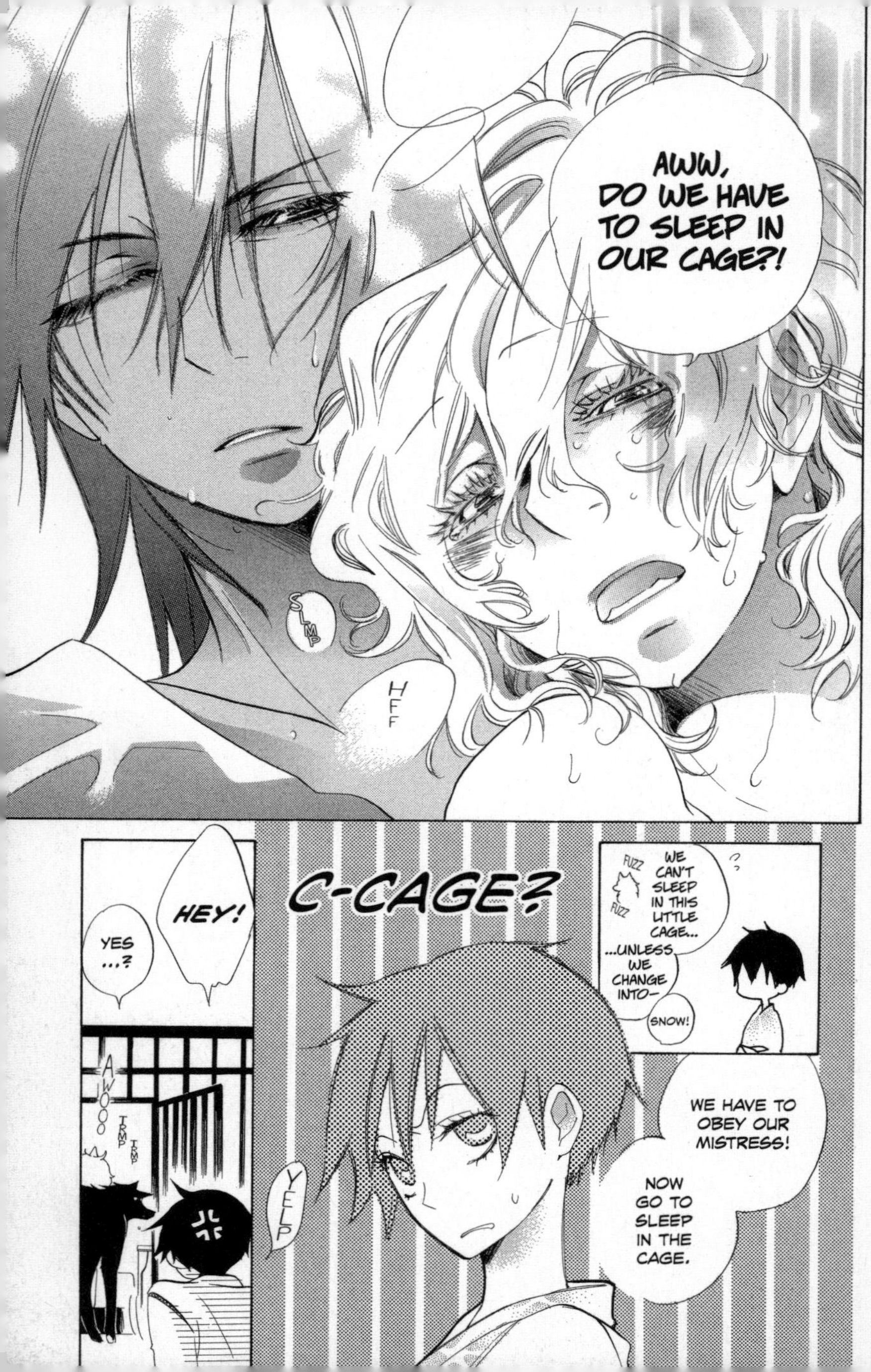
AWW, DO WE HAVE TO SLEEP IN OUR CAGE?!
SLMP
HFF
FUZZ FUZZ
WE CAN'T SLEEP IN THIS LITTLE CAGE...
...UNLESS WE CHANGE INTO—
SNOW!
C-CAGE?
WE HAVE TO OBEY OUR MISTRESS!
NOW GO TO SLEEP IN THE CAGE.
HEY!
YES ...?
AWOOO
TMP TMP
YELP

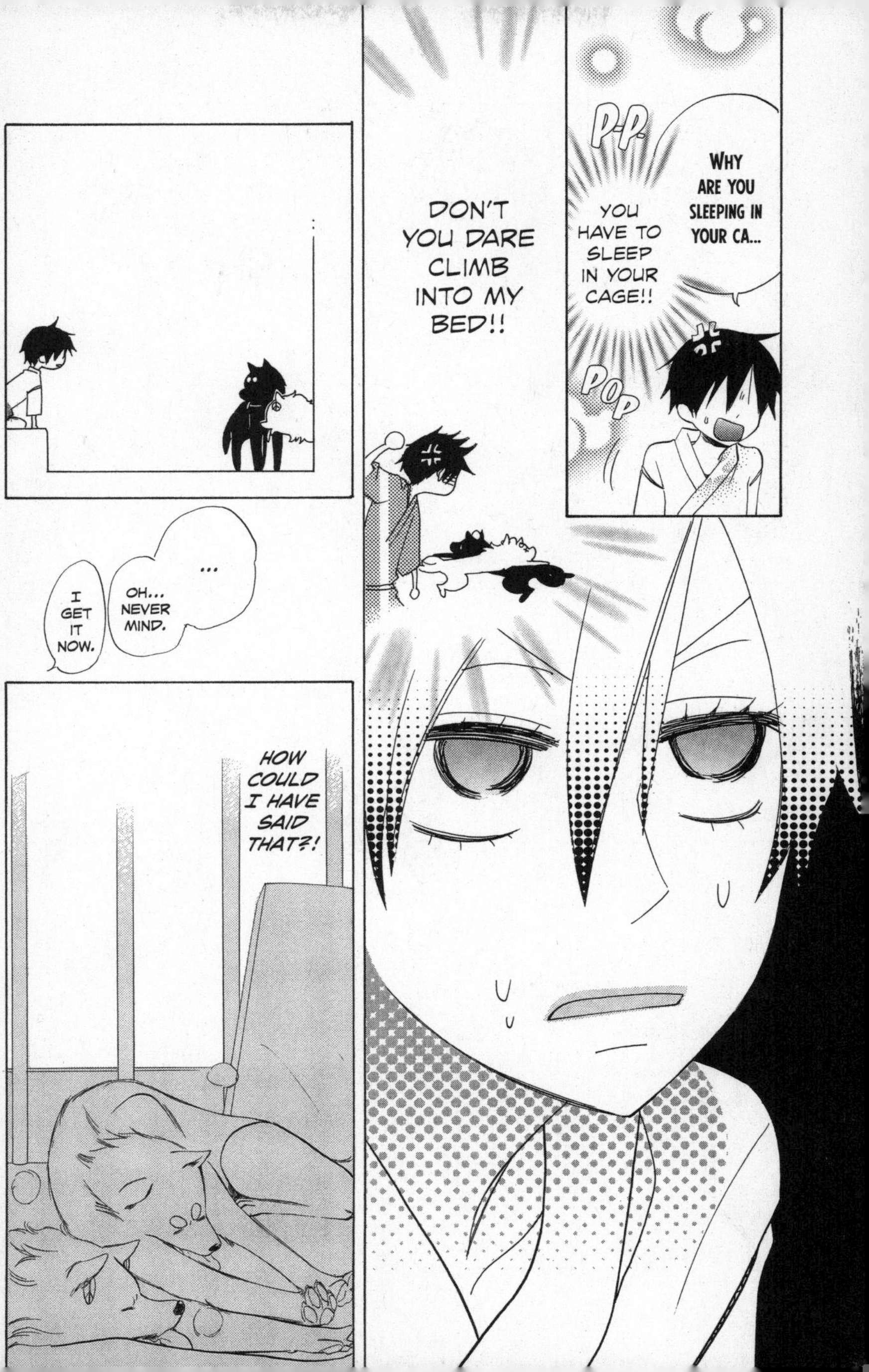
P-P-
WHY ARE YOU SLEEPING IN YOUR CA...
YOU HAVE TO SLEEP IN YOUR CAGE!!
POP
DON'T YOU DARE CLIMB INTO MY BED!!
...
OH... NEVER MIND.
I GET IT NOW.
HOW COULD I HAVE SAID THAT?!

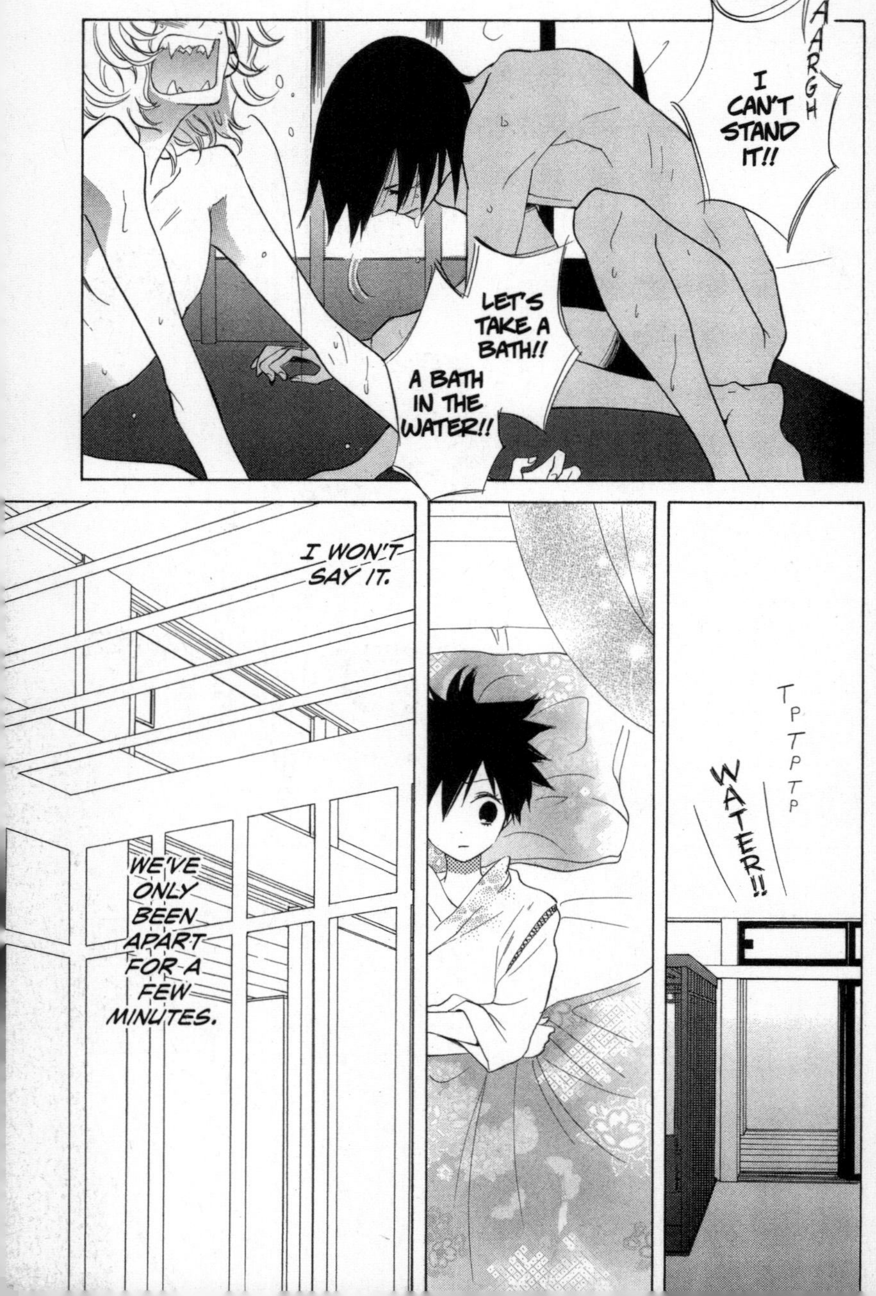
AARGH
I CAN'T STAND IT!!
LET'S TAKE A BATH!!
A BATH IN THE WATER!!
TPTPTP
WATER!!
I WON'T SAY IT.
WE'VE ONLY BEEN APART FOR A FEW MINUTES.

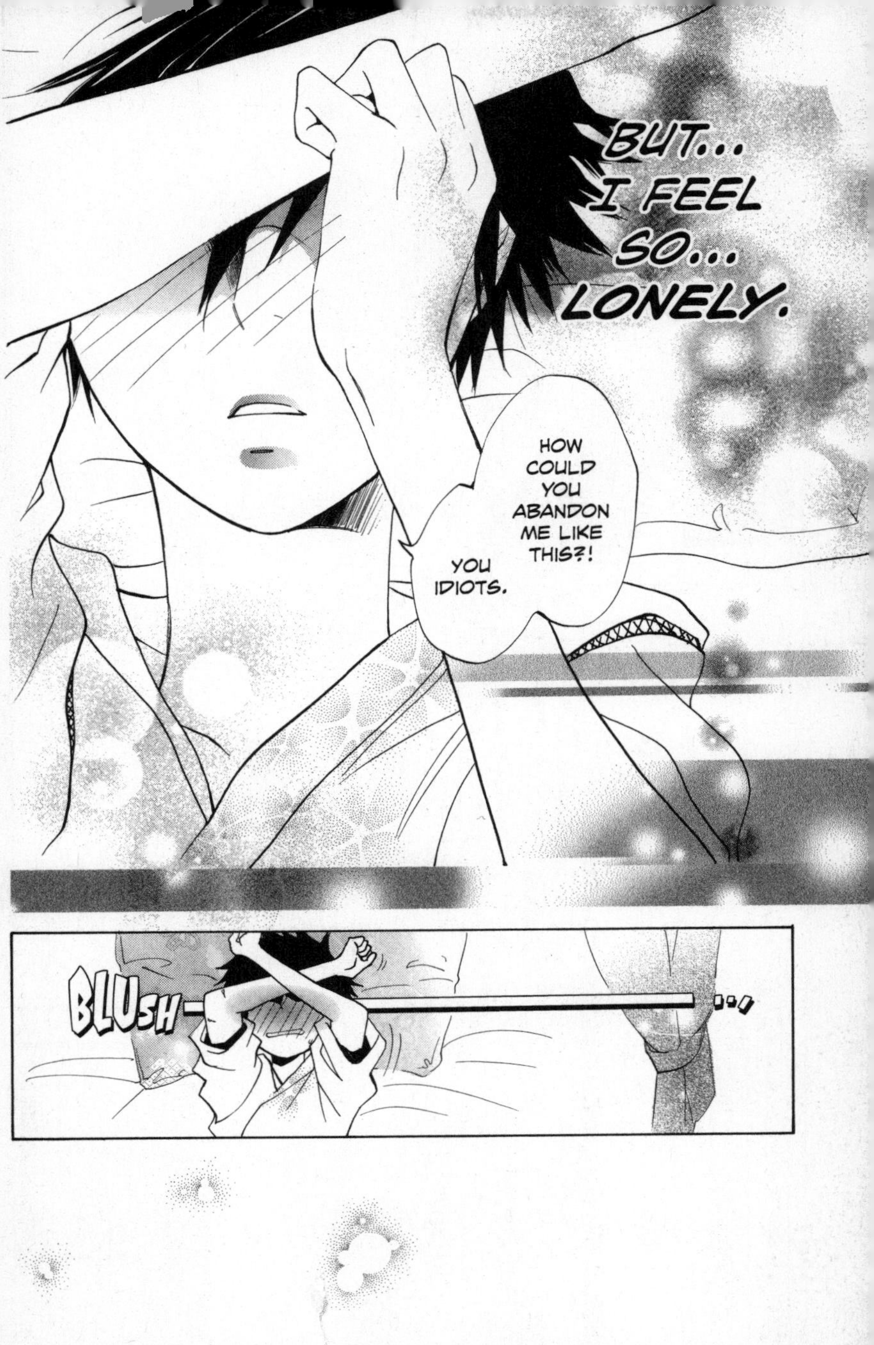
BUT... I FEEL SO... LONELY.
HOW COULD YOU ABANDON ME LIKE THIS?!
YOU IDIOTS.
BLUSH
...!

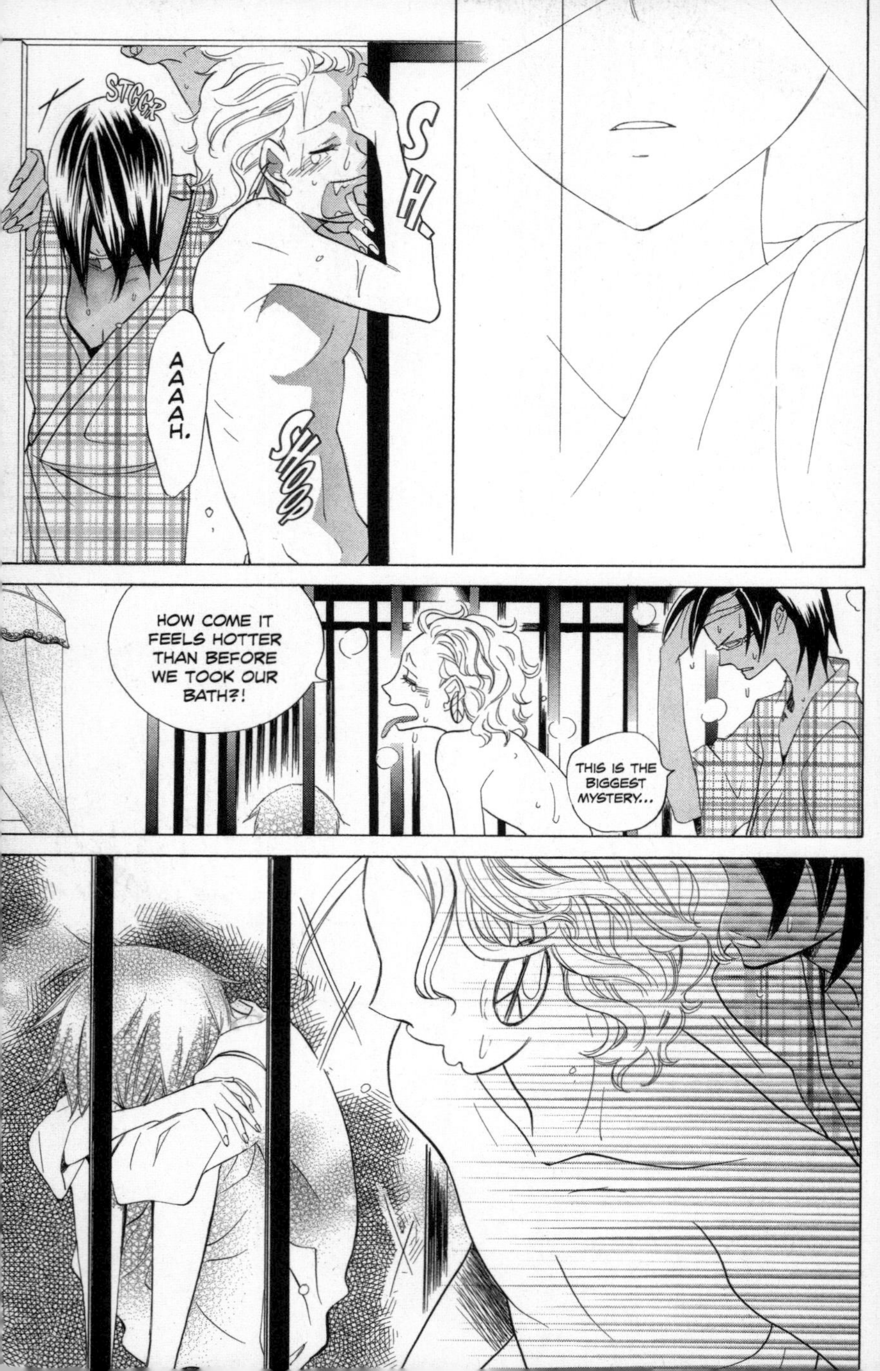
SHH
STGGR
AAAAH.
SHOOP
THIS IS THE BIGGEST MYSTERY...
HOW COME IT FEELS HOTTER THAN BEFORE WE TOOK OUR BATH?!

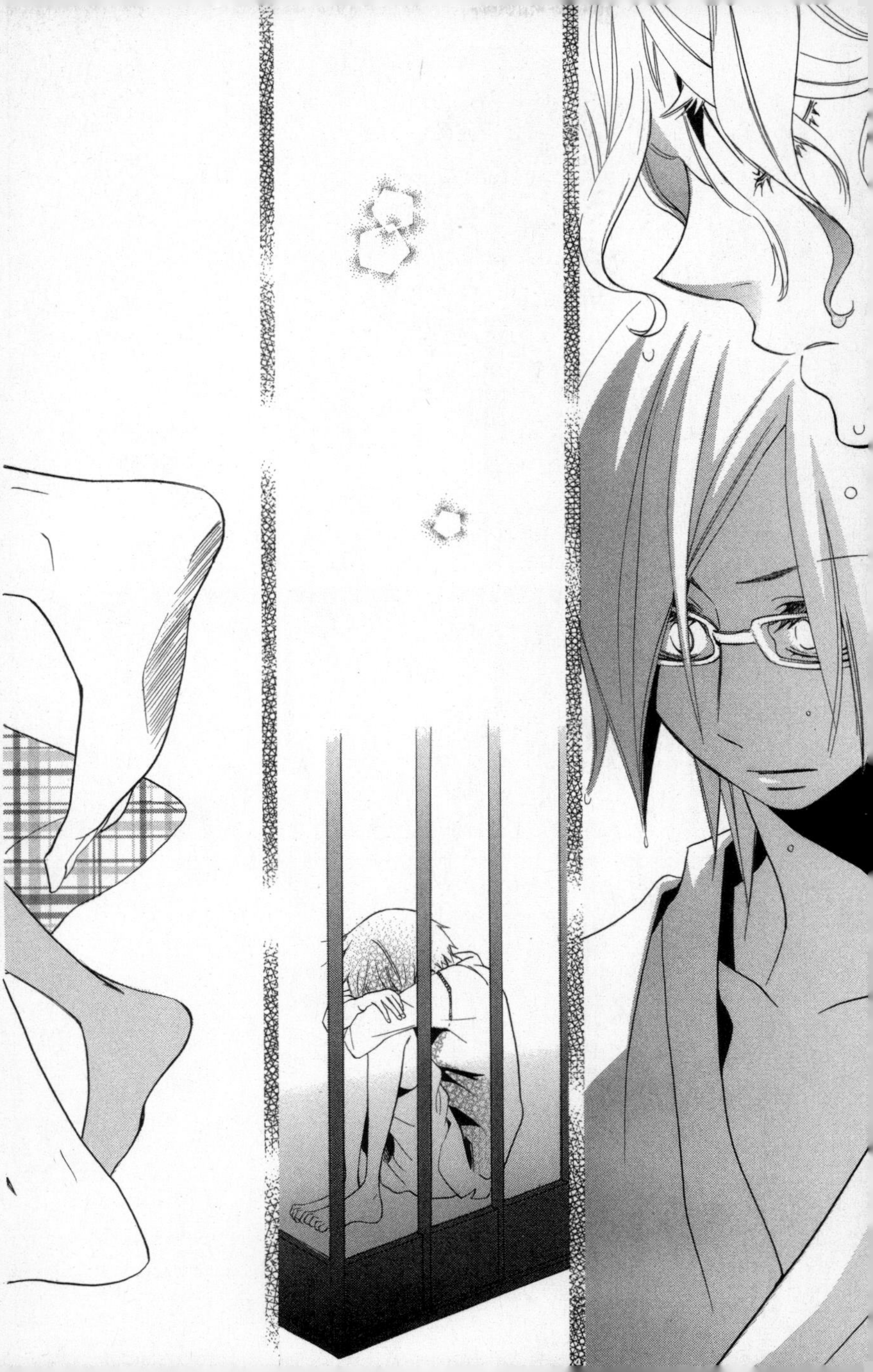

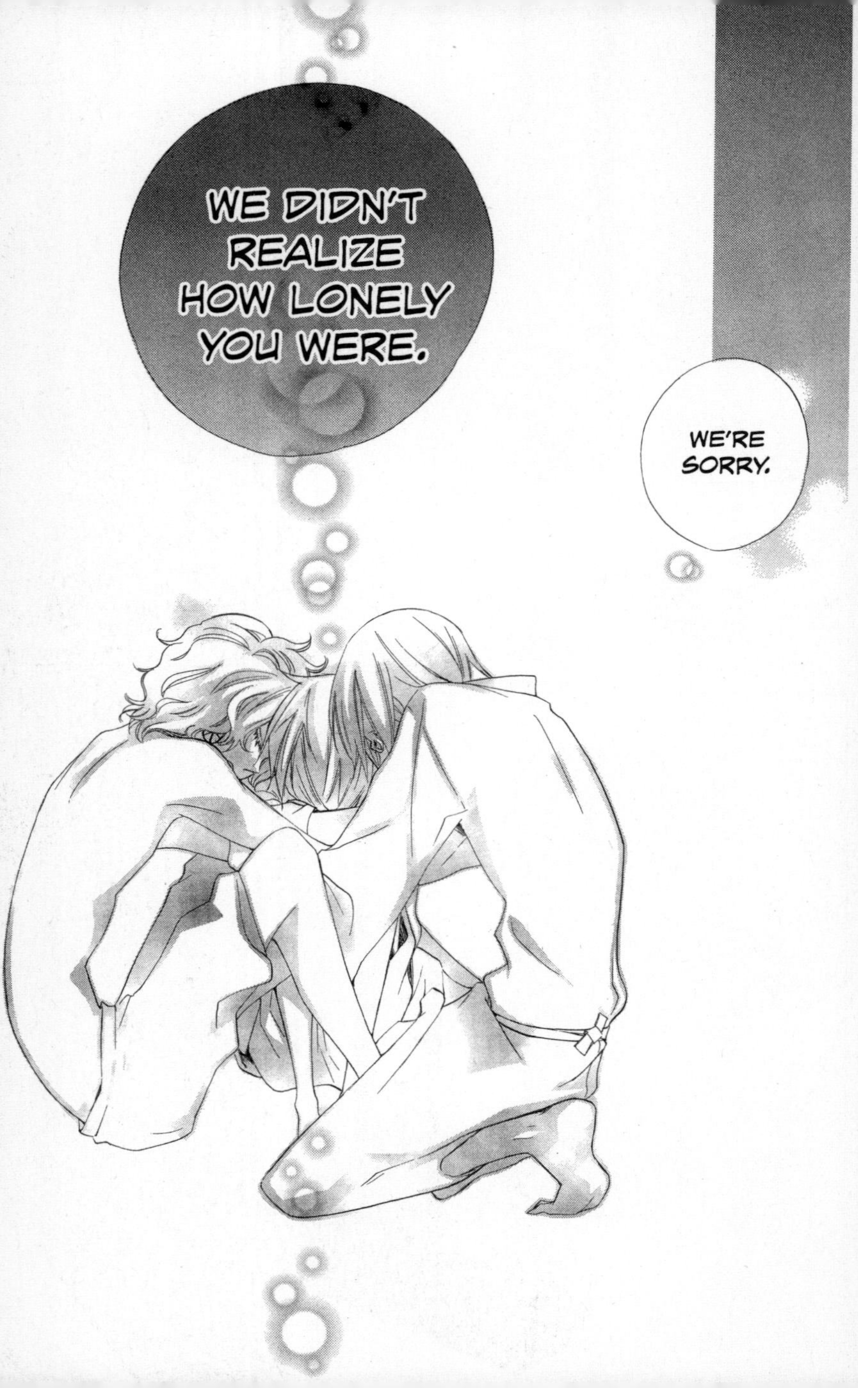
WE'RE SORRY.
WE DIDN'T REALIZE HOW LONELY YOU WERE.

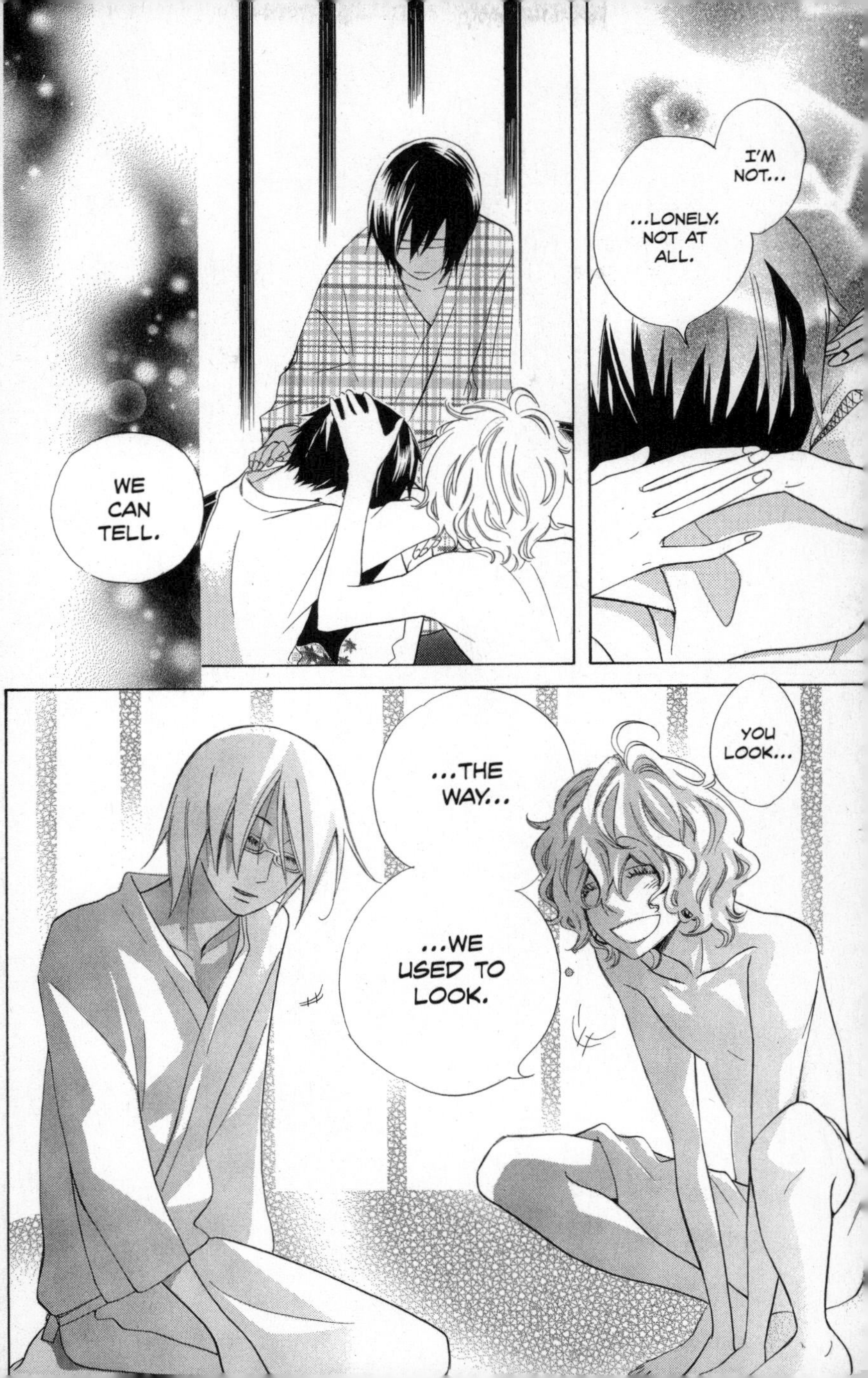
I'M NOT...
...LONELY. NOT AT ALL.
WE CAN TELL.
YOU LOOK...
...THE WAY...
...WE USED TO LOOK.

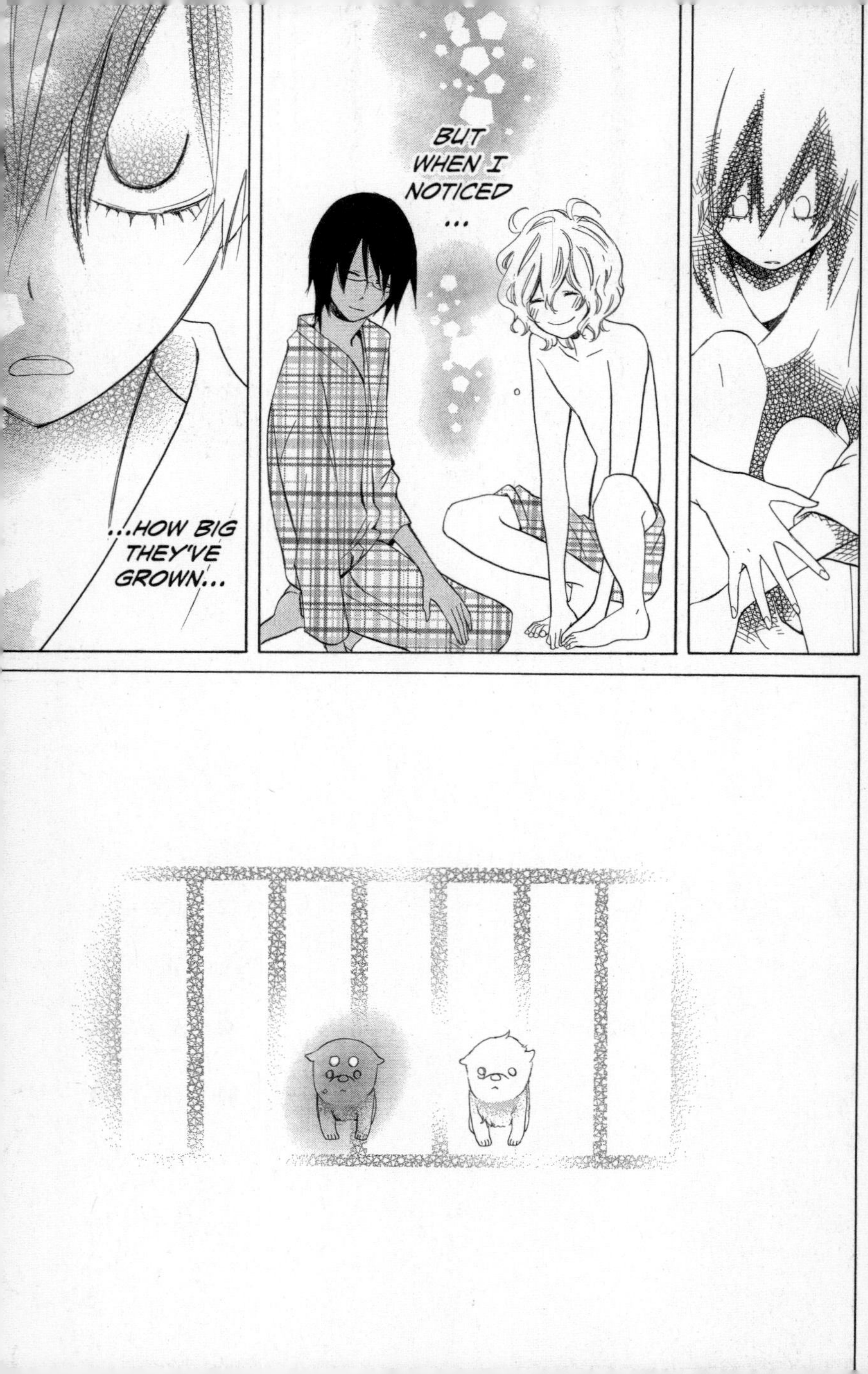
BUT WHEN I NOTICED ...
...HOW BIG THEY'VE GROWN...

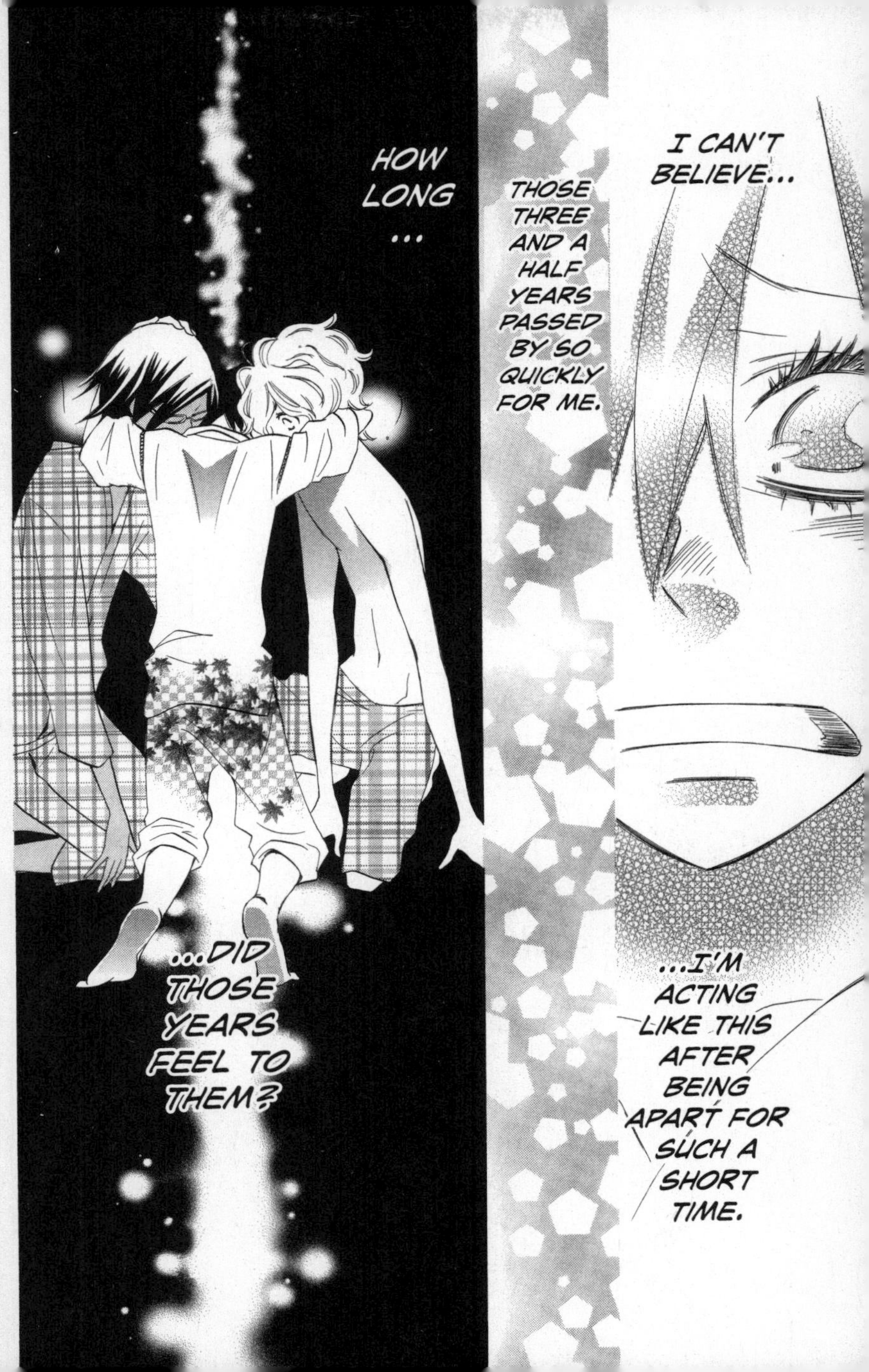
I CAN'T BELIEVE...
...I'M ACTING LIKE THIS AFTER BEING APART FOR SUCH A SHORT TIME.
THOSE THREE AND A HALF YEARS PASSED BY SO QUICKLY FOR ME.
HOW LONG...
...DID THOSE YEARS FEEL TO THEM?

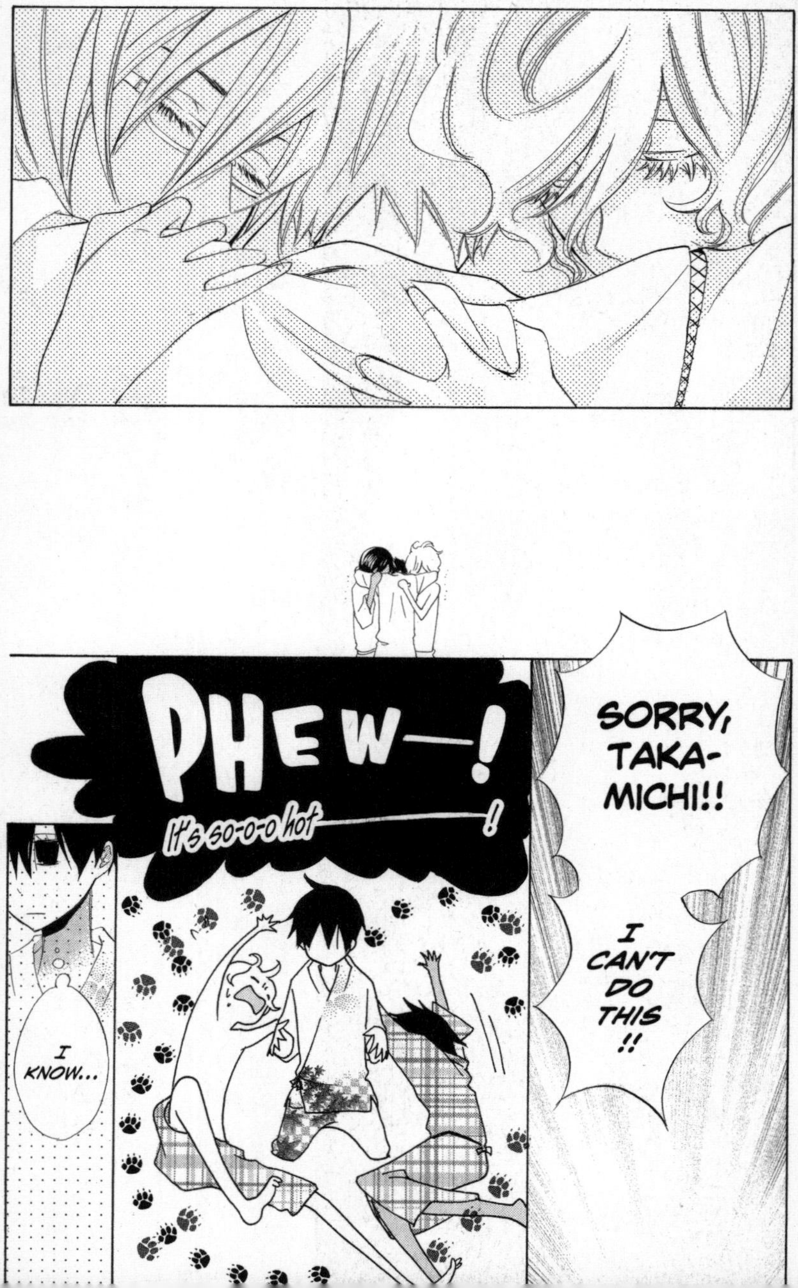
SORRY, TAKA-MICHI!!
I CAN'T DO THIS!!
PHEW—!
It's so-o-o hot——!
I KNOW...

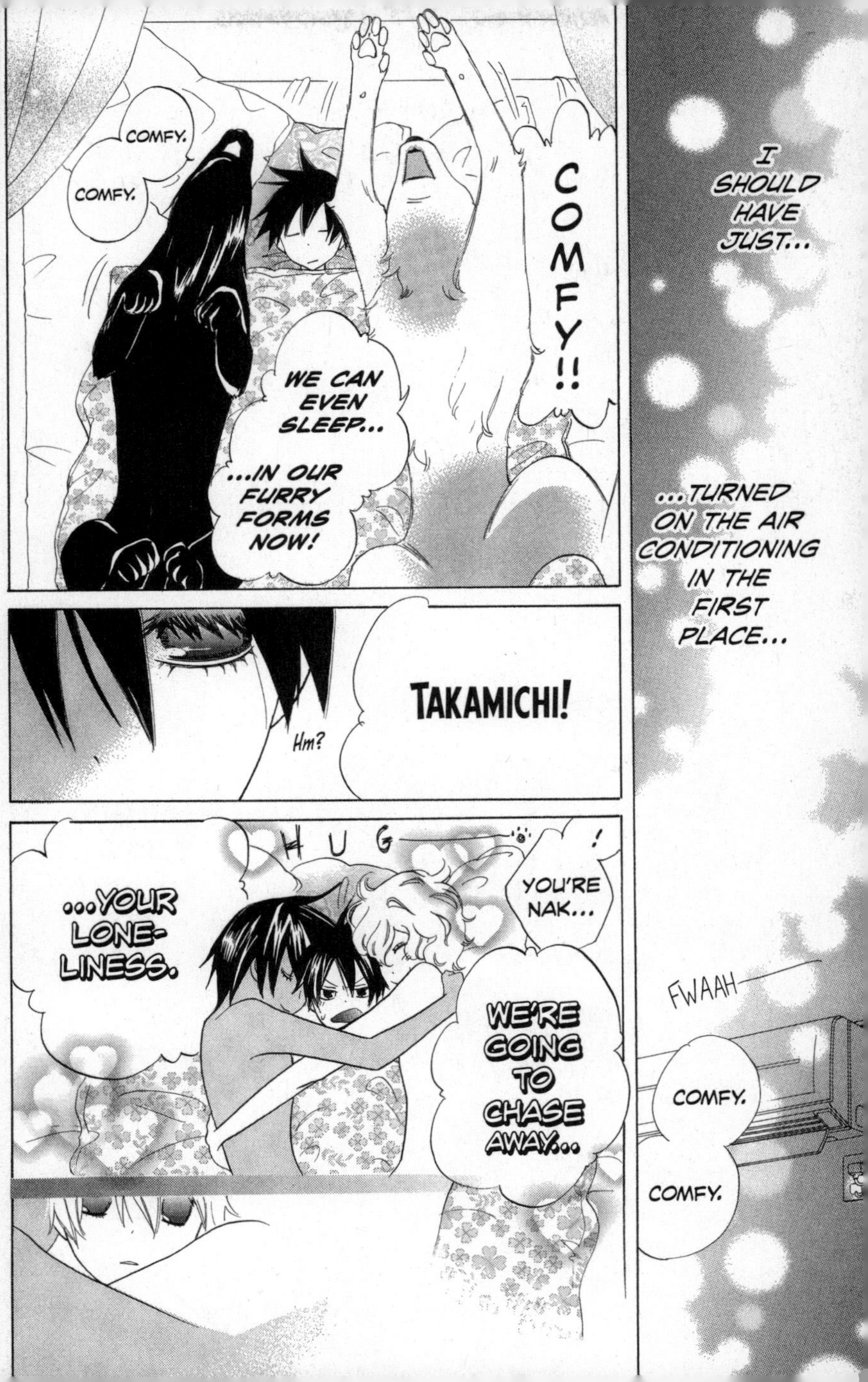
I SHOULD HAVE JUST...
...TURNED ON THE AIR CONDITIONING IN THE FIRST PLACE...
FWAAH
COMFY.
COMFY.
COMFY!!
COMFY.
COMFY.
WE CAN EVEN SLEEP...
...IN OUR FURRY FORMS NOW!
TAKAMICHI!
Hm?
!
YOU'RE NAK...
HUG
WE'RE GOING TO CHASE AWAY...
...YOUR LONE-LINESS.

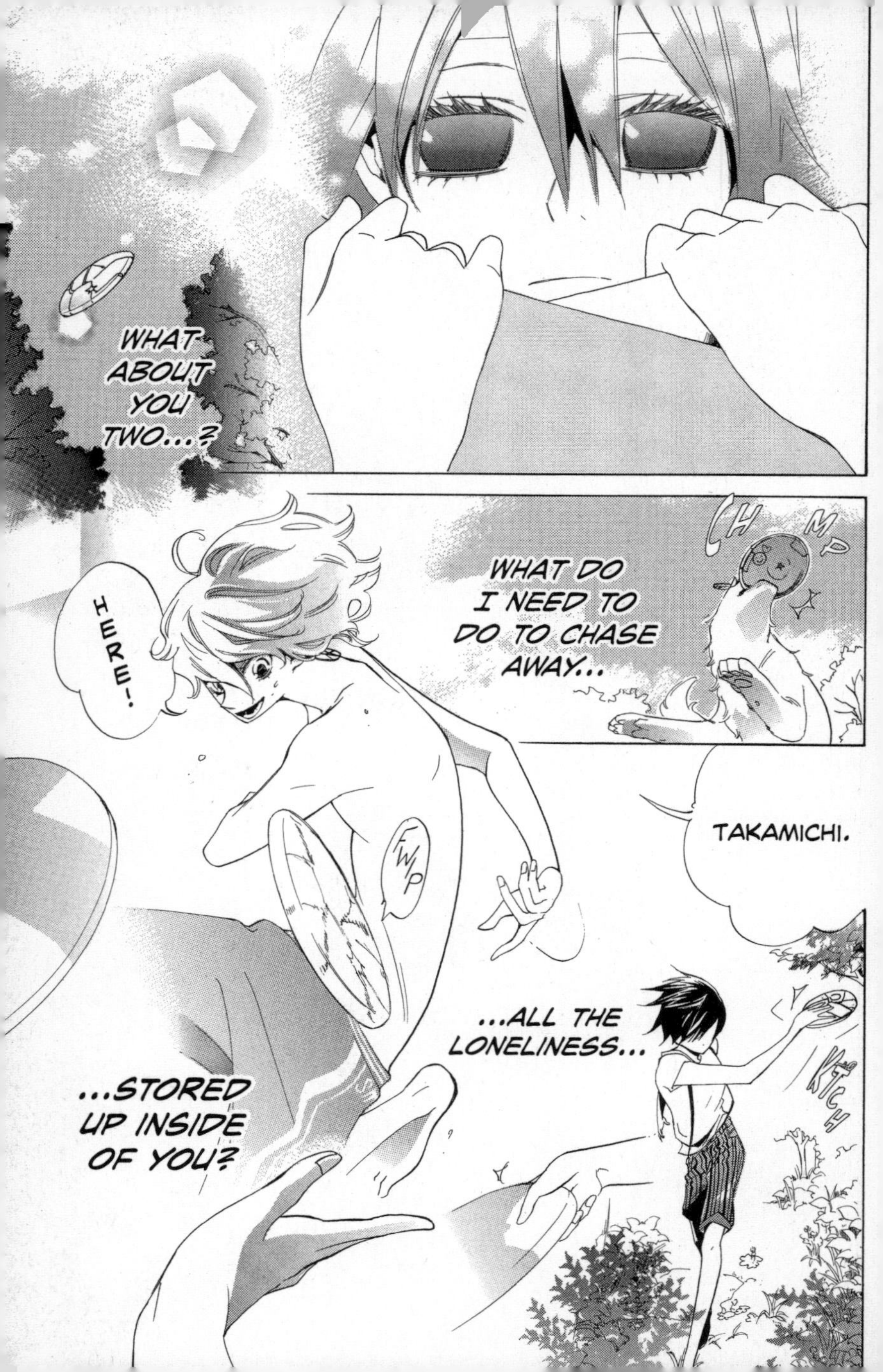
WHAT ABOUT YOU TWO...?
CHOMP
WHAT DO I NEED TO DO TO CHASE AWAY...
TAKAMICHI.
...ALL THE LONELINESS...
KTCH
HERE!
FWP
...STORED UP INSIDE OF YOU?

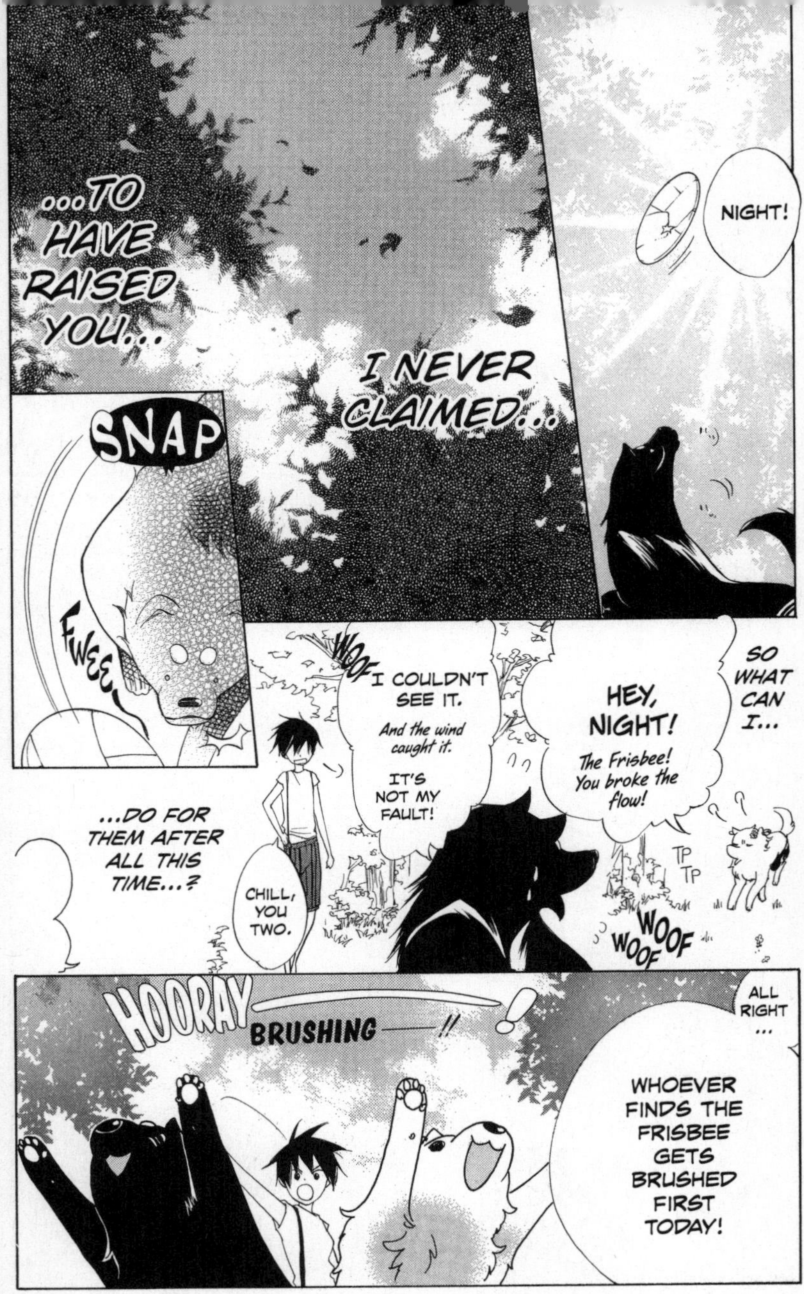
NIGHT!
I NEVER CLAIMED...
...TO HAVE RAISED YOU...
SNAP
FWEE
SO WHAT CAN I...
HEY, NIGHT! The Frisbee! You broke the flow!
WOOF
I COULDN'T SEE IT. And the wind caught it. IT'S NOT MY FAULT!
TP TP
WOOF WOOF
CHILL, YOU TWO.
...DO FOR THEM AFTER ALL THIS TIME...?
ALL RIGHT...
WHOEVER FINDS THE FRISBEE GETS BRUSHED FIRST TODAY!
HOORAY—!
BRUSHING—!!

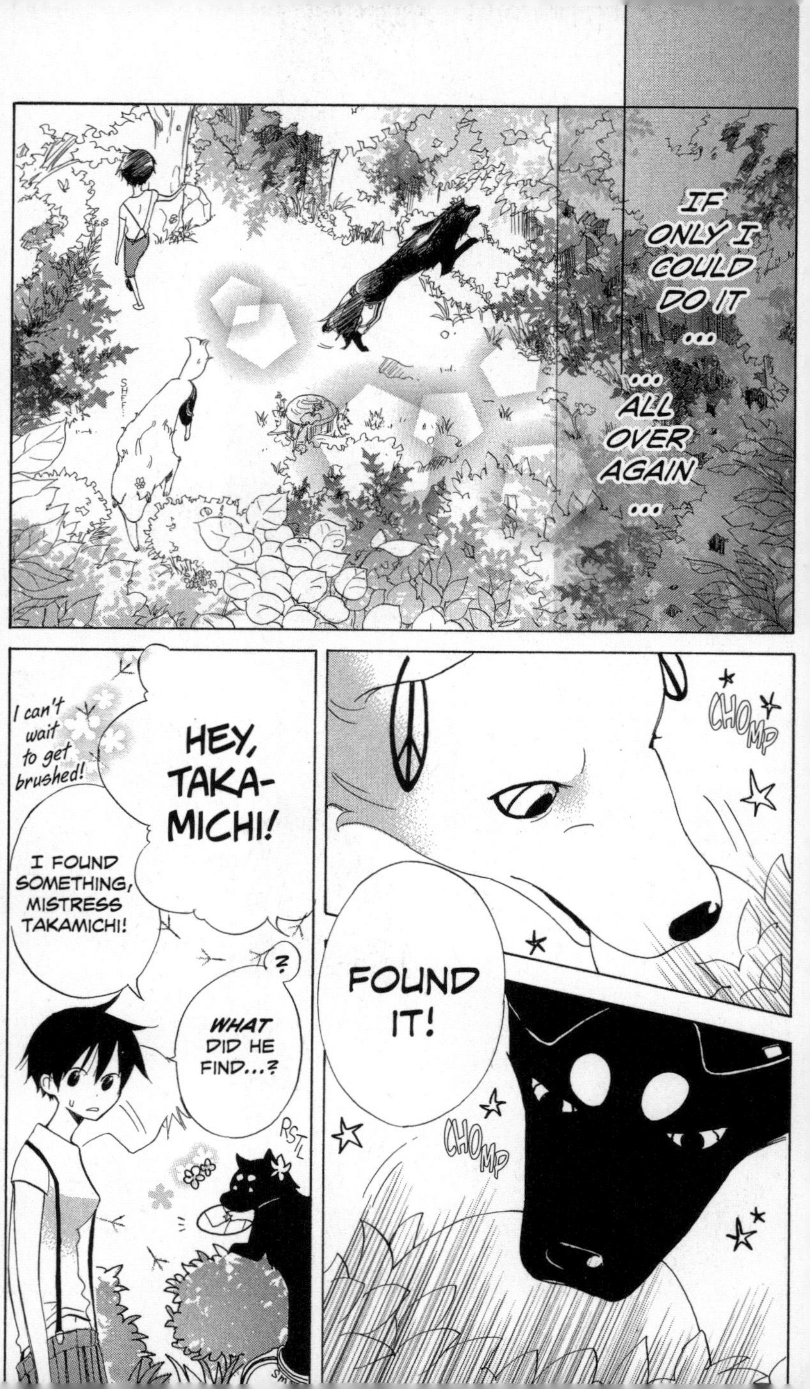
IF ONLY I COULD DO IT ...
... ALL OVER AGAIN ...
SHFF...
CHOMP
FOUND IT!
CHOMP
HEY, TAKA-MICHI!
I can't wait to get brushed!
I FOUND SOMETHING, MISTRESS TAKAMICHI!
?
*WHAT* DID HE FIND...?
RSTL

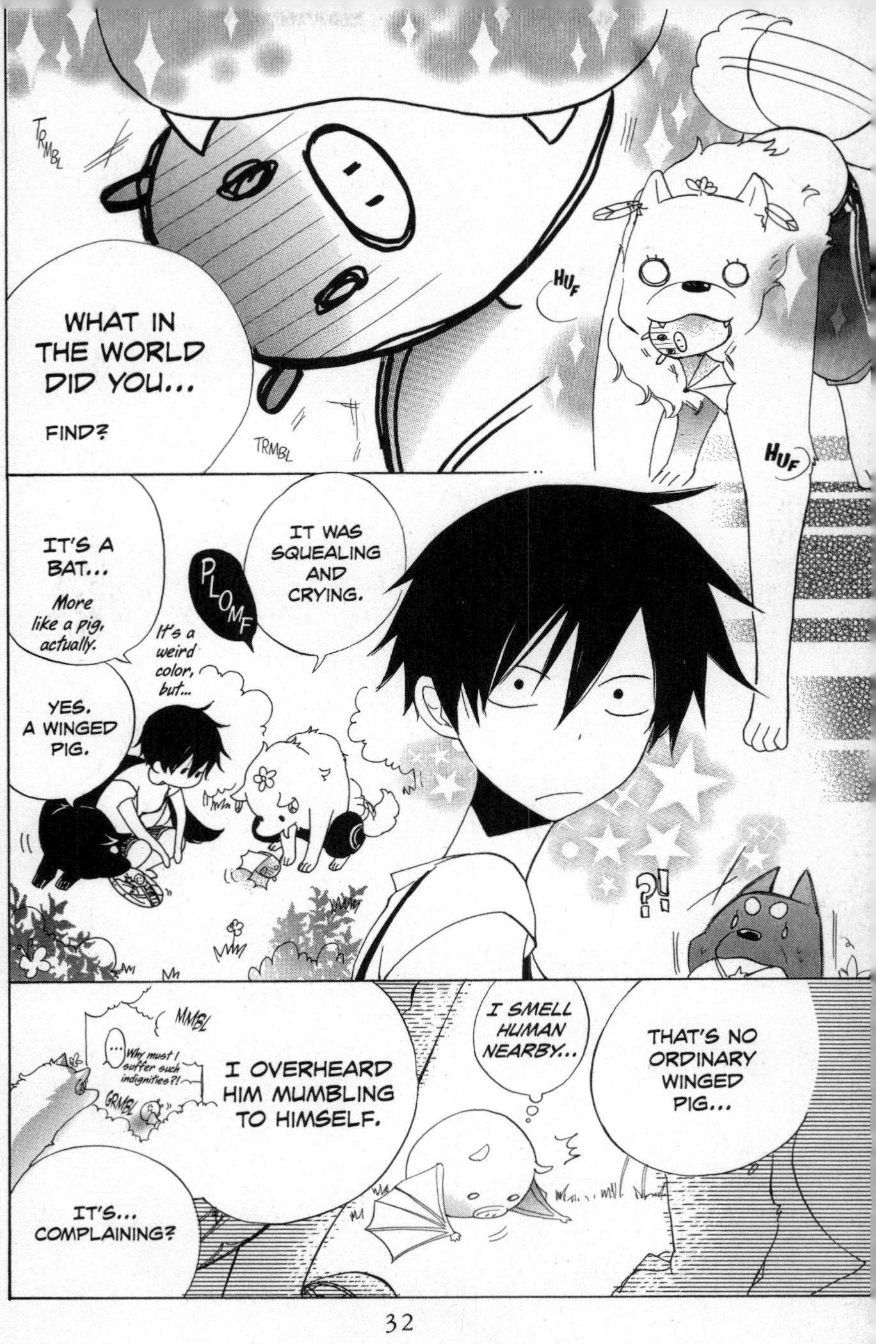
HUF
HUF
WHAT IN THE WORLD DID YOU...
FIND?
TRMBL
TRMBL
?!
IT WAS SQUEALING AND CRYING.
PLOMF
IT'S A BAT...
More like a pig, actually.
It's a weird color, but...
YES. A WINGED PIG.
THAT'S NO ORDINARY WINGED PIG...
I SMELL HUMAN NEARBY...
I OVERHEARD HIM MUMBLING TO HIMSELF.
MMBL
...
Why must I suffer such indignities?!
GRMBL
IT'S... COMPLAINING?

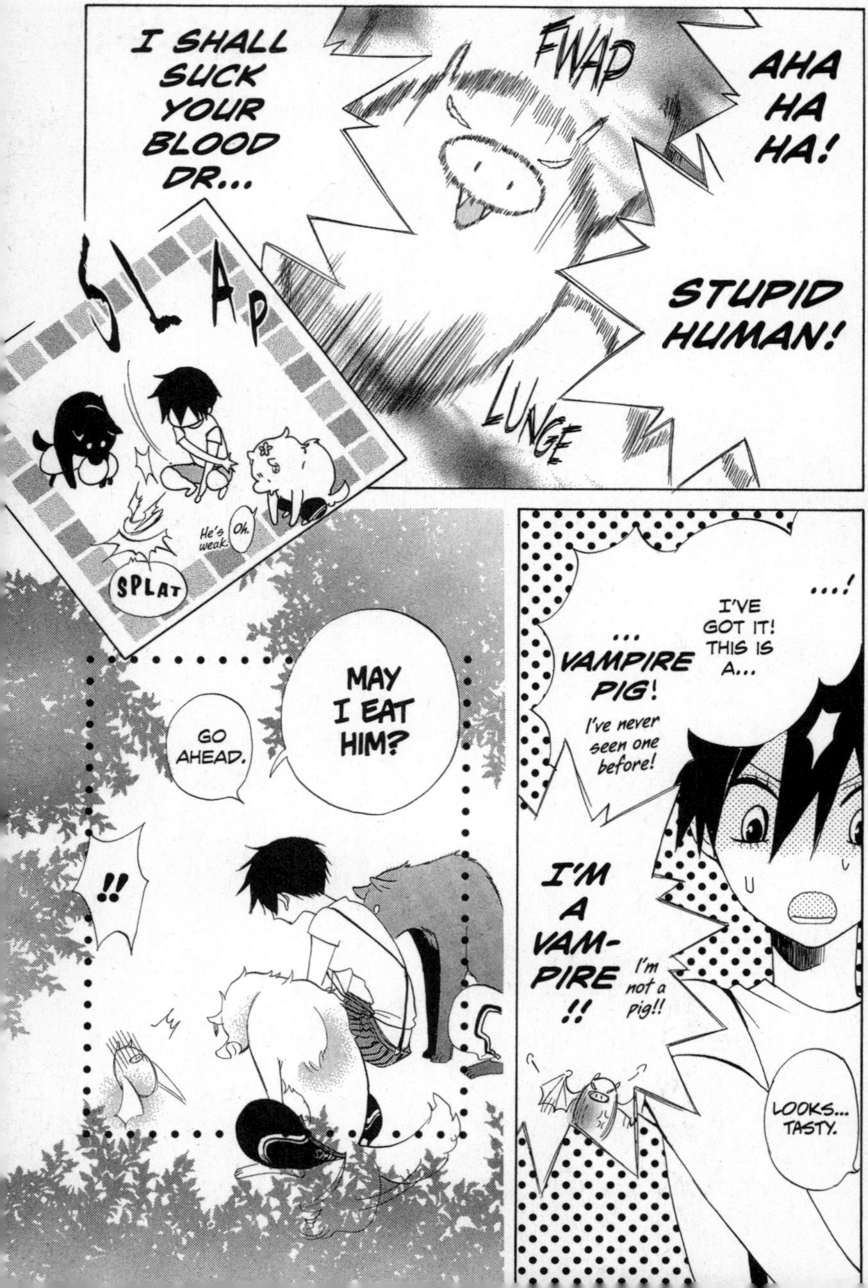
AHA HA HA!
FWAP
I SHALL SUCK YOUR BLOOD DR...
STUPID HUMAN!
LUNGE
SLAP
Oh.
He's weak.
SPLAT
...!
I'VE GOT IT! THIS IS A...
...VAMPIRE PIG!
I've never seen one before!
I'M A VAMPIRE!!
I'm not a pig!!
LOOKS... TASTY.
MAY I EAT HIM?
GO AHEAD.
!!

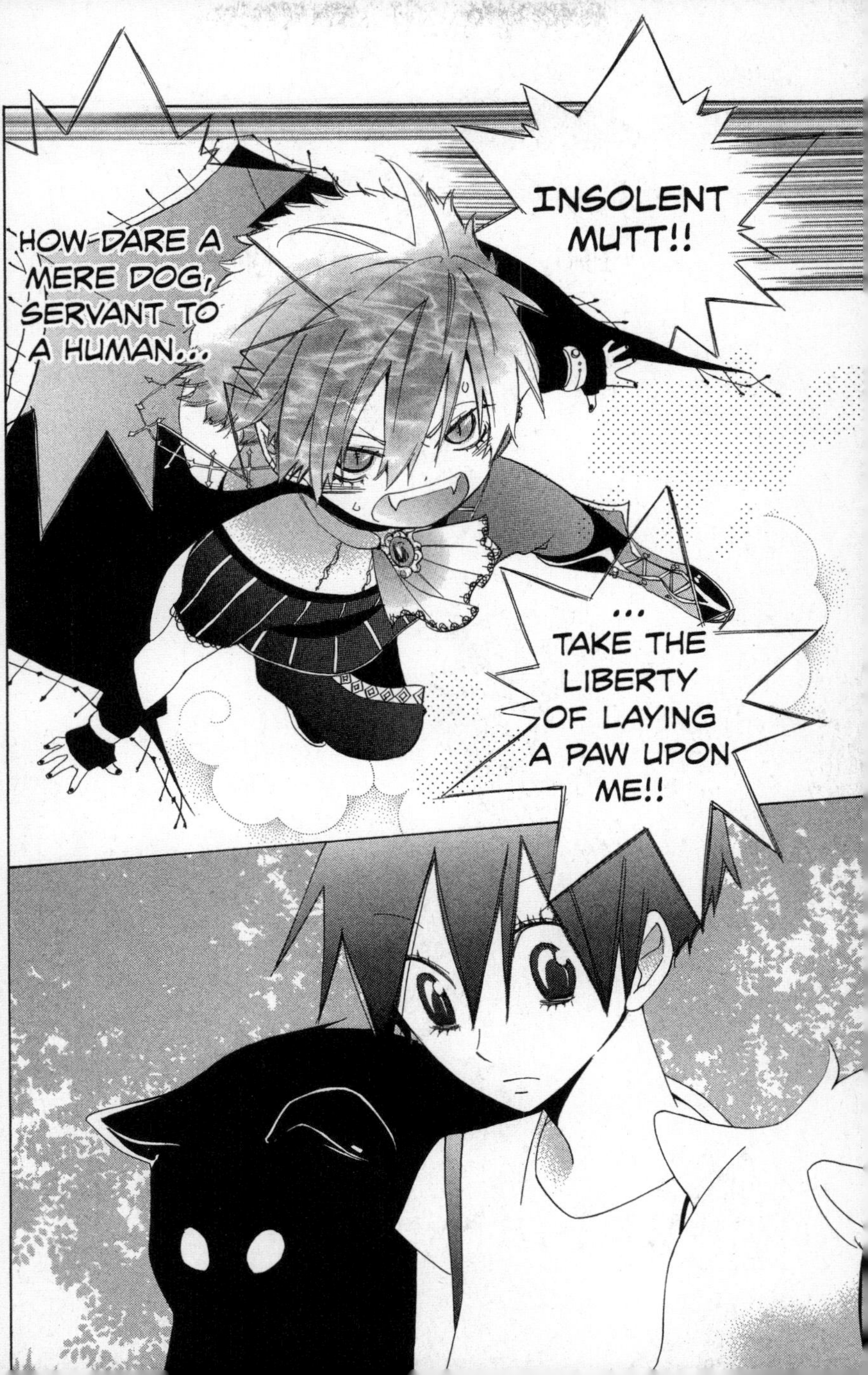
INSOLENT MUTT!!
HOW DARE A MERE DOG, SERVANT TO A HUMAN...
... TAKE THE LIBERTY OF LAYING A PAW UPON ME!!

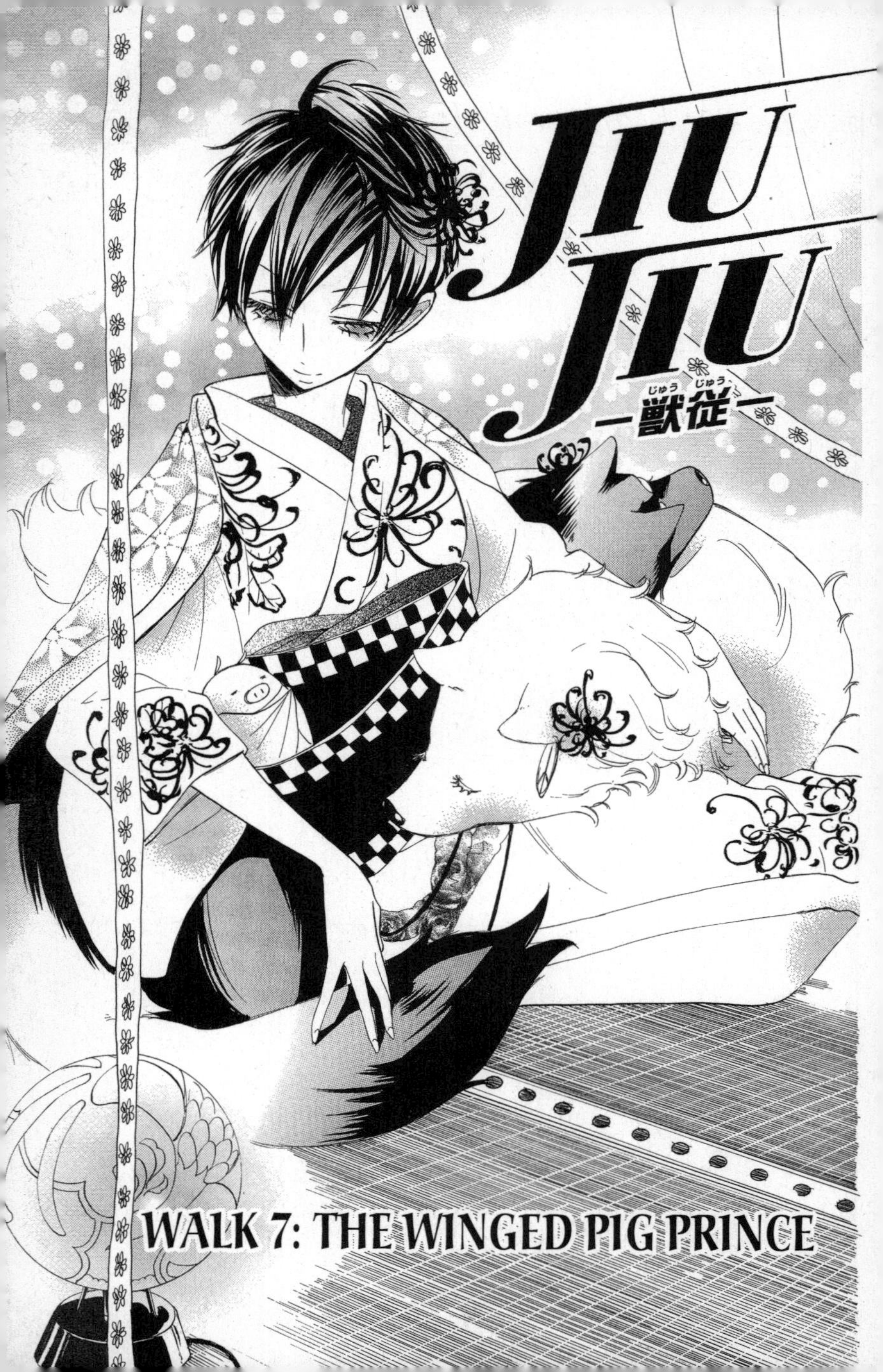
JIU JIU
じゅう じゅう
—獣従—
WALK 7: THE WINGED PIG PRINCE

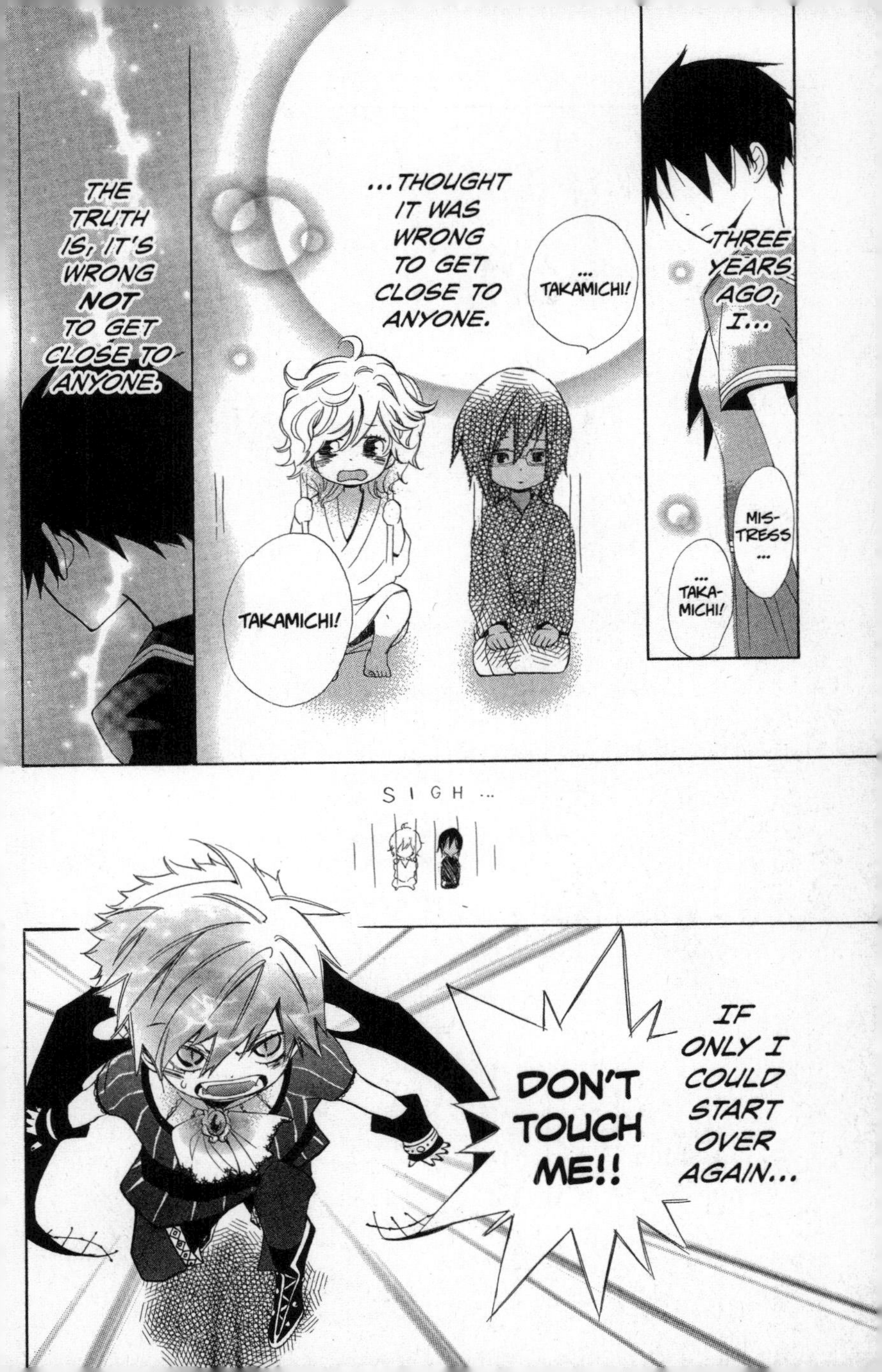
THREE YEARS AGO, I...
MIS-TRESS...
...TAKA-MICHI!
...THOUGHT IT WAS WRONG TO GET CLOSE TO ANYONE.
...TAKAMICHI!
TAKAMICHI!
THE TRUTH IS, IT'S WRONG **NOT** TO GET CLOSE TO ANYONE.
SIGH...
IF ONLY I COULD START OVER AGAIN...
DON'T TOUCH ME!!

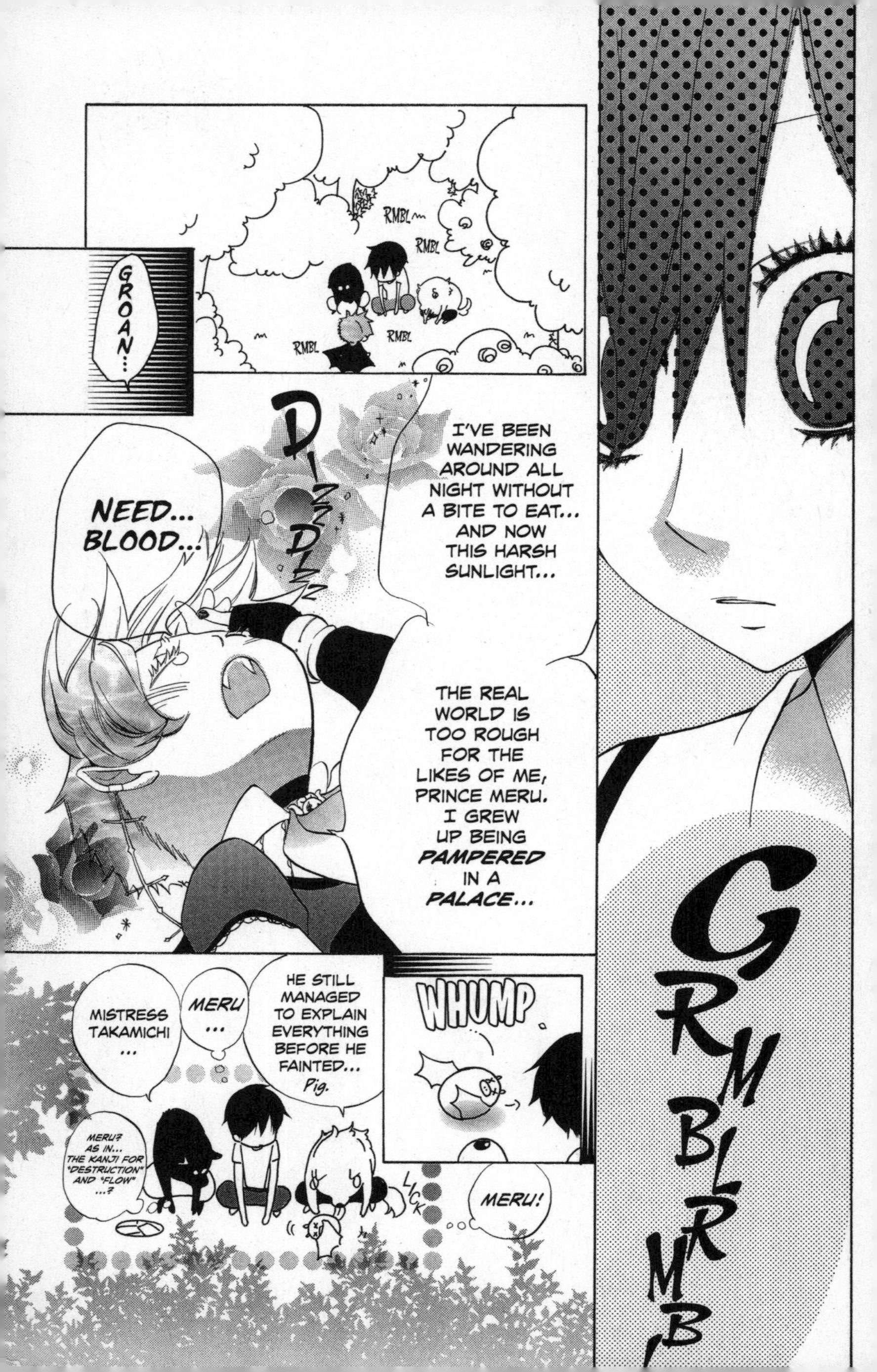
GRMBLRMB
RMBL
RMBL
RMBL
RMBL
GROAN...
I'VE BEEN WANDERING AROUND ALL NIGHT WITHOUT A BITE TO EAT... AND NOW THIS HARSH SUNLIGHT...
DIZZ DIZZ
NEED... BLOOD...
THE REAL WORLD IS TOO ROUGH FOR THE LIKES OF ME, PRINCE MERU. I GREW UP BEING PAMPERED IN A PALACE...
WHUMP
HE STILL MANAGED TO EXPLAIN EVERYTHING BEFORE HE FAINTED... Pig.
MERU...
MISTRESS TAKAMICHI...
MERU!
LICK
MERU? AS IN... THE KANJI FOR "DESTRUCTION" AND "FLOW"...?

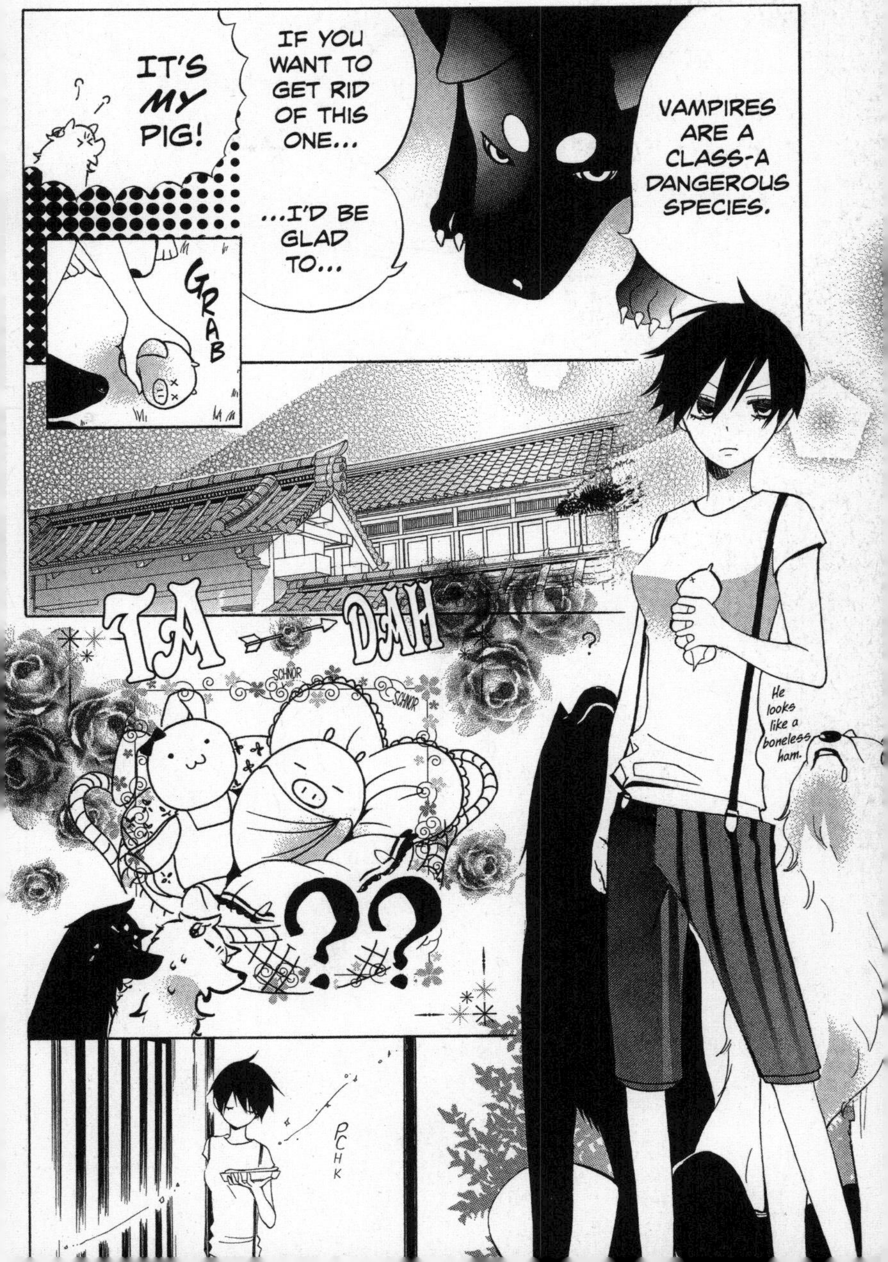
VAMPIRES ARE A CLASS-A DANGEROUS SPECIES.
IF YOU WANT TO GET RID OF THIS ONE...
...I'D BE GLAD TO...
IT'S *MY* PIG!
GRAB
TA DAH
SCHNOR
SCHNOR
He looks like a boneless ham.
PCHK

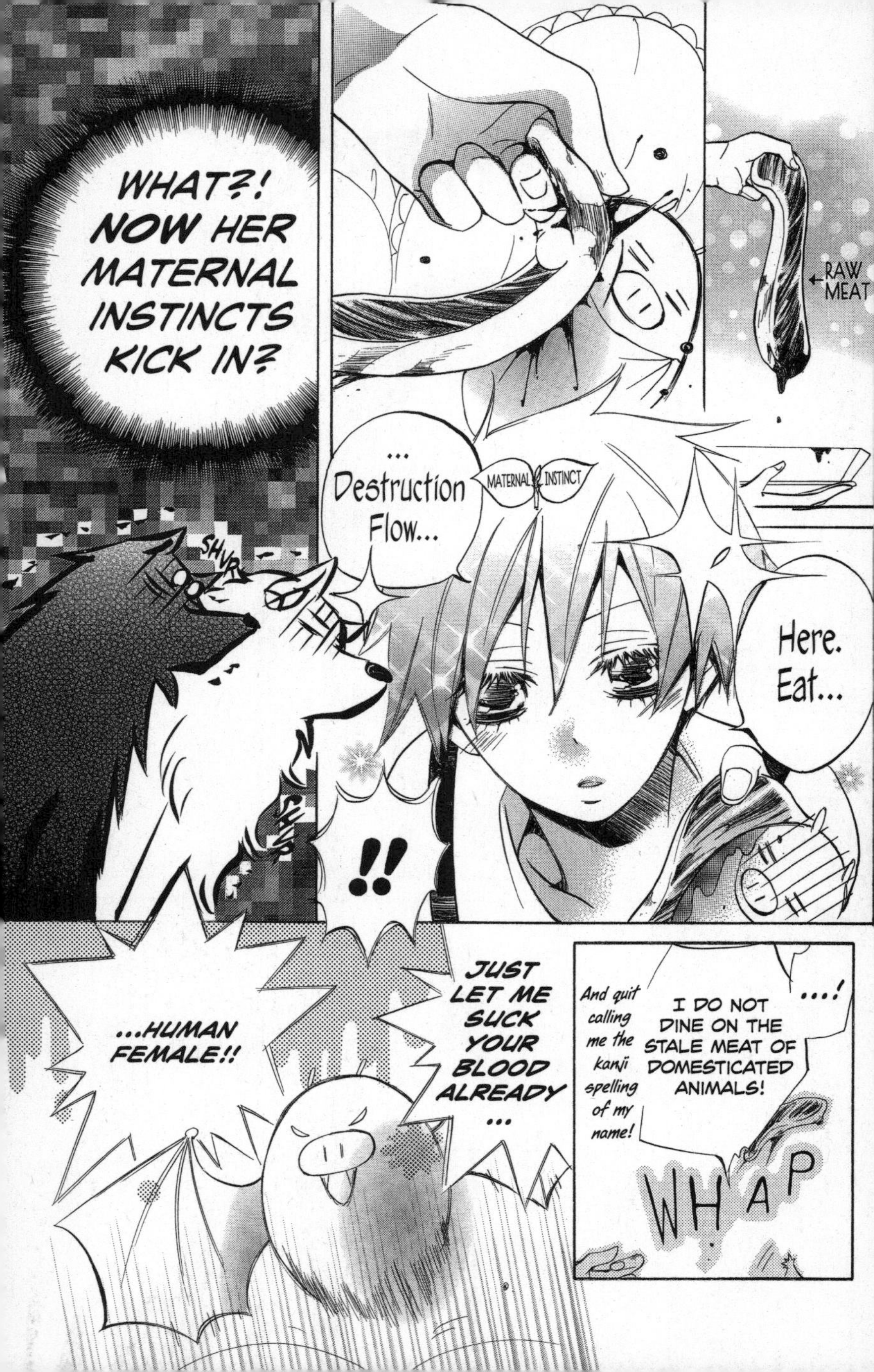
← RAW MEAT
Here. Eat...
MATERNAL INSTINCT
... Destruction Flow...
!!
SHVR
SHVR
WHAT?! NOW HER MATERNAL INSTINCTS KICK IN?
...!
I DO NOT DINE ON THE STALE MEAT OF DOMESTICATED ANIMALS!
And quit calling me the kanji spelling of my name!
WHAP
JUST LET ME SUCK YOUR BLOOD ALREADY...
...HUMAN FEMALE!!

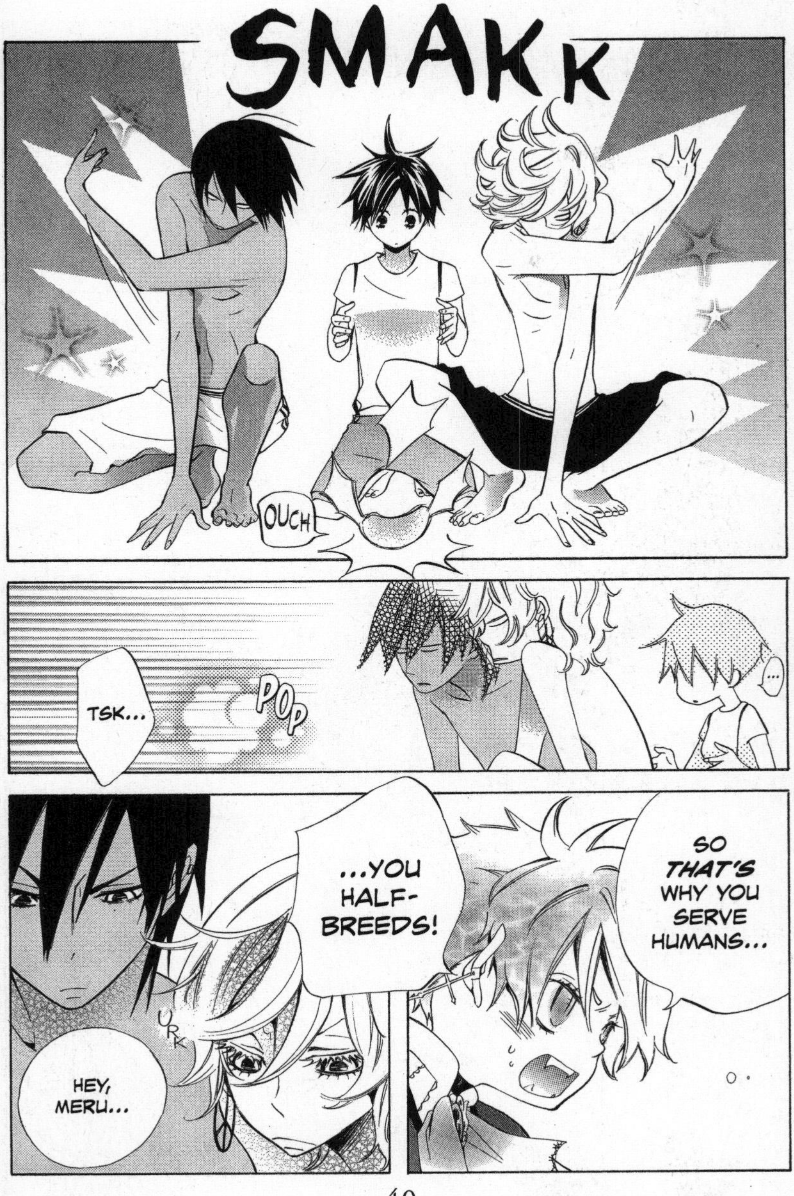
SMAKK
OUCH
...
POP
TSK...
SO *THAT'S* WHY YOU SERVE HUMANS...
...YOU HALF-BREEDS!
URK
HEY, MERU...

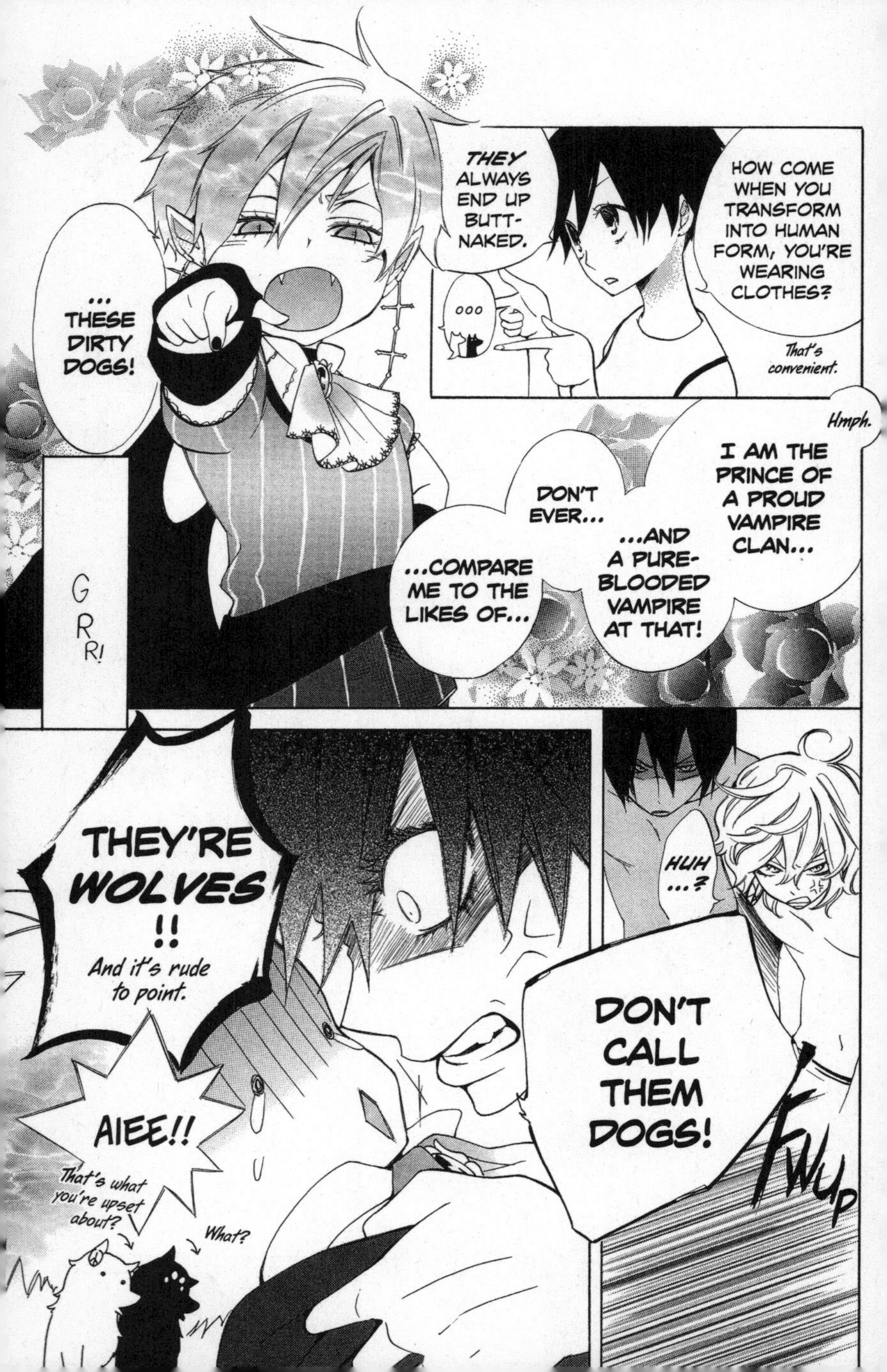
HOW COME WHEN YOU TRANSFORM INTO HUMAN FORM, YOU'RE WEARING CLOTHES?
*THEY* ALWAYS END UP BUTT-NAKED.
ooo
That's convenient.
Hmph.
I AM THE PRINCE OF A PROUD VAMPIRE CLAN...
...AND A PURE-BLOODED VAMPIRE AT THAT!
DON'T EVER...
...COMPARE ME TO THE LIKES OF...
... THESE DIRTY DOGS!
GRR!
HUH ...?
FWUP
DON'T CALL THEM DOGS!
THEY'RE *WOLVES* !!
And it's rude to point.
AIEE!!
That's what you're upset about?
What?

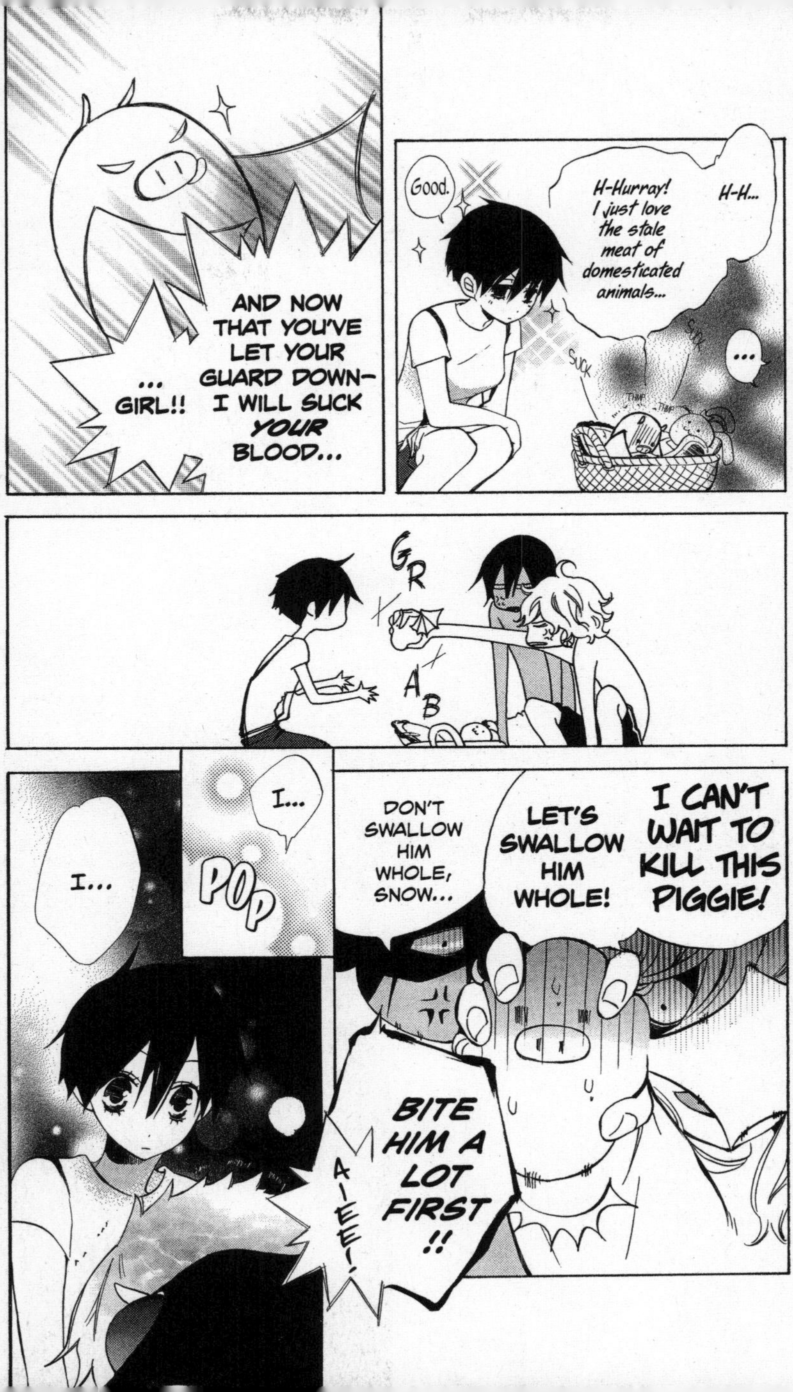
H-H...
H-Hurray! I just love the stale meat of domesticated animals...
Good.
SUCK
SUCK
...
THMP
THMP
AND NOW THAT YOU'VE LET YOUR GUARD DOWN— I WILL SUCK YOUR BLOOD...
... GIRL!!
GRAB
I CAN'T WAIT TO KILL THIS PIGGIE!
LET'S SWALLOW HIM WHOLE!
DON'T SWALLOW HIM WHOLE, SNOW...
BITE HIM A LOT FIRST!!
AIEE!
I...
POP
I...

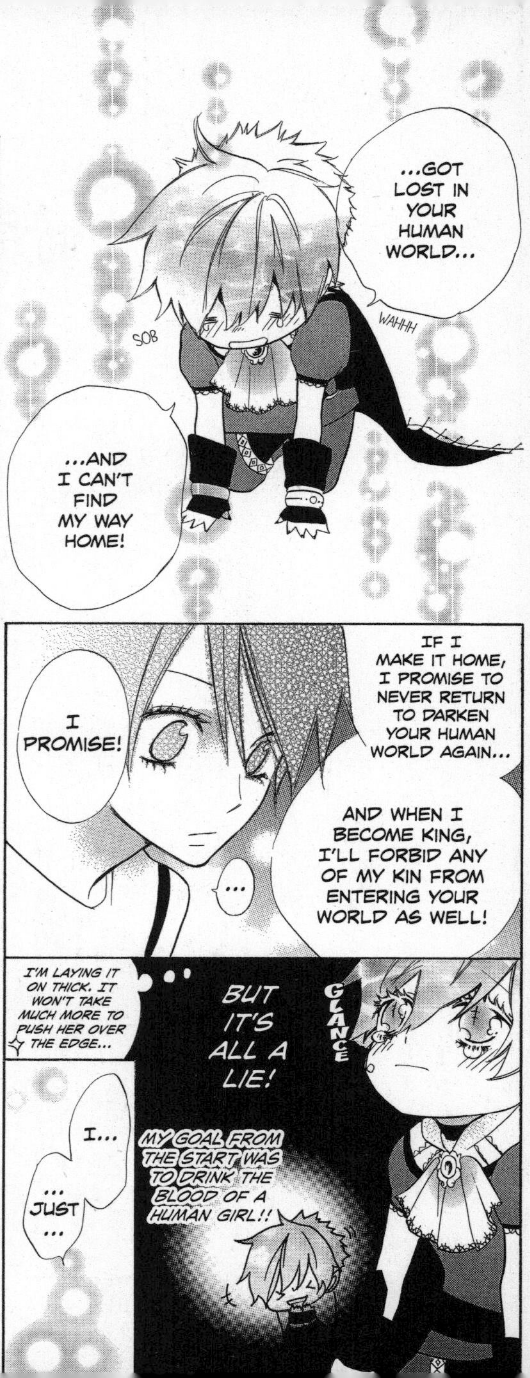
...GOT LOST IN YOUR HUMAN WORLD...
WAHHH
SOB
...AND I CAN'T FIND MY WAY HOME!
IF I MAKE IT HOME, I PROMISE TO NEVER RETURN TO DARKEN YOUR HUMAN WORLD AGAIN...
AND WHEN I BECOME KING, I'LL FORBID ANY OF MY KIN FROM ENTERING YOUR WORLD AS WELL!
...
I PROMISE!
GLANCE
BUT IT'S ALL A LIE!
I'M LAYING IT ON THICK. IT WON'T TAKE MUCH MORE TO PUSH HER OVER THE EDGE...
MY GOAL FROM THE START WAS TO DRINK THE BLOOD OF A HUMAN GIRL!!
I...
...JUST...

Unexpected Q&A corner

I was so happy to receive two letters from my readers who read Jiu Jiu vol. 1 and wrote to me asking, "May I ask you a question?"!! Two!! Two...?!

Okay, focus, focus... So, anyway, I thought I'd take this opportunity to answer their questions in this sidebar.

Did Takamichi give Snow those earrings ☮ he wears?

That's something I wasn't able to include in the "Night's Diary" episode... but I hope to explain it sometime soon, so please be patient...!

Why does Takamichi call Moon "Paper Moon"?

Well, because, basically, she's saying he's no "New Moon" but just a "Waxing Crescent."

Who's the elder brother, Snow or Night?

Both Snow and Night think they were born first. Only their mother knows for sure.

That's it!

Yamaguchi Prefecture Rie-sama.
Shiga Prefecture Hina-sama.

I'm sorry I didn't really answer your questions clearly... but thanks so much for asking!!

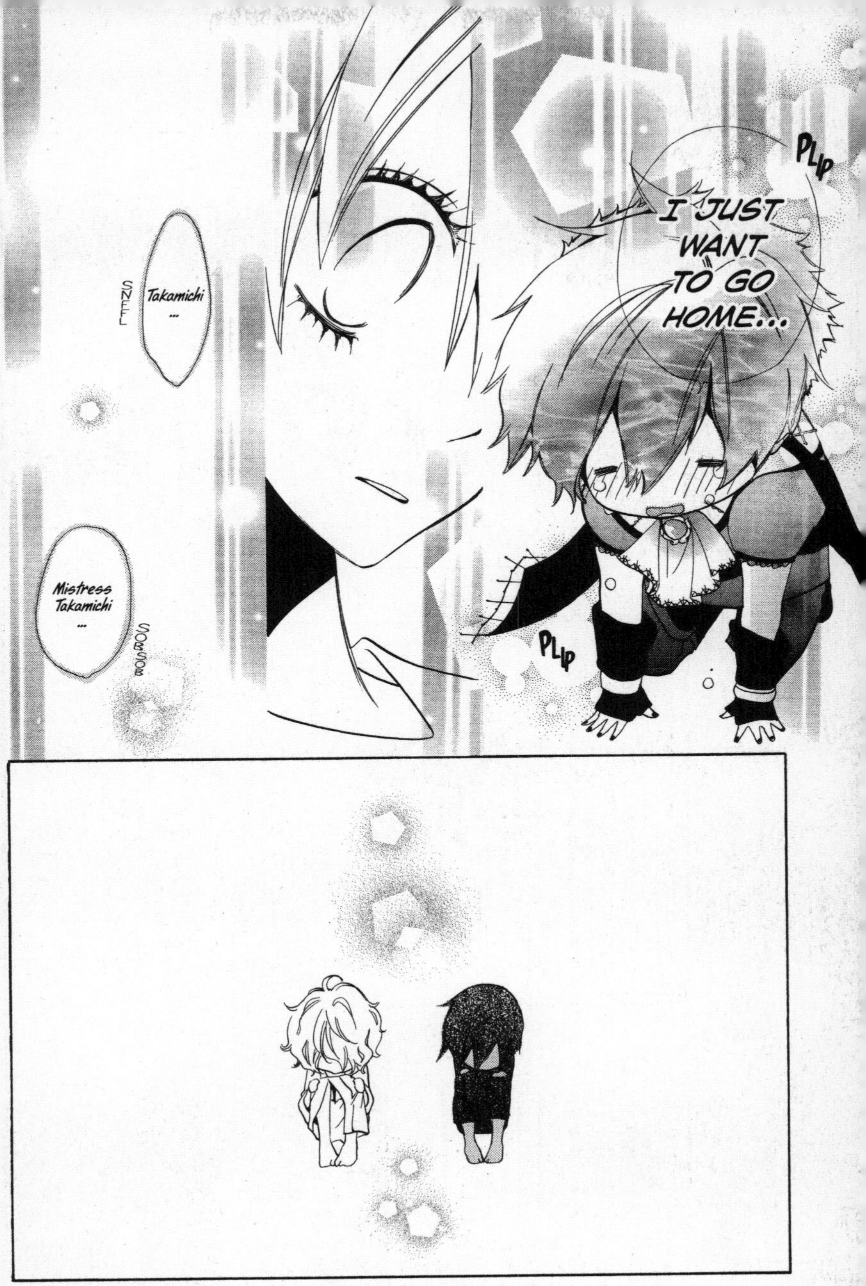
PLIP
I JUST WANT TO GO HOME...
PLIP
Takamichi ...
SNFFL
Mistress Takamichi ...
SOB SOB

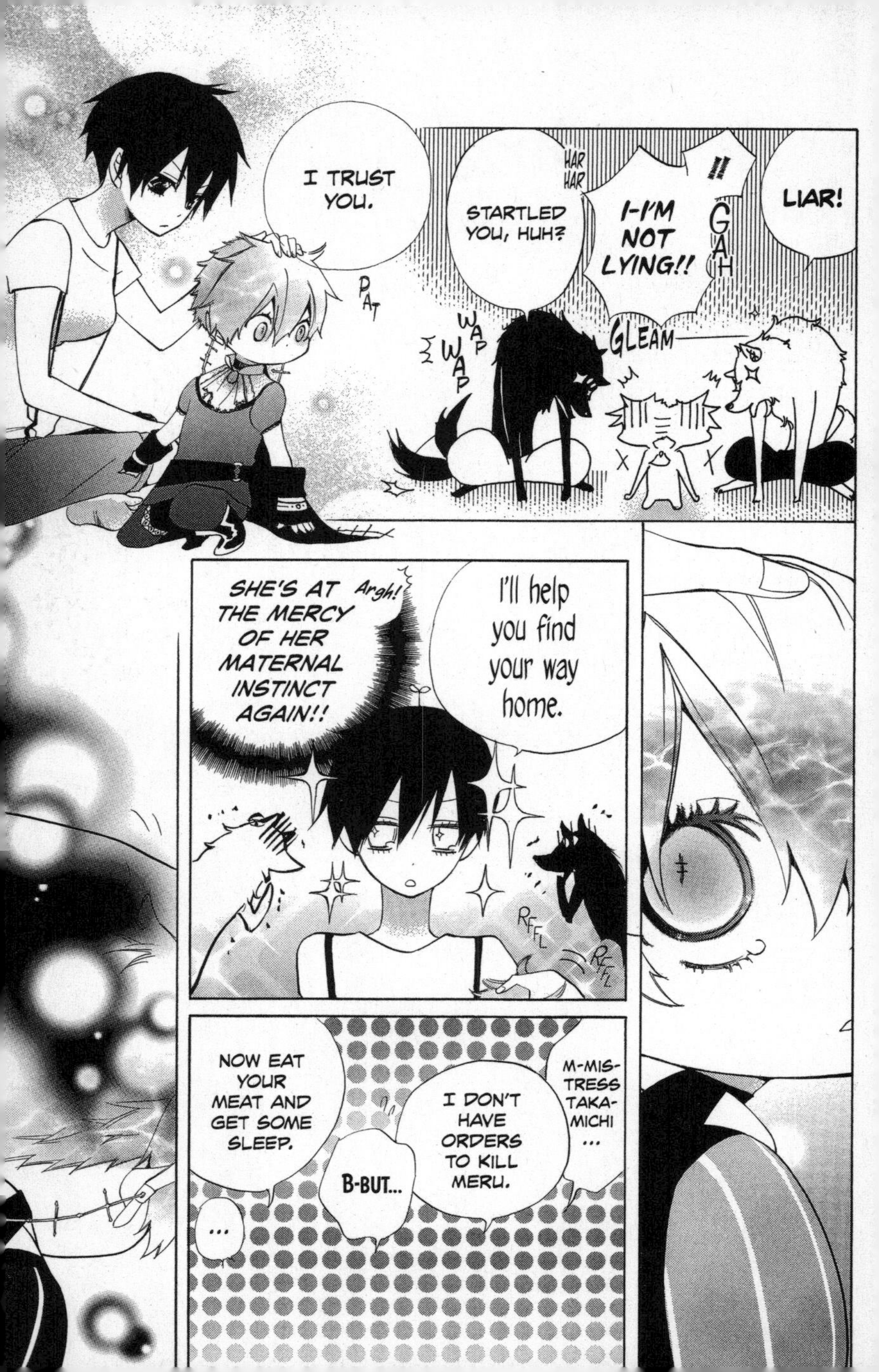
LIAR!
!!
GAH
I-I'M NOT LYING!!
HAR HAR
STARTLED YOU, HUH?
GLEAM
WAP WAP
I TRUST YOU.
PAT
I'll help you find your way home.
Argh!
SHE'S AT THE MERCY OF HER MATERNAL INSTINCT AGAIN!!
RFFL
RFFL
M-MISTRESS TAKAMICHI...
I DON'T HAVE ORDERS TO KILL MERU.
B-BUT...
NOW EAT YOUR MEAT AND GET SOME SLEEP.
...

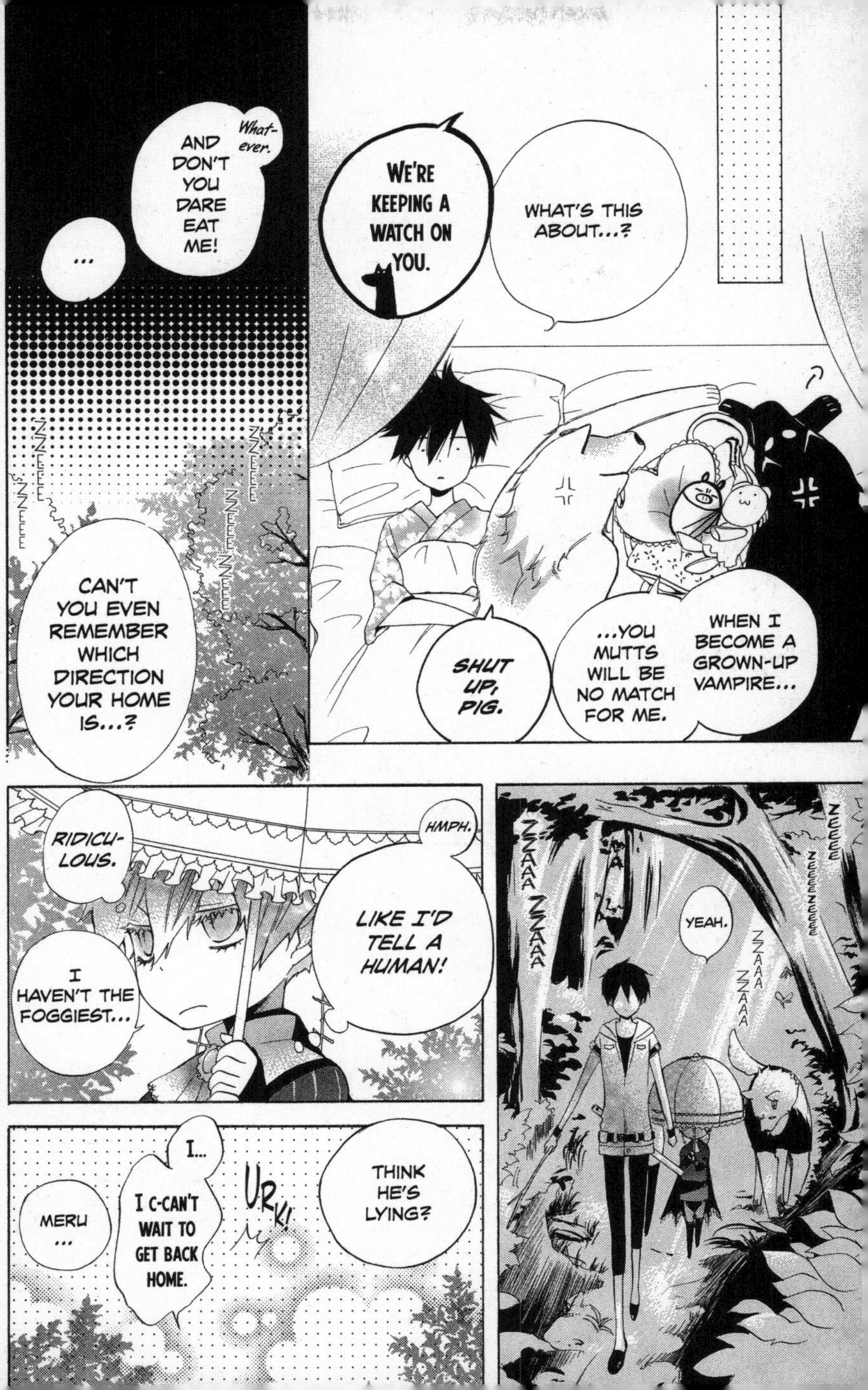
WHAT'S THIS ABOUT...?
WE'RE KEEPING A WATCH ON YOU.
WHEN I BECOME A GROWN-UP VAMPIRE...
...YOU MUTTS WILL BE NO MATCH FOR ME.
SHUT UP, PIG.
Whatever.
AND DON'T YOU DARE EAT ME!
...
ZZZEEE
ZZZEEE
ZZEEE
ZZEEE
CAN'T YOU EVEN REMEMBER WHICH DIRECTION YOUR HOME IS...?
ZEEEE
ZEEEEZEEEE
ZZAAA ZZAAA
YEAH.
ZZAAA ZZAAA
HMPH.
LIKE I'D TELL A HUMAN!
RIDICU-LOUS.
I HAVEN'T THE FOGGIEST...
THINK HE'S LYING?
URK!
I...
I C-CAN'T WAIT TO GET BACK HOME.
MERU...

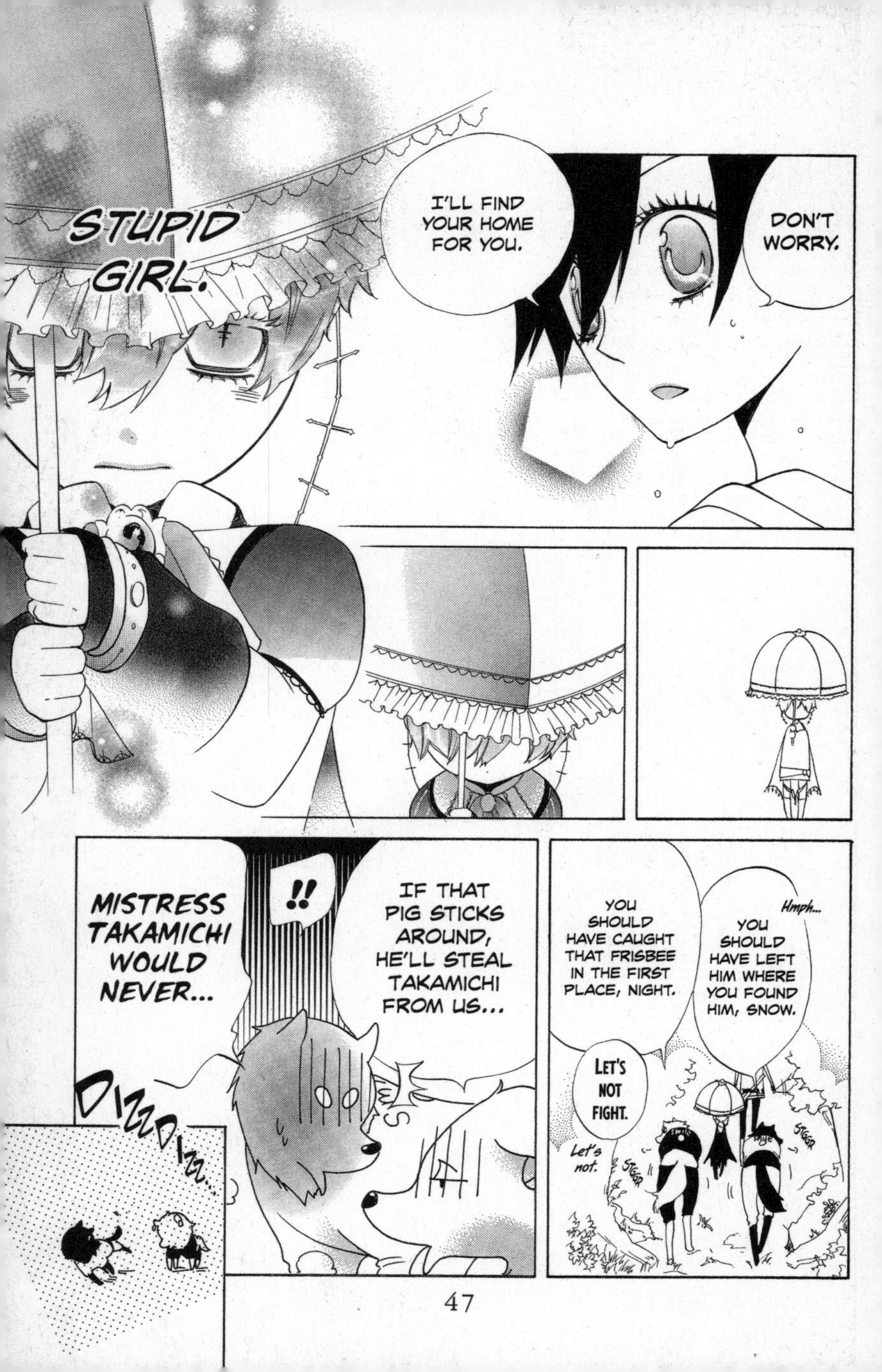
DON'T WORRY.
I'LL FIND YOUR HOME FOR YOU.
STUPID GIRL.
Hmph...
YOU SHOULD HAVE LEFT HIM WHERE YOU FOUND HIM, SNOW.
YOU SHOULD HAVE CAUGHT THAT FRISBEE IN THE FIRST PLACE, NIGHT.
LET'S NOT FIGHT.
Let's not.
STGGR
STGGR
IF THAT PIG STICKS AROUND, HE'LL STEAL TAKAMICHI FROM US...
!!
MISTRESS TAKAMICHI WOULD NEVER...
DIZZDIZZ...

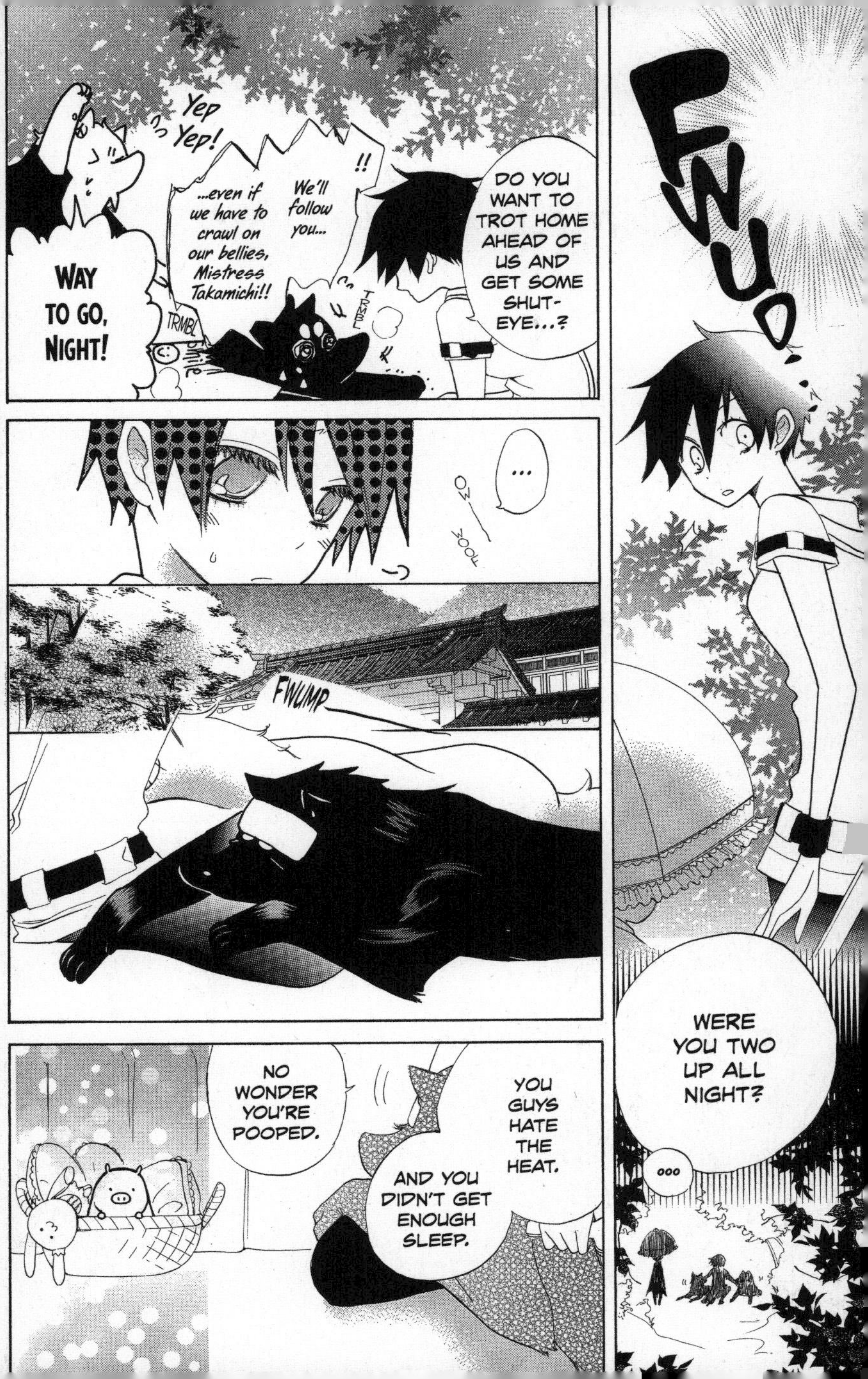
FWUD
...
WERE YOU TWO UP ALL NIGHT?
ooo
DO YOU WANT TO TROT HOME AHEAD OF US AND GET SOME SHUT-EYE...?
!!
We'll follow you...
...even if we have to crawl on our bellies, Mistress Takamichi!!
Yep Yep!
WAY TO GO, NIGHT!
TRMBL
TRMBL
...
OW— WOOL
FWUMP
YOU GUYS HATE THE HEAT.
AND YOU DIDN'T GET ENOUGH SLEEP.
NO WONDER YOU'RE POOPED.

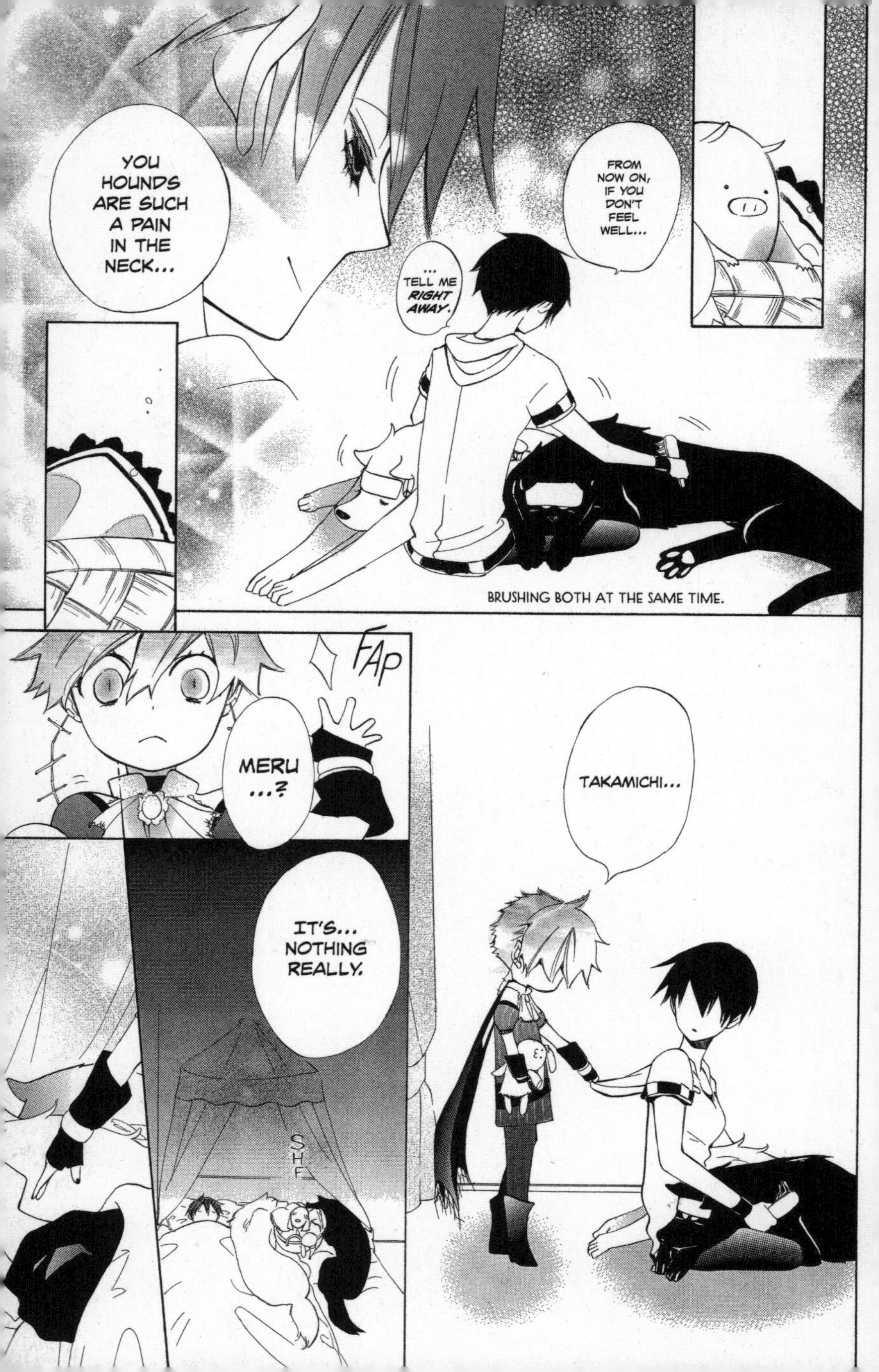
FROM NOW ON, IF YOU DON'T FEEL WELL...
...TELL ME RIGHT AWAY.
YOU HOUNDS ARE SUCH A PAIN IN THE NECK...
BRUSHING BOTH AT THE SAME TIME.
TAKAMICHI...
FAP
MERU...?
IT'S... NOTHING REALLY.
SHF

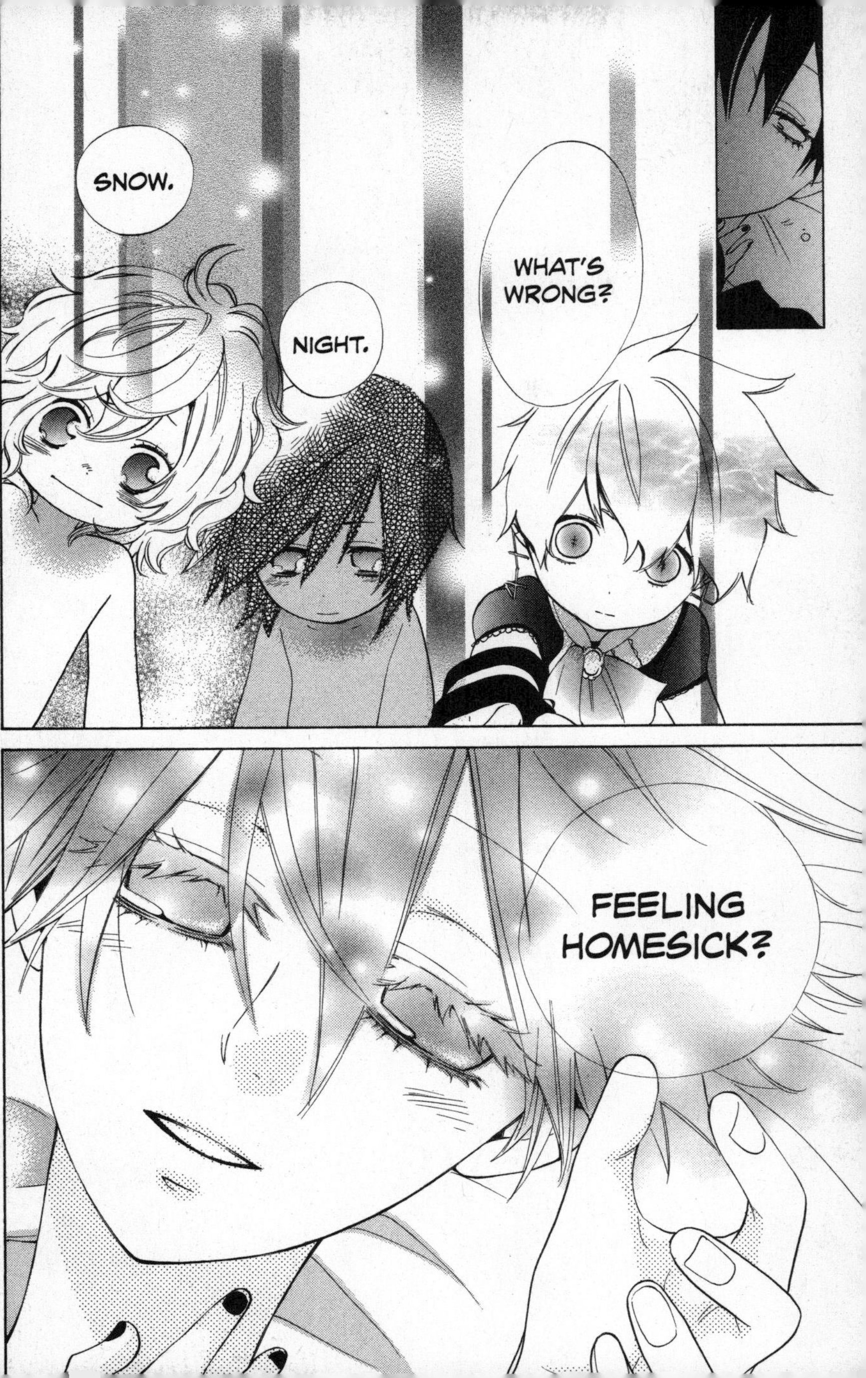
WHAT'S WRONG?
NIGHT.
SNOW.
FEELING HOMESICK?

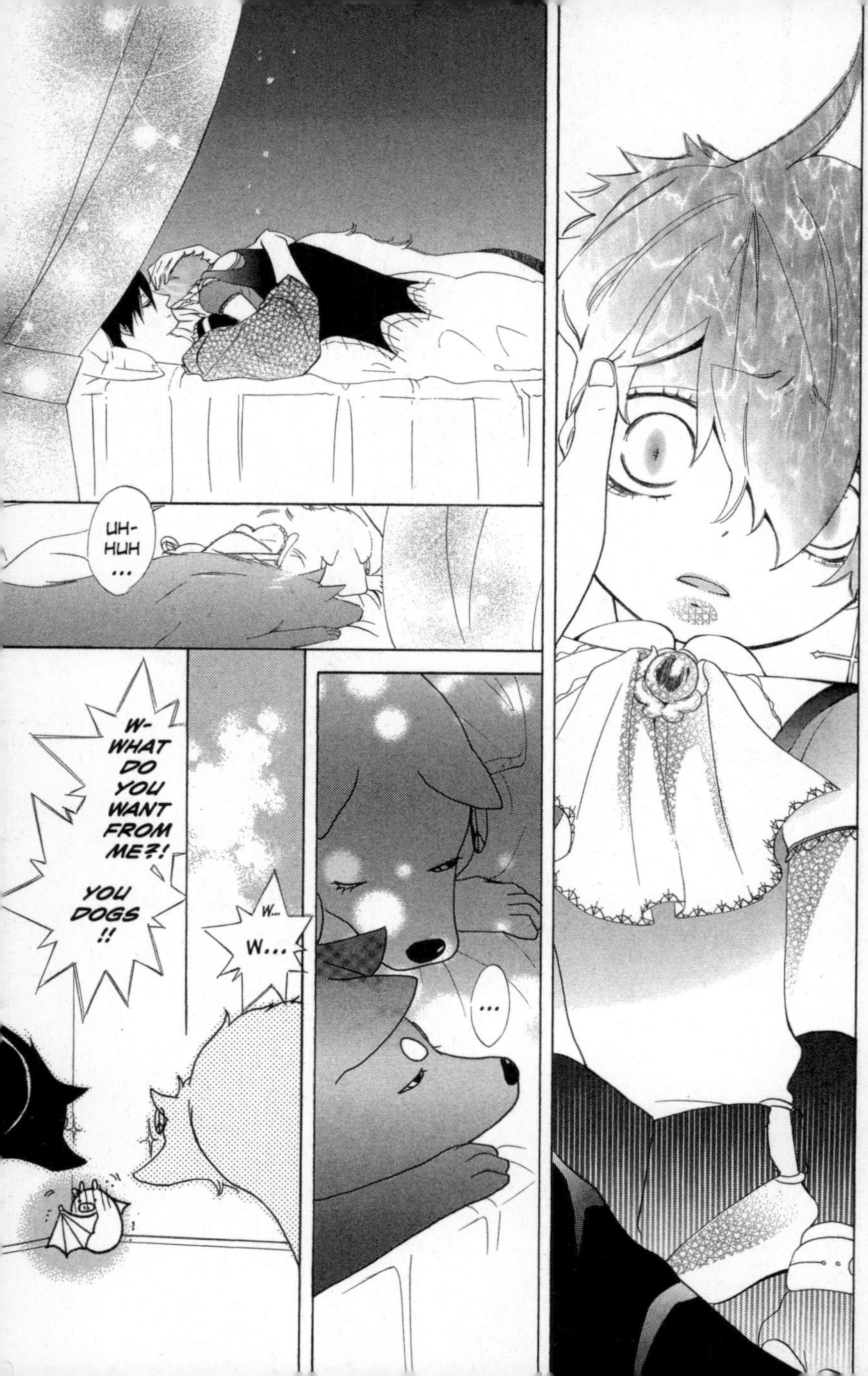
UH-HUH ...
...
W... W...
W-WHAT DO YOU WANT FROM ME?! YOU DOGS!!

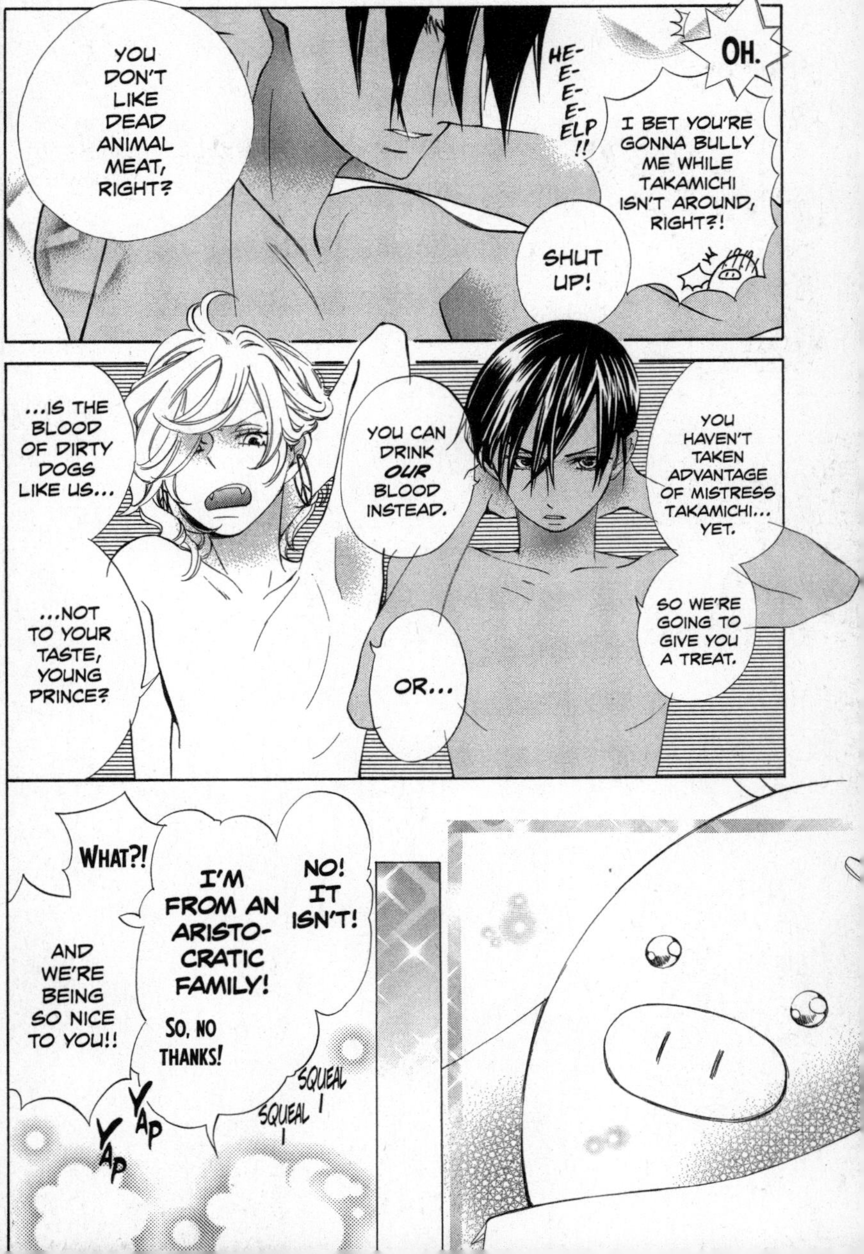
OH.
I BET YOU'RE GONNA BULLY ME WHILE TAKAMICHI ISN'T AROUND, RIGHT?!
HE-E-E-E-ELP!!
SHUT UP!
YOU DON'T LIKE DEAD ANIMAL MEAT, RIGHT?
YOU HAVEN'T TAKEN ADVANTAGE OF MISTRESS TAKAMICHI... YET.
SO WE'RE GOING TO GIVE YOU A TREAT.
YOU CAN DRINK OUR BLOOD INSTEAD.
OR...
...IS THE BLOOD OF DIRTY DOGS LIKE US...
...NOT TO YOUR TASTE, YOUNG PRINCE?
NO! IT ISN'T!
I'M FROM AN ARISTO-CRATIC FAMILY!
SO, NO THANKS!
SQUEAL
SQUEAL
WHAT?!
AND WE'RE BEING SO NICE TO YOU!!
YAP
YAP

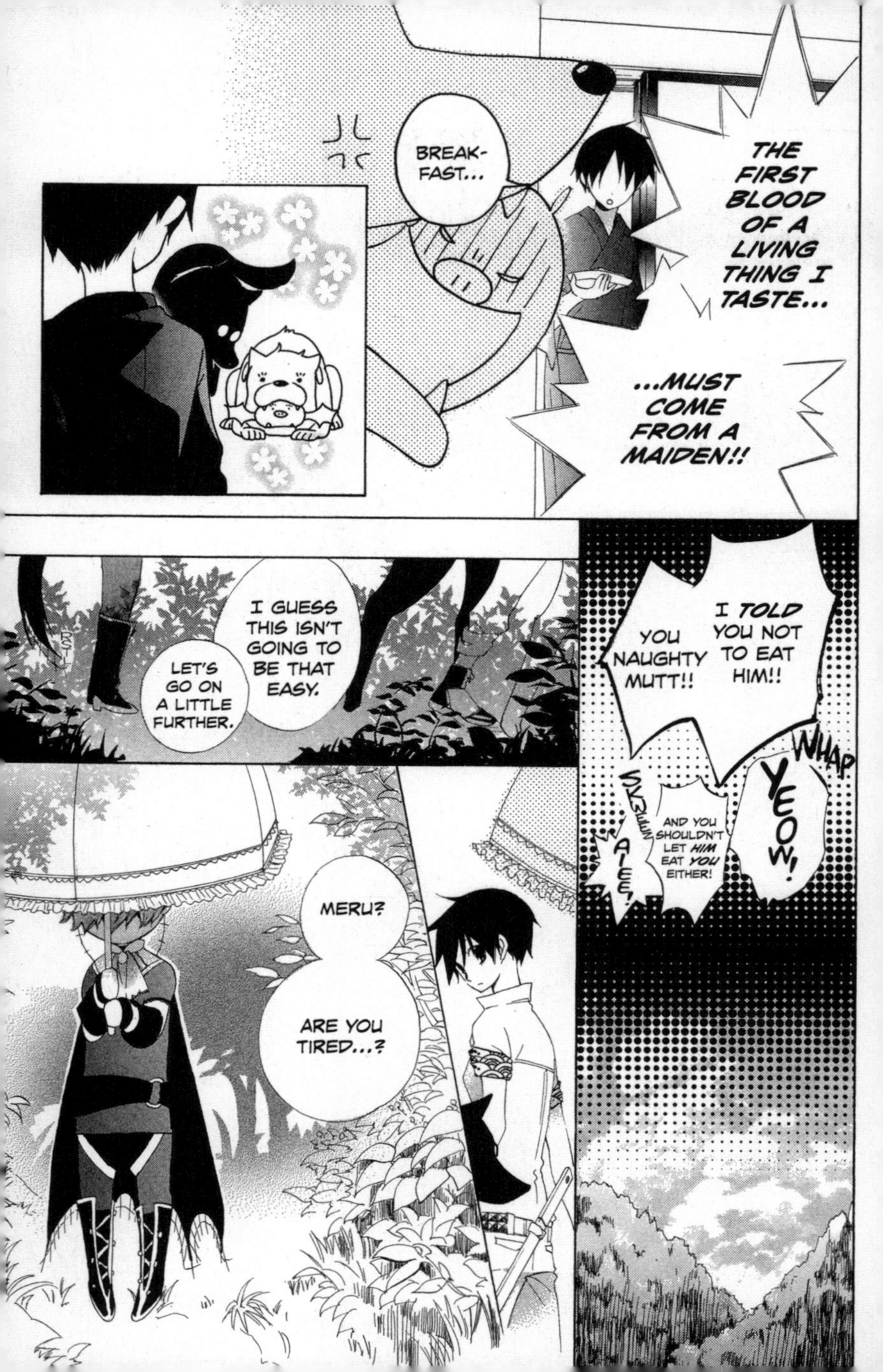
THE FIRST BLOOD OF A LIVING THING I TASTE...
...MUST COME FROM A MAIDEN!!
BREAK-FAST...
I TOLD YOU NOT TO EAT HIM!!
YOU NAUGHTY MUTT!!
WHAP
YEOW!
AND YOU SHOULDN'T LET HIM EAT YOU EITHER!
AIEE!
I GUESS THIS ISN'T GOING TO BE THAT EASY.
LET'S GO ON A LITTLE FURTHER.
MERU?
ARE YOU TIRED...?

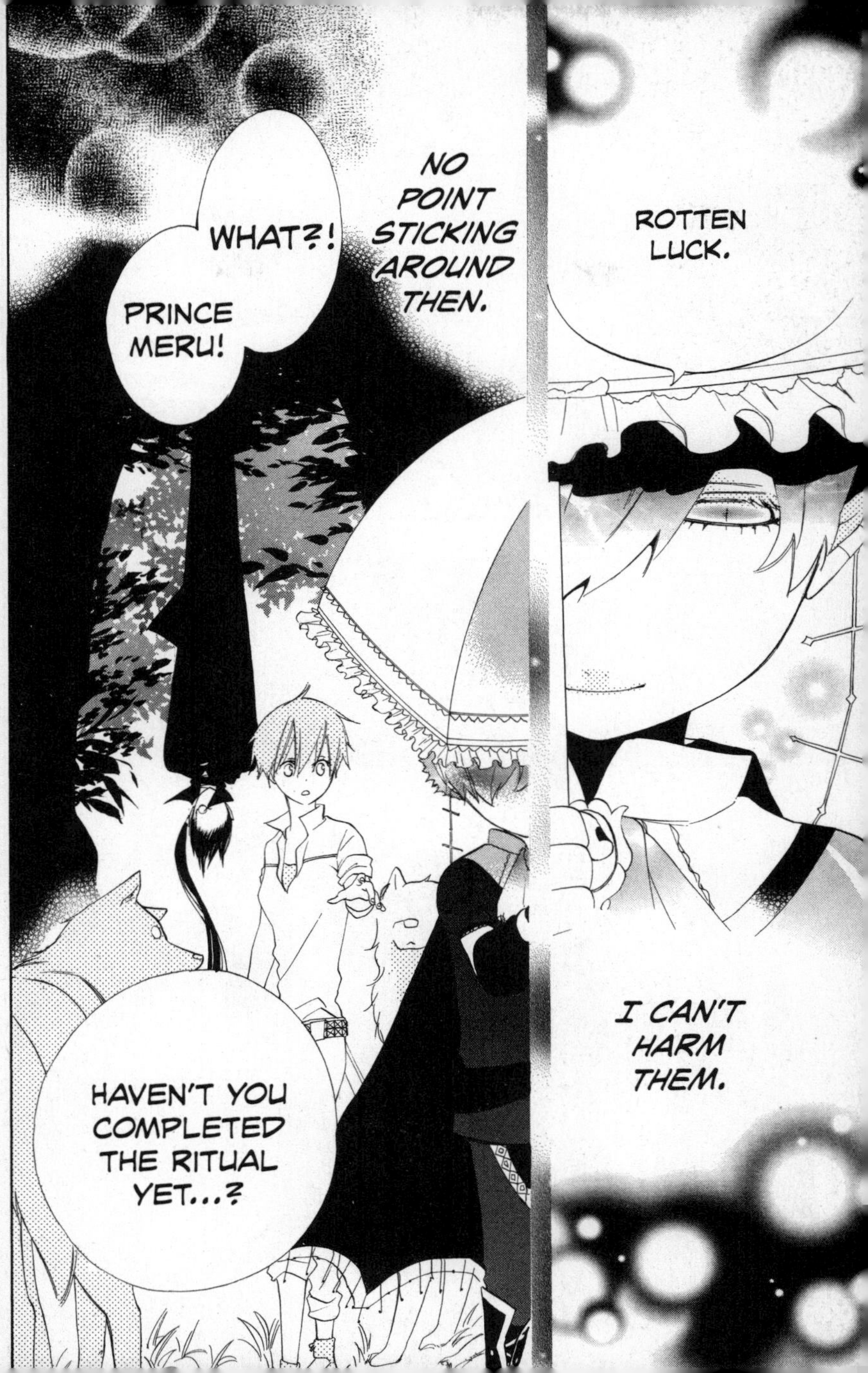
ROTTEN LUCK.
I CAN'T HARM THEM.
NO POINT STICKING AROUND THEN.
WHAT?!
PRINCE MERU!
HAVEN'T YOU COMPLETED THE RITUAL YET...?

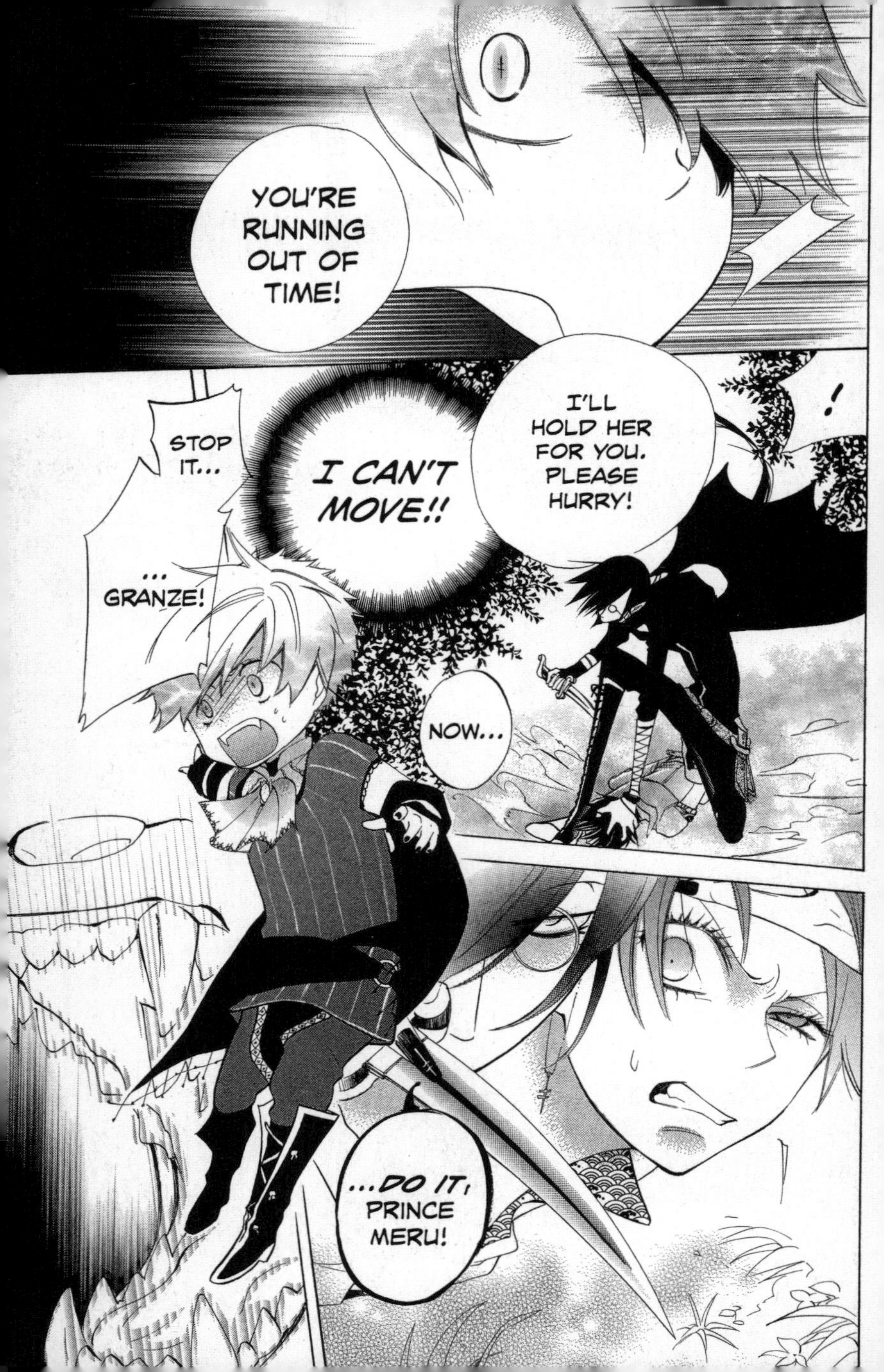
YOU'RE RUNNING OUT OF TIME!
!
I'LL HOLD HER FOR YOU. PLEASE HURRY!
NOW...
I CAN'T MOVE!!
STOP IT...
...GRANZE!
...DO IT, PRINCE MERU!

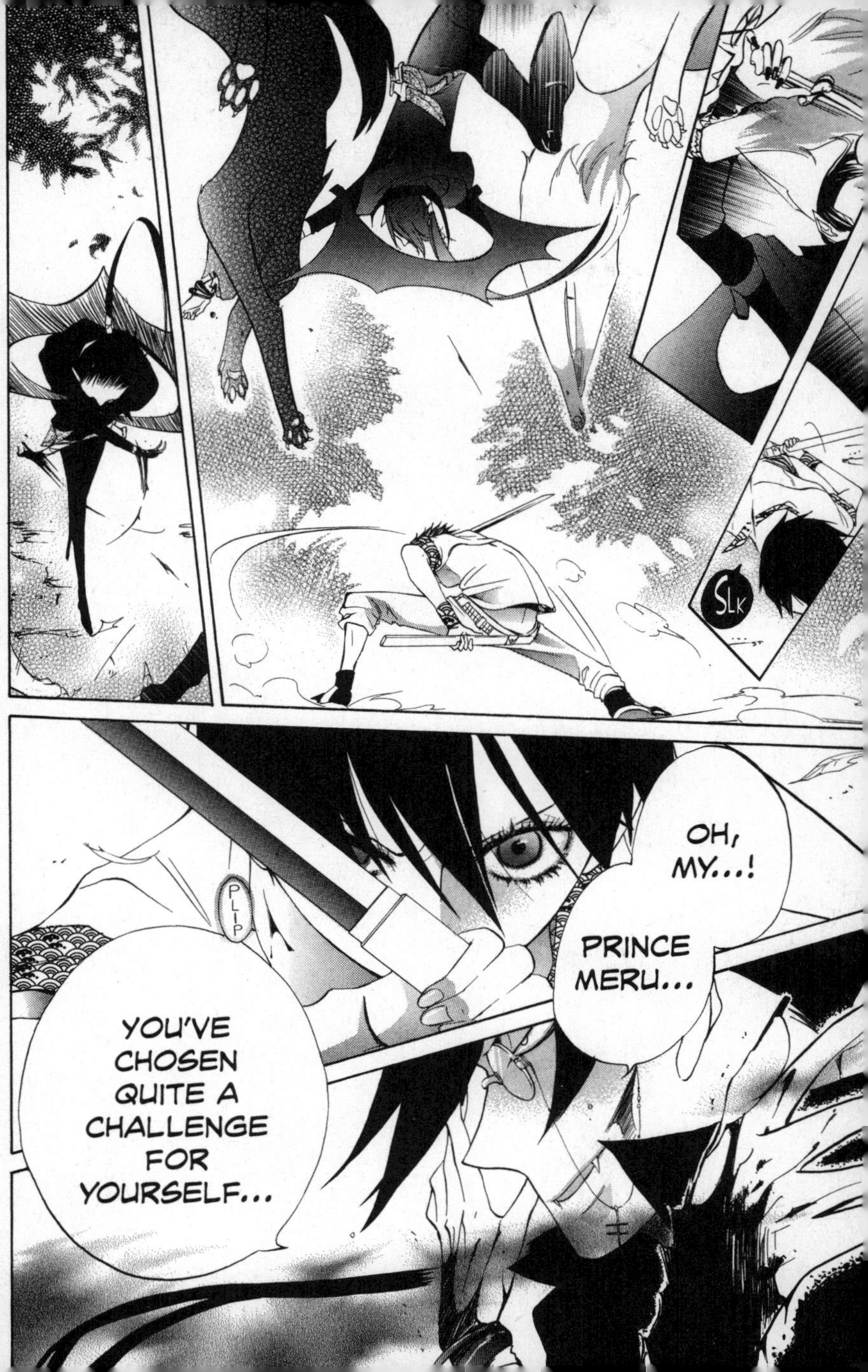
SLK
OH, MY...!
PRINCE MERU...
PLIP
YOU'VE CHOSEN QUITE A CHALLENGE FOR YOURSELF...

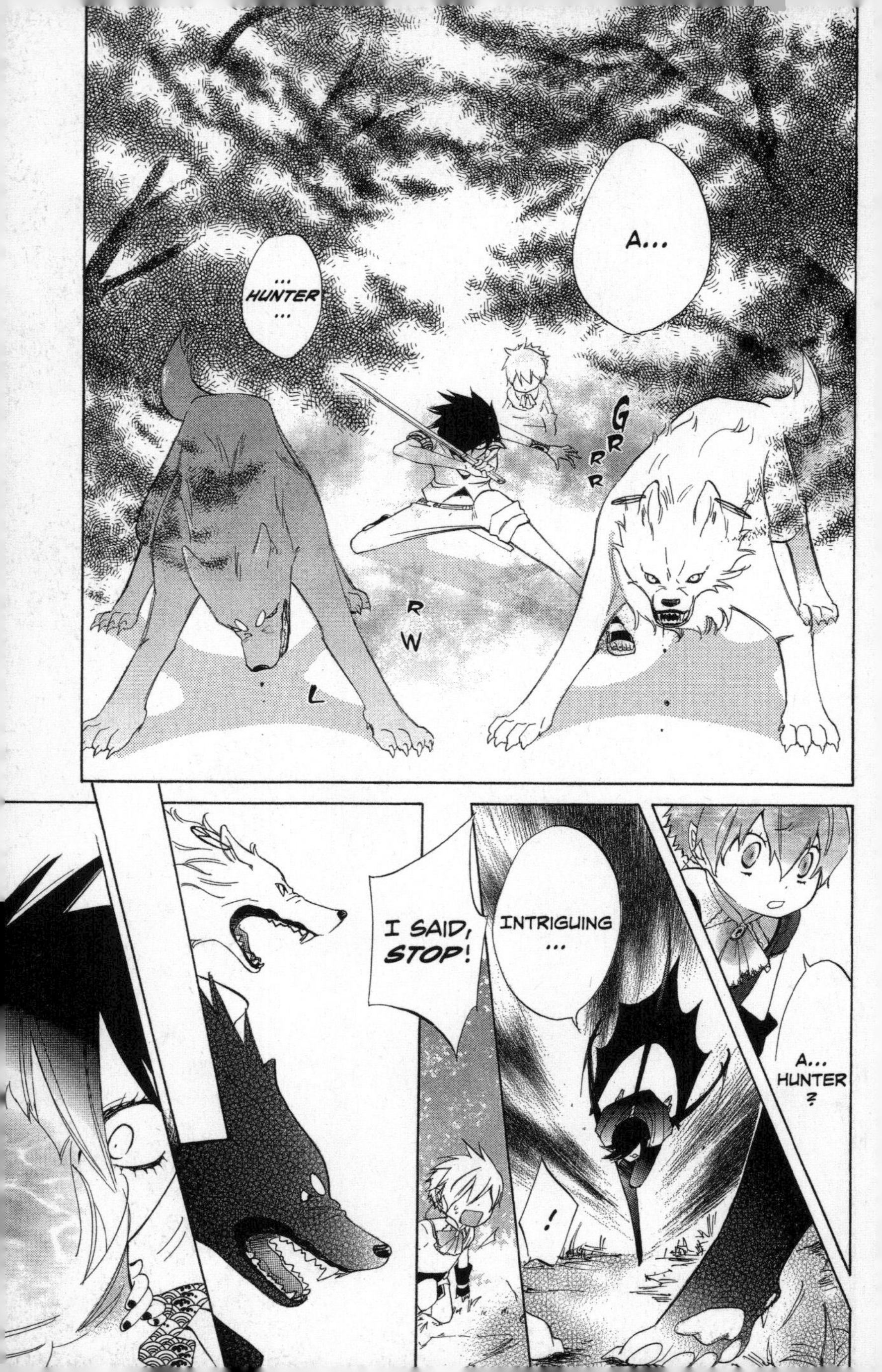
A...
... HUNTER ...
GRRR
RWL
A... HUNTER?
INTRIGUING...
!
I SAID, STOP!

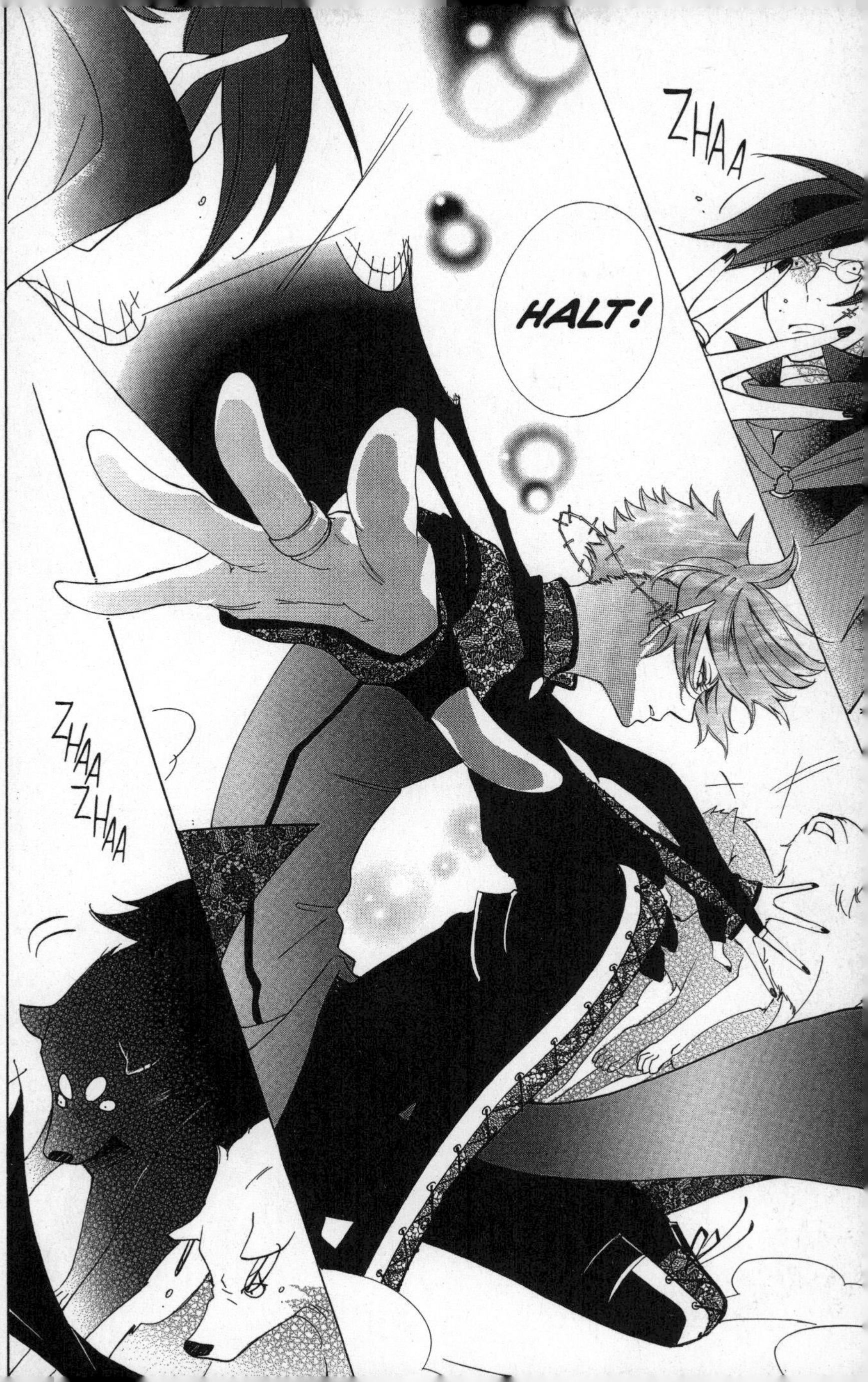
ZHAA
HALT!
ZHAA ZHAA
ZHAA

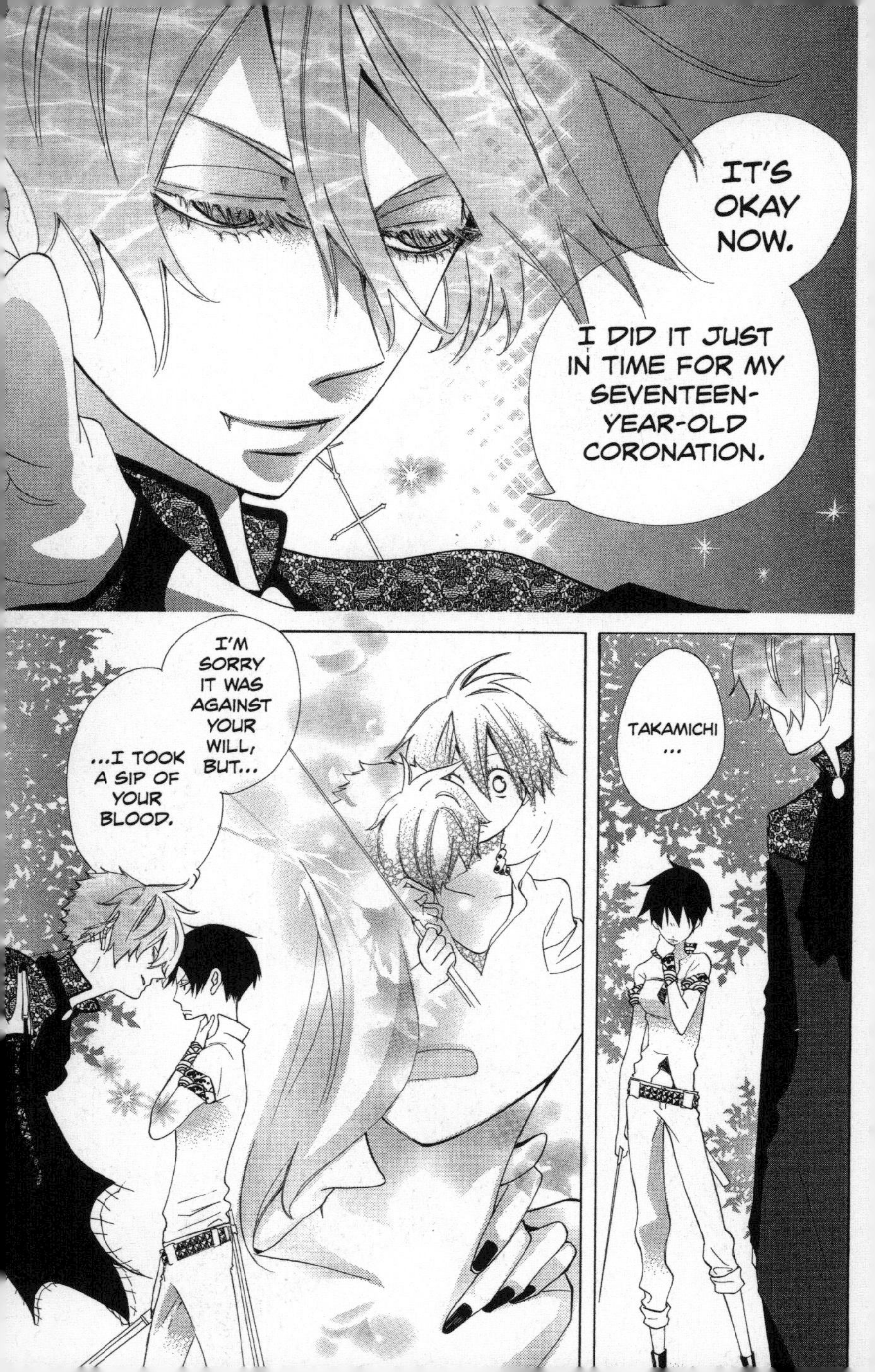
IT'S JUST OKAY NOW.
I DID IT JUST IN TIME FOR MY SEVENTEEN-YEAR-OLD CORONATION.
TAKAMICHI...
I'M SORRY IT WAS AGAINST YOUR WILL, BUT...
...I TOOK A SIP OF YOUR BLOOD.

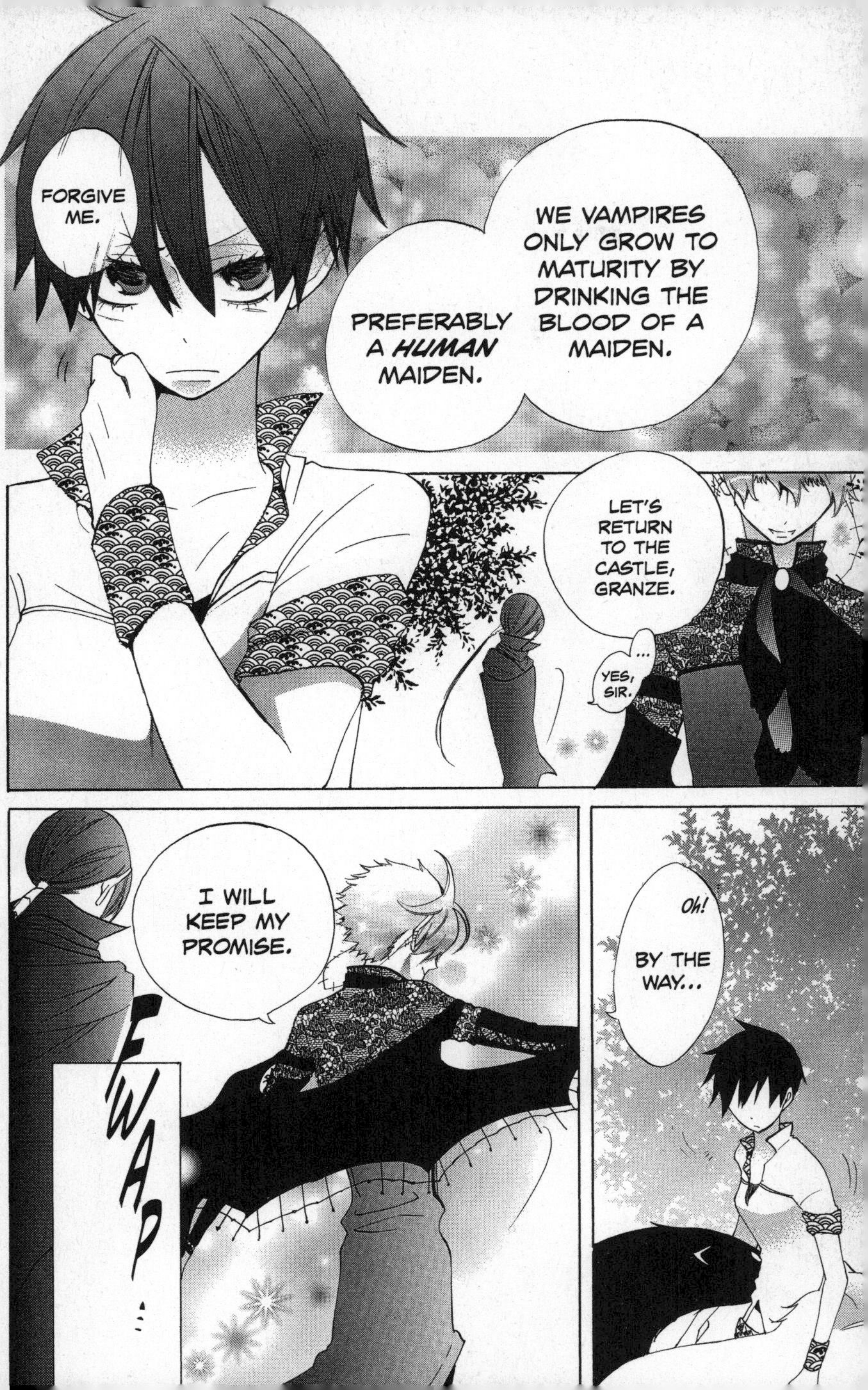
WE VAMPIRES ONLY GROW TO MATURITY BY DRINKING THE BLOOD OF A MAIDEN.
PREFERABLY A *HUMAN* MAIDEN.
FORGIVE ME.
LET'S RETURN TO THE CASTLE, GRANZE.
... YES, SIR.
*Oh!*
BY THE WAY...
I WILL KEEP MY PROMISE.
FWAP...

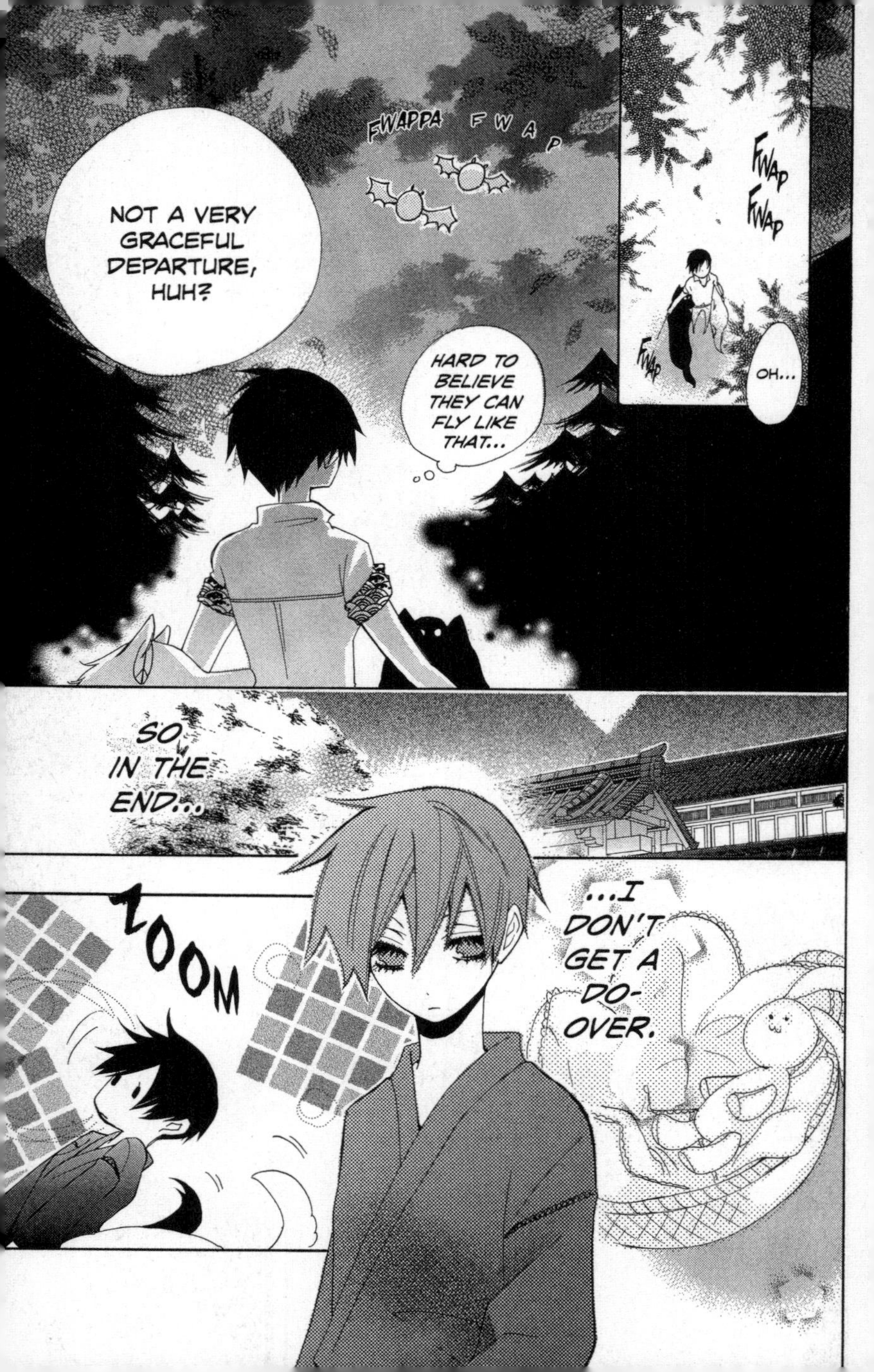
FWAP FWAP
FWAP
OH...
FWAPPA FWAP
NOT A VERY GRACEFUL DEPARTURE, HUH?
HARD TO BELIEVE THEY CAN FLY LIKE THAT...
SO IN THE END...
...I DON'T GET A DO-OVER.
ZOOM

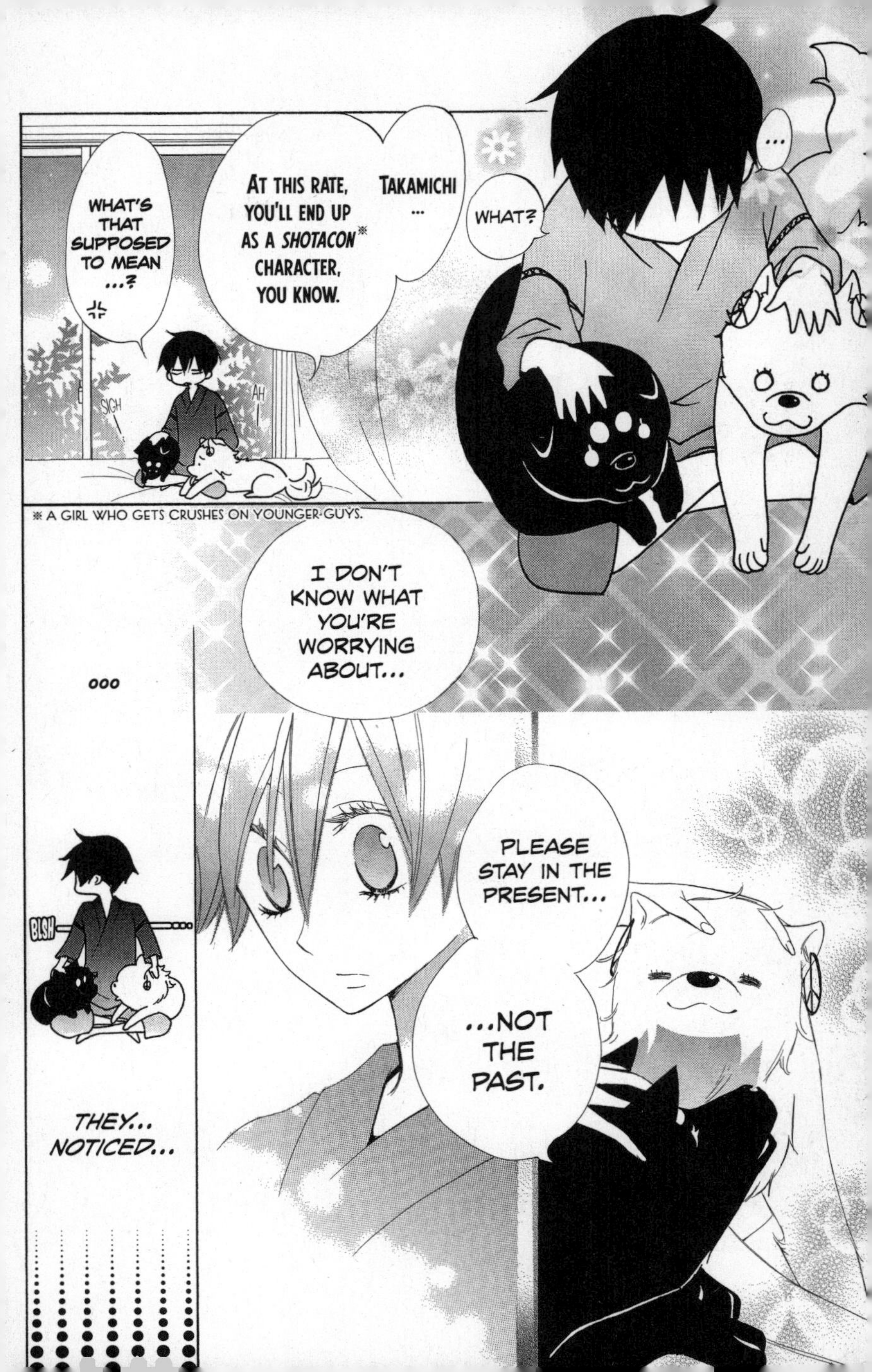
...
WHAT?
I DON'T KNOW WHAT YOU'RE WORRYING ABOUT...
TAKAMICHI ...
AT THIS RATE, YOU'LL END UP AS A *SHOTACON*※ CHARACTER, YOU KNOW.
AH
SIGH
WHAT'S THAT SUPPOSED TO MEAN ...?
PLEASE STAY IN THE PRESENT...
...NOT THE PAST.
ooo
BLSH
THEY... NOTICED...

※ A GIRL WHO GETS CRUSHES ON YOUNGER GUYS.

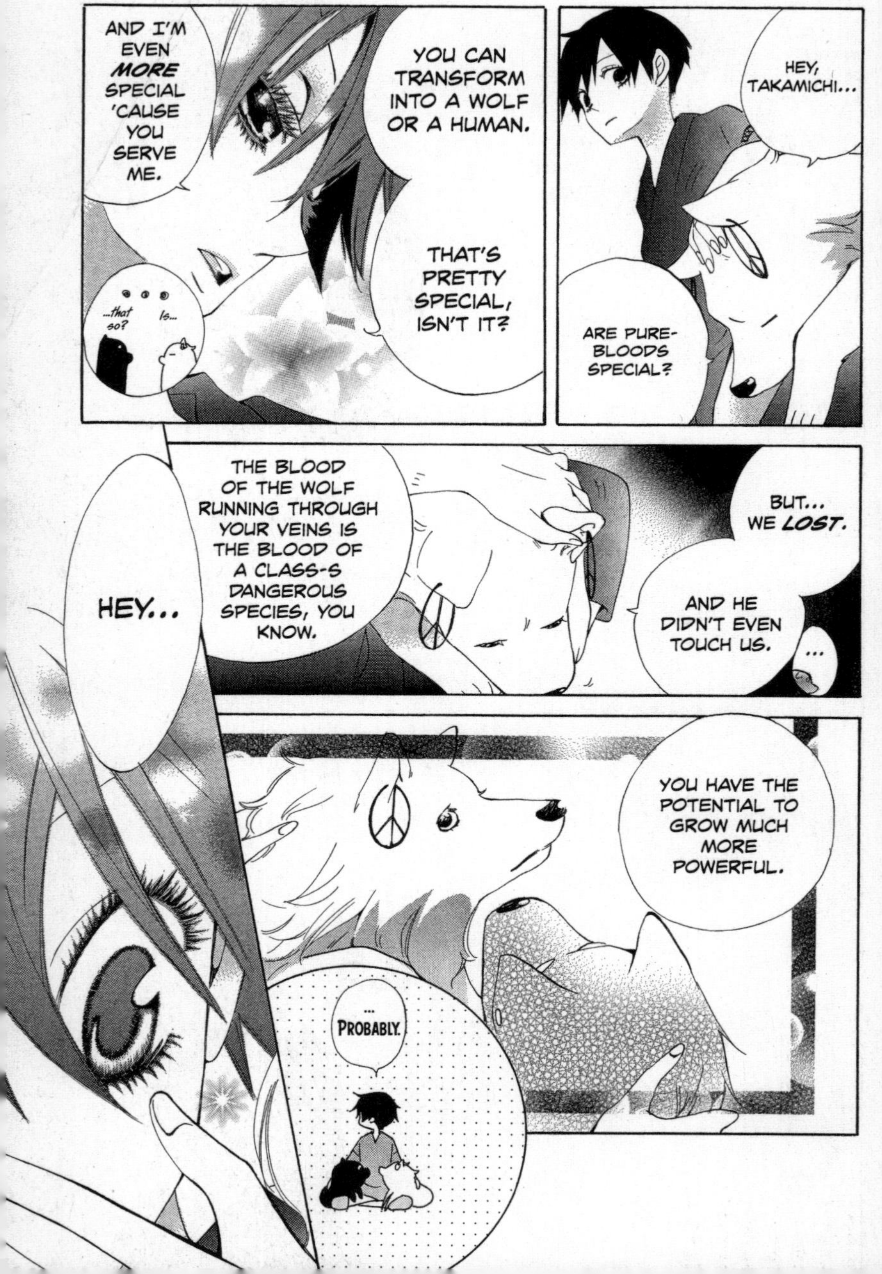
HEY, TAKAMICHI...
ARE PURE-BLOODS SPECIAL?
YOU CAN TRANSFORM INTO A WOLF OR A HUMAN.
THAT'S PRETTY SPECIAL, ISN'T IT?
AND I'M EVEN *MORE* SPECIAL 'CAUSE YOU SERVE ME.
Is...
...that so?
BUT... WE *LOST*.
AND HE DIDN'T EVEN TOUCH US.
...
THE BLOOD OF THE WOLF RUNNING THROUGH YOUR VEINS IS THE BLOOD OF A CLASS-S DANGEROUS SPECIES, YOU KNOW.
HEY...
YOU HAVE THE POTENTIAL TO GROW MUCH MORE POWERFUL.
...PROBABLY.

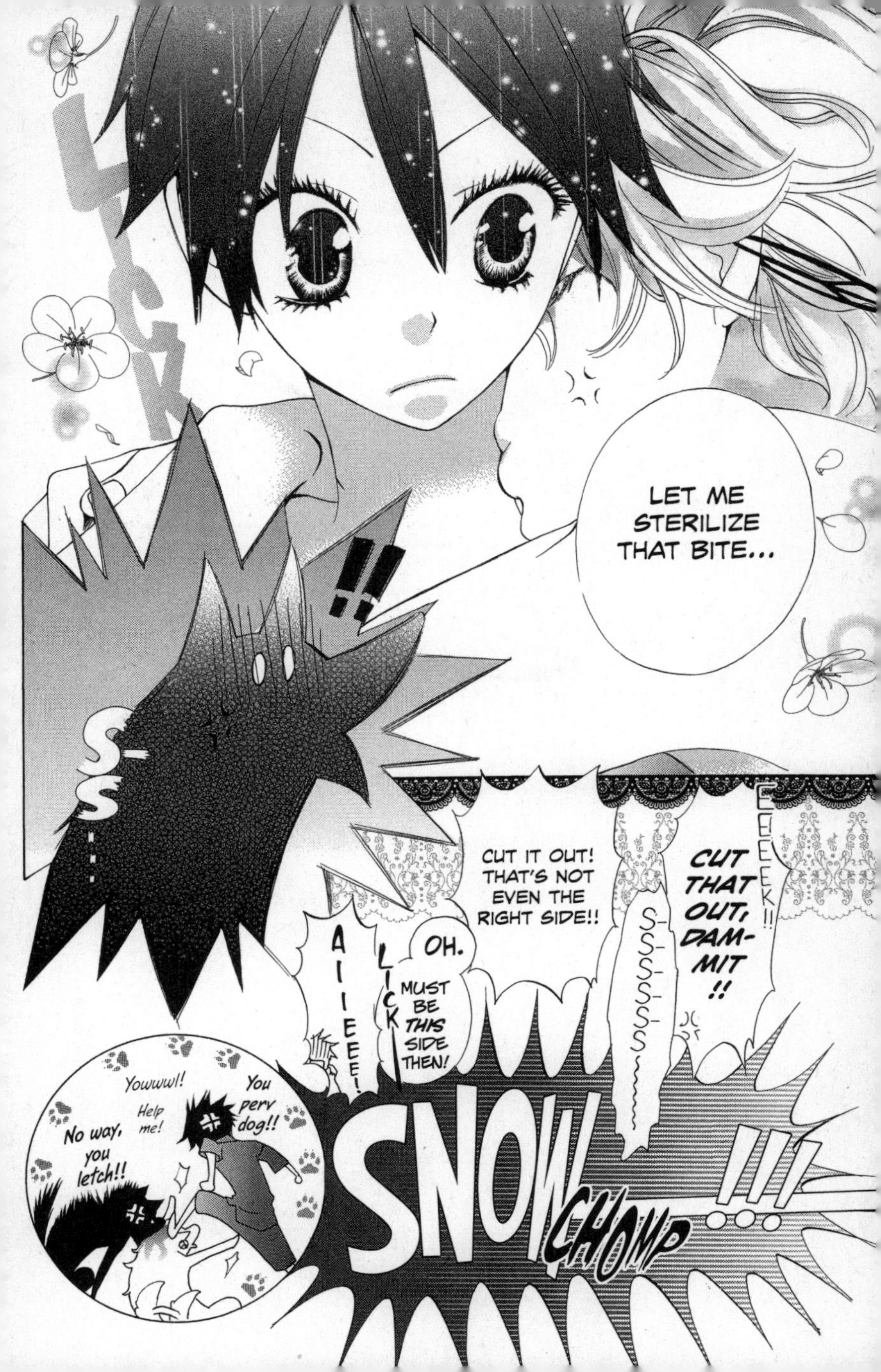
LET ME STERILIZE THAT BITE...
LICK
!!
S-S...
EEEEEK!!
CUT THAT OUT, DAM-MIT!!
SSSSSS
CUT IT OUT! THAT'S NOT EVEN THE RIGHT SIDE!!
OH.
MUST BE THIS SIDE THEN!
LICK
AIIEEE!
SNOW
CHOMP
!!!
You perv dog!!
Yowwwl!
Help me!
No way, you letch!!

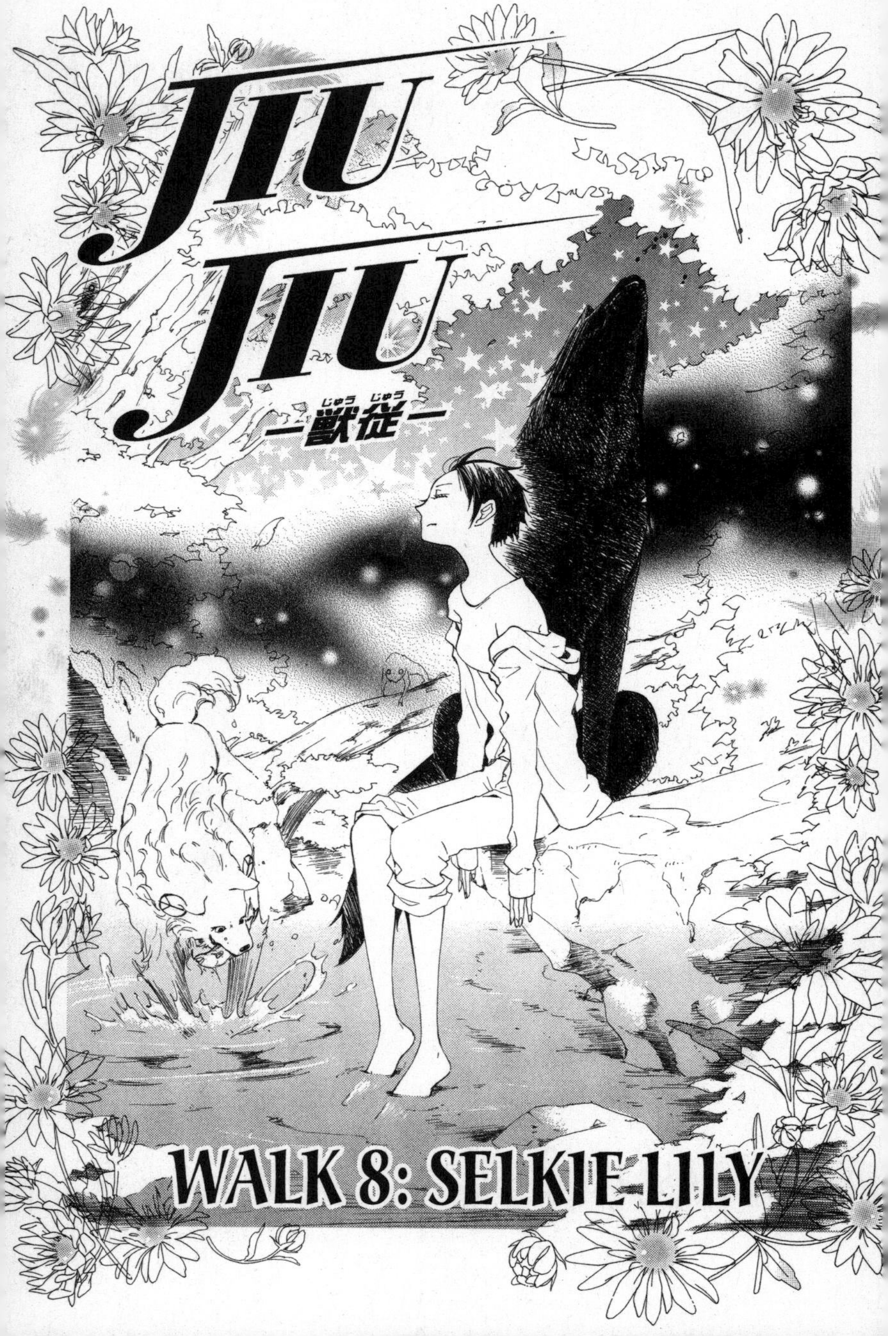
JIU JIU
じゅう じゅう
—獣従—
WALK 8: SELKIE LILY

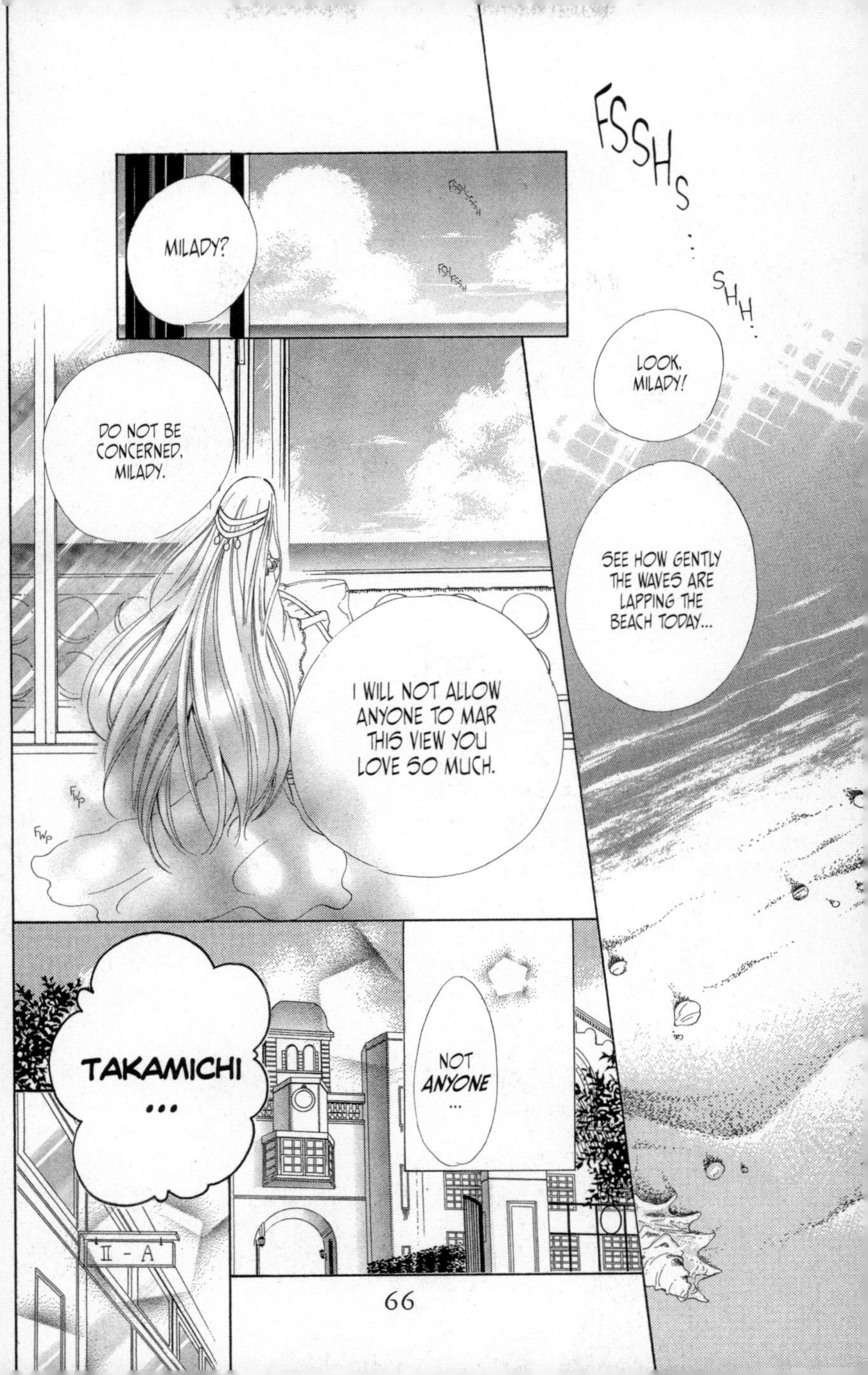
FSSHS
SHH
LOOK, MILADY!
SEE HOW GENTLY THE WAVES ARE LAPPING THE BEACH TODAY...
MILADY?
DO NOT BE CONCERNED, MILADY.
I WILL NOT ALLOW ANYONE TO MAR THIS VIEW YOU LOVE SO MUCH.
FWP
FWP
NOT *ANYONE* ...
TAKAMICHI ...
II - A

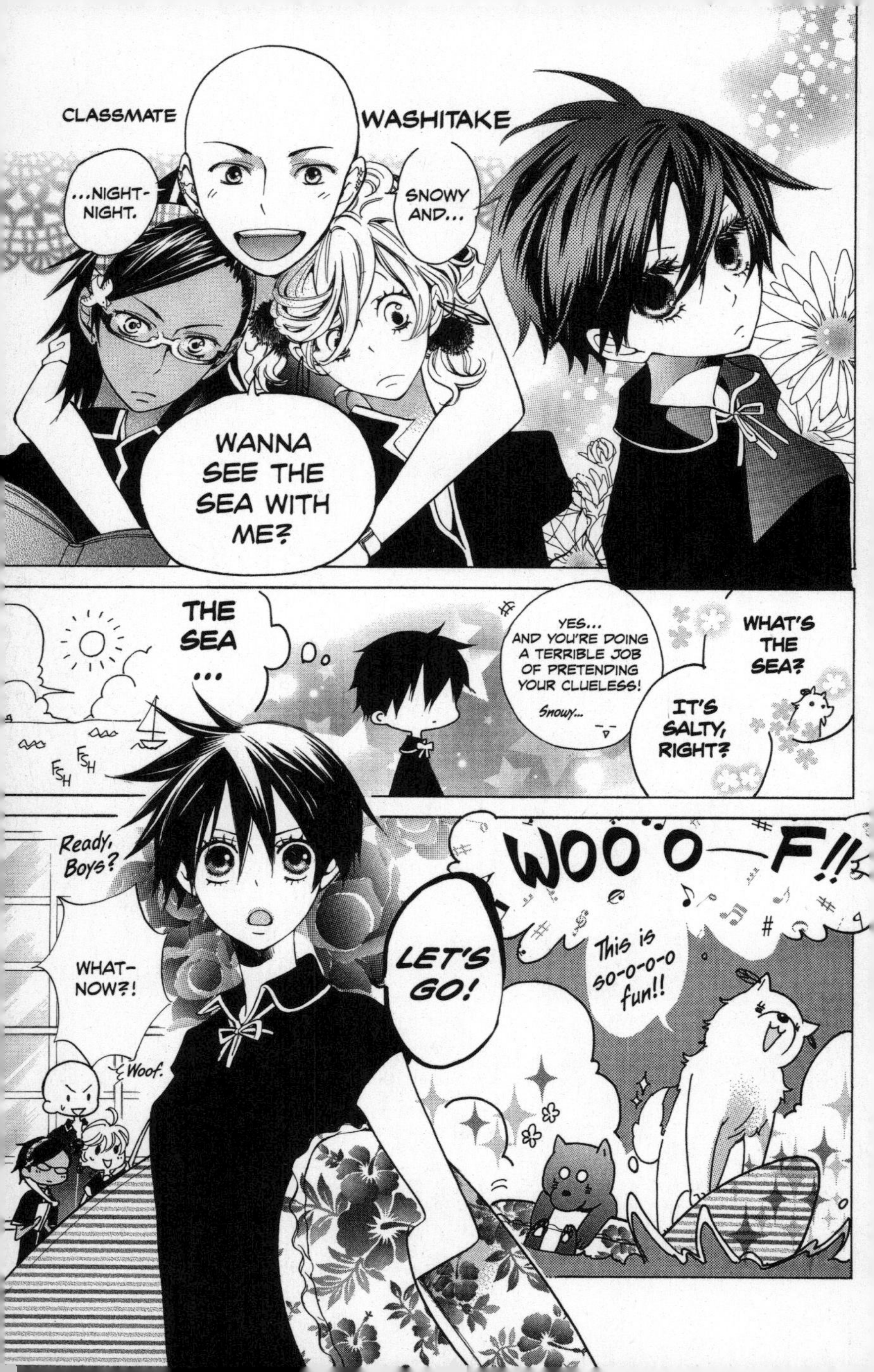
CLASSMATE WASHITAKE
SNOWY AND...
...NIGHT-NIGHT.
WANNA SEE THE SEA WITH ME?
WHAT'S THE SEA?
IT'S SALTY, RIGHT?
YES... AND YOU'RE DOING A TERRIBLE JOB OF PRETENDING YOUR CLUELESS!
Snowy...
THE SEA ...
FSH
FSH
WOO O—F!!
This is so-o-o-o fun!!
LET'S GO!
Ready, Boys?
WHAT-NOW?!
Woof.

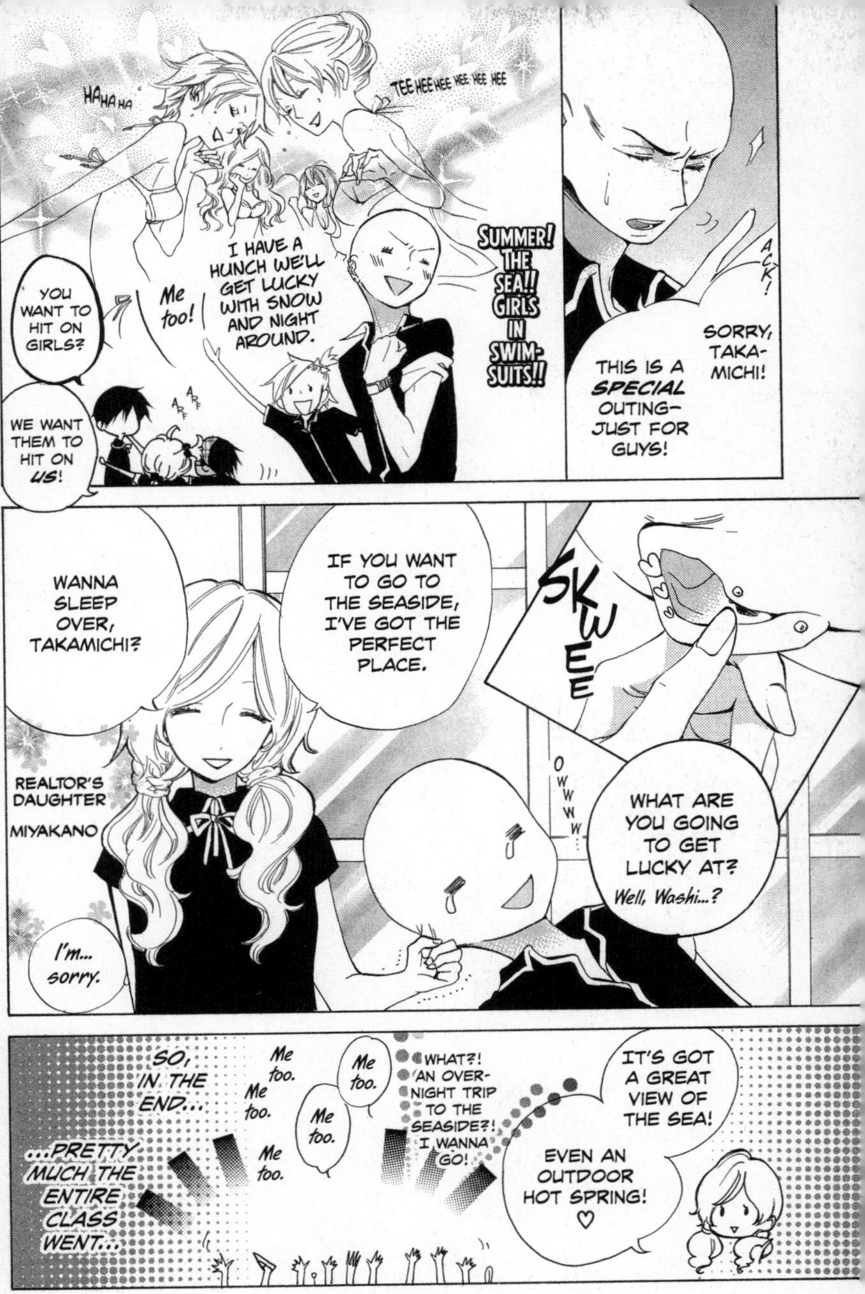
ACK!
SORRY, TAKAMICHI!
THIS IS A SPECIAL OUTING—JUST FOR GUYS!
TEE HEE HEE HEE HEE HEE
HA HA HA HA
SUMMER! THE SEA!! GIRLS IN SWIM-SUITS!!
I HAVE A HUNCH WE'LL GET LUCKY WITH SNOW AND NIGHT AROUND.
Me too!
YOU WANT TO HIT ON GIRLS?
ARF ARF
WE WANT THEM TO HIT ON US!
SKWEE
WHAT ARE YOU GOING TO GET LUCKY AT?
Well, Washi...?
OWWW
IF YOU WANT TO GO TO THE SEASIDE, I'VE GOT THE PERFECT PLACE.
WANNA SLEEP OVER, TAKAMICHI?
REALTOR'S DAUGHTER
MIYAKANO
I'm... sorry.
IT'S GOT A GREAT VIEW OF THE SEA!
EVEN AN OUTDOOR HOT SPRING! ♡
WHAT?! AN OVER-NIGHT TRIP TO THE SEASIDE?! I WANNA GO!
Me too.
Me too.
Me too.
Me too.
Me too.
SO, IN THE END...
...PRETTY MUCH THE ENTIRE CLASS WENT...

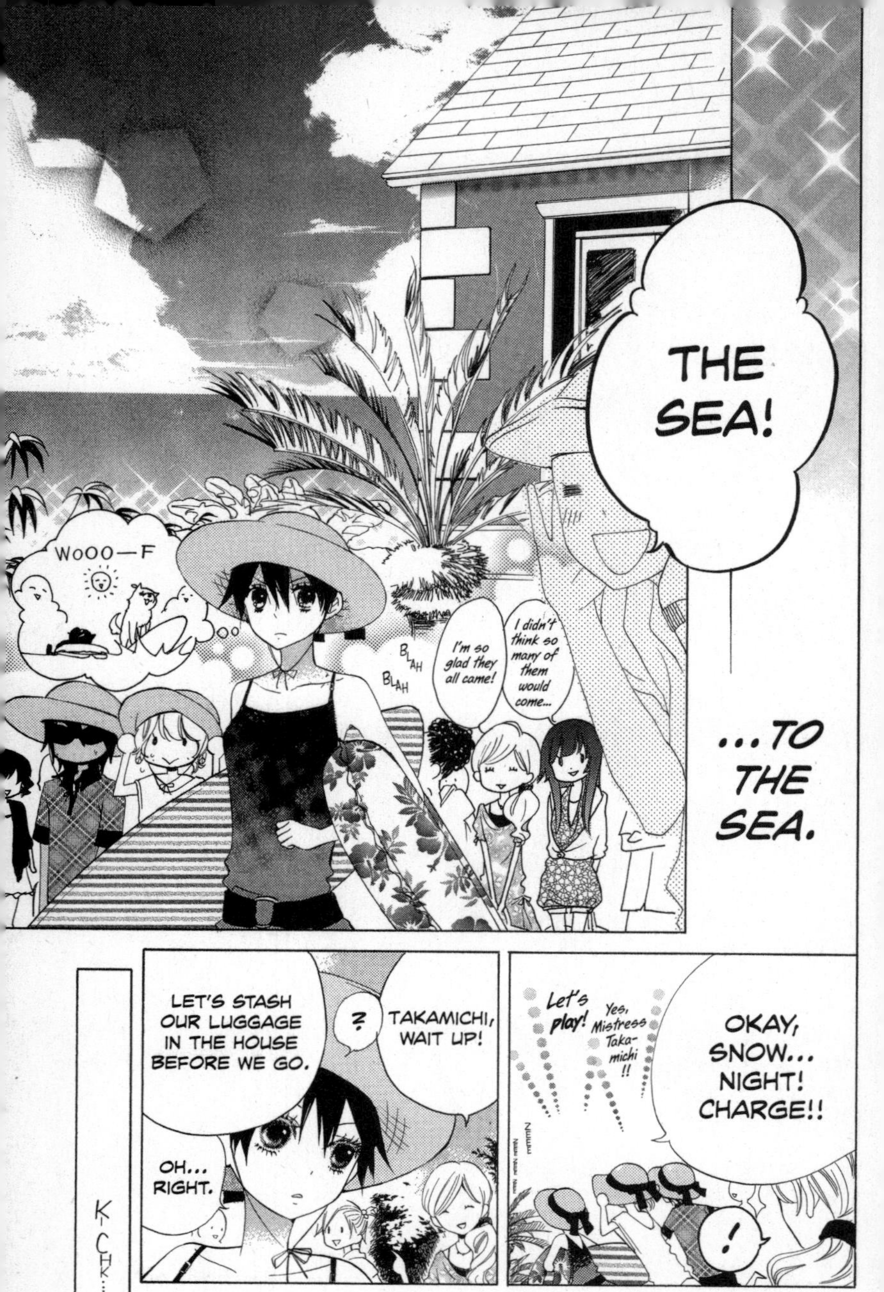
THE SEA!
...TO THE SEA.
I didn't think so many of them would come...
I'm so glad they all came!
BLAH BLAH
WOOO—F
OKAY, SNOW... NIGHT! CHARGE!!
Yes, Mistress Takamichi!!
Let's play!
!
TAKAMICHI, WAIT UP!
?
LET'S STASH OUR LUGGAGE IN THE HOUSE BEFORE WE GO.
OH... RIGHT.
KI-CHK...

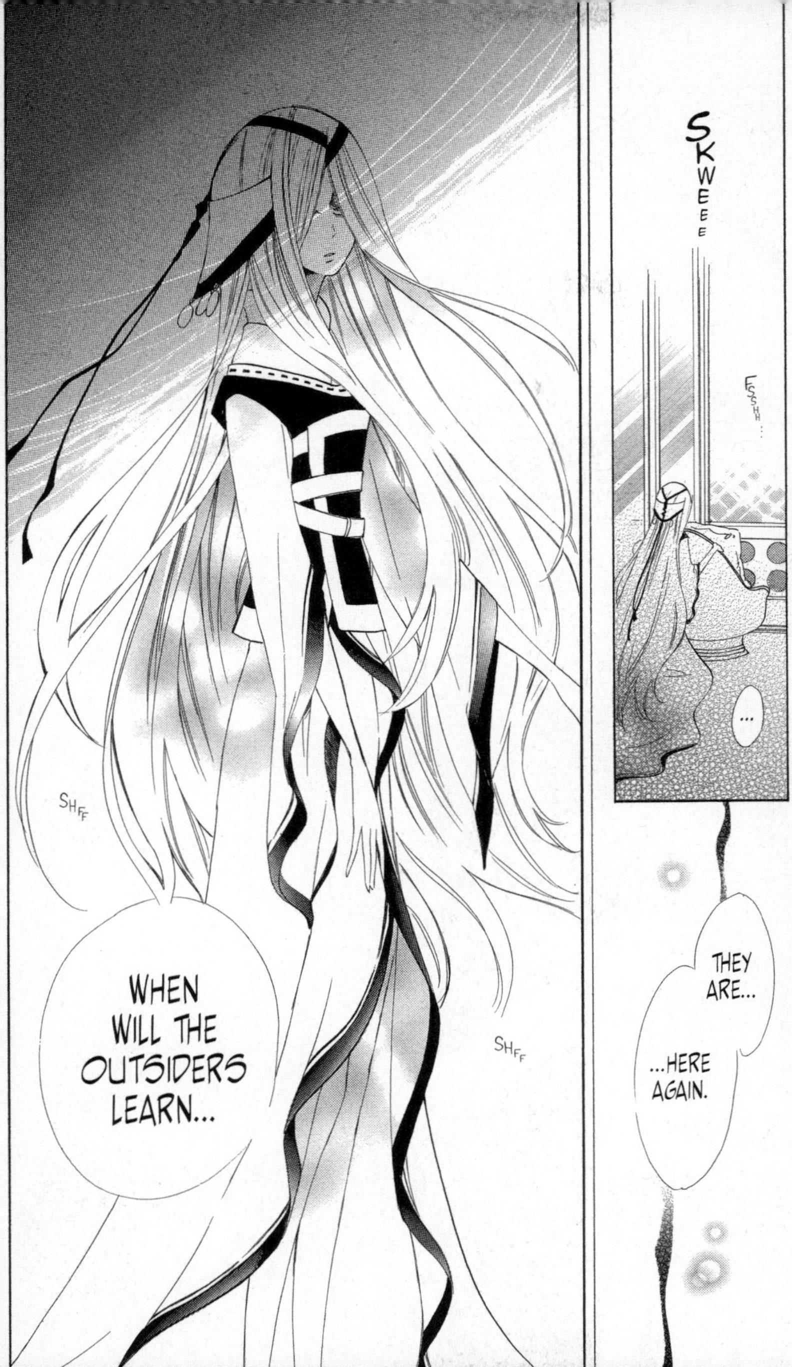
SKWEEE
FSSSH...
...
THEY ARE...
...HERE AGAIN.
SHFF
WHEN WILL THE OUTSIDERS LEARN...
SHFF

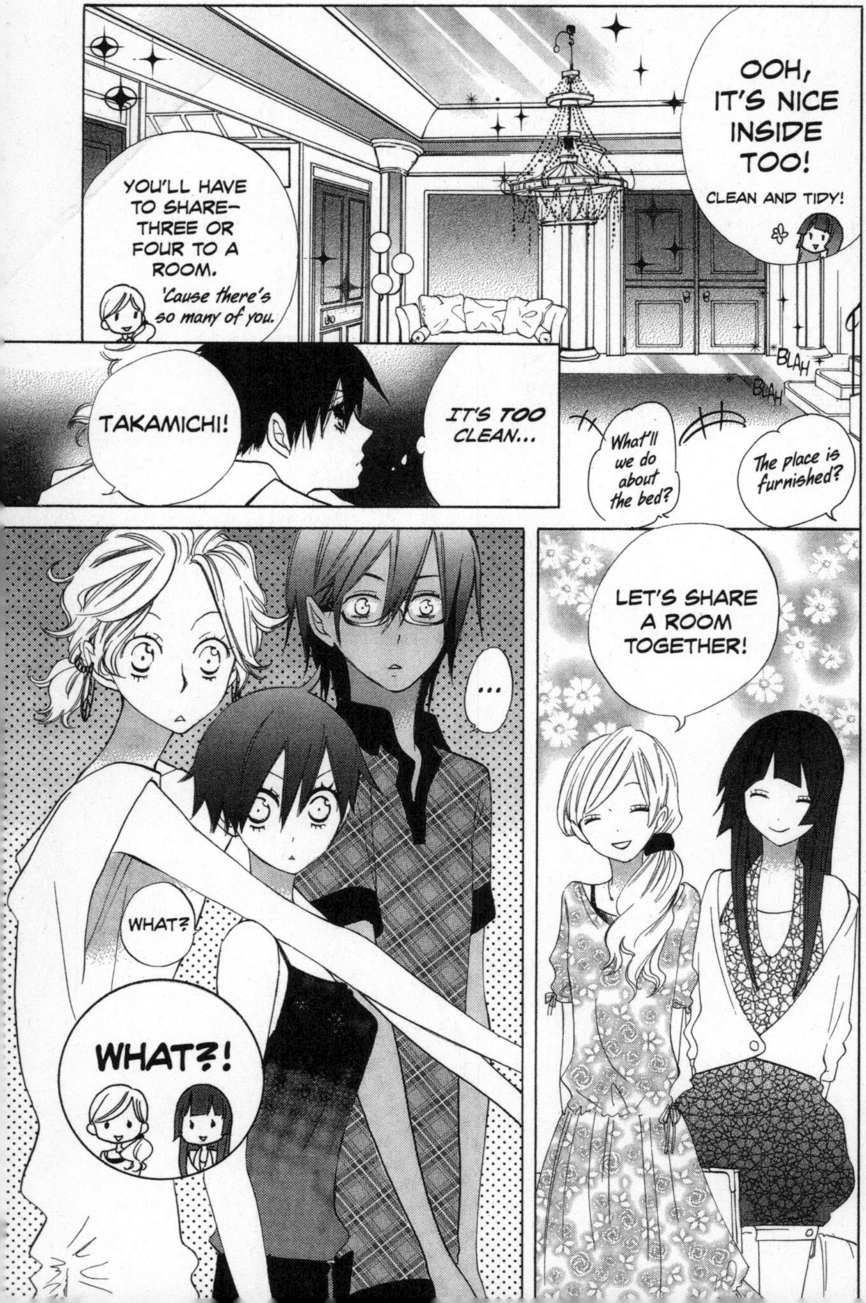
OOH, IT'S NICE INSIDE TOO!
CLEAN AND TIDY!
YOU'LL HAVE TO SHARE—THREE OR FOUR TO A ROOM.
'Cause there's so many of you.
BLAH BLAH
The place is furnished?
What'll we do about the bed?
IT'S TOO CLEAN...
TAKAMICHI!
LET'S SHARE A ROOM TOGETHER!
...
WHAT?
WHAT?!

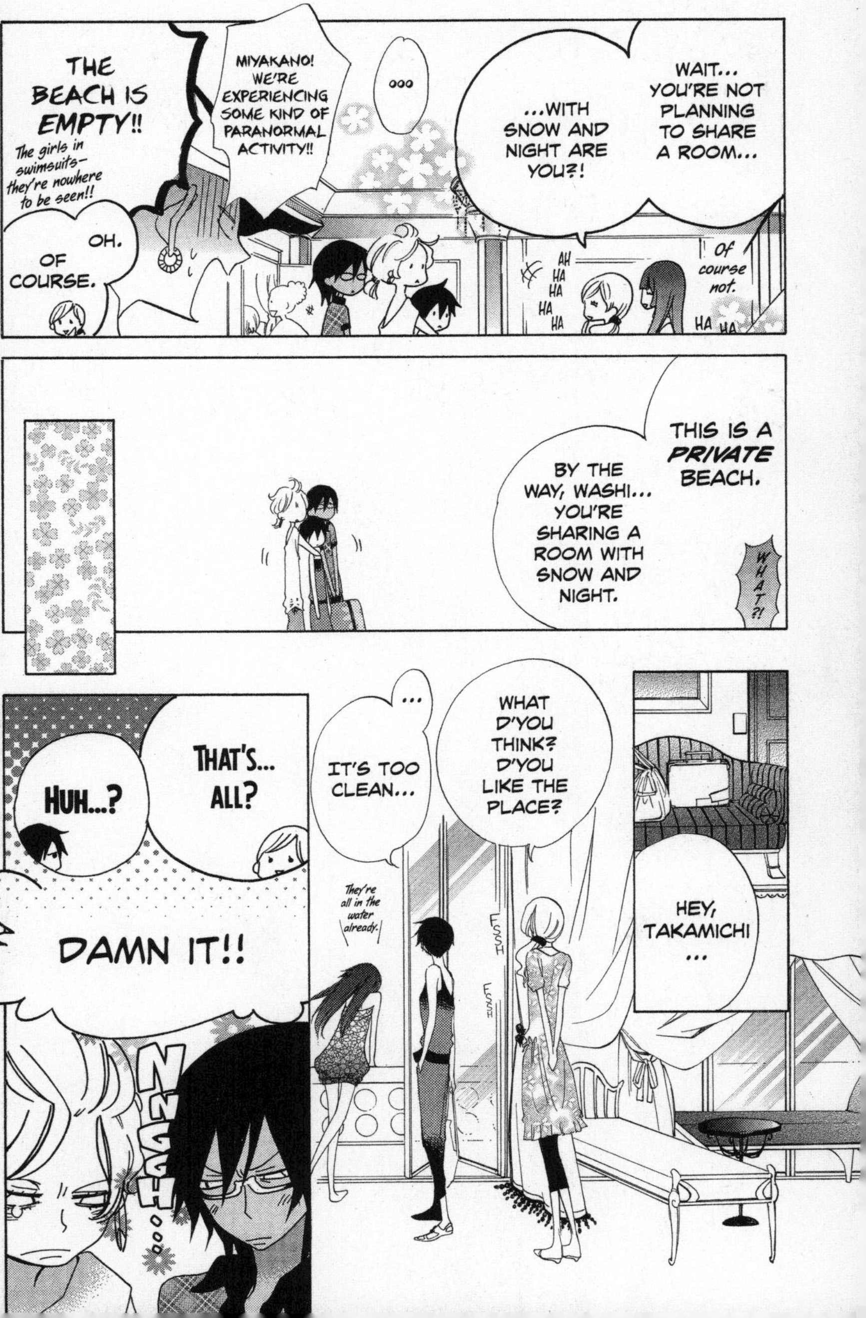
WAIT... YOU'RE NOT PLANNING TO SHARE A ROOM...
...WITH SNOW AND NIGHT ARE YOU?!
Of course not.
AH HA HA HA HA
HA HA
ooo
MIYAKANO! WE'RE EXPERIENCING SOME KIND OF PARANORMAL ACTIVITY!!
THE BEACH IS EMPTY!!
The girls in swimsuits— they're nowhere to be seen!!
OH. OF COURSE.
THIS IS A PRIVATE BEACH.
WHAT?!
BY THE WAY, WASHI... YOU'RE SHARING A ROOM WITH SNOW AND NIGHT.
HEY, TAKAMICHI ...
WHAT D'YOU THINK? D'YOU LIKE THE PLACE?
...
IT'S TOO CLEAN...
They're all in the water already.
FSSH
FSSH
THAT'S... ALL?
HUH...?
DAMN IT!!
NNGH ooo

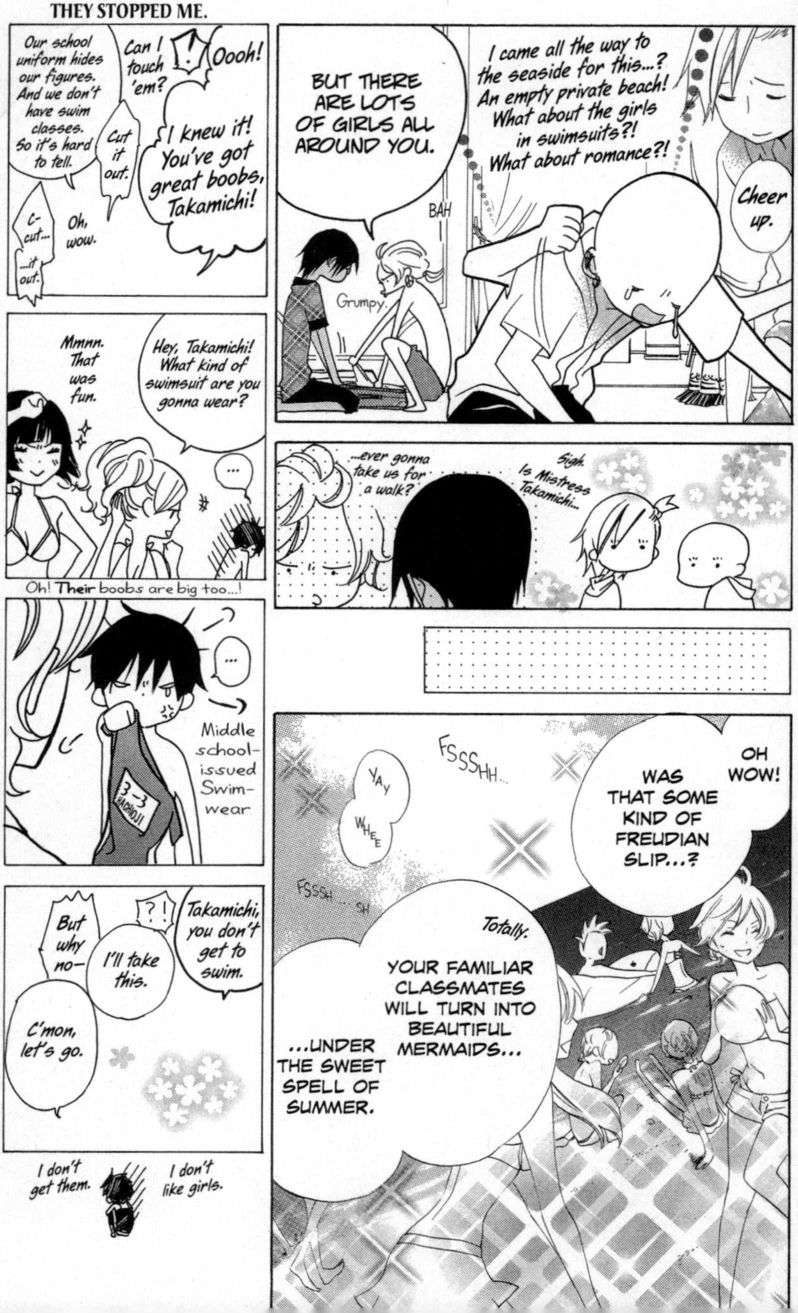
Cheer up.
I came all the way to the seaside for this...? An empty private beach! What about the girls in swimsuits?! What about romance?!
BAH
BUT THERE ARE LOTS OF GIRLS ALL AROUND YOU.
Grumpy.
Sigh. Is Mistress Takamichi...
...ever gonna take us for a walk?
OH WOW!
WAS THAT SOME KIND OF FREUDIAN SLIP...?
FSSSHH...
YAY
WHEE
Totally.
YOUR FAMILIAR CLASSMATES WILL TURN INTO BEAUTIFUL MERMAIDS...
...UNDER THE SWEET SPELL OF SUMMER.
FSSSH...SH
THEY STOPPED ME.
Oooh!
!
Can I touch 'em?
I knew it! You've got great boobs, Takamichi!
Our school uniform hides our figures. And we don't have swim classes. So it's hard to tell.
Cut it out.
Oh, wow.
C-cut...
...it out.
Hey, Takamichi! What kind of swimsuit are you gonna wear?
Mmmn. That was fun.
...
Oh! Their boobs are big too...!
...
Middle school-issued Swimwear
3-3 HACHIOJI
Takamichi, you don't get to swim.
?!
I'll take this.
But why no—
C'mon, let's go.
I don't like girls.
I don't get them.

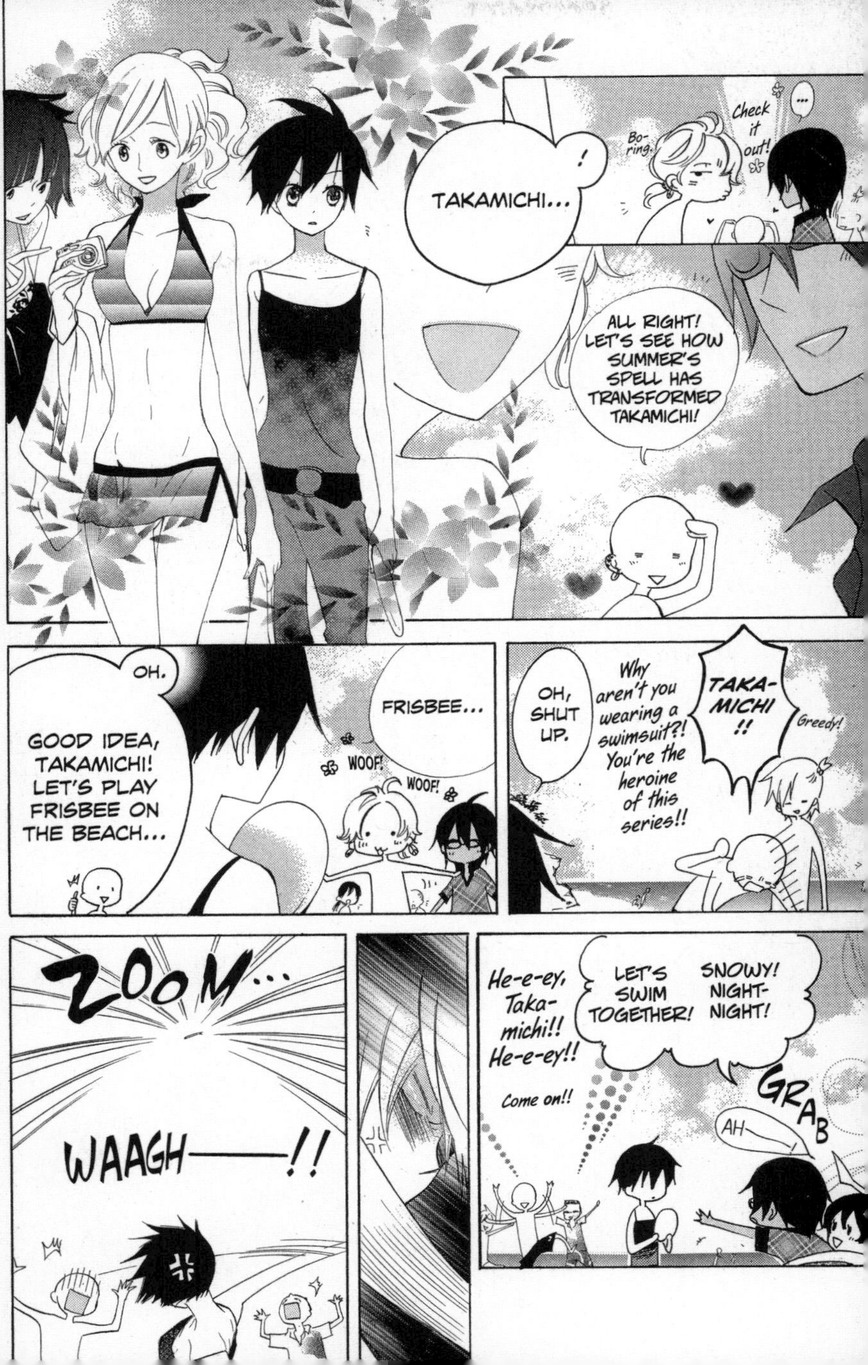
...
Check it out!
Bo-ring.
ALL RIGHT! LET'S SEE HOW SUMMER'S SPELL HAS TRANSFORMED TAKAMICHI!
!
TAKAMICHI...
TAKA-MICHI !!
Greedy!
Why aren't you wearing a swimsuit?! You're the heroine of this series!!
OH, SHUT UP.
FRISBEE...
OH.
GOOD IDEA, TAKAMICHI! LET'S PLAY FRISBEE ON THE BEACH...
WOOF!
WOOF!
SNOWY! NIGHT-NIGHT!
LET'S SWIM TOGETHER!
He-e-ey, Taka-michi!! He-e-ey!!
Come on!!
GRAB
AH—!
ZOOM...
WAAGH——!!

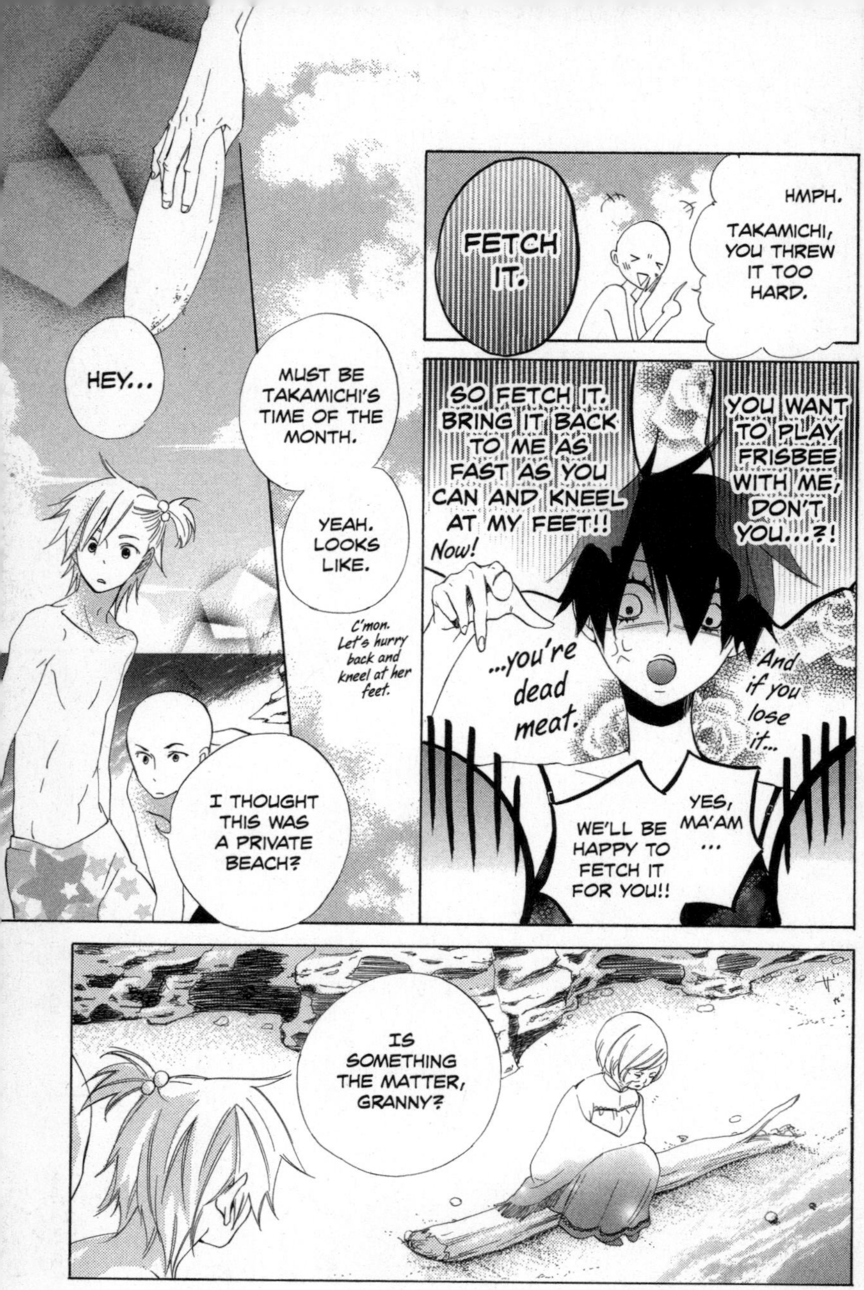

HMPH.
TAKAMICHI, YOU THREW IT TOO HARD.
FETCH IT.
YOU WANT TO PLAY FRISBEE WITH ME, DON'T YOU...?!
SO FETCH IT. BRING IT BACK TO ME AS FAST AS YOU CAN AND KNEEL AT MY FEET!!
Now!
And if you lose it...
...you're dead meat.
YES, MA'AM ...
WE'LL BE HAPPY TO FETCH IT FOR YOU!!
MUST BE TAKAMICHI'S TIME OF THE MONTH.
YEAH. LOOKS LIKE.
C'mon. Let's hurry back and kneel at her feet.
HEY...
I THOUGHT THIS WAS A PRIVATE BEACH?
IS SOMETHING THE MATTER, GRANNY?

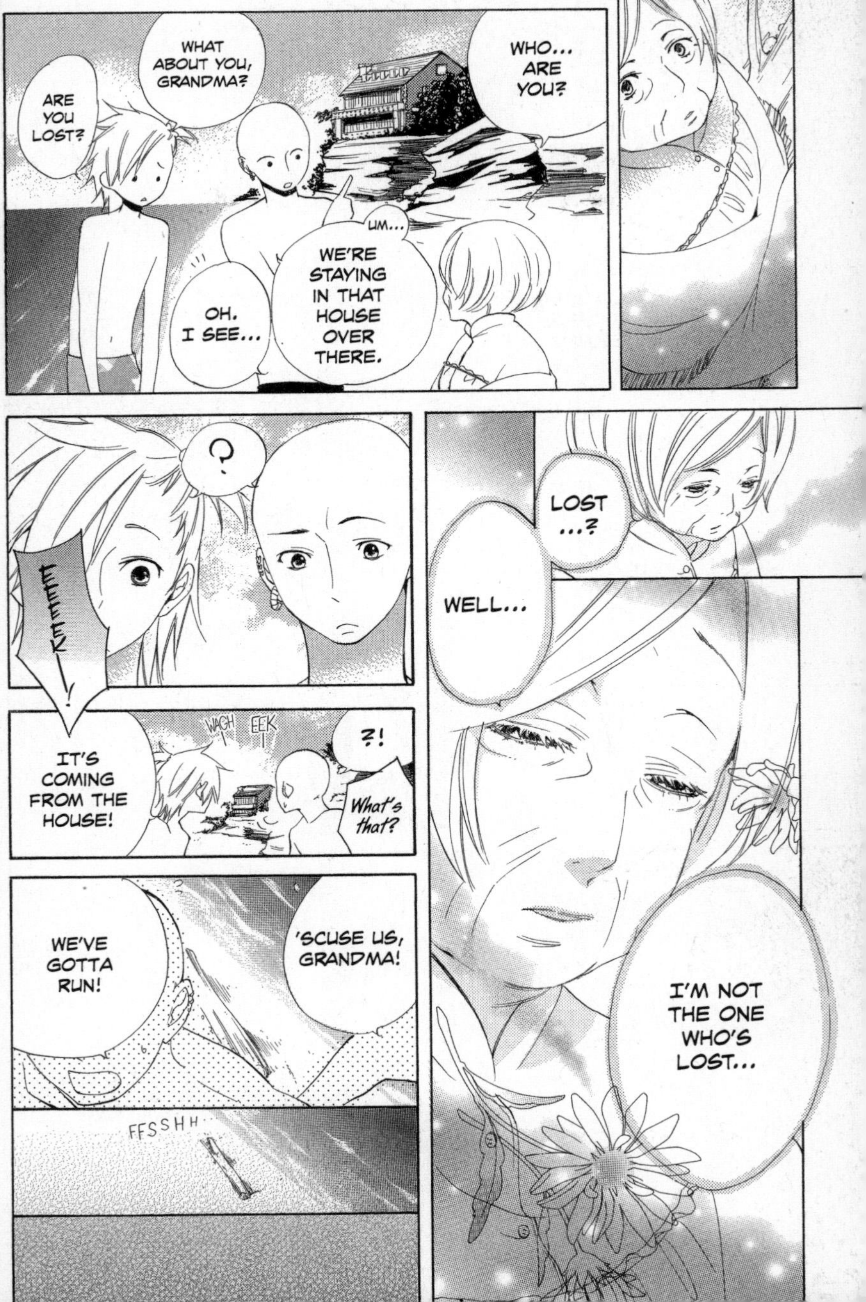
WHO... ARE YOU?
WHAT ABOUT YOU, GRANDMA?
ARE YOU LOST?
UM...
WE'RE STAYING IN THAT HOUSE OVER THERE.
OH. I SEE...
LOST ...?
WELL...
I'M NOT THE ONE WHO'S LOST...
?
EEEEK!
?!
What's that?
WAGH
EEK
IT'S COMING FROM THE HOUSE!
'SCUSE US, GRANDMA!
WE'VE GOTTA RUN!
FFSSHH

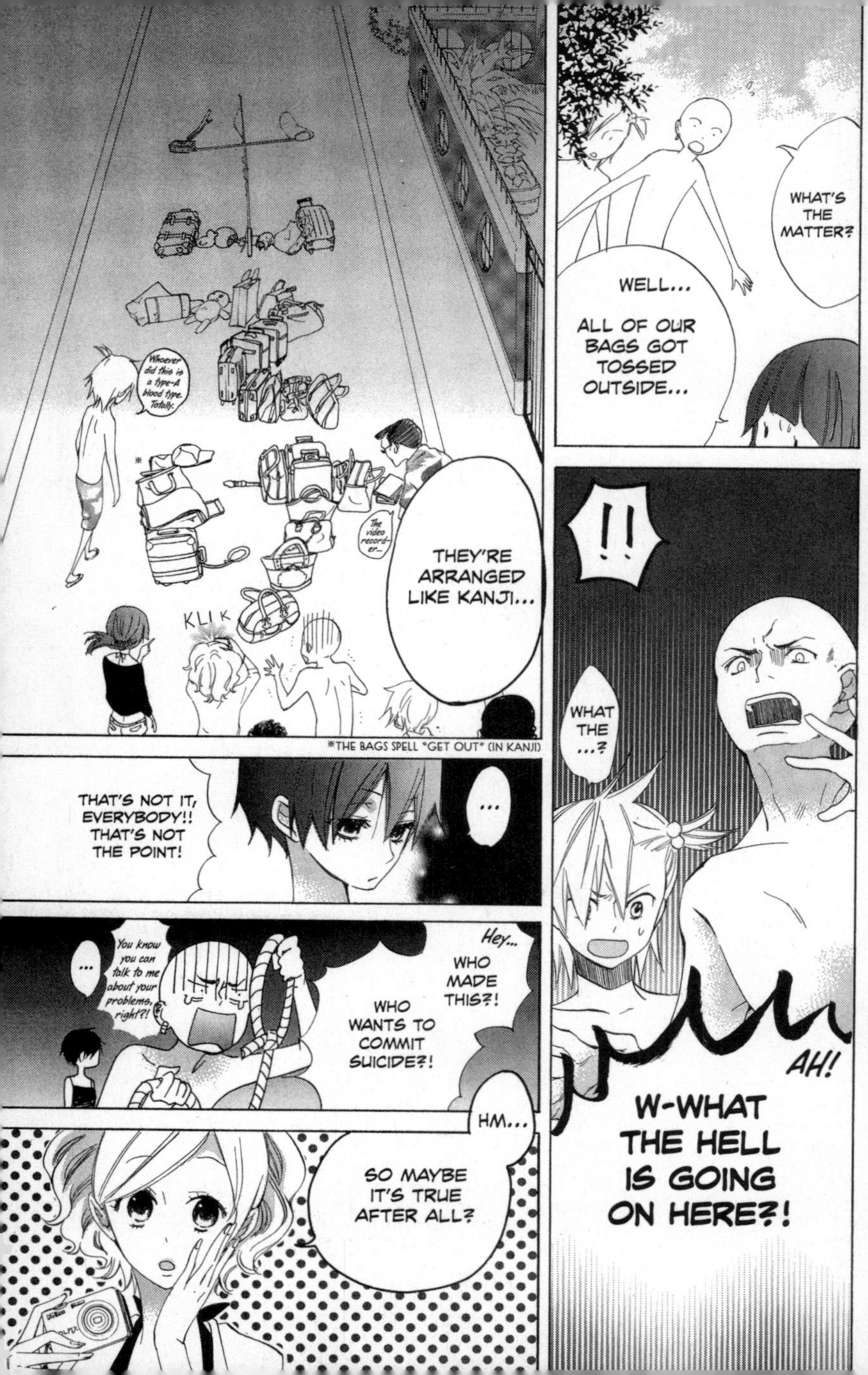
WHAT'S THE MATTER?
WELL...
ALL OF OUR BAGS GOT TOSSED OUTSIDE...
Whoever did this is a type-A blood type. Totally.
THEY'RE ARRANGED LIKE KANJI...
The video recorder...
KLIK
※THE BAGS SPELL "GET OUT" (IN KANJI)
!!
WHAT THE ...?
AH!
W-WHAT THE HELL IS GOING ON HERE?!
THAT'S NOT IT, EVERYBODY!! THAT'S NOT THE POINT!
...
Hey...
WHO MADE THIS?!
WHO WANTS TO COMMIT SUICIDE?!
You know you can talk to me about your problems, right?!
...
HM...
SO MAYBE IT'S TRUE AFTER ALL?

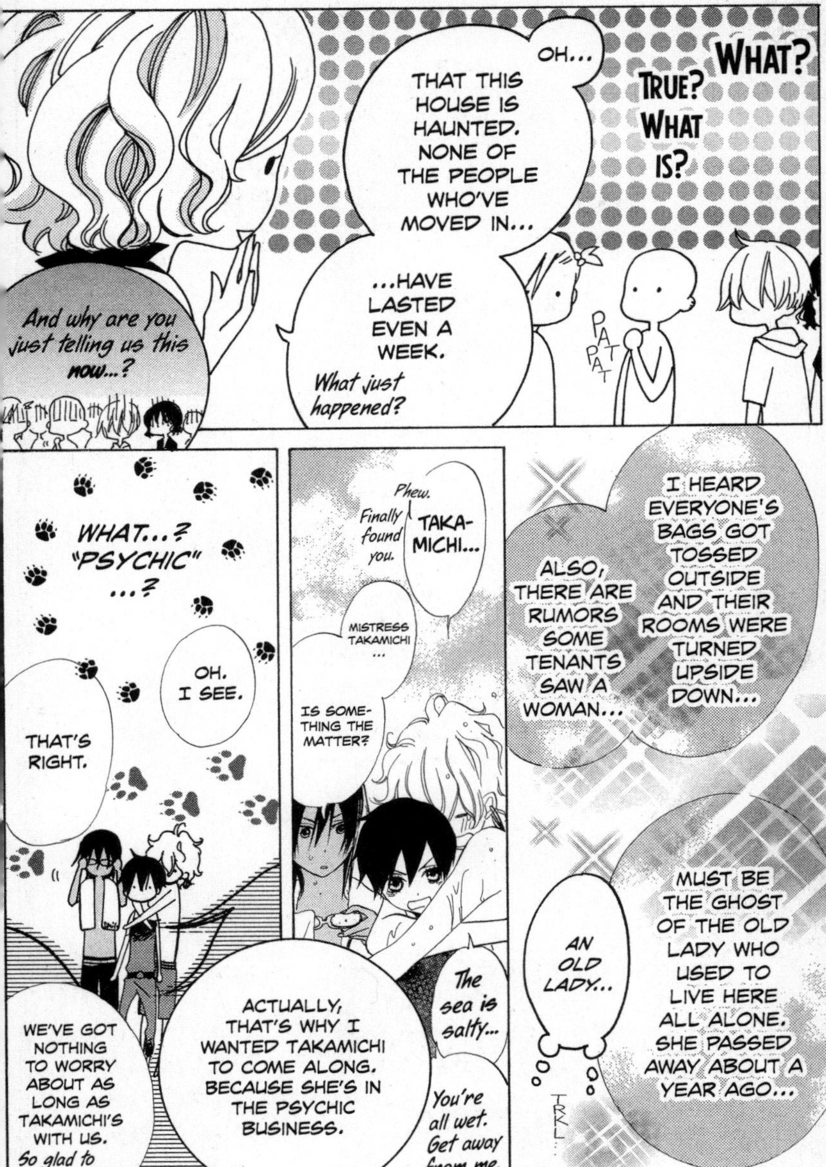
WHAT?
TRUE? WHAT IS?
OH...
THAT THIS HOUSE IS HAUNTED. NONE OF THE PEOPLE WHO'VE MOVED IN...
...HAVE LASTED EVEN A WEEK.
What just happened?
PAT PAT
And why are you just telling us this now...?
I HEARD EVERYONE'S BAGS GOT TOSSED OUTSIDE AND THEIR ROOMS WERE TURNED UPSIDE DOWN...
ALSO, THERE ARE RUMORS SOME TENANTS SAW A WOMAN...
MUST BE THE GHOST OF THE OLD LADY WHO USED TO LIVE HERE ALL ALONE. SHE PASSED AWAY ABOUT A YEAR AGO...
AN OLD LADY...
TRKL
TAKA-MICHI...
Phew. Finally found you.
MISTRESS TAKAMICHI...
IS SOME-THING THE MATTER?
The sea is salty...
You're all wet. Get away from me.
ACTUALLY, THAT'S WHY I WANTED TAKAMICHI TO COME ALONG. BECAUSE SHE'S IN THE PSYCHIC BUSINESS.
WHAT...? "PSYCHIC" ...?
OH. I SEE.
THAT'S RIGHT.
WE'VE GOT NOTHING TO WORRY ABOUT AS LONG AS TAKAMICHI'S WITH US.
So glad to hear it...

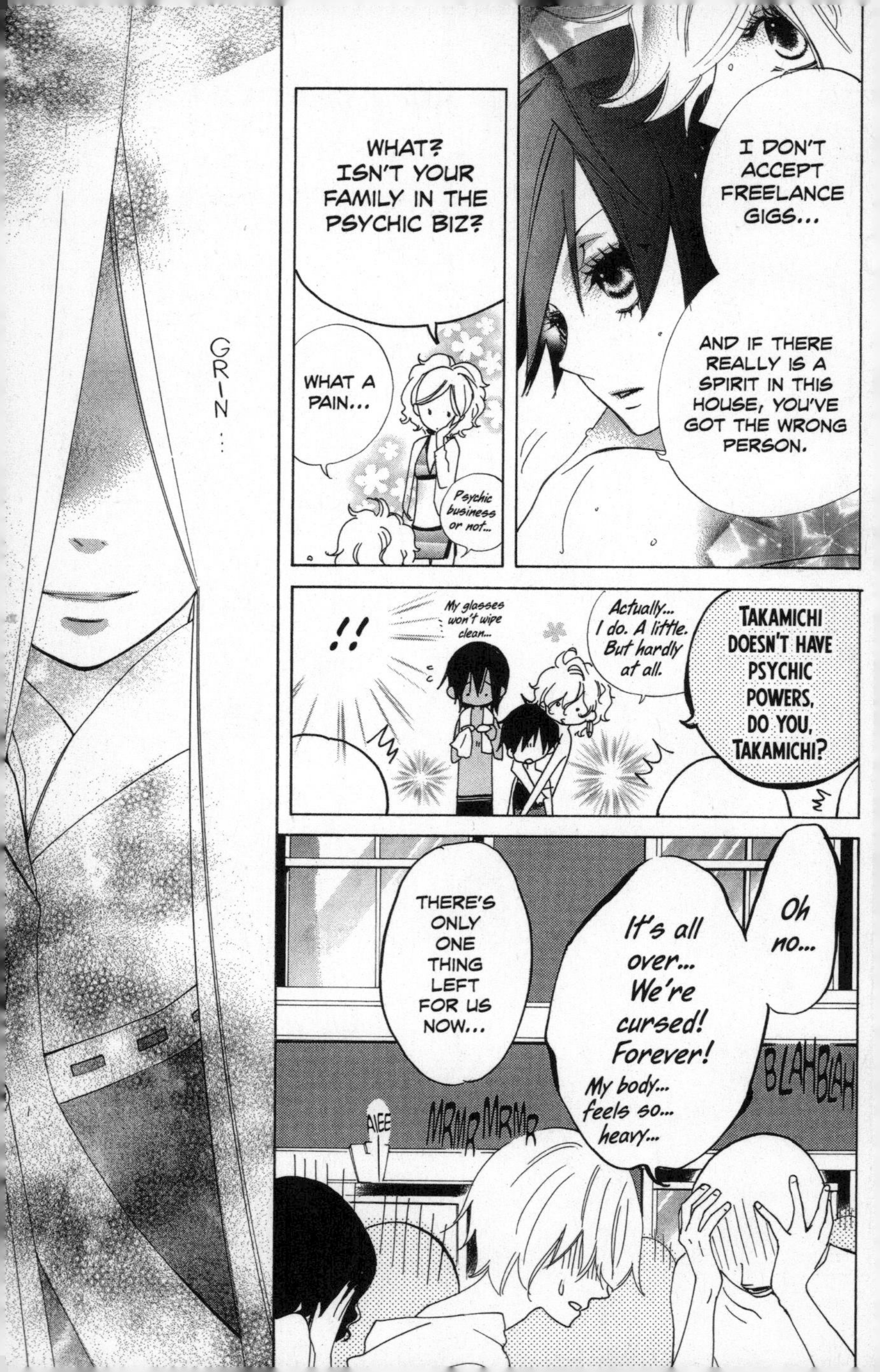
I DON'T ACCEPT FREELANCE GIGS...
AND IF THERE REALLY IS A SPIRIT IN THIS HOUSE, YOU'VE GOT THE WRONG PERSON.
WHAT? ISN'T YOUR FAMILY IN THE PSYCHIC BIZ?
WHAT A PAIN...
Psychic business or not...
TAKAMICHI DOESN'T HAVE PSYCHIC POWERS, DO YOU, TAKAMICHI?
Actually... I do. A little. But hardly at all.
My glasses won't wipe clean...
!!
Oh no...
It's all over... We're cursed! Forever!
My body... feels so... heavy...
BLAHBLAH
THERE'S ONLY ONE THING LEFT FOR US NOW...
MRMR MRMR
AIEE
GRIN...

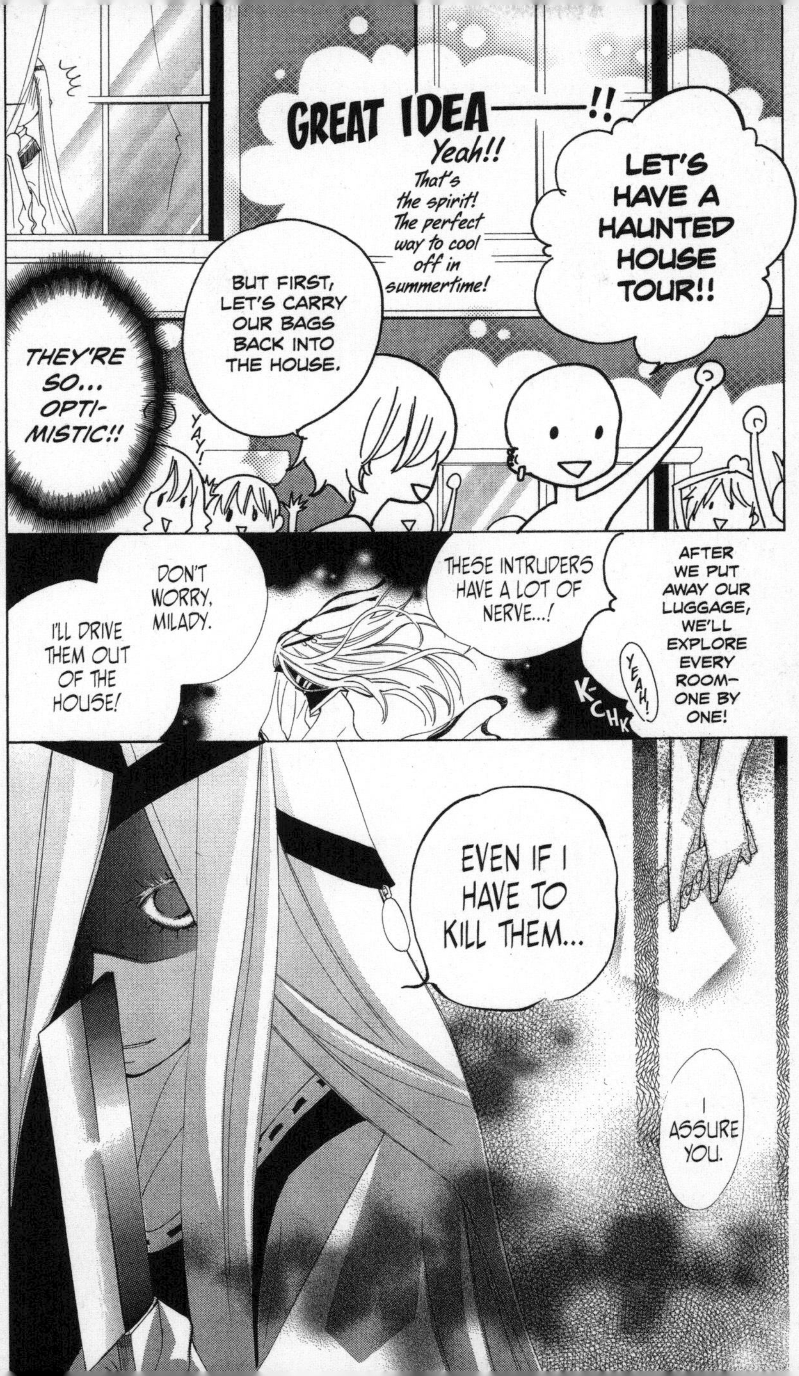
LET'S HAVE A HAUNTED HOUSE TOUR!!
GREAT IDEA——!!
Yeah!!
That's the spirit! The perfect way to cool off in summertime!
BUT FIRST, LET'S CARRY OUR BAGS BACK INTO THE HOUSE.
YAY!
THEY'RE SO... OPTI-MISTIC!!
AFTER WE PUT AWAY OUR LUGGAGE, WE'LL EXPLORE EVERY ROOM—ONE BY ONE!
YEAH!
K-CHK
THESE INTRUDERS HAVE A LOT OF NERVE...!
DON'T WORRY, MILADY.
I'LL DRIVE THEM OUT OF THE HOUSE!
EVEN IF I HAVE TO KILL THEM...
I ASSURE YOU.

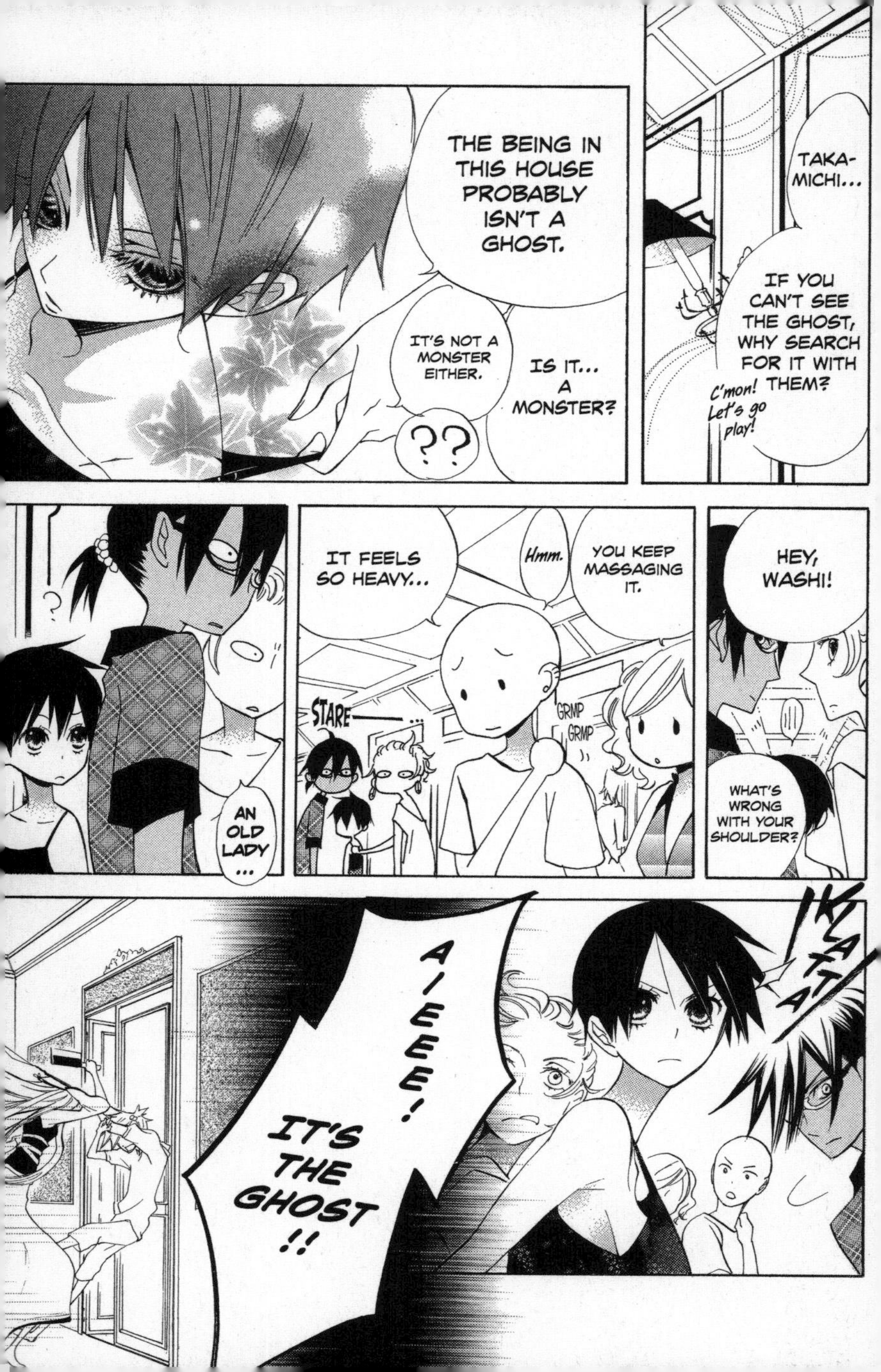
TAKA-MICHI...
IF YOU CAN'T SEE THE GHOST, WHY SEARCH FOR IT WITH THEM?
C'mon! Let's go play!
THE BEING IN THIS HOUSE PROBABLY ISN'T A GHOST.
IS IT... A MONSTER?
IT'S NOT A MONSTER EITHER.
??
HEY, WASHI!
WHAT'S WRONG WITH YOUR SHOULDER?
YOU KEEP MASSAGING IT.
Hmm.
IT FEELS SO HEAVY...
GRMP GRMP
STARE—— ...
AN OLD LADY ...
KLATTA
AIEEE! IT'S THE GHOST!!

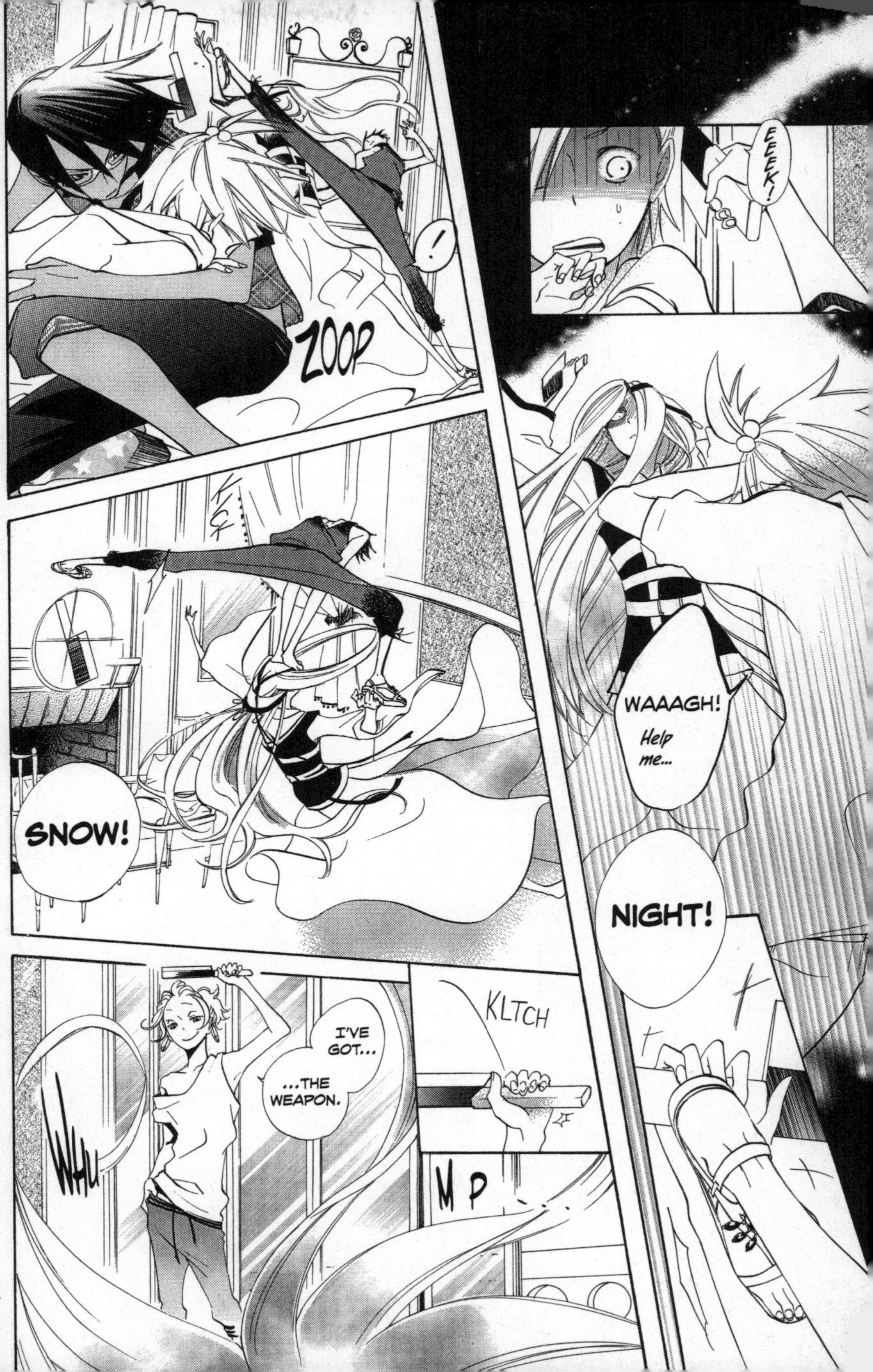
EEEK!
!
ZOOP
WAAAGH!
Help me...
NIGHT!
SNOW!
KLTCH
I'VE GOT...
...THE WEAPON.
WHU
MP

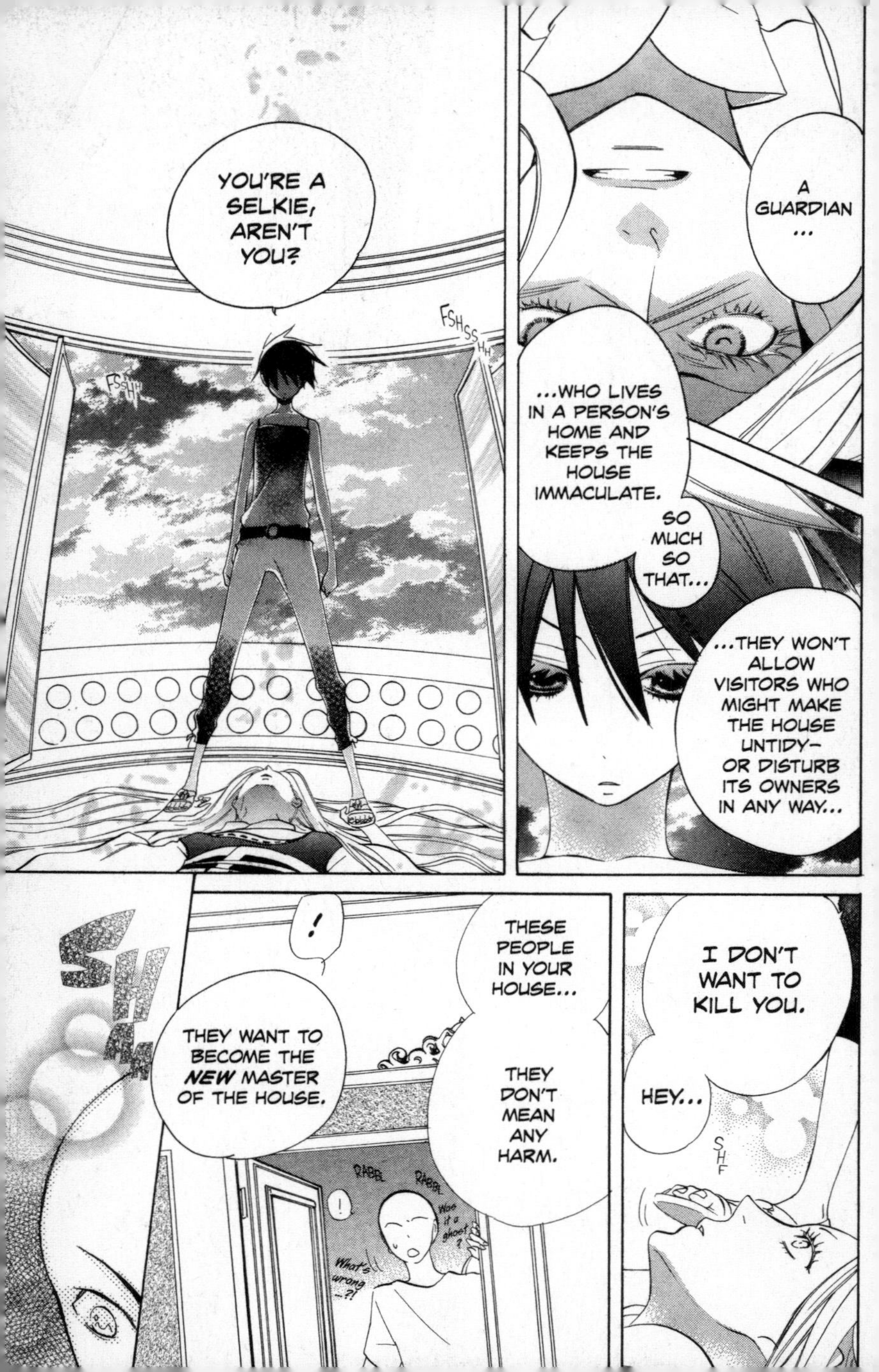
A GUARDIAN...
...WHO LIVES IN A PERSON'S HOME AND KEEPS THE HOUSE IMMACULATE.
SO MUCH SO THAT...
...THEY WON'T ALLOW VISITORS WHO MIGHT MAKE THE HOUSE UNTIDY—OR DISTURB ITS OWNERS IN ANY WAY...
YOU'RE A SELKIE, AREN'T YOU?
FSHSSHH
FSSHH
I DON'T WANT TO KILL YOU.
HEY...
SHF
THESE PEOPLE IN YOUR HOUSE...
!
THEY DON'T MEAN ANY HARM.
THEY WANT TO BECOME THE *NEW* MASTER OF THE HOUSE.
RABBL RABBL
!
Was it a ghost?
What's wrong..?!

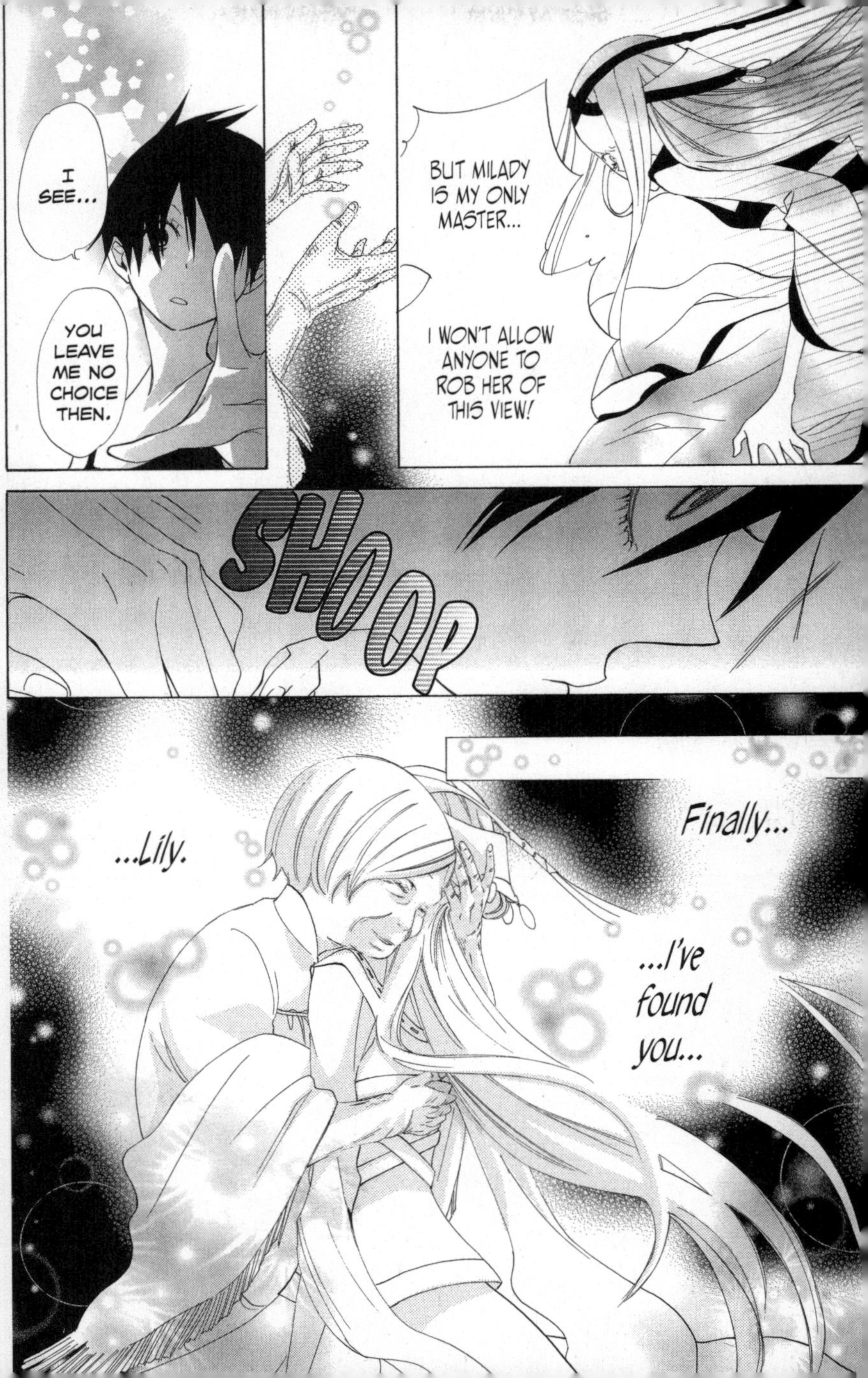
BUT MILADY IS MY ONLY MASTER...
I WON'T ALLOW ANYONE TO ROB HER OF THIS VIEW!
I SEE...
YOU LEAVE ME NO CHOICE THEN.
SHOOOP
Finally...
...Lily.
...I've found you...

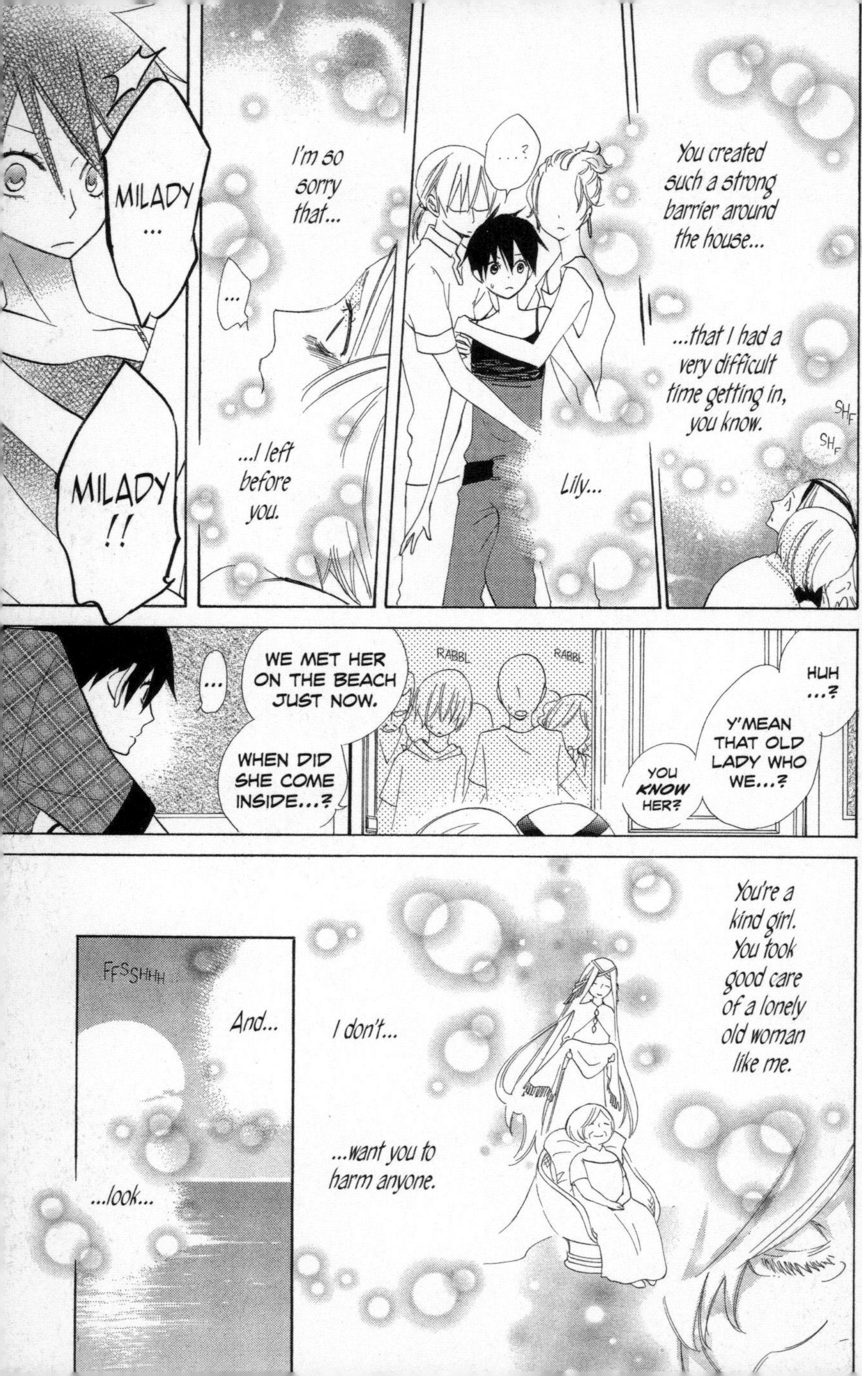
You created such a strong barrier around the house...
...that I had a very difficult time getting in, you know.
SHF
SHF
...?
Lily...
I'm so sorry that...
...
...I left before you.
MILADY...
MILADY!!
HUH...?
Y'MEAN THAT OLD LADY WHO WE...?
YOU KNOW HER?
RABBL
RABBL
WE MET HER ON THE BEACH JUST NOW.
WHEN DID SHE COME INSIDE...?
...
You're a kind girl. You took good care of a lonely old woman like me.
I don't...
...want you to harm anyone.
And...
FFSSHHH
...look...

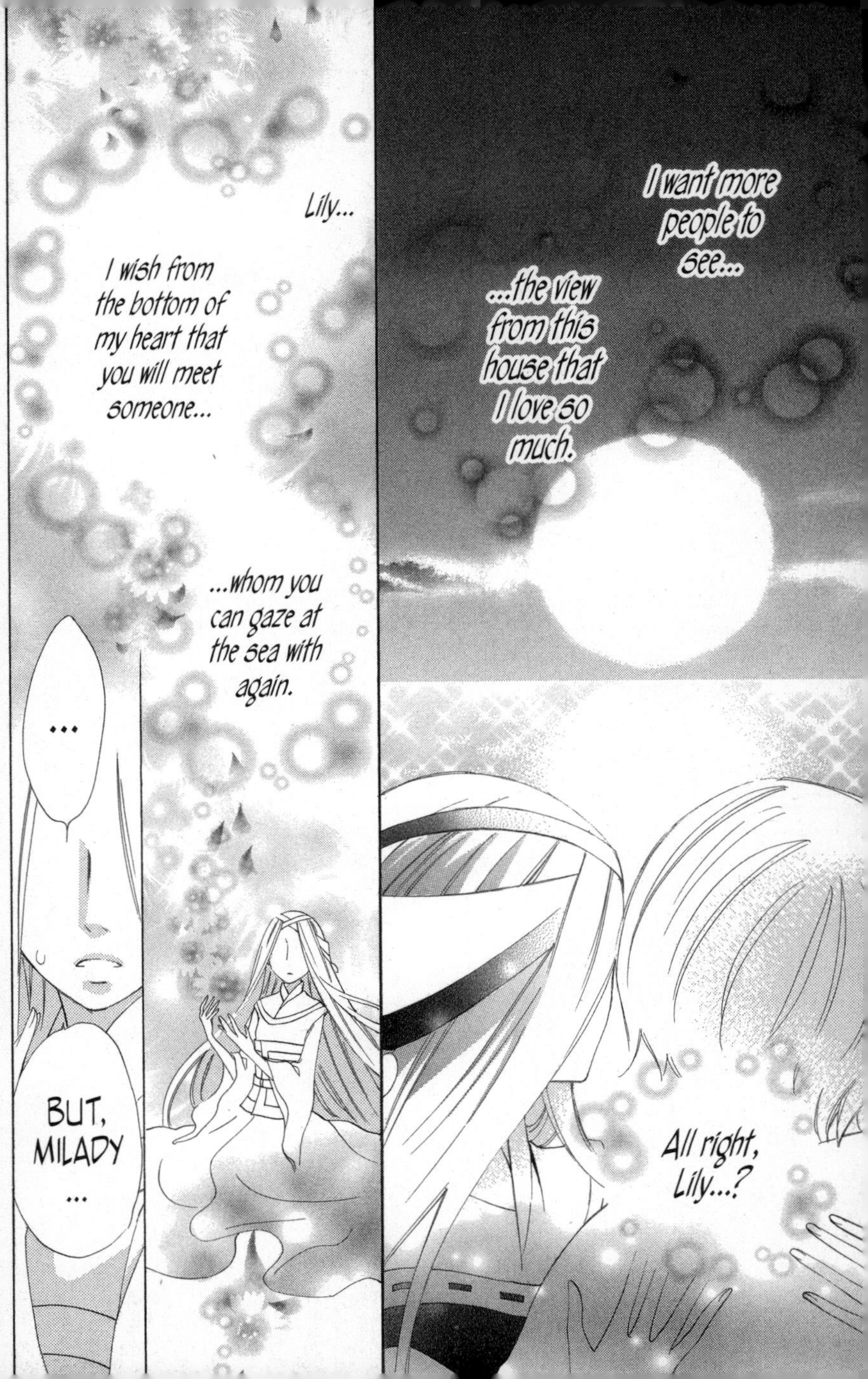
I want more people to see...
...the view from this house that I love so much.
All right, Lily...?
Lily...
I wish from the bottom of my heart that you will meet someone...
...whom you can gaze at the sea with again.
...
BUT, MILADY ...

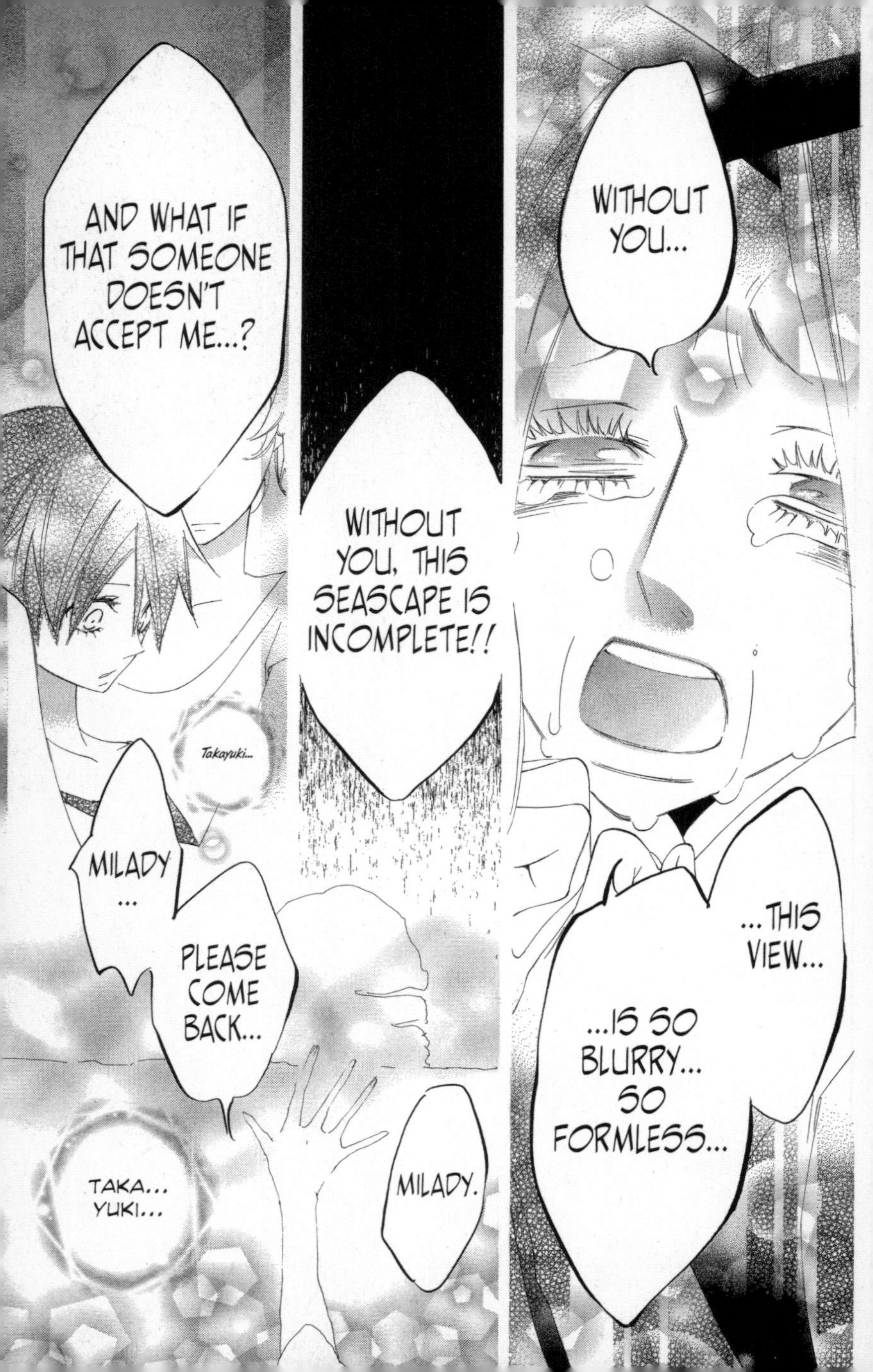
WITHOUT YOU...
...THIS VIEW...
...IS SO BLURRY... SO FORMLESS...
WITHOUT YOU, THIS SEASCAPE IS INCOMPLETE!!
AND WHAT IF THAT SOMEONE DOESN'T ACCEPT ME...?
Takayuki...
MILADY...
PLEASE COME BACK...
MILADY.
TAKA... YUKI...

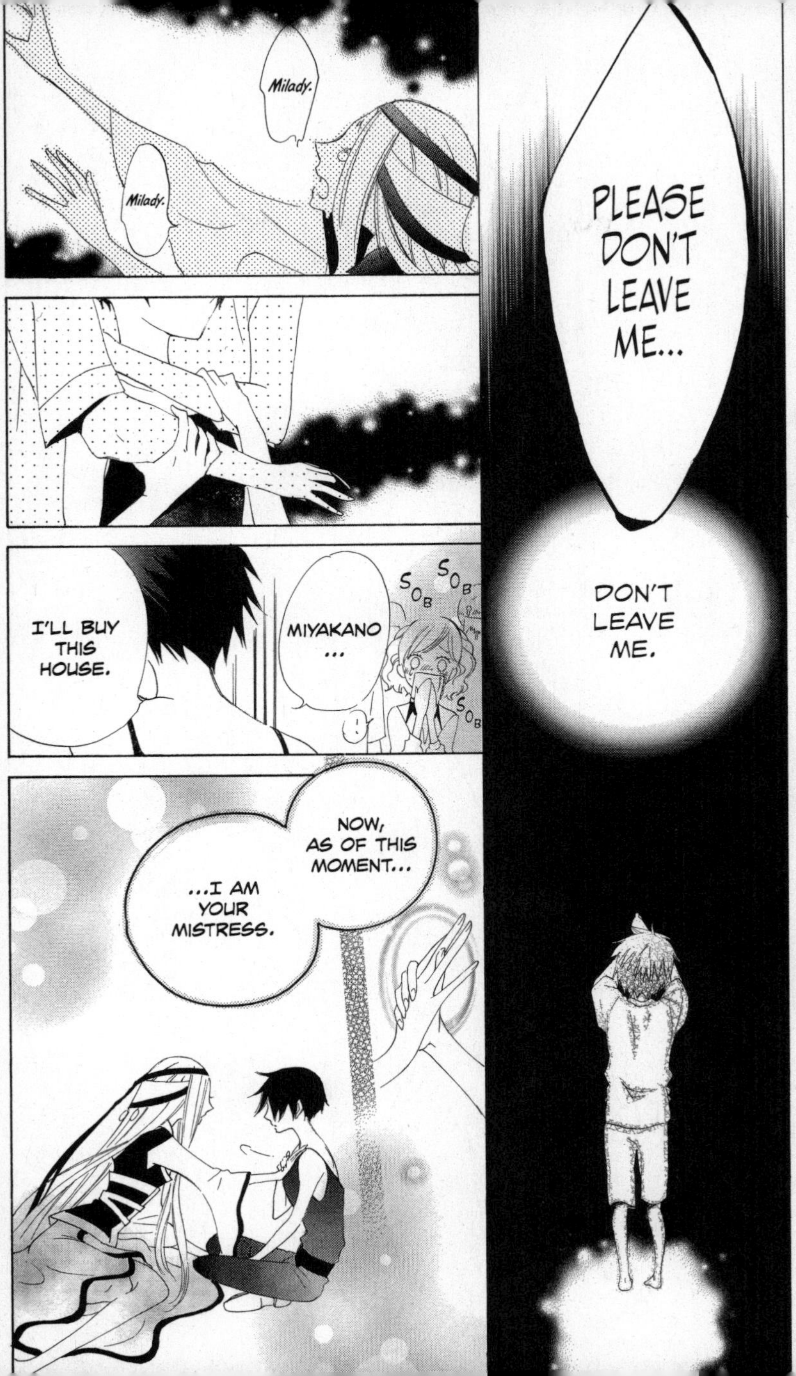
PLEASE DON'T LEAVE ME...
DON'T LEAVE ME.
Milady.
Milady.
SOB SOB
SOB
MIYAKANO ...
I'LL BUY THIS HOUSE.
NOW, AS OF THIS MOMENT...
...I AM YOUR MISTRESS.

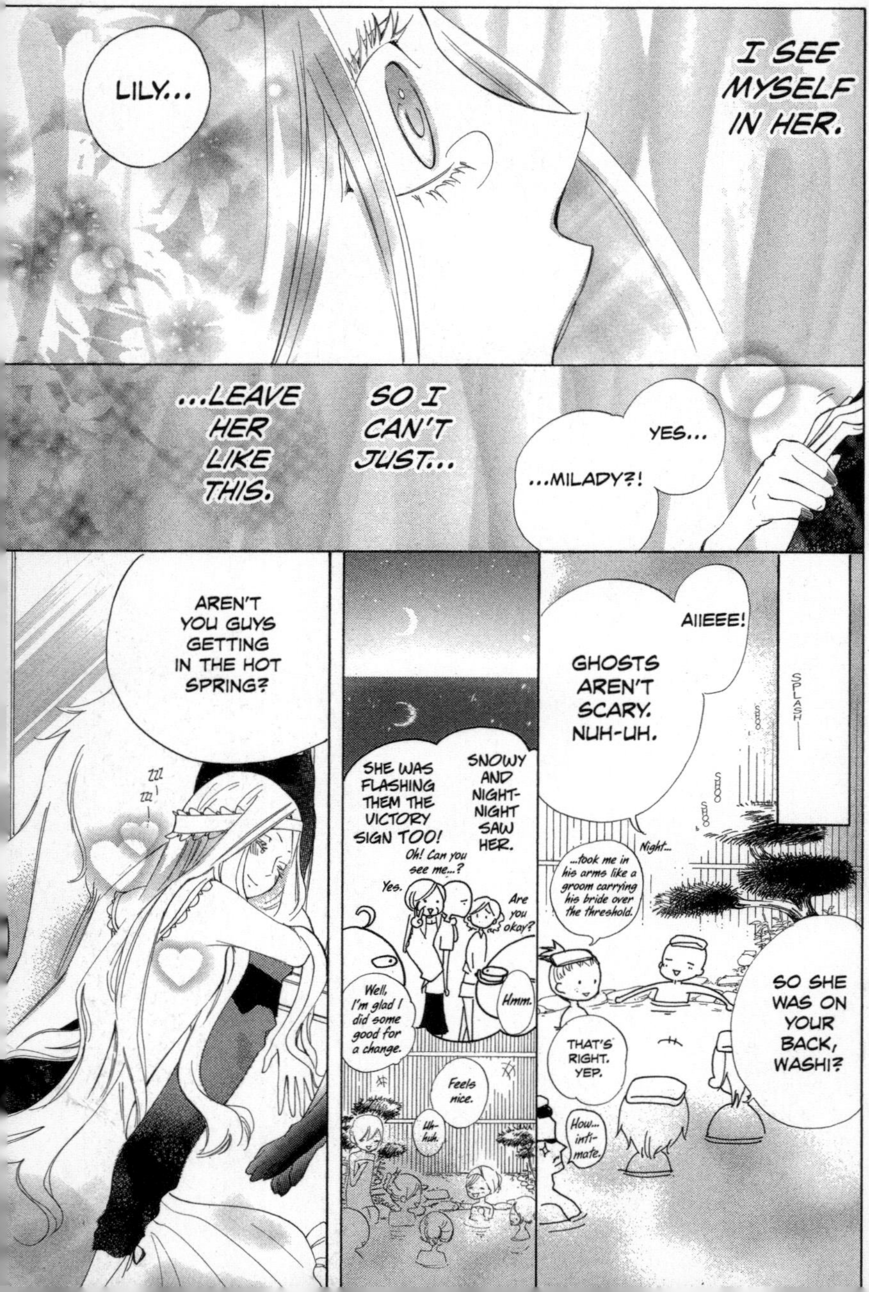
I SEE MYSELF IN HER.
LILY...
YES...
...MILADY?!
SO I CAN'T JUST...
...LEAVE HER LIKE THIS.
SPLASH
SHOO
SHOO
SHOO
AIIEEE!
GHOSTS AREN'T SCARY. NUH-UH.
Night...
...took me in his arms like a groom carrying his bride over the threshold.
SO SHE WAS ON YOUR BACK, WASHI?
THAT'S RIGHT. YEP.
How... inti-mate.
SNOWY AND NIGHT-NIGHT SAW HER.
SHE WAS FLASHING THEM THE VICTORY SIGN TOO!
Oh! Can you see me...?
Yes.
Are you okay?
Hmm.
Well, I'm glad I did some good for a change.
Feels nice.
Uh-huh.
AREN'T YOU GUYS GETTING IN THE HOT SPRING?
zzz
zzz

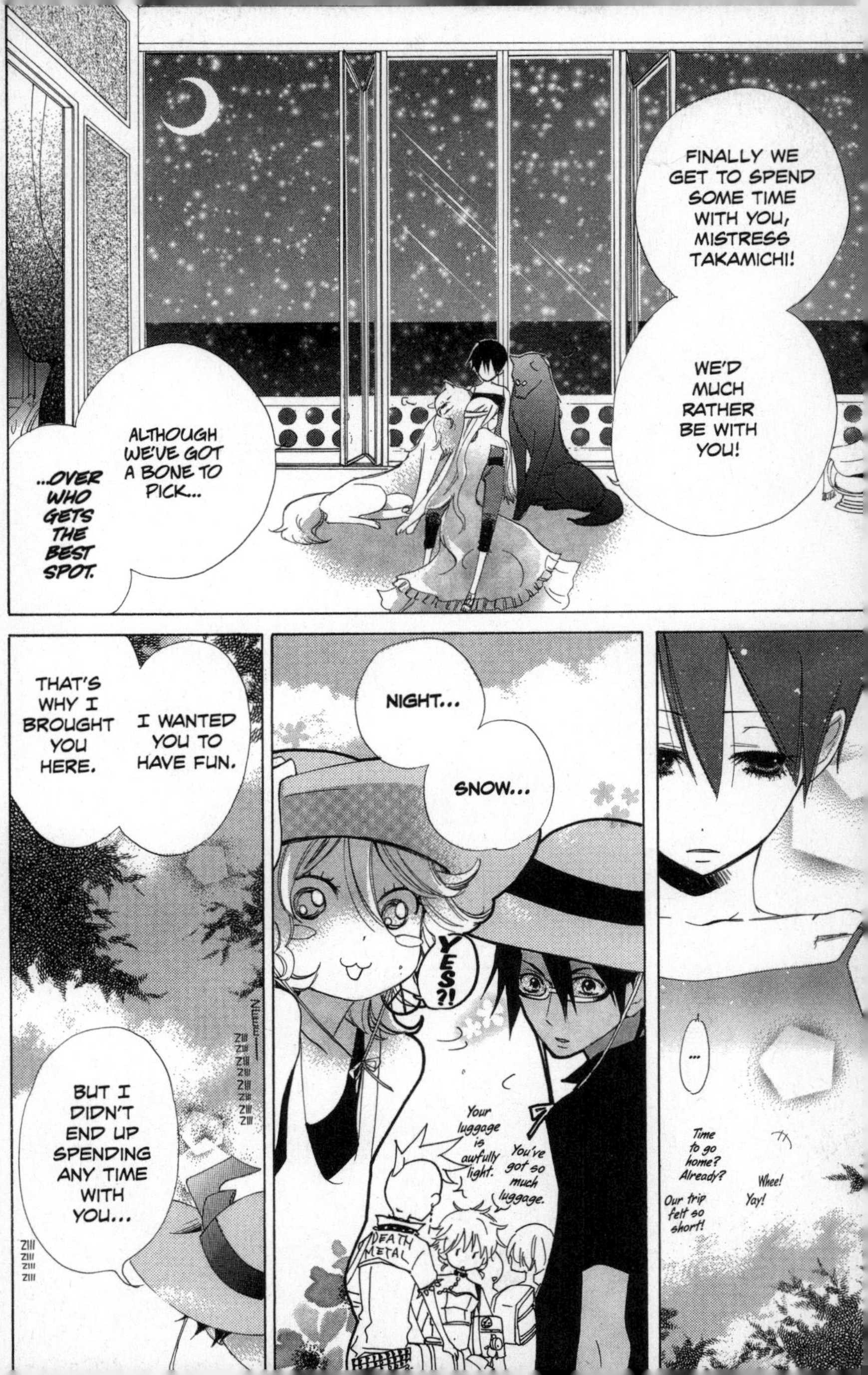
FINALLY WE GET TO SPEND SOME TIME WITH YOU, MISTRESS TAKAMICHI!
WE'D MUCH RATHER BE WITH YOU!
ALTHOUGH WE'VE GOT A BONE TO PICK...
...OVER WHO GETS THE BEST SPOT.
...
Time to go home? Already?
Our trip felt so short!
Whee!
Yay!
NIGHT...
SNOW...
YES?!
Your luggage is awfully light.
You've got so much luggage.
DEATH METAL
I WANTED YOU TO HAVE FUN.
THAT'S WHY I BROUGHT YOU HERE.
BUT I DIDN'T END UP SPENDING ANY TIME WITH YOU...
ZIII ZIII ZIII ZIII ZIII ZIII
ZIII ZIII ZIII ZIII

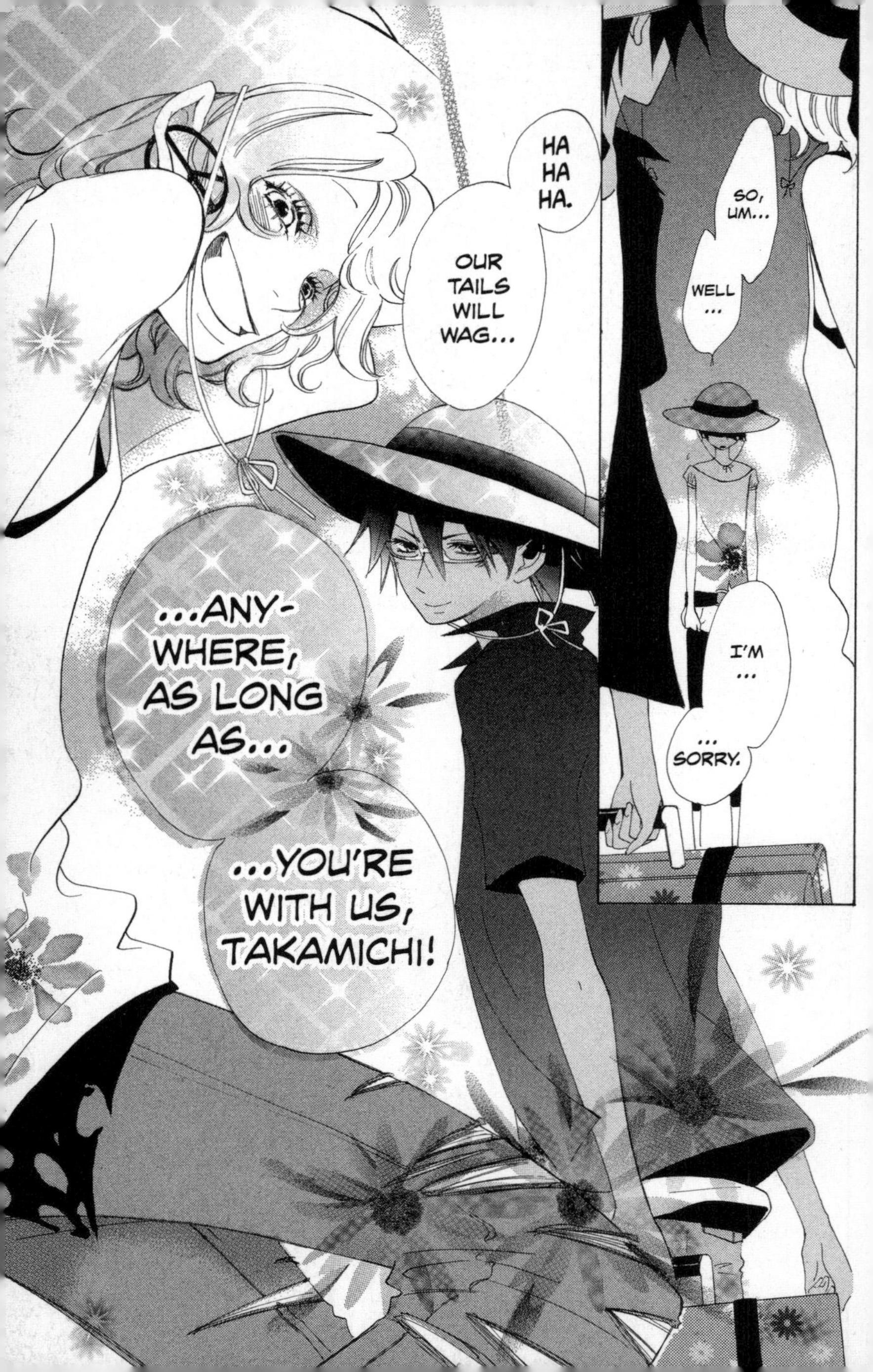
SO, UM...
WELL...
I'M...
...SORRY.
HA HA HA.
OUR TAILS WILL WAG...
...ANY-WHERE, AS LONG AS...
...YOU'RE WITH US, TAKAMICHI!

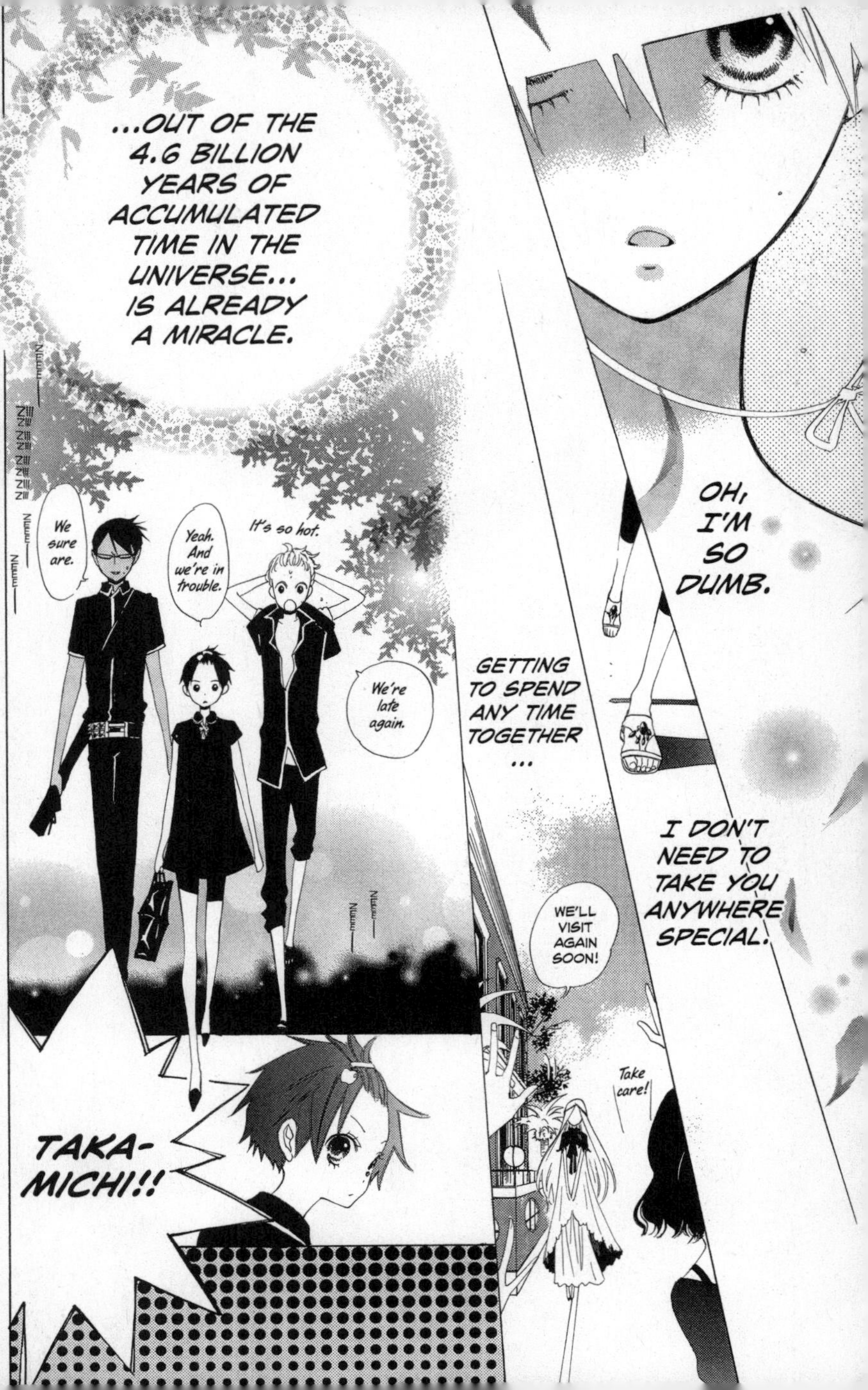
OH, I'M SO DUMB.
I DON'T NEED TO TAKE YOU ANYWHERE SPECIAL.
GETTING TO SPEND ANY TIME TOGETHER ...
WE'LL VISIT AGAIN SOON!
Take care!
...OUT OF THE 4.6 BILLION YEARS OF ACCUMULATED TIME IN THE UNIVERSE... IS ALREADY A MIRACLE.
It's so hot.
We're late again.
Yeah. And we're in trouble.
We sure are.
TAKA-MICHI!!

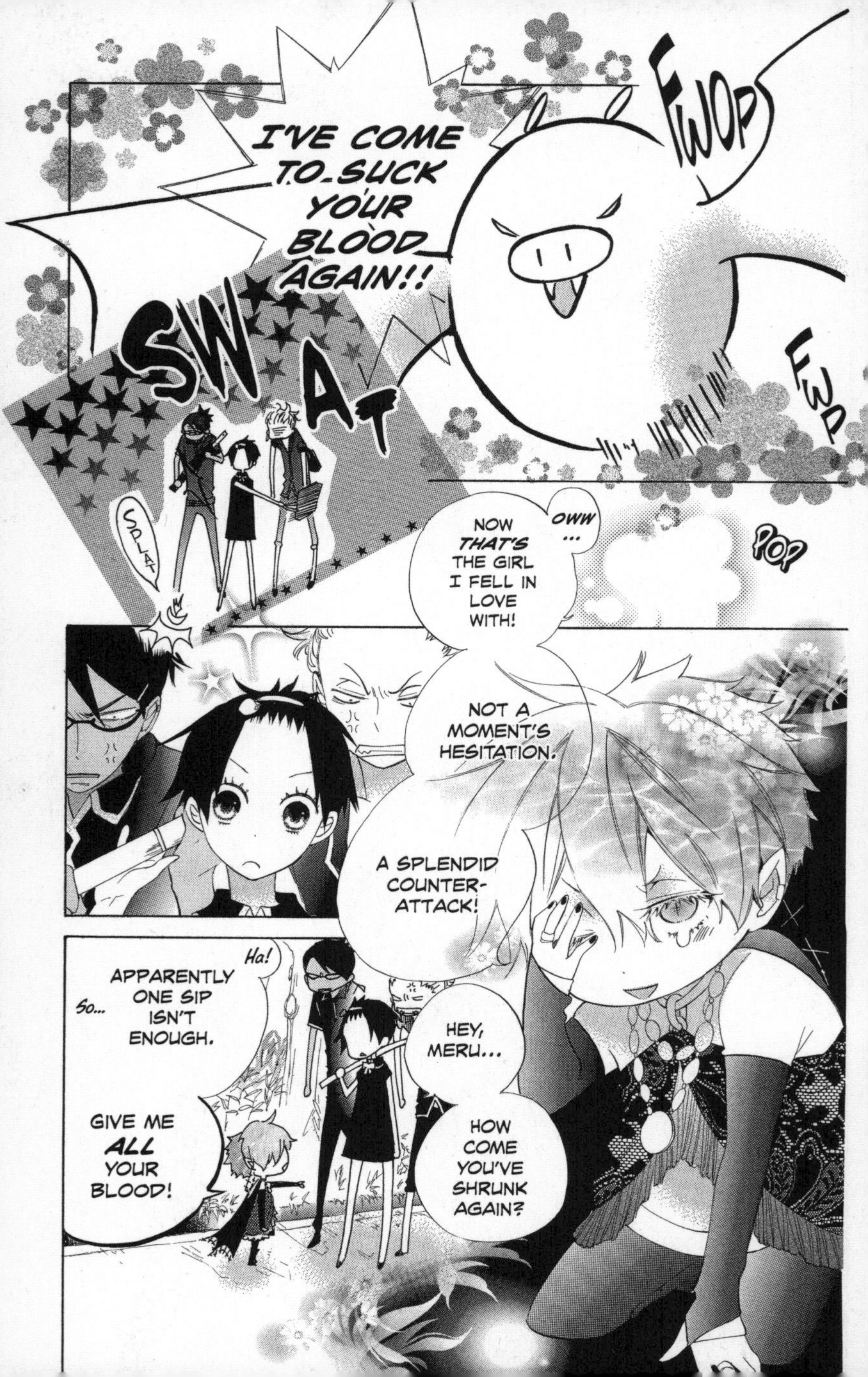
FWOPS
I'VE COME TO SUCK YOUR BLOOD AGAIN!!
FWP
SWAT
SPLAT
POP
OWW...
NOW *THAT'S* THE GIRL I FELL IN LOVE WITH!
NOT A MOMENT'S HESITATION.
A SPLENDID COUNTER-ATTACK!
HEY, MERU...
HOW COME YOU'VE SHRUNK AGAIN?
Ha!
So...
APPARENTLY ONE SIP ISN'T ENOUGH.
GIVE ME ***ALL*** YOUR BLOOD!

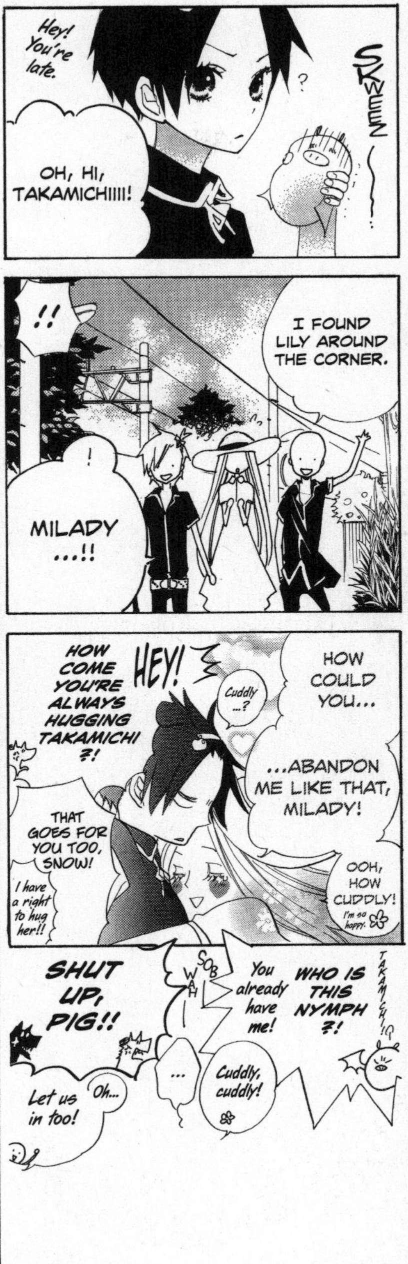
SKWEEN
?
Hey! You're late.
OH, HI, TAKAMICHIIIII!
I FOUND LILY AROUND THE CORNER.
!!
!
MILADY ...!!
HOW COULD YOU...
...ABANDON ME LIKE THAT, MILADY!
Cuddly ...?
HEY!
HOW COME YOU'RE ALWAYS HUGGING TAKAMICHI?!
THAT GOES FOR YOU TOO, SNOW!
OOH, HOW CUDDLY! I'm so happy.
I have a right to hug her!!
TAKAMICHI!?
WHO IS THIS NYMPH?!
You already have me!
SOB
WAH
SHUT UP, PIG!!
Cuddly, cuddly!
...
Oh...
Let us in too!

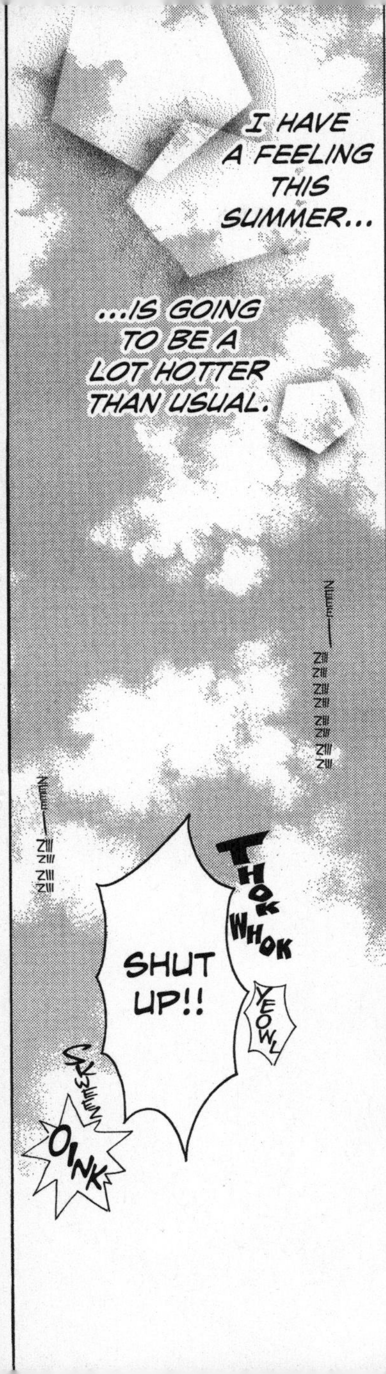
I HAVE A FEELING THIS SUMMER...
...IS GOING TO BE A LOT HOTTER THAN USUAL.
THOK
WHOK
SHUT UP!!
YEOWL
SKWEE
OINK

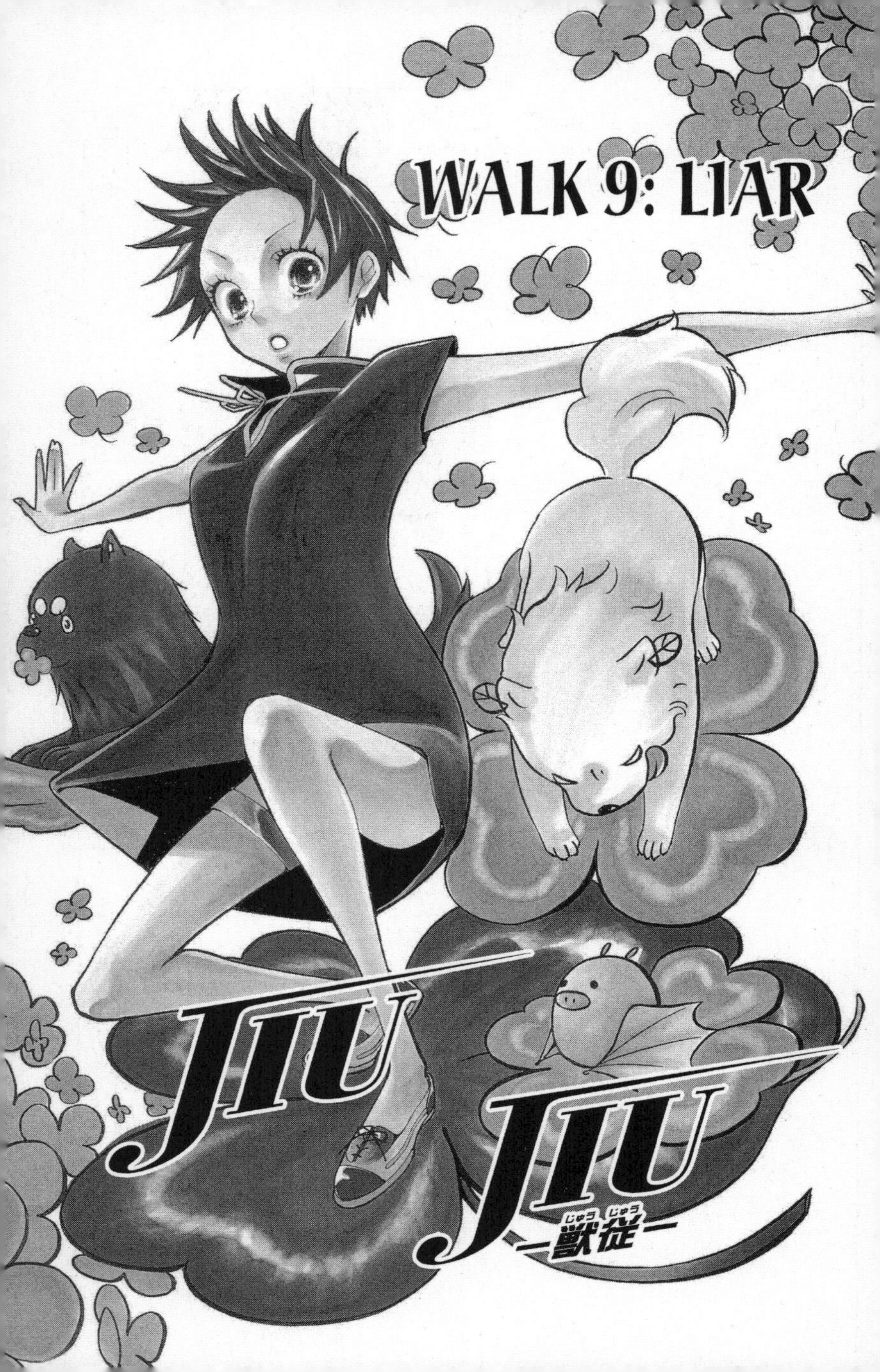
WALK 9: LIAR
JIU JIU
獣従

# HAVEN'T THE FOGGIEST

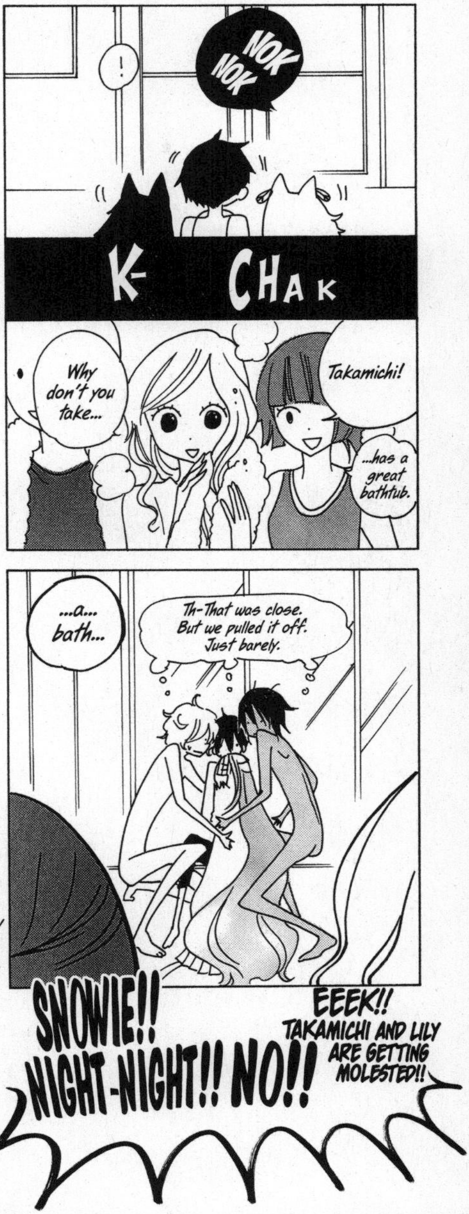
NOK NOK
!
K-CHAK
Takamichi!
...has a great bathtub.
Why don't you take...
Th-That was close. But we pulled it off. Just barely.
...a... bath...
EEEK!! TAKAMICHI AND LILY ARE GETTING MOLESTED!!
SNOWIE!! NIGHT-NIGHT!! NO!!

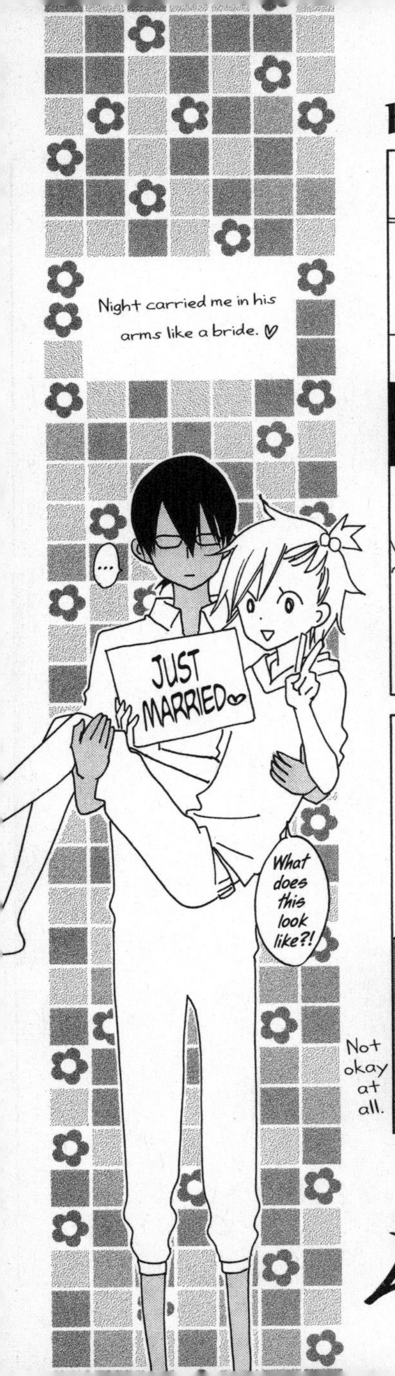
Night carried me in his arms like a bride. ♥
...
JUST MARRIED
What does this look like?!
Not okay at all.

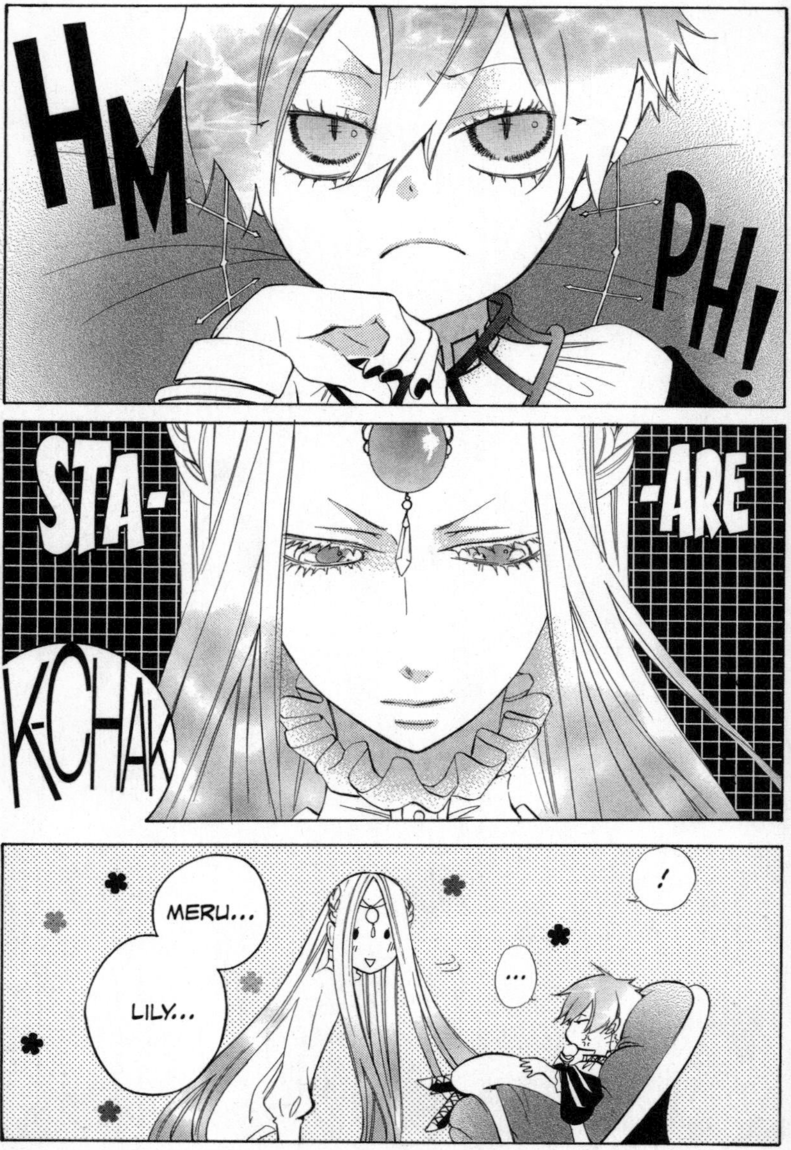
HMPH!
STA-
-ARE
K-CHAK
!
...
MERU...
LILY...

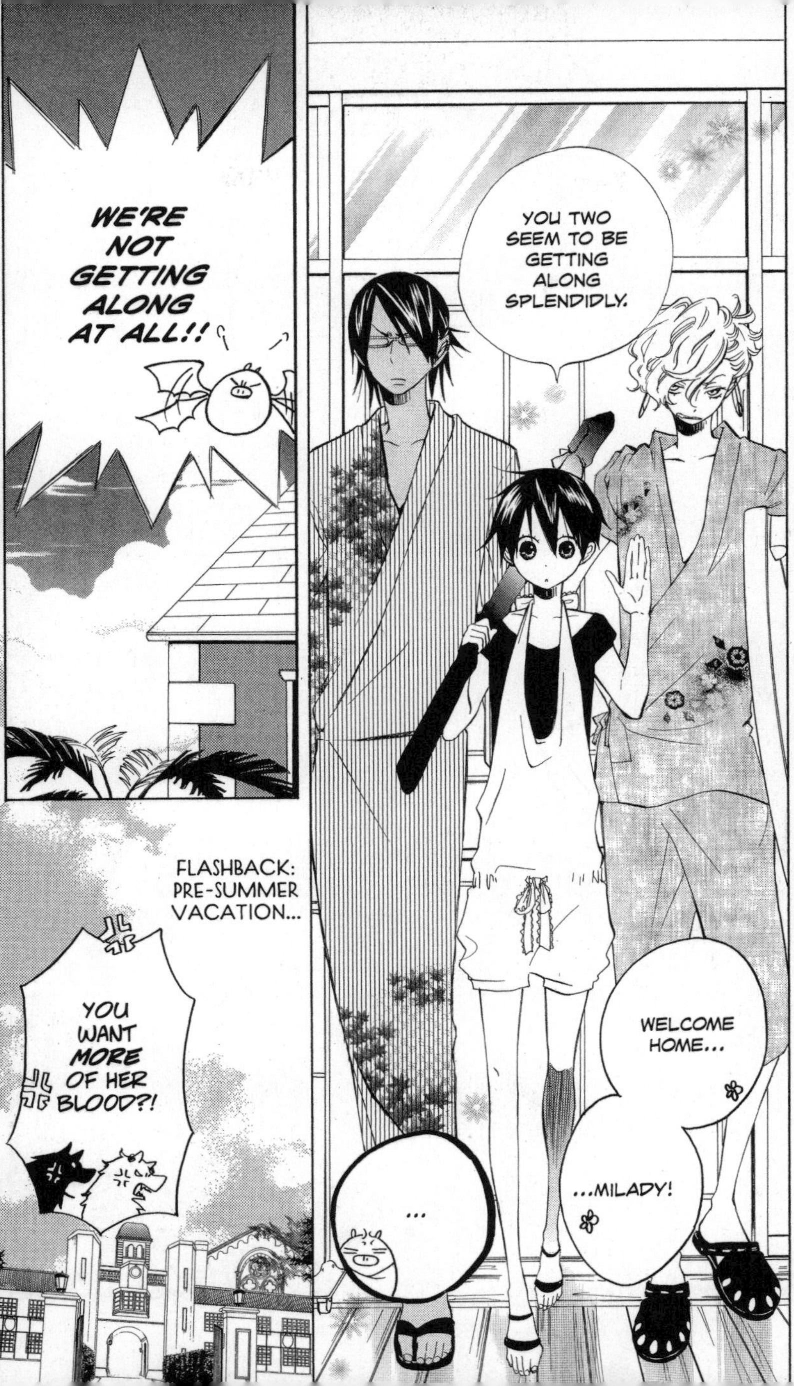
YOU TWO SEEM TO BE GETTING ALONG SPLENDIDLY.
WELCOME HOME...
...MILADY!
...
WE'RE NOT GETTING ALONG AT ALL!!
FLASHBACK: PRE-SUMMER VACATION...
YOU WANT MORE OF HER BLOOD?!

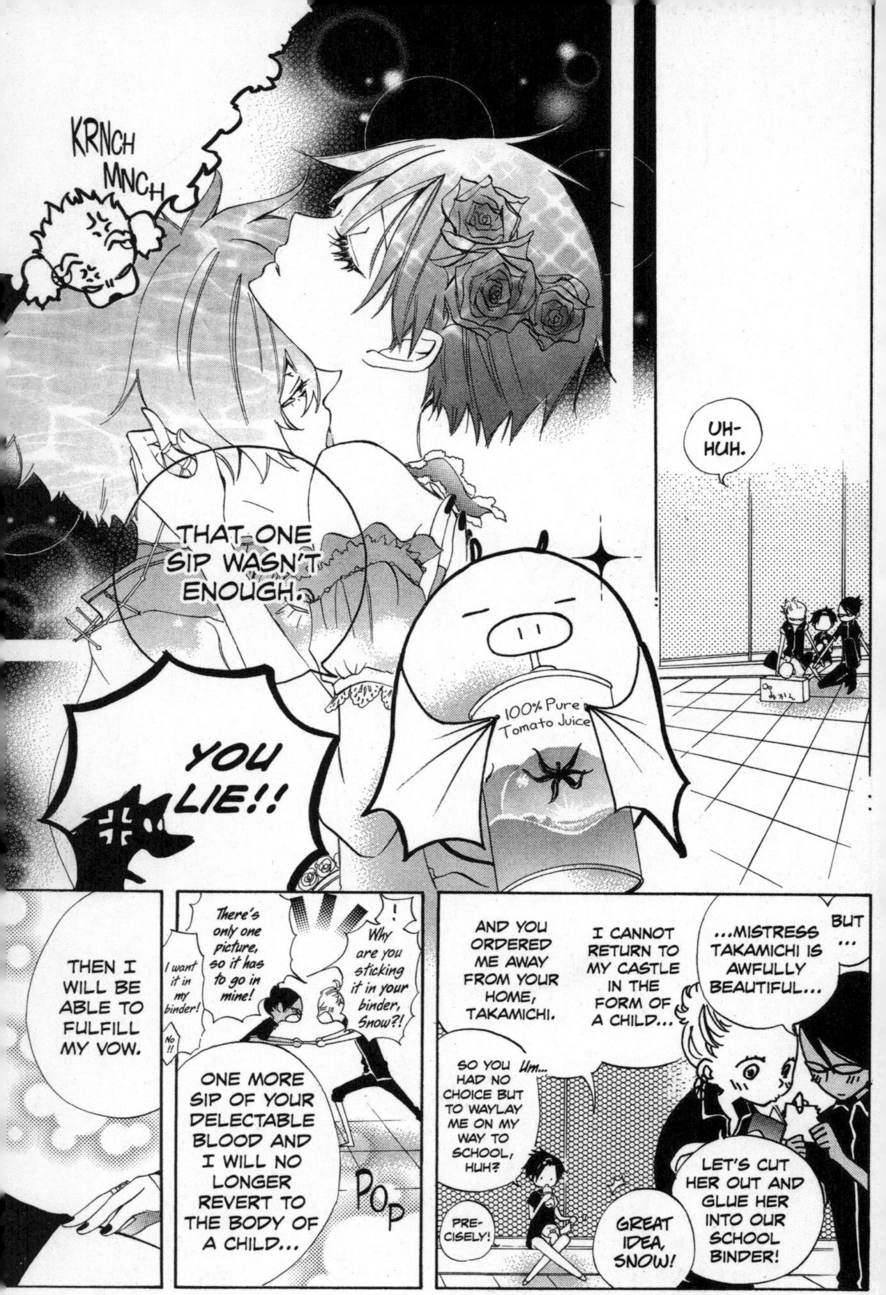
UH-HUH.
KRNCH MNCH
THAT ONE SIP WASN'T ENOUGH.
YOU LIE!!
100% Pure Tomato Juice
BUT ...
...MISTRESS TAKAMICHI IS AWFULLY BEAUTIFUL...
I CANNOT RETURN TO MY CASTLE IN THE FORM OF A CHILD...
AND YOU ORDERED ME AWAY FROM YOUR HOME, TAKAMICHI.
LET'S CUT HER OUT AND GLUE HER INTO OUR SCHOOL BINDER!
GREAT IDEA, SNOW!
Um...
SO YOU HAD NO CHOICE BUT TO WAYLAY ME ON MY WAY TO SCHOOL, HUH?
PRE-CISELY!
!
Why are you sticking it in your binder, Snow?!
There's only one picture, so it has to go in mine!
I want it in my binder!
No!!
ONE MORE SIP OF YOUR DELECTABLE BLOOD AND I WILL NO LONGER REVERT TO THE BODY OF A CHILD...
POP
THEN I WILL BE ABLE TO FULFILL MY VOW.

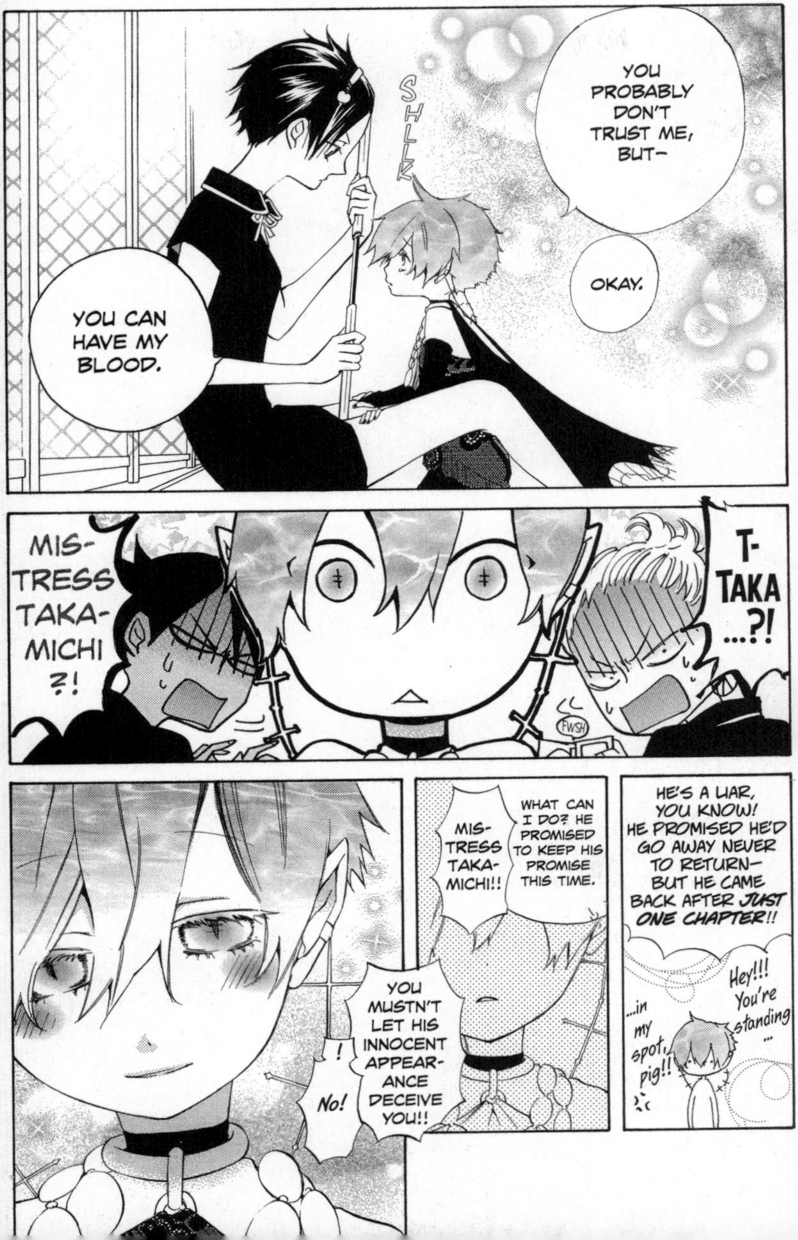
YOU PROBABLY DON'T TRUST ME, BUT-
SHLLK
OKAY.
YOU CAN HAVE MY BLOOD.
T-TAKA...?!
FWSH
MIS-TRESS TAKA-MICHI ?!
HE'S A LIAR, YOU KNOW! HE PROMISED HE'D GO AWAY NEVER TO RETURN— BUT HE CAME BACK AFTER *JUST ONE CHAPTER*!!
Hey!!! You're standing...
...in my spot, pig!!
WHAT CAN I DO? HE PROMISED TO KEEP HIS PROMISE THIS TIME.
MIS-TRESS TAKA-MICHI!!
YOU MUSTN'T LET HIS INNOCENT APPEAR-ANCE DECEIVE YOU!!
!
No!

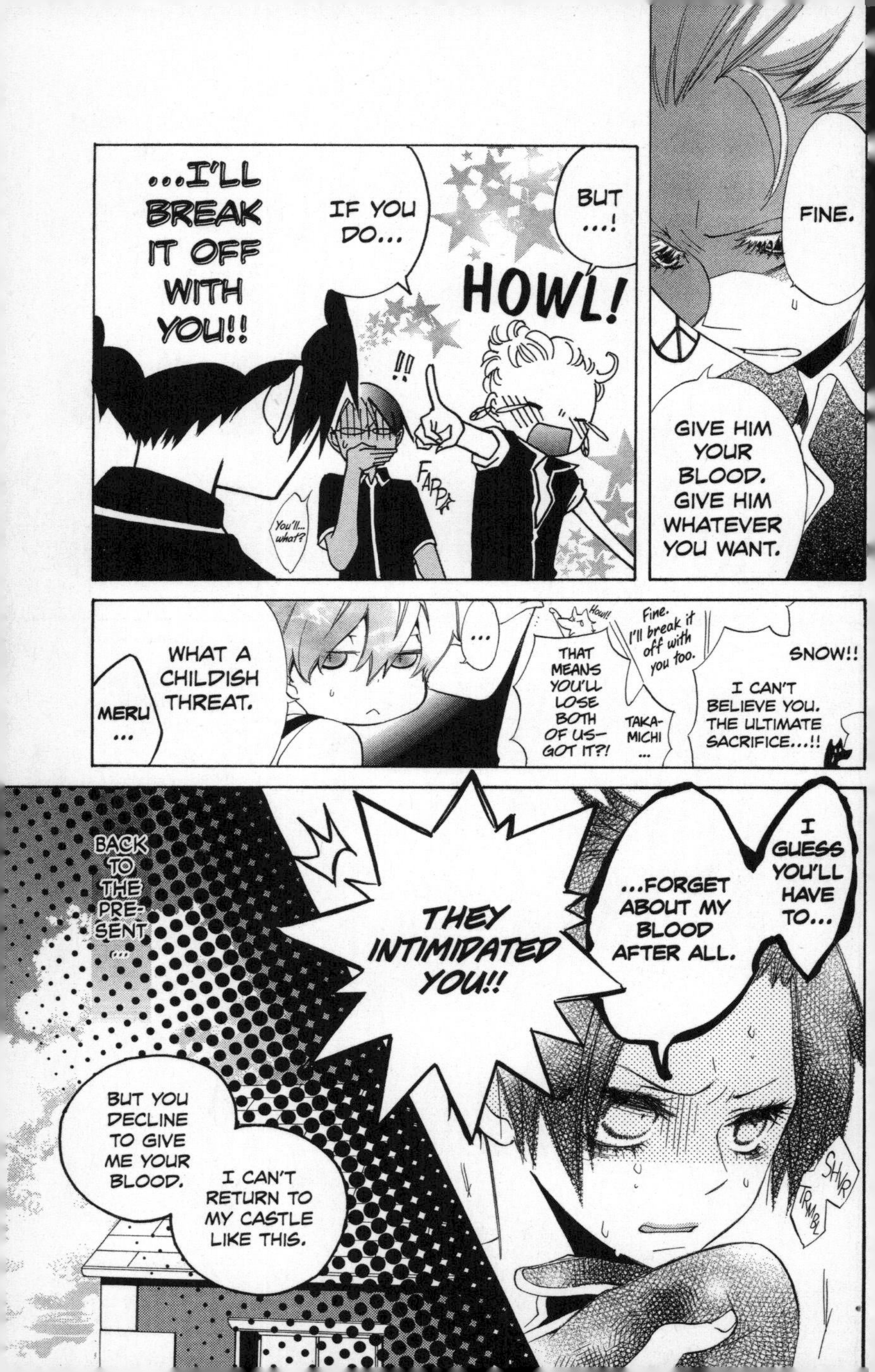
FINE.
GIVE HIM YOUR BLOOD. GIVE HIM WHATEVER YOU WANT.
BUT ...!
HOWL!
IF YOU DO...
...I'LL BREAK IT OFF WITH YOU!!
!!
You'll... what?
SNOW!!
I CAN'T BELIEVE YOU. THE ULTIMATE SACRIFICE...!!
Fine. I'll break it off with you too.
Howl!
TAKA-MICHI ...
THAT MEANS YOU'LL LOSE BOTH OF US-GOT IT?!
...
WHAT A CHILDISH THREAT.
MERU ...
I GUESS YOU'LL HAVE TO...
...FORGET ABOUT MY BLOOD AFTER ALL.
THEY INTIMIDATED YOU!!
BACK TO THE PRE-SENT ...
SHVR
TRMBL
BUT YOU DECLINE TO GIVE ME YOUR BLOOD.
I CAN'T RETURN TO MY CASTLE LIKE THIS.

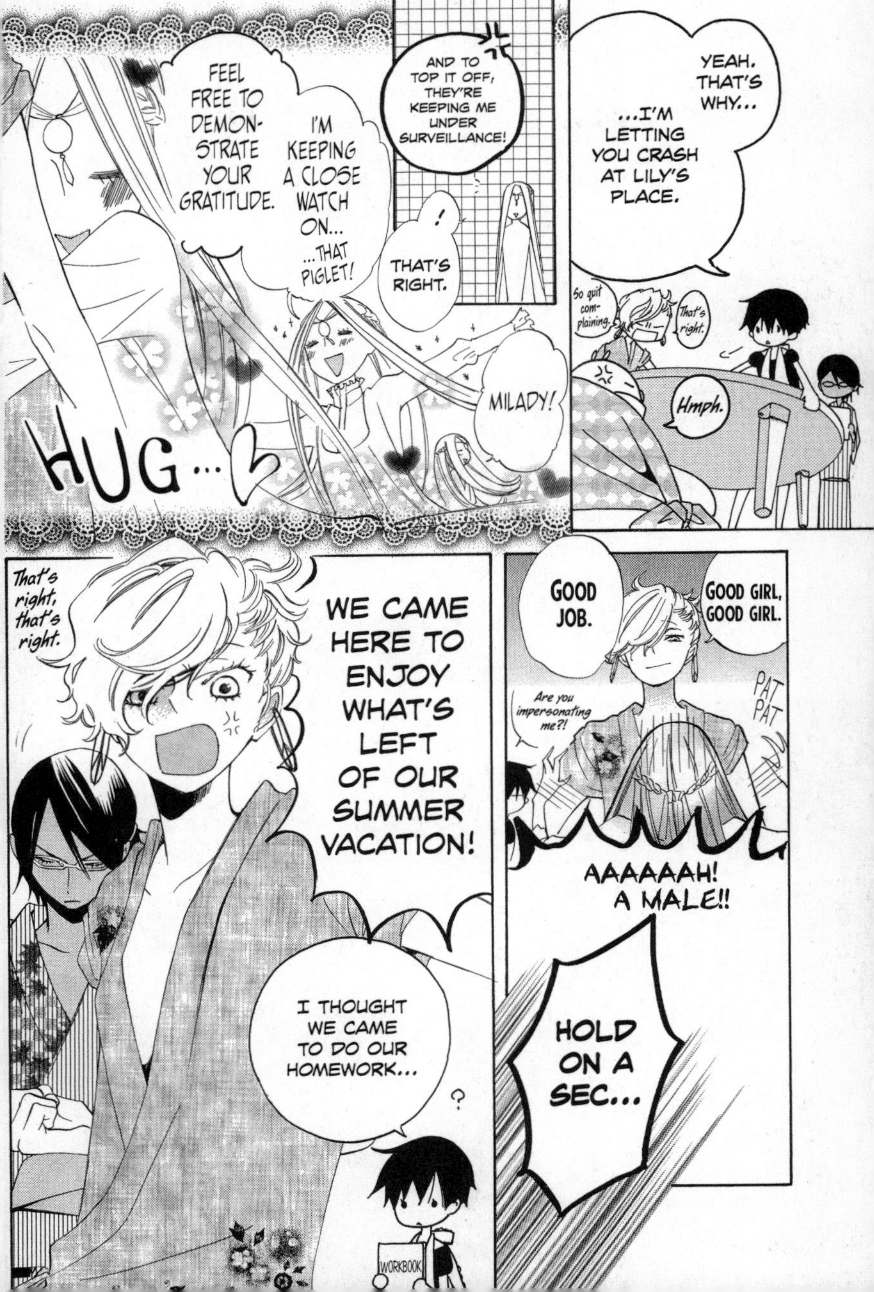
YEAH. THAT'S WHY...
...I'M LETTING YOU CRASH AT LILY'S PLACE.
So quit complaining.
That's right.
Hmph.
AND TO TOP IT OFF, THEY'RE KEEPING ME UNDER SURVEILLANCE!
!
THAT'S RIGHT.
I'M KEEPING A CLOSE WATCH ON... ...THAT PIGLET!
FEEL FREE TO DEMON-STRATE YOUR GRATITUDE.
MILADY!
HUG...
GOOD GIRL, GOOD GIRL.
GOOD JOB.
PAT PAT
Are you impersonating me?!
AAAAAAH! A MALE!!
HOLD ON A SEC...
WE CAME HERE TO ENJOY WHAT'S LEFT OF OUR SUMMER VACATION!
That's right, that's right.
I THOUGHT WE CAME TO DO OUR HOMEWORK...
?
WORKBOOK

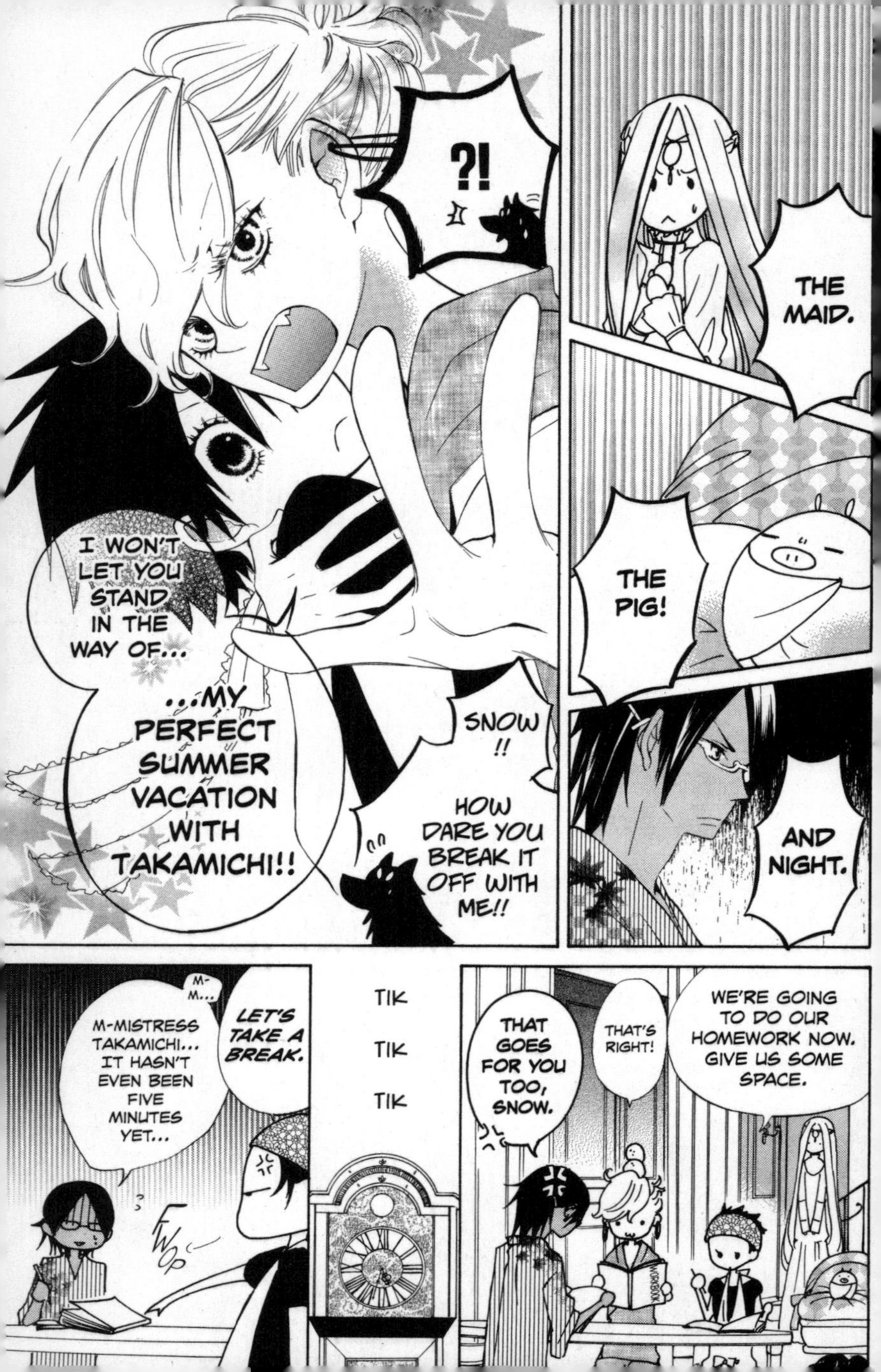
THE MAID.
THE PIG!
AND NIGHT.
?!
SNOW!!
HOW DARE YOU BREAK IT OFF WITH ME!!
I WON'T LET YOU STAND IN THE WAY OF...
...MY PERFECT SUMMER VACATION WITH TAKAMICHI!!
WE'RE GOING TO DO OUR HOMEWORK NOW. GIVE US SOME SPACE.
THAT'S RIGHT!
THAT GOES FOR YOU TOO, SNOW.
WORKBOOK
TIK
TIK
TIK
LET'S TAKE A BREAK.
M-M...
M-MISTRESS TAKAMICHI... IT HASN'T EVEN BEEN FIVE MINUTES YET...
FWOP

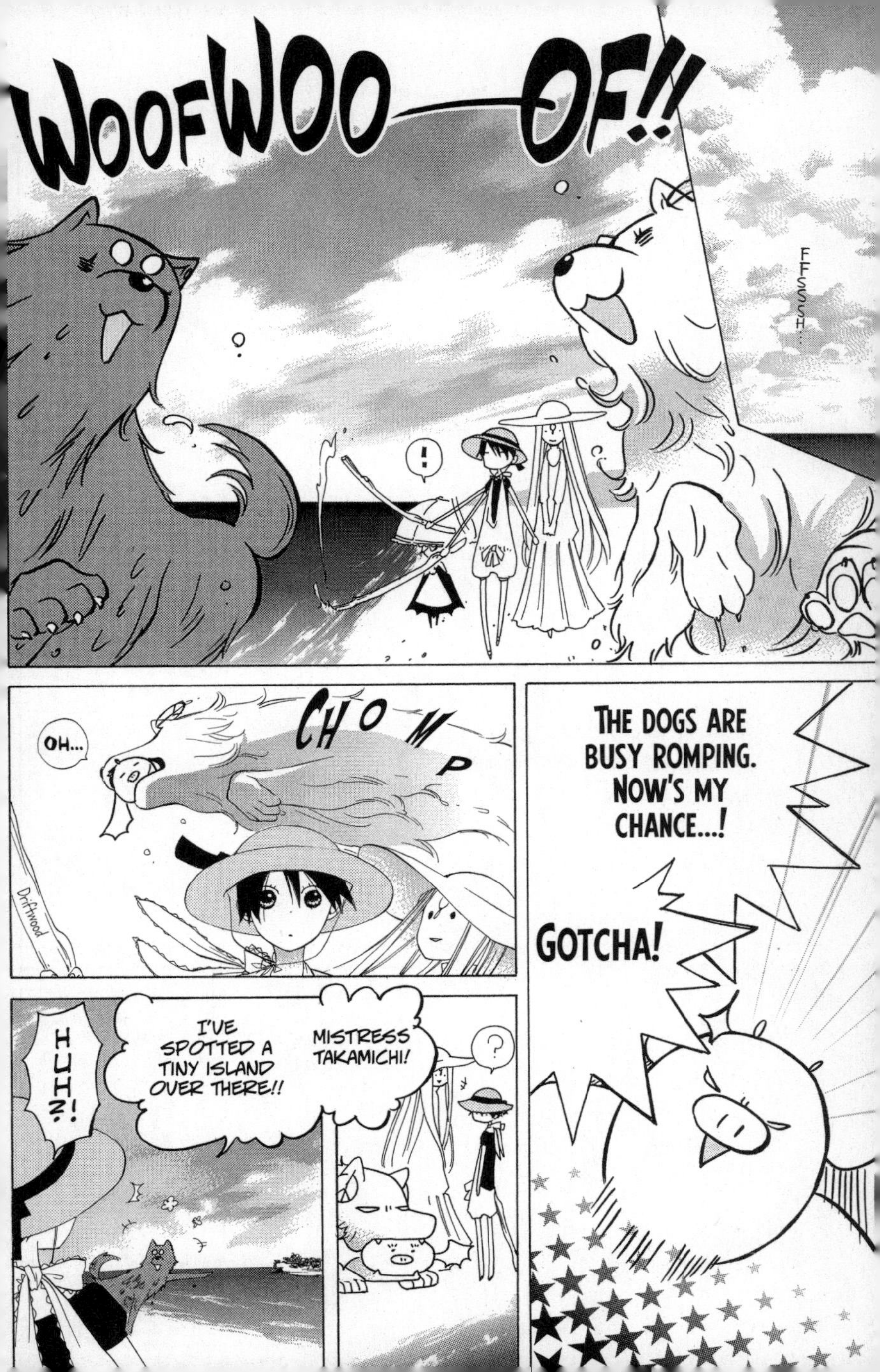
WOOFWOO—OF!!
FFSSSSH...
!
THE DOGS ARE BUSY ROMPING. NOW'S MY CHANCE...!
GOTCHA!
CHOMP
OH...
Driftwood
?
MISTRESS TAKAMICHI!
I'VE SPOTTED A TINY ISLAND OVER THERE!!
HUH?!

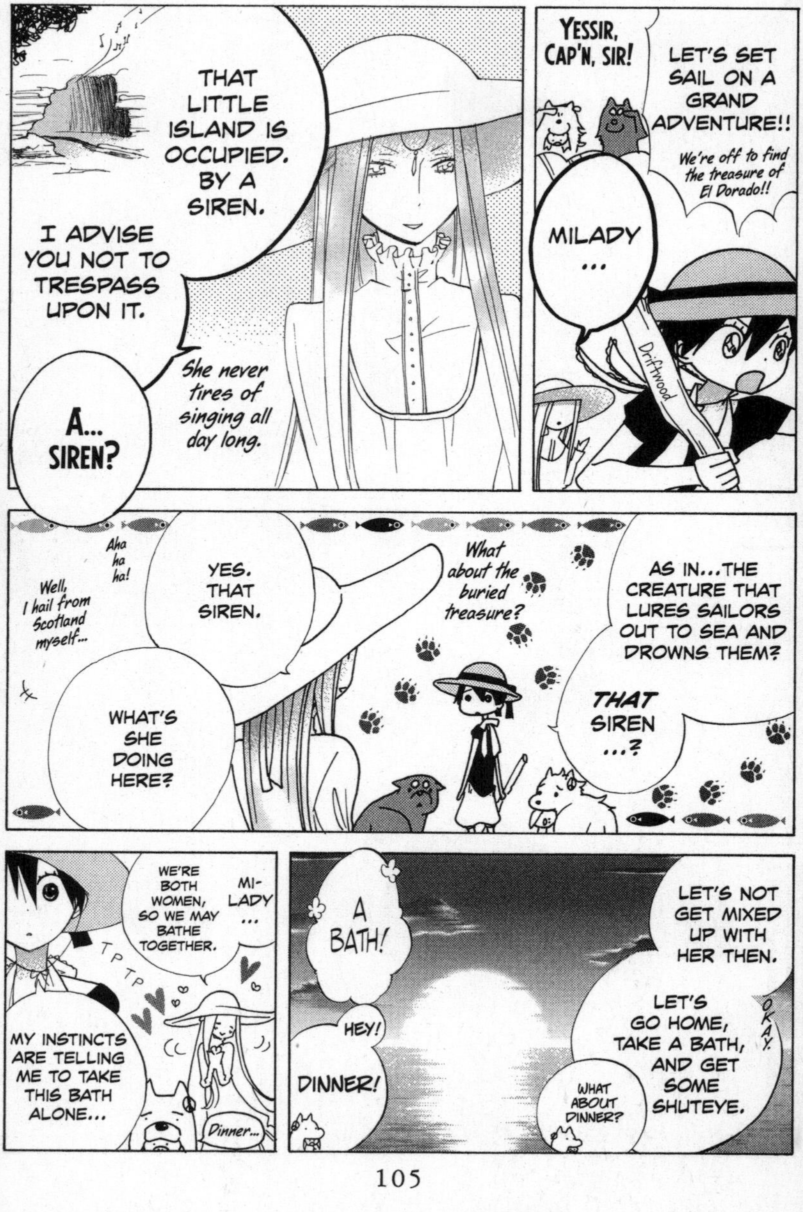

LET'S SET SAIL ON A GRAND ADVENTURE!!
We're off to find the treasure of El Dorado!!
YESSIR, CAP'N, SIR!
MILADY ...
Driftwood
THAT LITTLE ISLAND IS OCCUPIED. BY A SIREN.
I ADVISE YOU NOT TO TRESPASS UPON IT.
She never tires of singing all day long.
A... SIREN?
AS IN...THE CREATURE THAT LURES SAILORS OUT TO SEA AND DROWNS THEM?
THAT SIREN ...?
What about the buried treasure?
YES. THAT SIREN.
Aha ha ha!
Well, I hail from Scotland myself...
WHAT'S SHE DOING HERE?
LET'S NOT GET MIXED UP WITH HER THEN.
OKAY.
LET'S GO HOME, TAKE A BATH, AND GET SOME SHUTEYE.
WHAT ABOUT DINNER?
A BATH!
HEY!
DINNER!
MI-LADY ...
WE'RE BOTH WOMEN, SO WE MAY BATHE TOGETHER.
TP TP
MY INSTINCTS ARE TELLING ME TO TAKE THIS BATH ALONE...
Dinner...

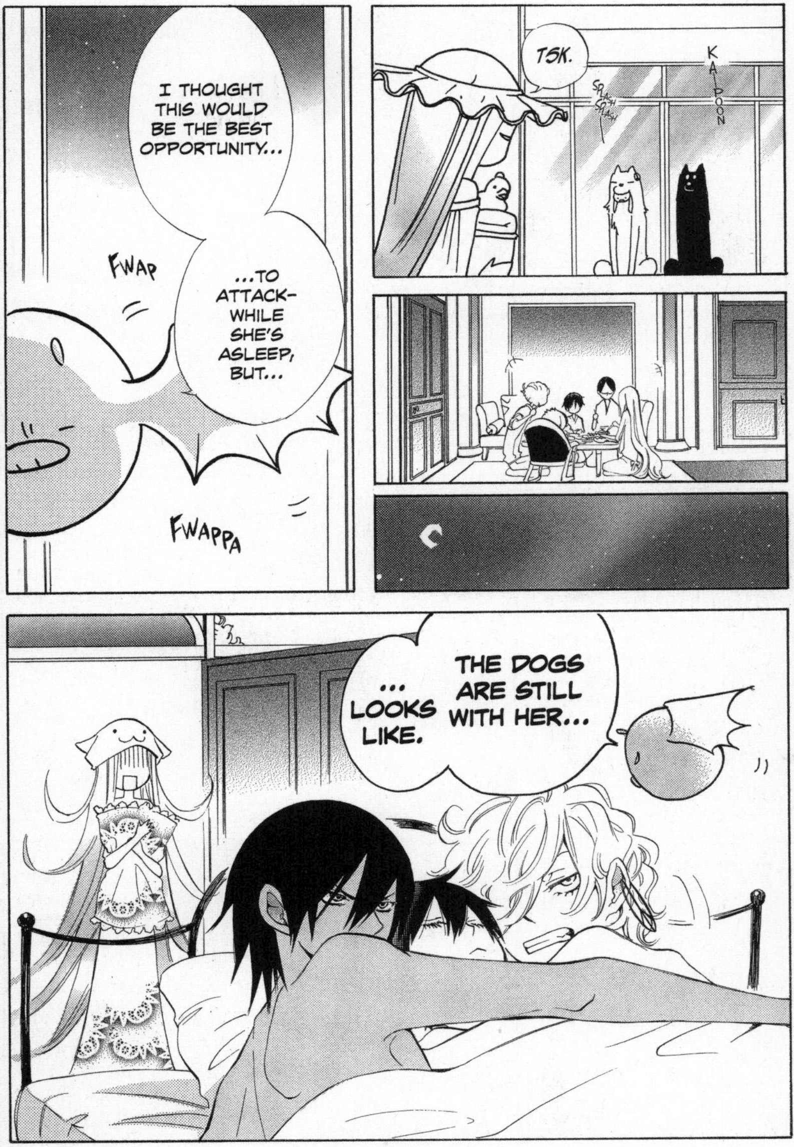
TSK.
SPLASH SPLASH
KAPOON
I THOUGHT THIS WOULD BE THE BEST OPPORTUNITY...
...TO ATTACK-WHILE SHE'S ASLEEP, BUT...
FWAP
FWAPPA
THE DOGS ARE STILL WITH HER...
...LOOKS LIKE.

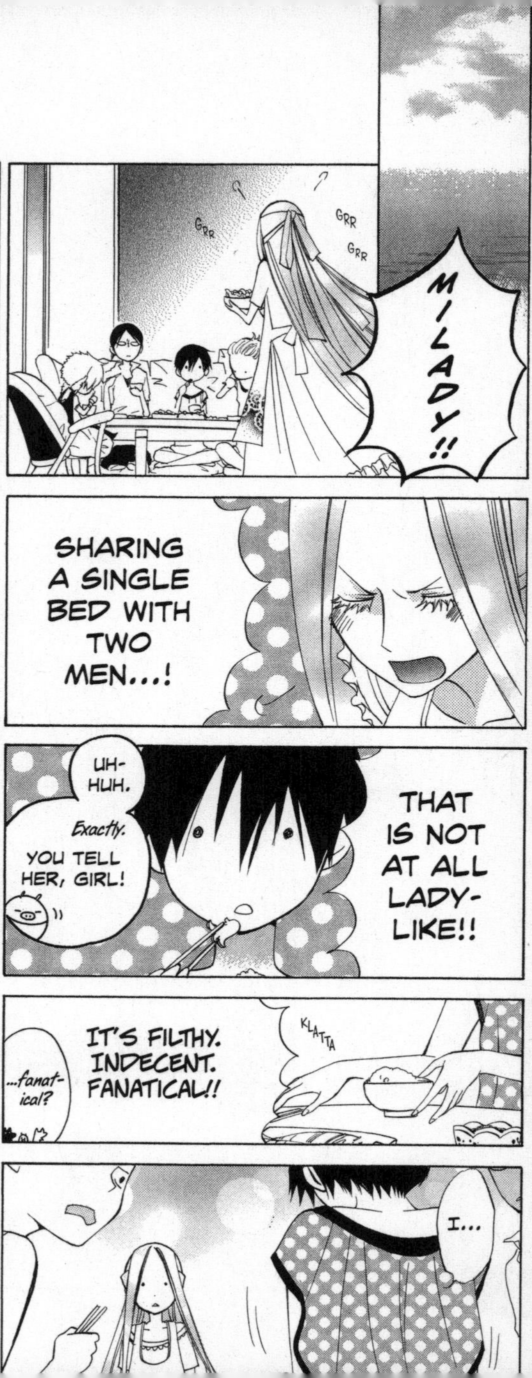
GRR
GRR
GRR
MILADY!!
SHARING A SINGLE BED WITH TWO MEN...!
THAT IS NOT AT ALL LADY-LIKE!!
UH-HUH.
Exactly.
YOU TELL HER, GIRL!
KLATTA
IT'S FILTHY. INDECENT. FANATICAL!!
...fanatical?
I...

DRY SPELL

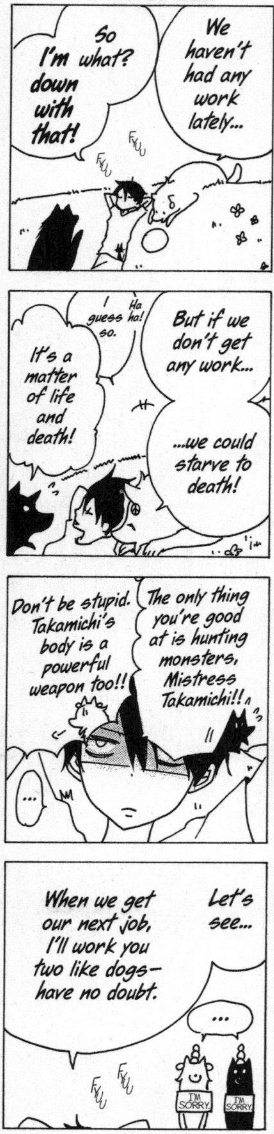
We haven't had any work lately...
So I'm what? down with that!
FYUU
FYUU
But if we don't get any work...
...we could starve to death!
I guess so.
Ha ha!
It's a matter of life and death!
The only thing you're good at is hunting monsters, Mistress Takamichi!!
Don't be stupid. Takamichi's body is a powerful weapon too!!
...
Let's see...
When we get our next job, I'll work you two like dogs—have no doubt.
...
I'M SORRY.
I'M SORRY.
FYUU
FYUU

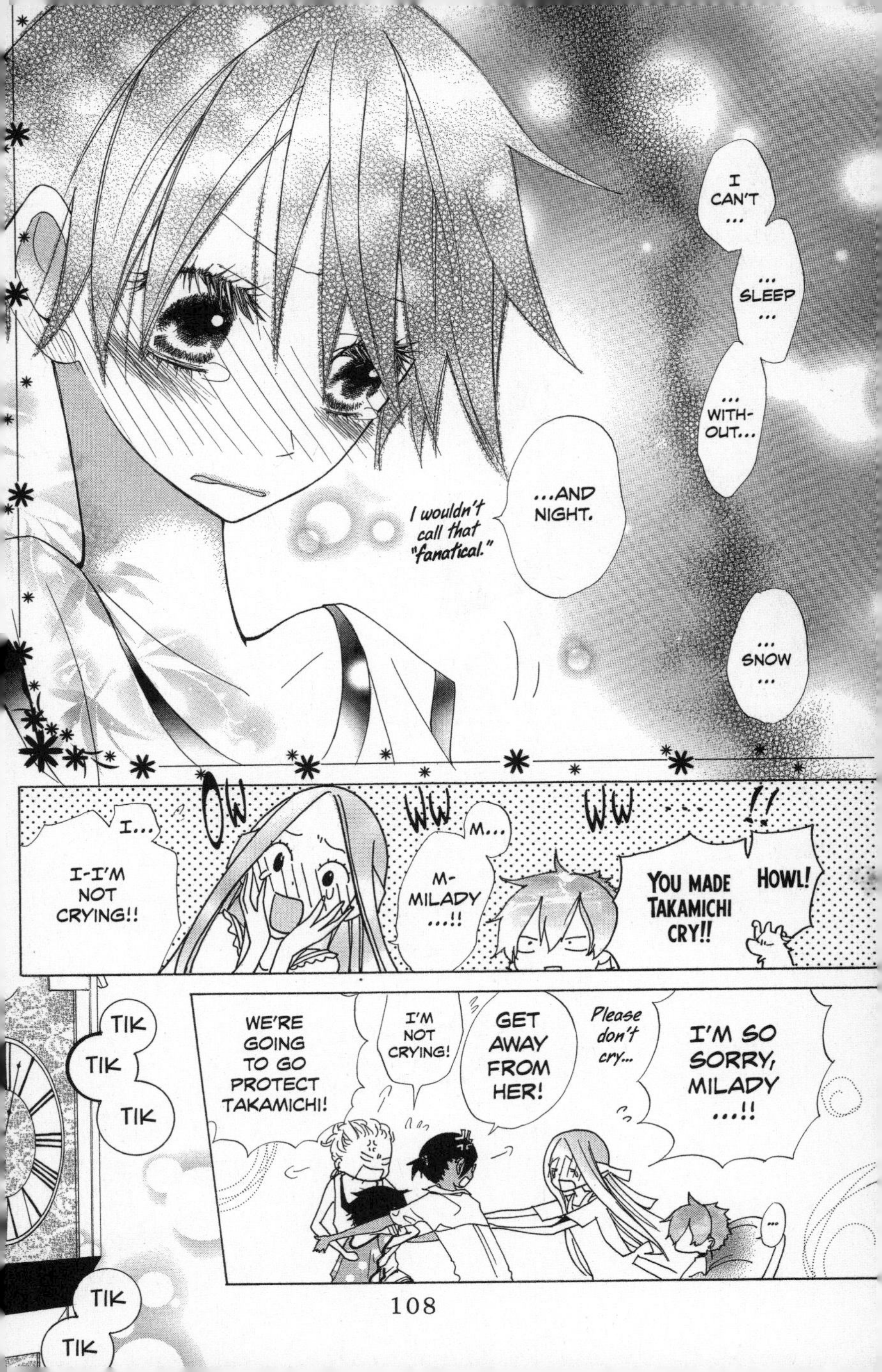
I CAN'T ...
... SLEEP ...
... WITH-OUT...
... SNOW ...
...AND NIGHT.
I wouldn't call that "fanatical."
HOWL!
YOU MADE TAKAMICHI CRY!!
!!
WW
M...
M-MILADY ...!!
WW
OW
I...
I-I'M NOT CRYING!!
I'M SO SORRY, MILADY ...!!
Please don't cry...
GET AWAY FROM HER!
I'M NOT CRYING!
WE'RE GOING TO GO PROTECT TAKAMICHI!
...
TIK
TIK
TIK
TIK
TIK

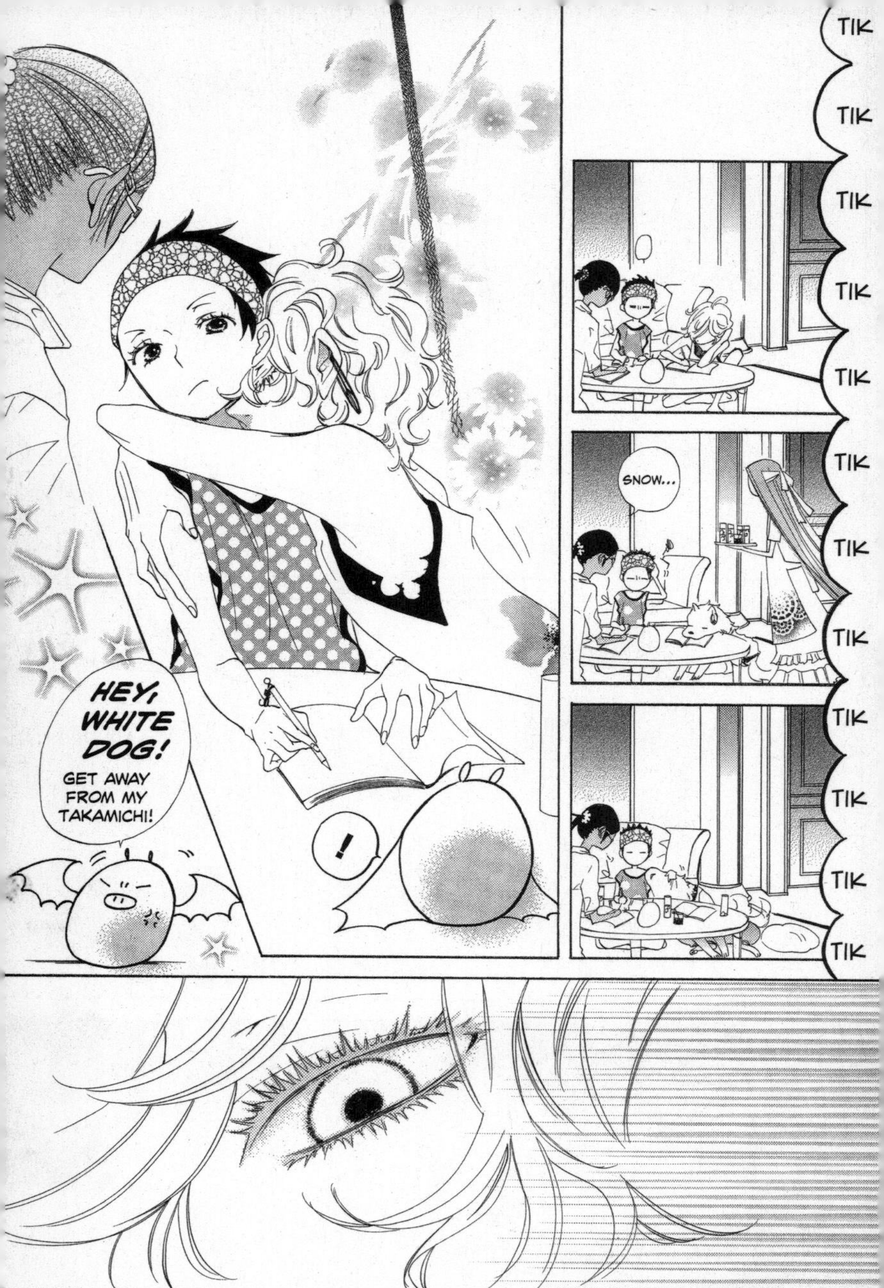
TIK
TIK
TIK
TIK
TIK
TIK
TIK
TIK
TIK
TIK
TIK
TIK
SNOW...
HEY, WHITE DOG! GET AWAY FROM MY TAKAMICHI!
!

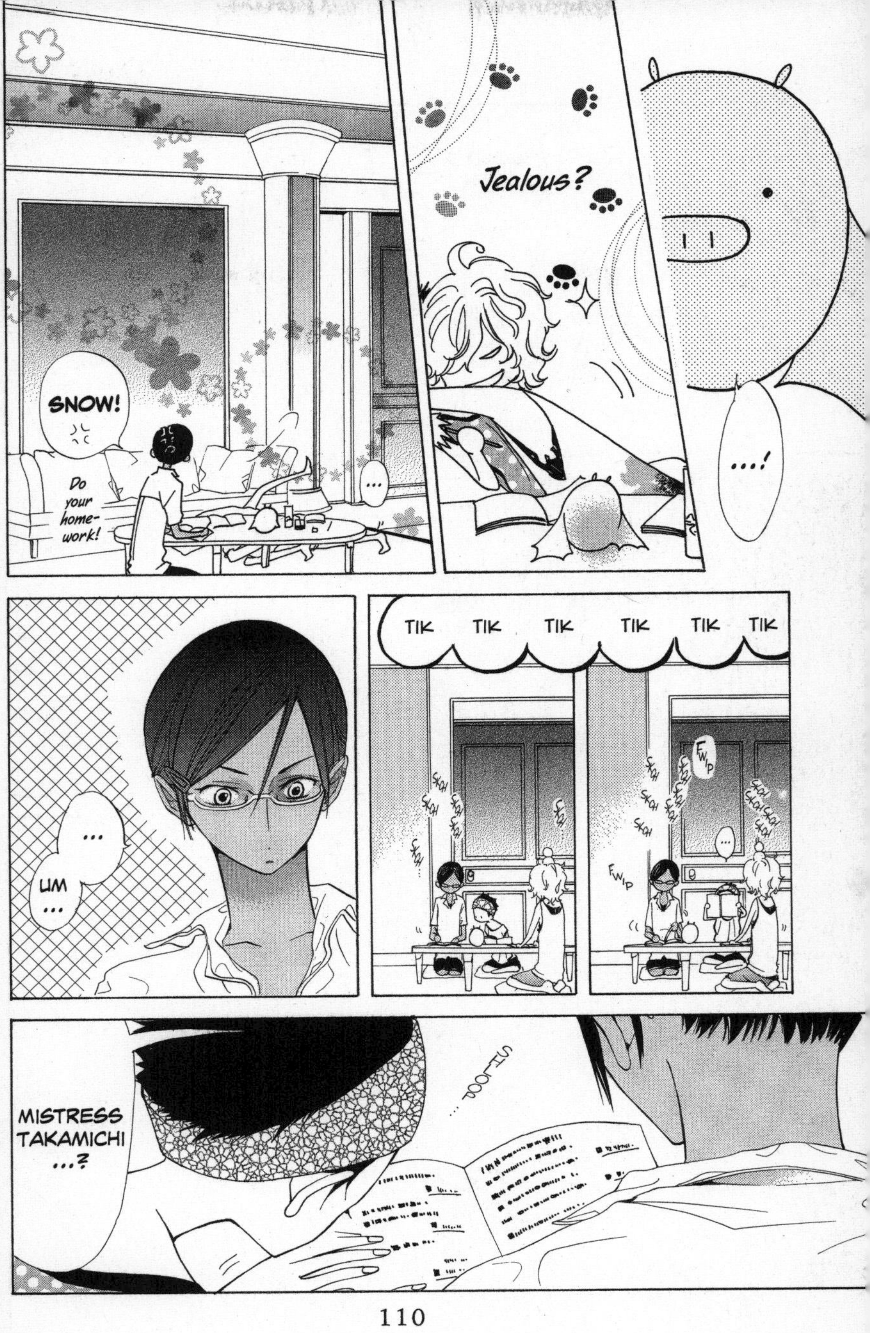
...!
Jealous?
SNOW!
...
Do your homework!
TIK TIK TIK TIK TIK TIK
FWIP
SKCH
...
FWIP
...
UM ...
SHOOP...
MISTRESS TAKAMICHI ...?

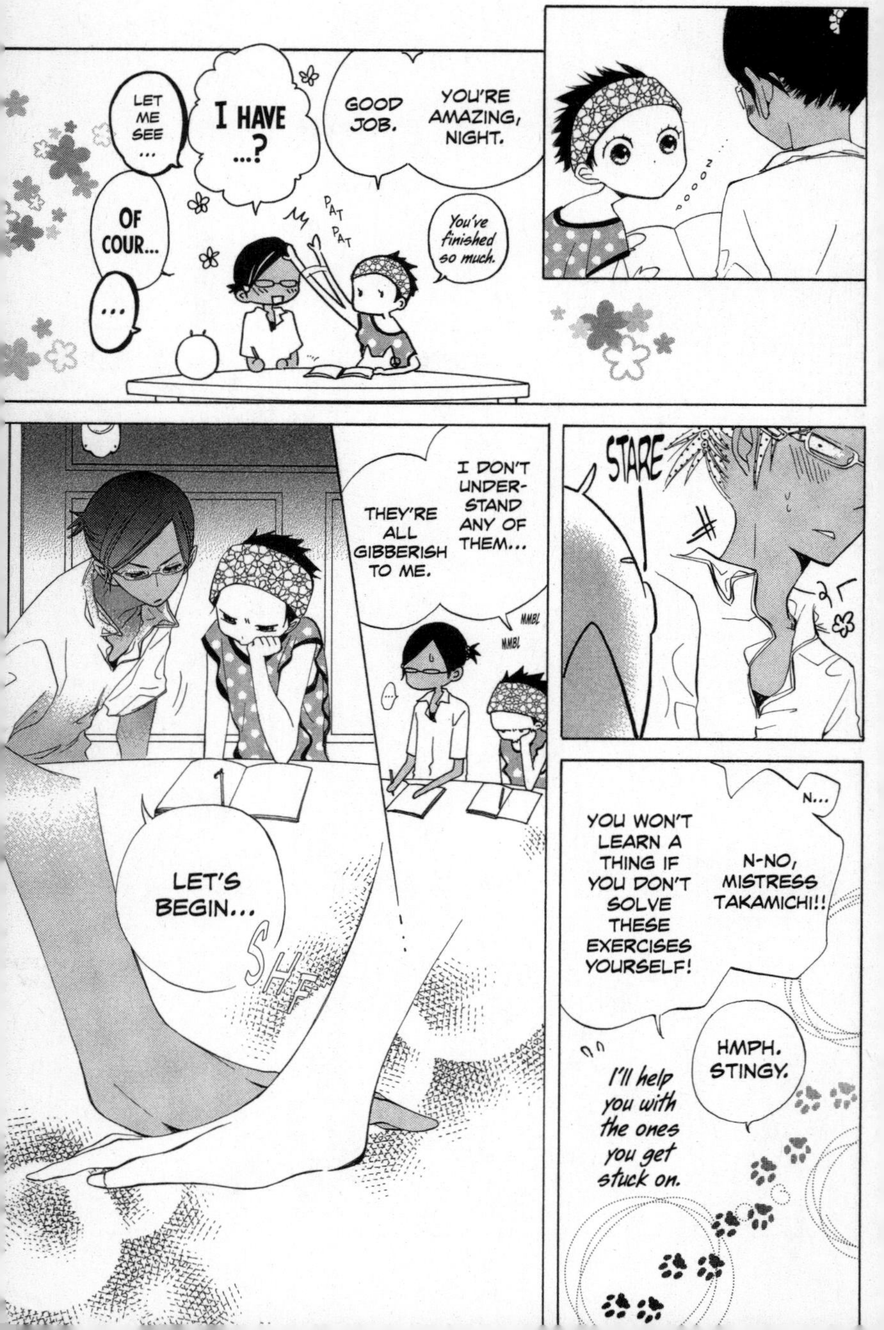
YOU'RE AMAZING, NIGHT.
GOOD JOB.
I HAVE ...?
LET ME SEE ...
PAT PAT
You've finished so much.
OF COUR...
...
STARE
N...
N-NO, MISTRESS TAKAMICHI!!
YOU WON'T LEARN A THING IF YOU DON'T SOLVE THESE EXERCISES YOURSELF!
HMPH. STINGY.
I'll help you with the ones you get stuck on.
I DON'T UNDERSTAND ANY OF THEM...
THEY'RE ALL GIBBERISH TO ME.
MMBL MMBL
...
LET'S BEGIN...
SHF

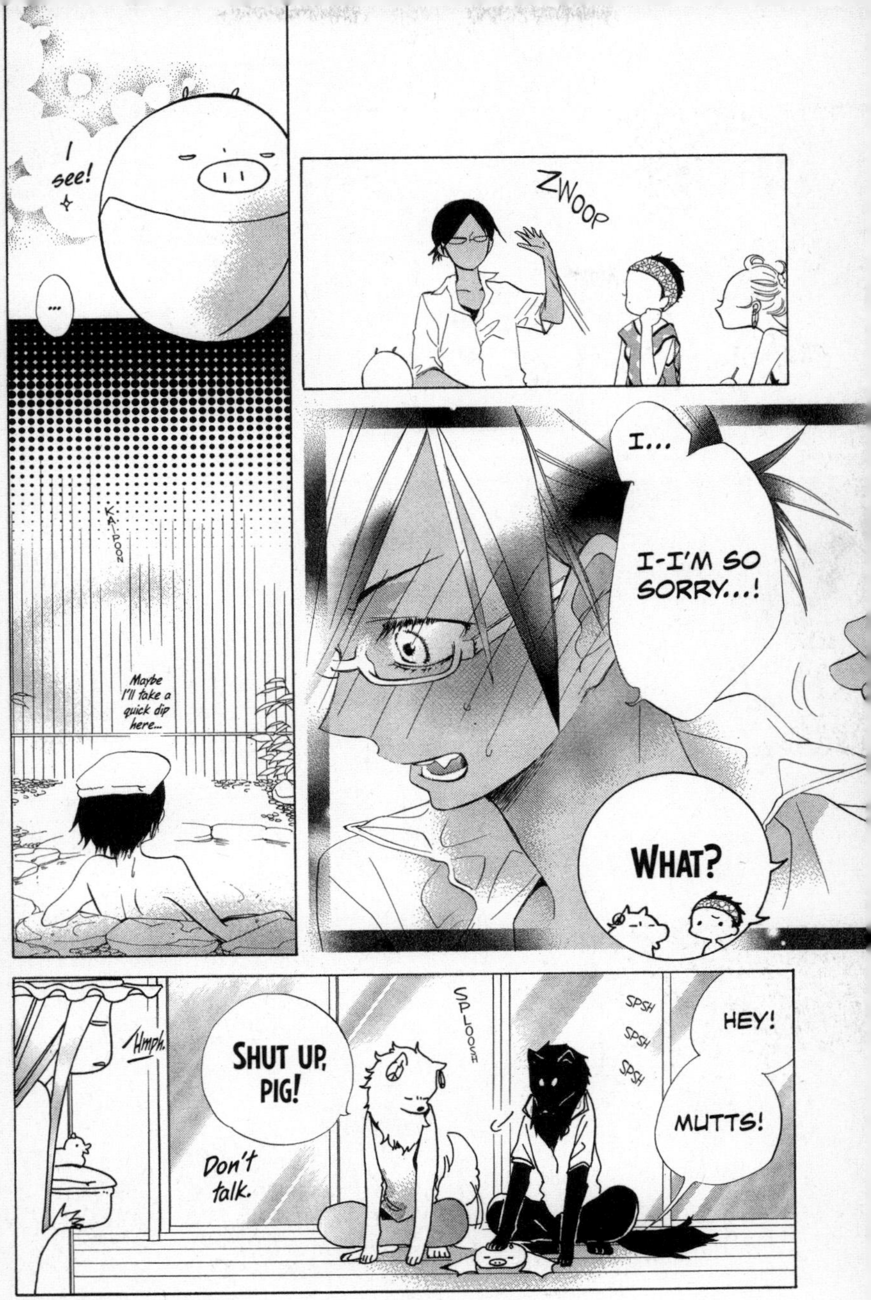
ZWOOP
I...
I-I'M SO SORRY...!
WHAT?
I see!
...
KA-POON
Maybe I'll take a quick dip here...
HEY!
MUTTS!
SPSH
SPSH
SPSH
SPLOOSH
SHUT UP, PIG!
Don't talk.
Hmph.



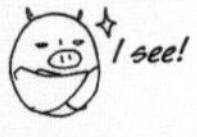
I see!

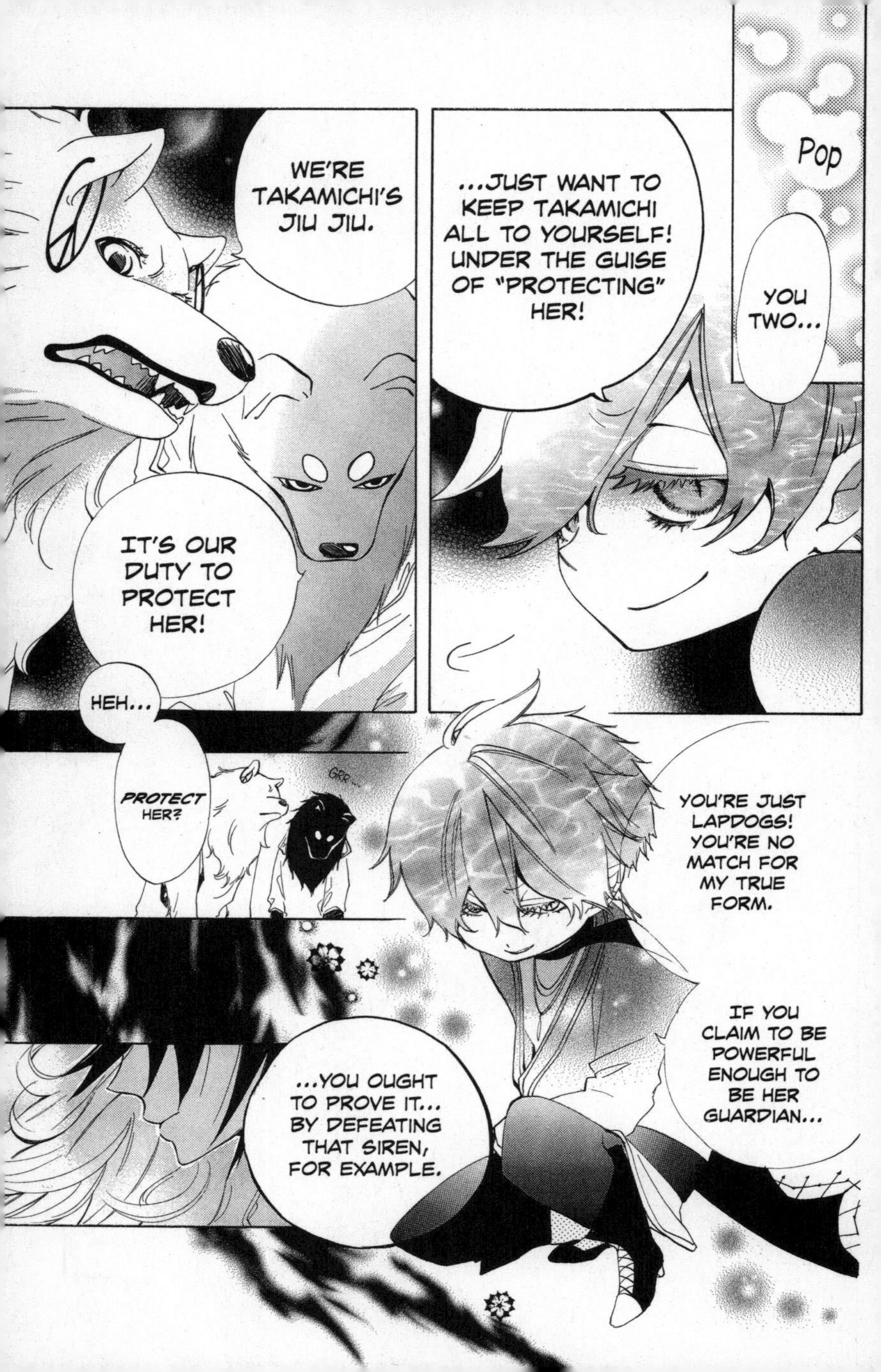
Pop
YOU TWO...
...JUST WANT TO KEEP TAKAMICHI ALL TO YOURSELF! UNDER THE GUISE OF "PROTECTING" HER!
WE'RE TAKAMICHI'S JIU JIU.
IT'S OUR DUTY TO PROTECT HER!
HEH...
*PROTECT* HER?
GRR...
YOU'RE JUST LAPDOGS! YOU'RE NO MATCH FOR MY TRUE FORM.
IF YOU CLAIM TO BE POWERFUL ENOUGH TO BE HER GUARDIAN...
...YOU OUGHT TO PROVE IT... BY DEFEATING THAT SIREN, FOR EXAMPLE.

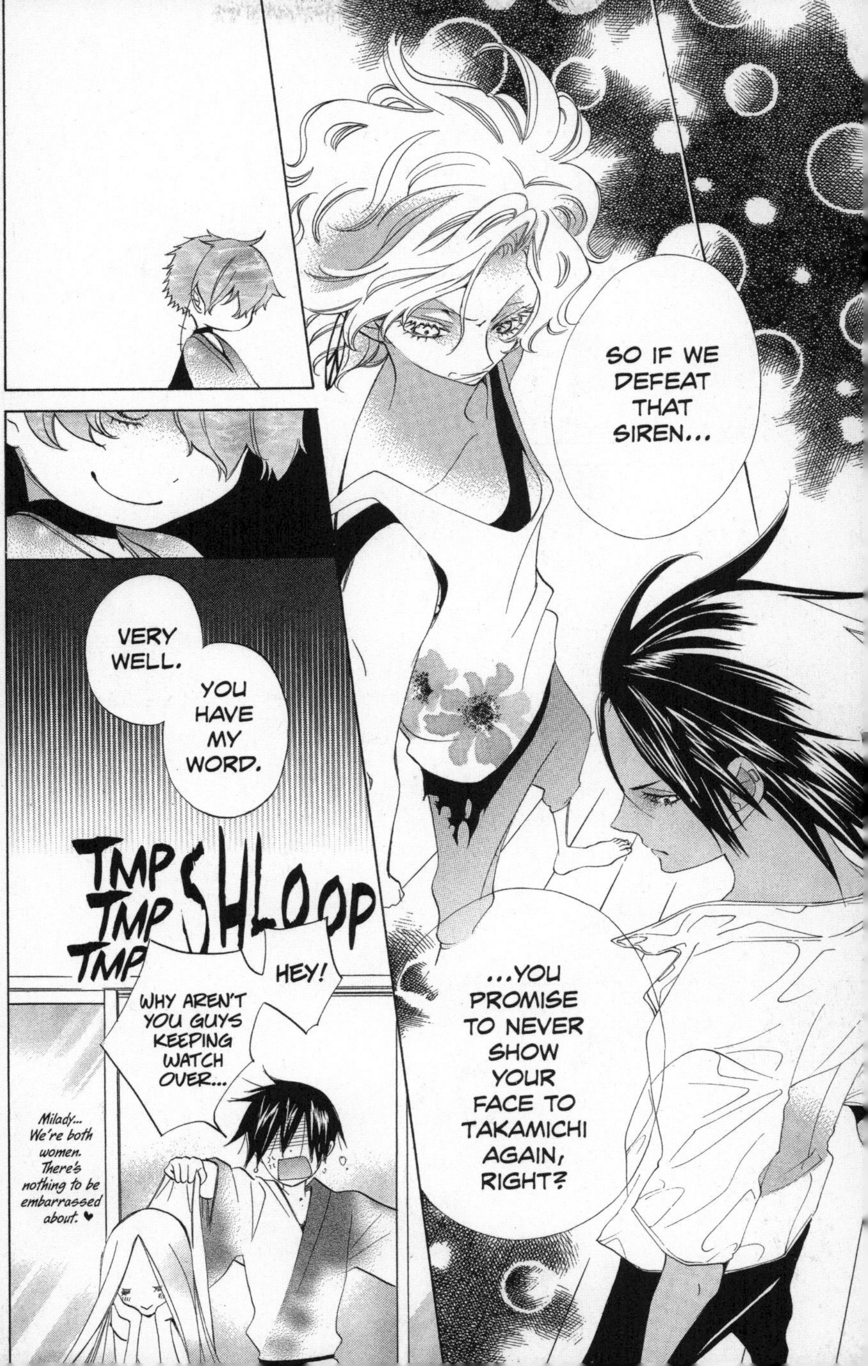

SO IF WE DEFEAT THAT SIREN...
...YOU PROMISE TO NEVER SHOW YOUR FACE TO TAKAMICHI AGAIN, RIGHT?
VERY WELL.
YOU HAVE MY WORD.
SHLOOP
TMP TMP TMP
HEY!
WHY AREN'T YOU GUYS KEEPING WATCH OVER...
Milady... We're both women. There's nothing to be embarrassed about. ♥

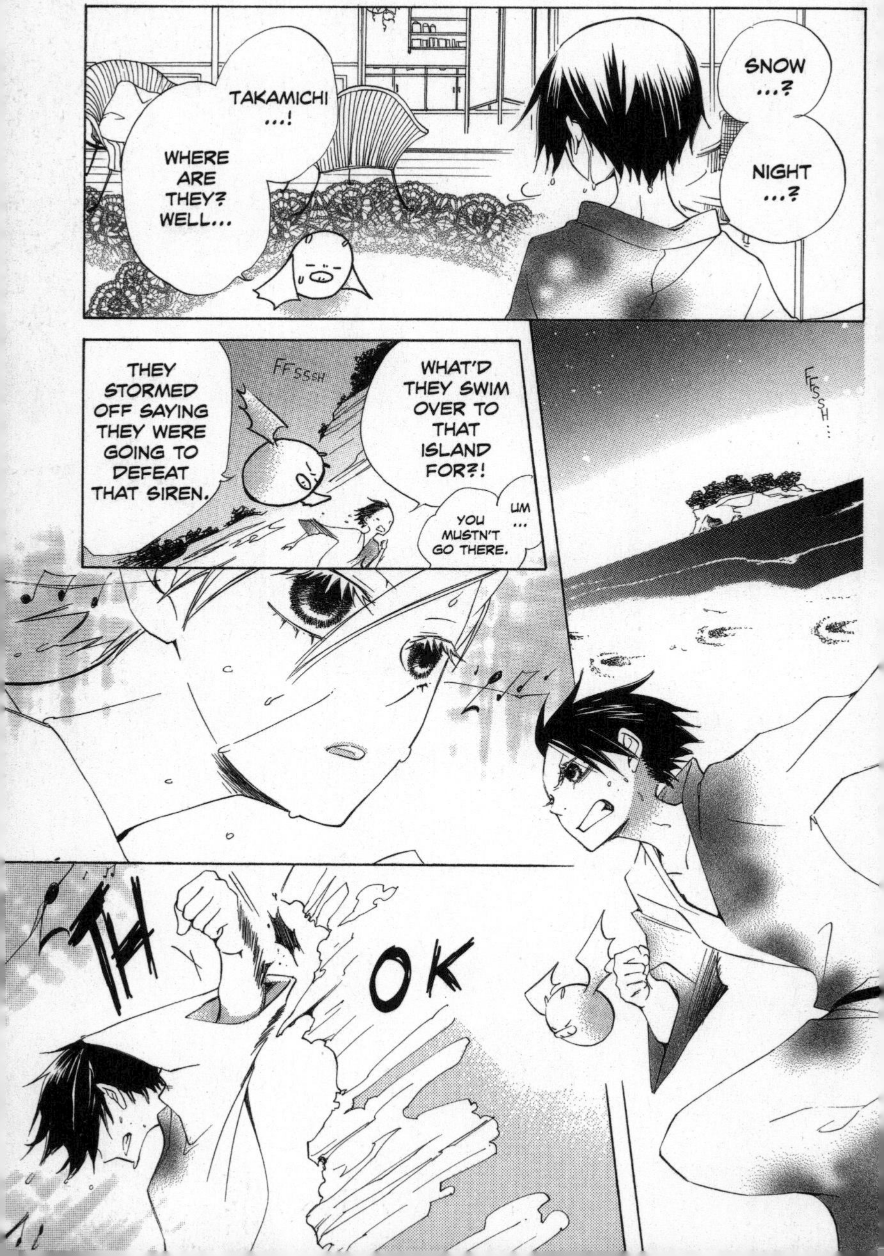
SNOW ...?
NIGHT ...?
TAKAMICHI ...!
WHERE ARE THEY? WELL...
FFSSSH...
THEY STORMED OFF SAYING THEY WERE GOING TO DEFEAT THAT SIREN.
FFSSSH
WHAT'D THEY SWIM OVER TO THAT ISLAND FOR?!
UM ... YOU MUSTN'T GO THERE.
THOK

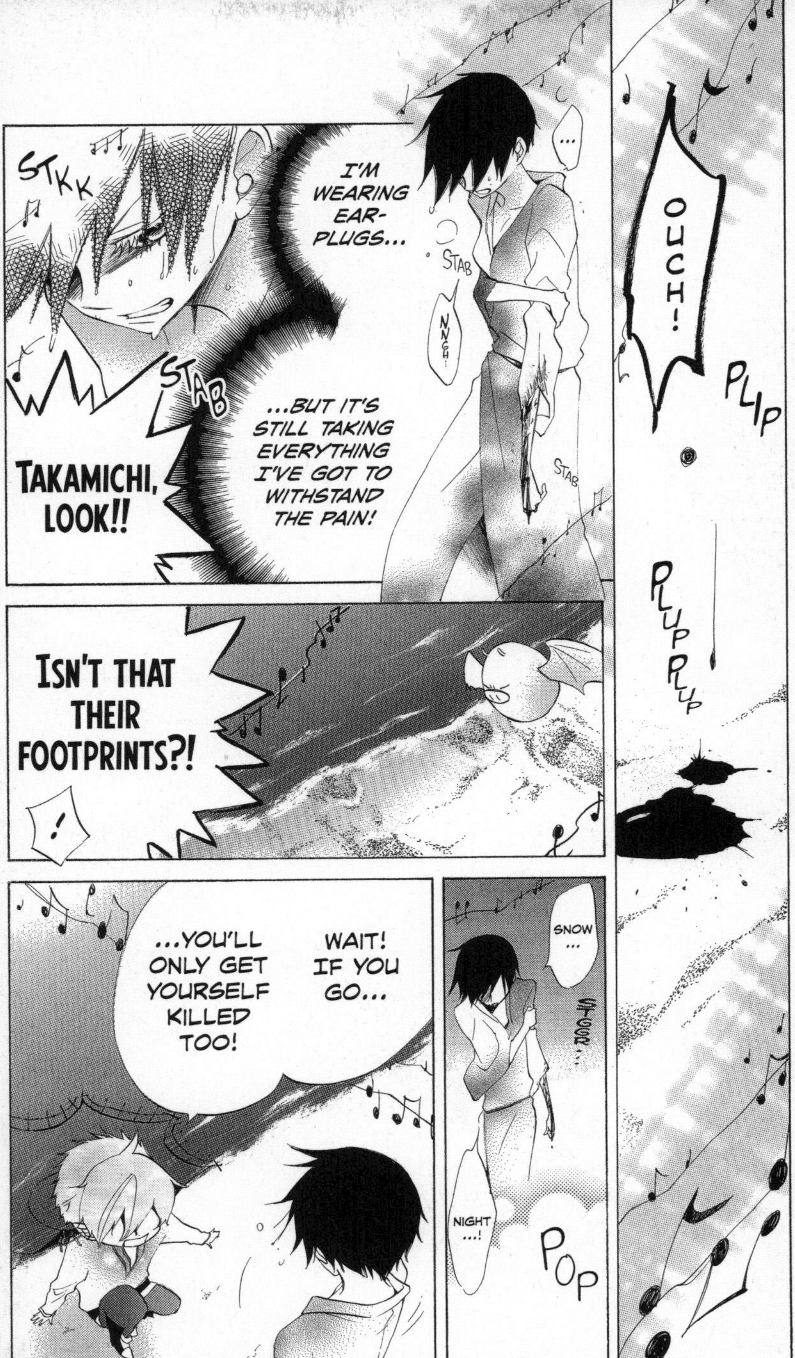
OUCH!
PLIP
PLUP PLUP
...
I'M WEARING EAR-PLUGS...
STAB
NNGH!
STKK
...BUT IT'S STILL TAKING EVERYTHING I'VE GOT TO WITHSTAND THE PAIN!
STAB
STAB
TAKAMICHI, LOOK!!
ISN'T THAT THEIR FOOTPRINTS?!
!
SNOW...
STGGR...
NIGHT...!
POP
WAIT! IF YOU GO...
...YOU'LL ONLY GET YOURSELF KILLED TOO!

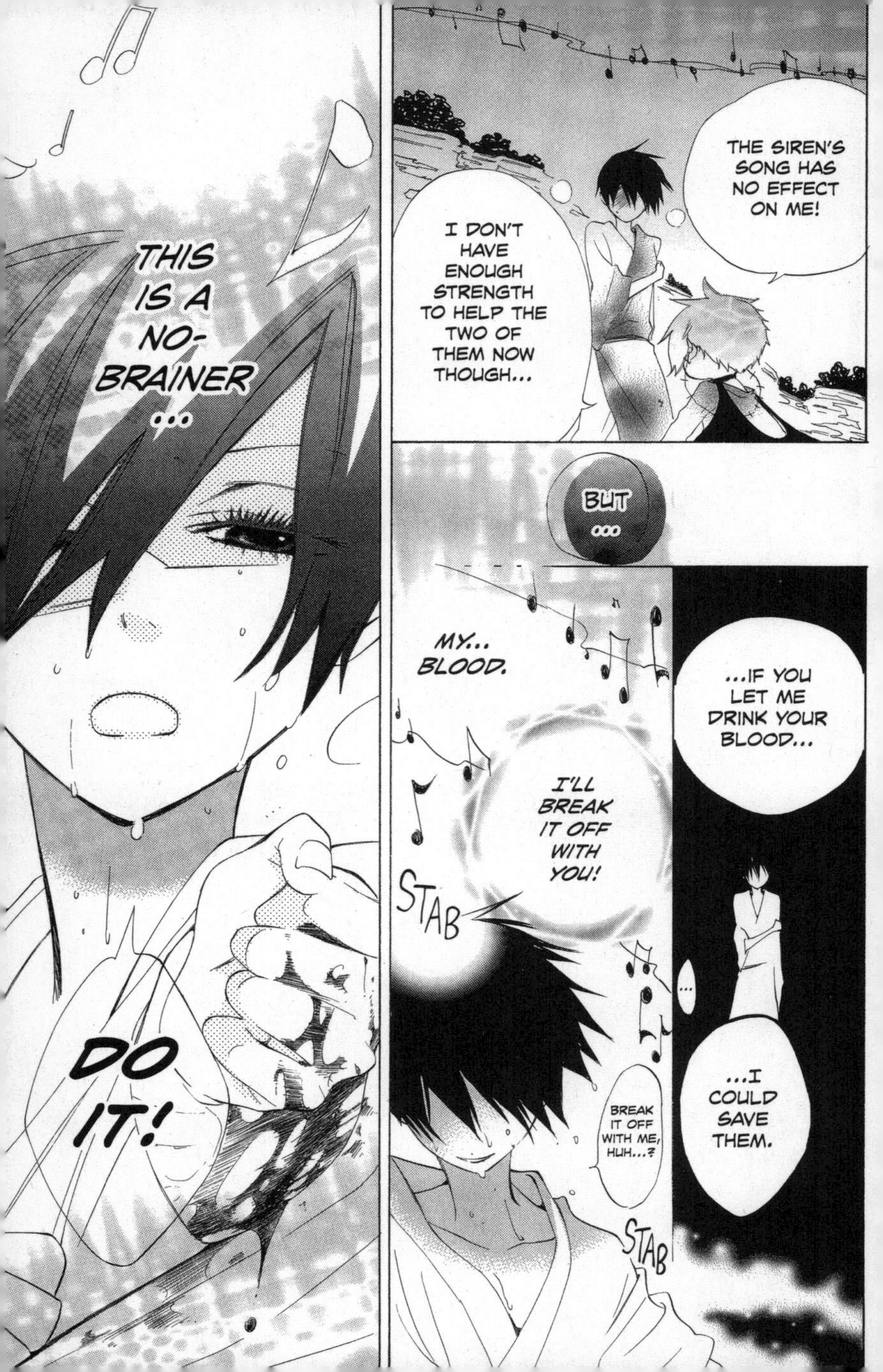
THE SIREN'S SONG HAS NO EFFECT ON ME!
I DON'T HAVE ENOUGH STRENGTH TO HELP THE TWO OF THEM NOW THOUGH...
BUT...
...IF YOU LET ME DRINK YOUR BLOOD...
...
...I COULD SAVE THEM.
MY... BLOOD.
I'LL BREAK IT OFF WITH YOU!
STAB
BREAK IT OFF WITH ME, HUH...?
STAB
THIS IS A NO-BRAINER...
DO IT!

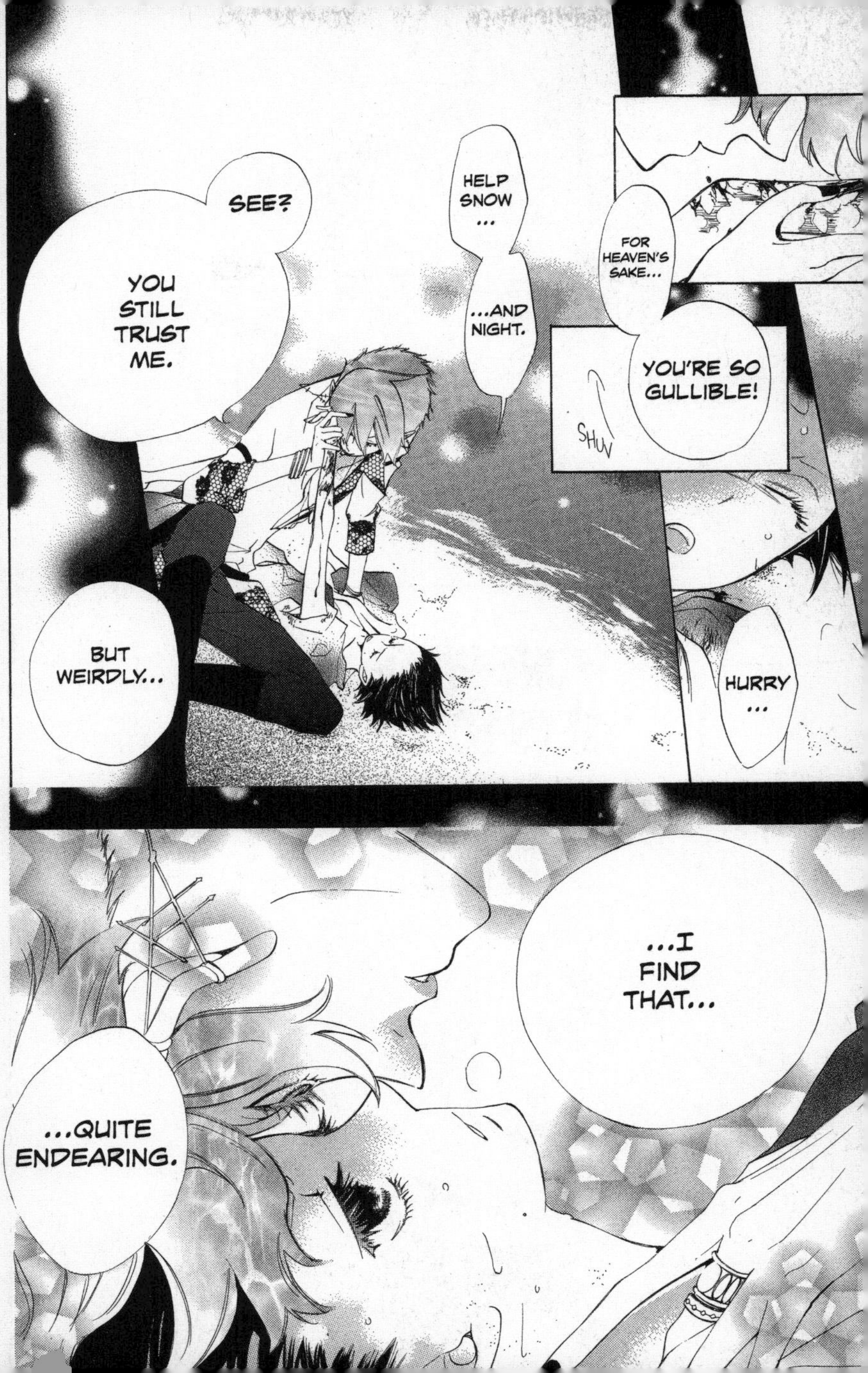
FOR HEAVEN'S SAKE...
YOU'RE SO GULLIBLE!
SHUV
HURRY...
HELP SNOW...
...AND NIGHT.
SEE?
YOU STILL TRUST ME.
BUT WEIRDLY...
...I FIND THAT...
...QUITE ENDEARING.

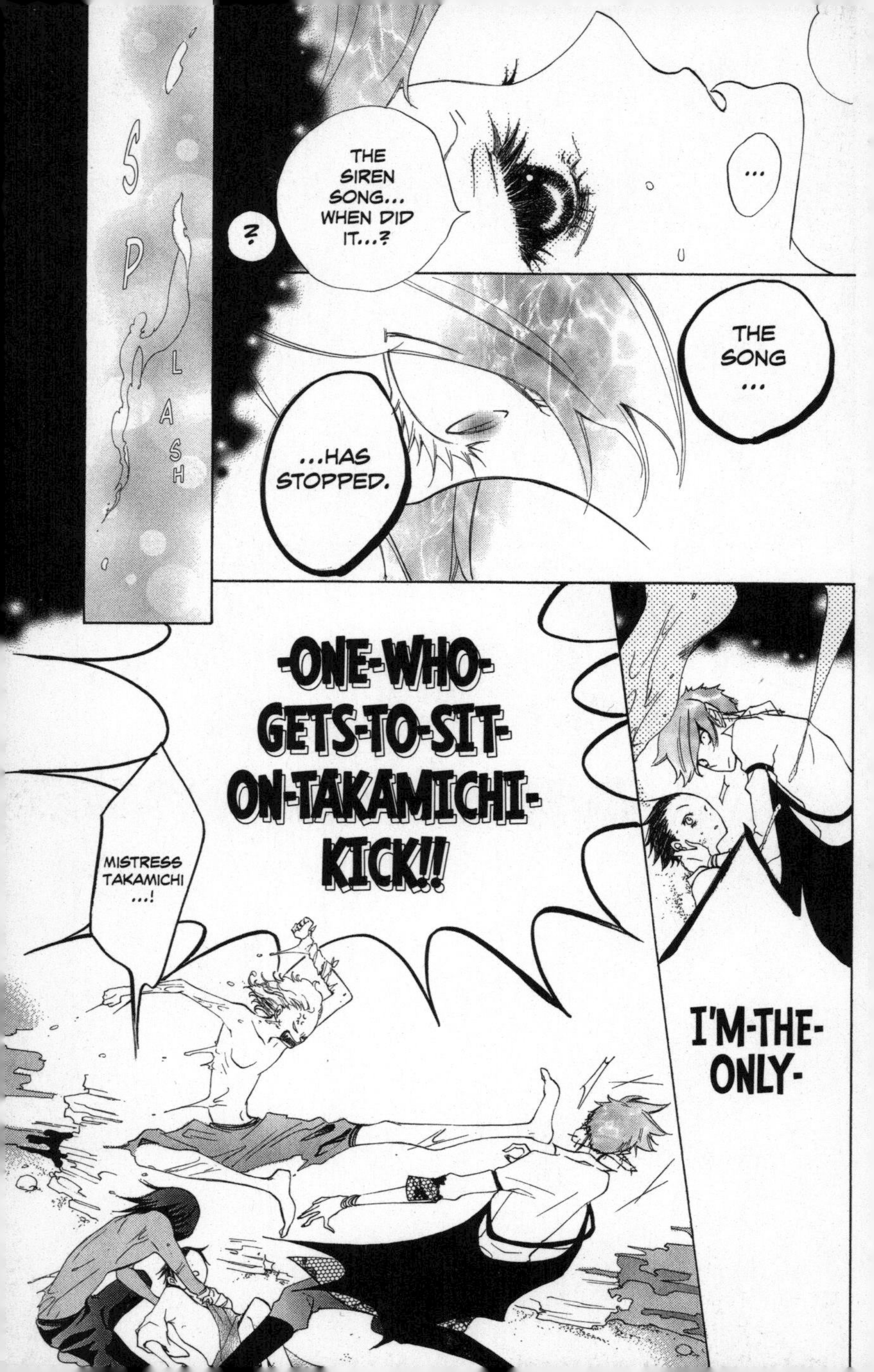
...
THE SIREN SONG... WHEN DID IT...?
?
THE SONG ...
...HAS STOPPED.
SPLASH
I'M-THE-ONLY-
-ONE-WHO-GETS-TO-SIT-ON-TAKAMICHI-KICK!!
MISTRESS TAKAMICHI ...!

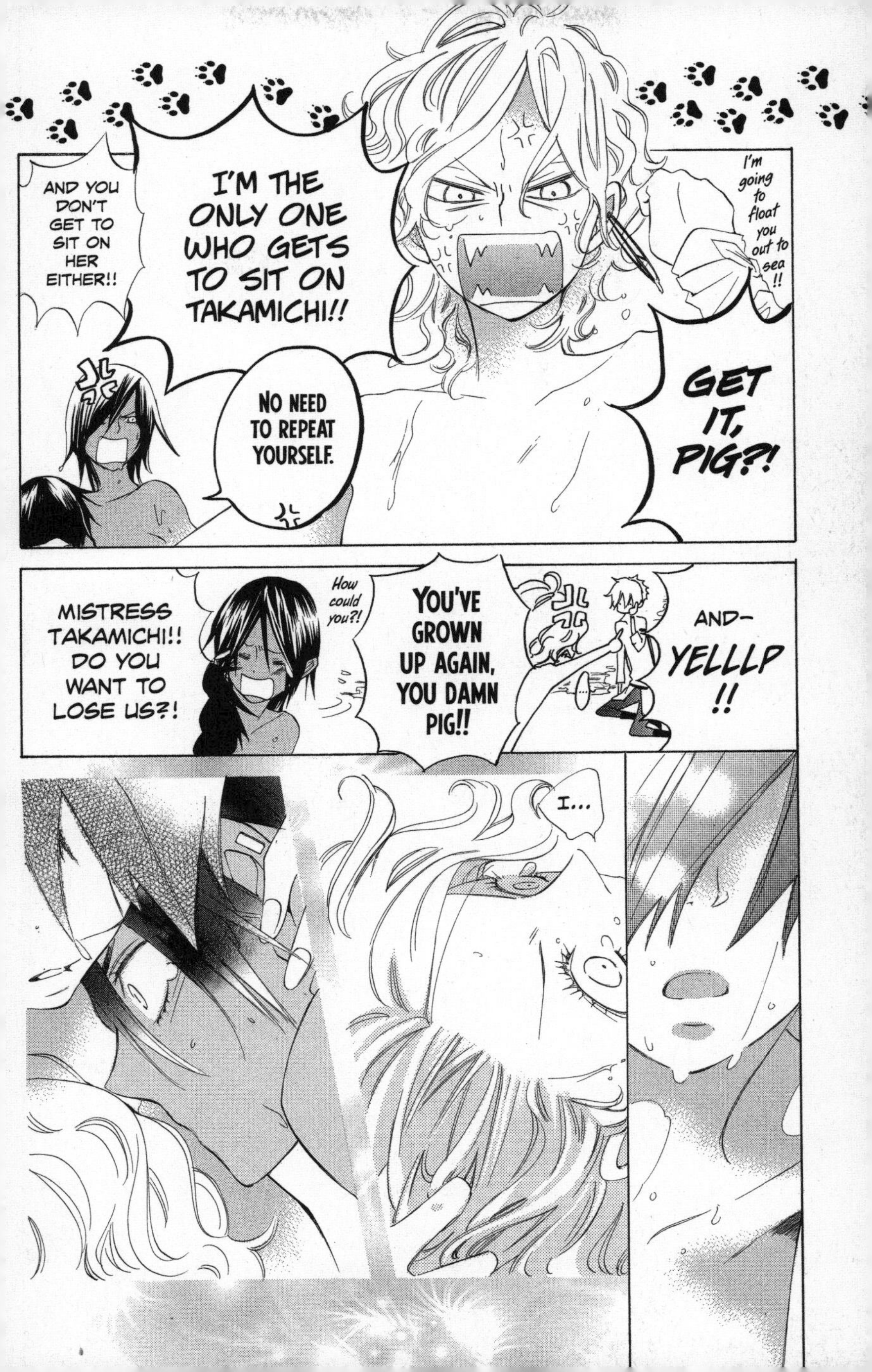
I'm going to float you out to sea!!
I'M THE ONLY ONE WHO GETS TO SIT ON TAKAMICHI!!
AND YOU DON'T GET TO SIT ON HER EITHER!!
GET IT, PIG?!
NO NEED TO REPEAT YOURSELF.
AND—
YELLLP!!
YOU'VE GROWN UP AGAIN, YOU DAMN PIG!!
How could you?!
MISTRESS TAKAMICHI!! DO YOU WANT TO LOSE US?!
I...

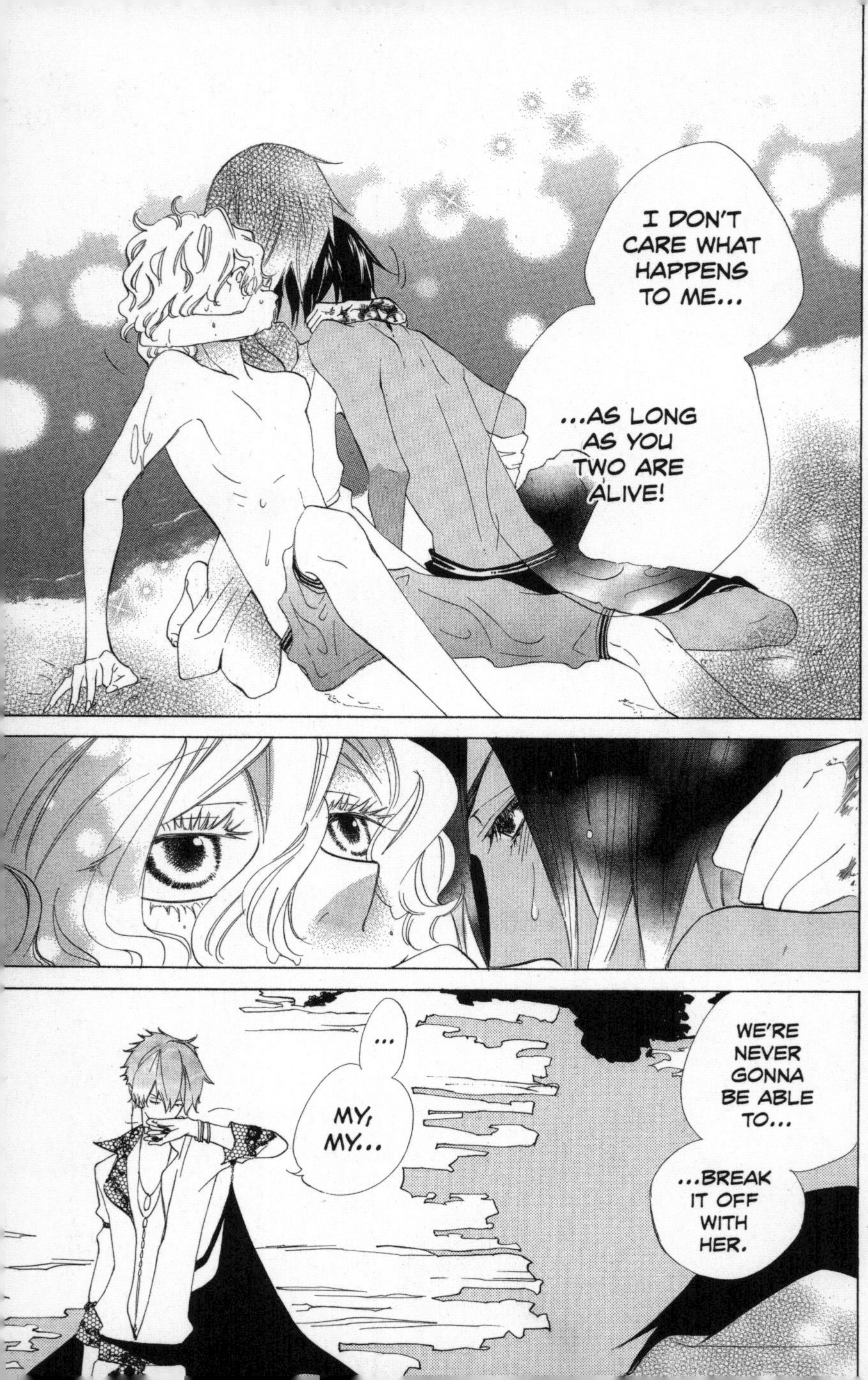
I DON'T CARE WHAT HAPPENS TO ME...
...AS LONG AS YOU TWO ARE ALIVE!
WE'RE NEVER GONNA BE ABLE TO...
...BREAK IT OFF WITH HER.
...
MY, MY...

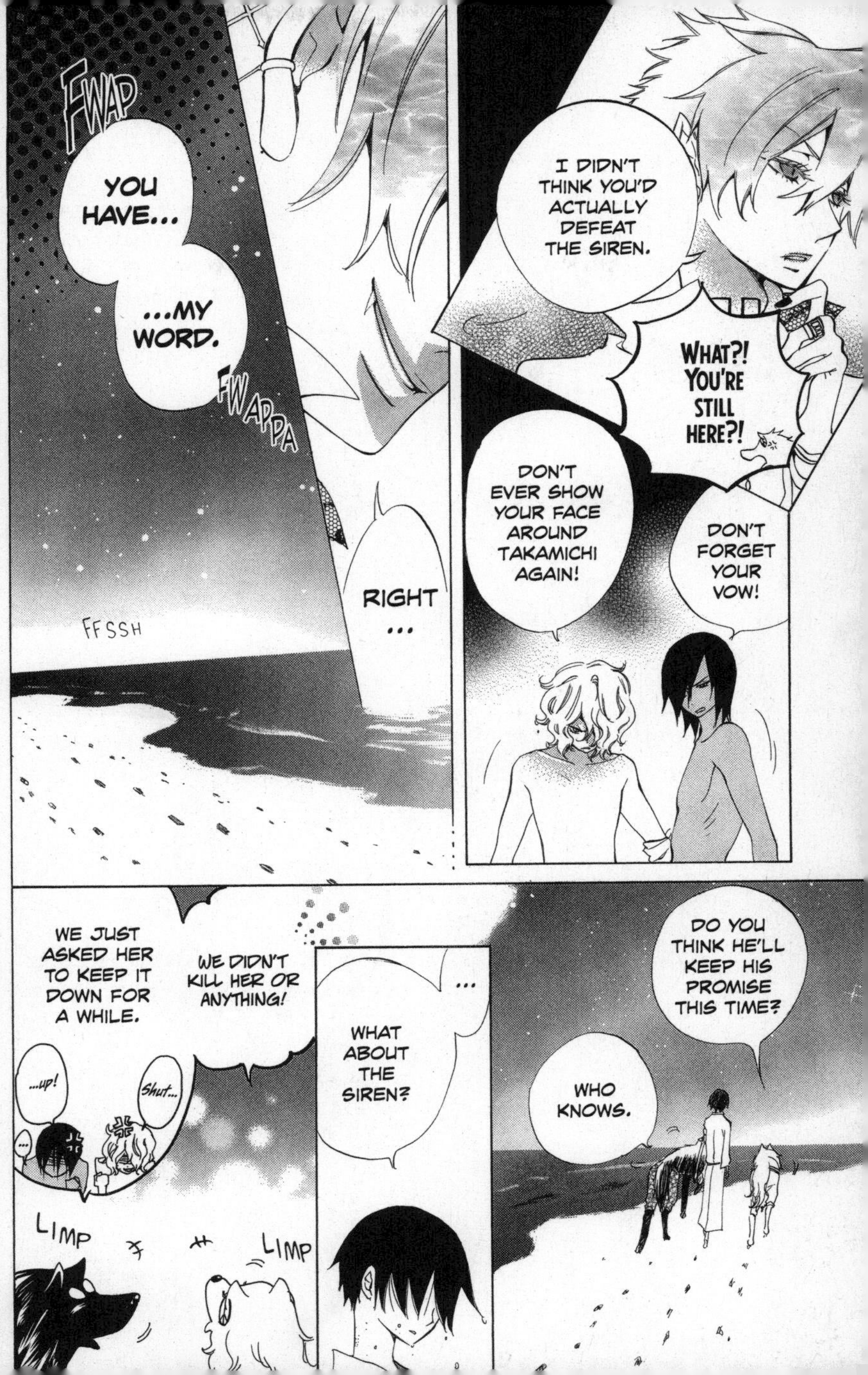
I DIDN'T THINK YOU'D ACTUALLY DEFEAT THE SIREN.
WHAT?! YOU'RE STILL HERE?!
DON'T FORGET YOUR VOW!
DON'T EVER SHOW YOUR FACE AROUND TAKAMICHI AGAIN!
FWAP
YOU HAVE...
...MY WORD.
FWAPPA
RIGHT...
FFSSH
DO YOU THINK HE'LL KEEP HIS PROMISE THIS TIME?
WHO KNOWS.
...
WHAT ABOUT THE SIREN?
WE DIDN'T KILL HER OR ANYTHING!
WE JUST ASKED HER TO KEEP IT DOWN FOR A WHILE.
Shut...
...up!
...
LIMP
LIMP

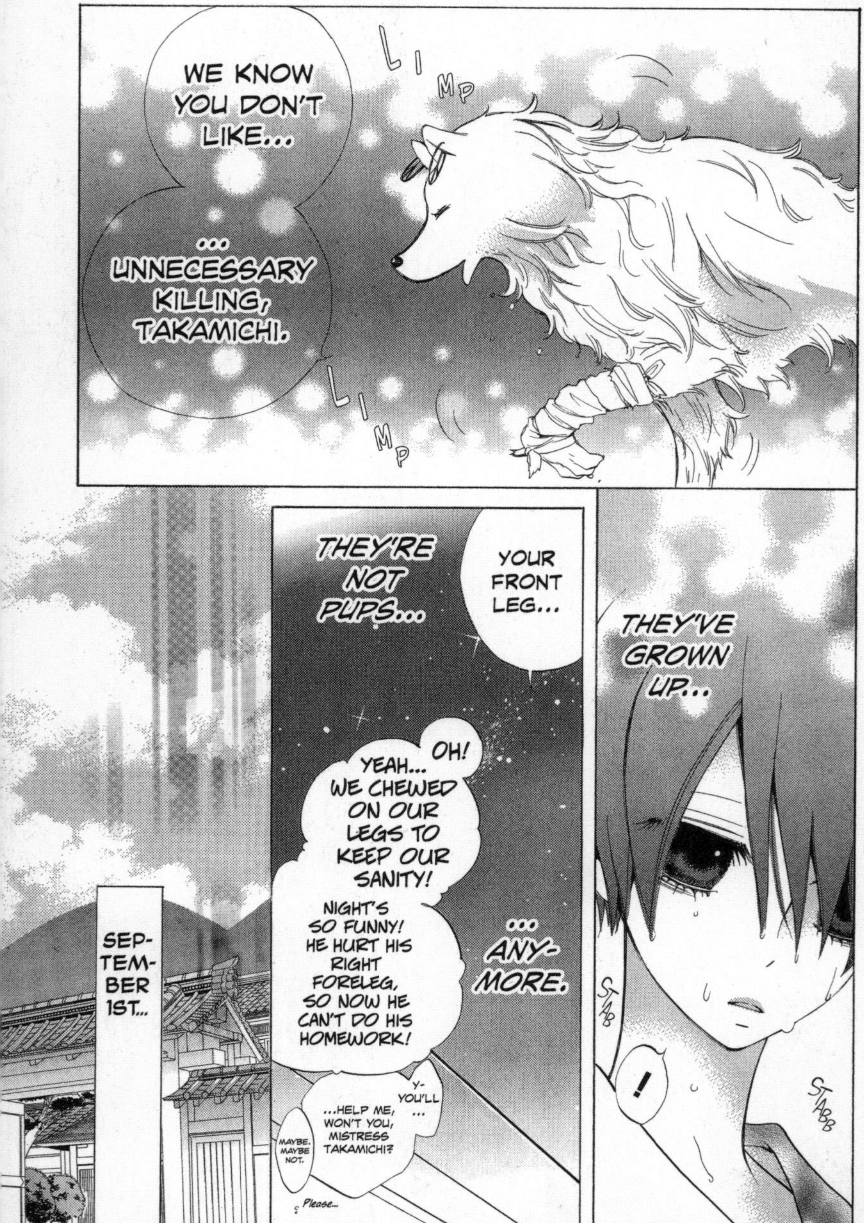
WE KNOW YOU DON'T LIKE...
...UNNECESSARY KILLING, TAKAMICHI.
LIMP
LIMP
THEY'VE GROWN UP...
STAB
!
STABB
YOUR FRONT LEG...
THEY'RE NOT PUPS...
OH!
YEAH... WE CHEWED ON OUR LEGS TO KEEP OUR SANITY!
...ANYMORE.
NIGHT'S SO FUNNY! HE HURT HIS RIGHT FORELEG, SO NOW HE CAN'T DO HIS HOMEWORK!
Y-YOU'LL...
...HELP ME, WON'T YOU, MISTRESS TAKAMICHI?
MAYBE. MAYBE NOT.
Please...
SEP-TEM-BER 1ST...

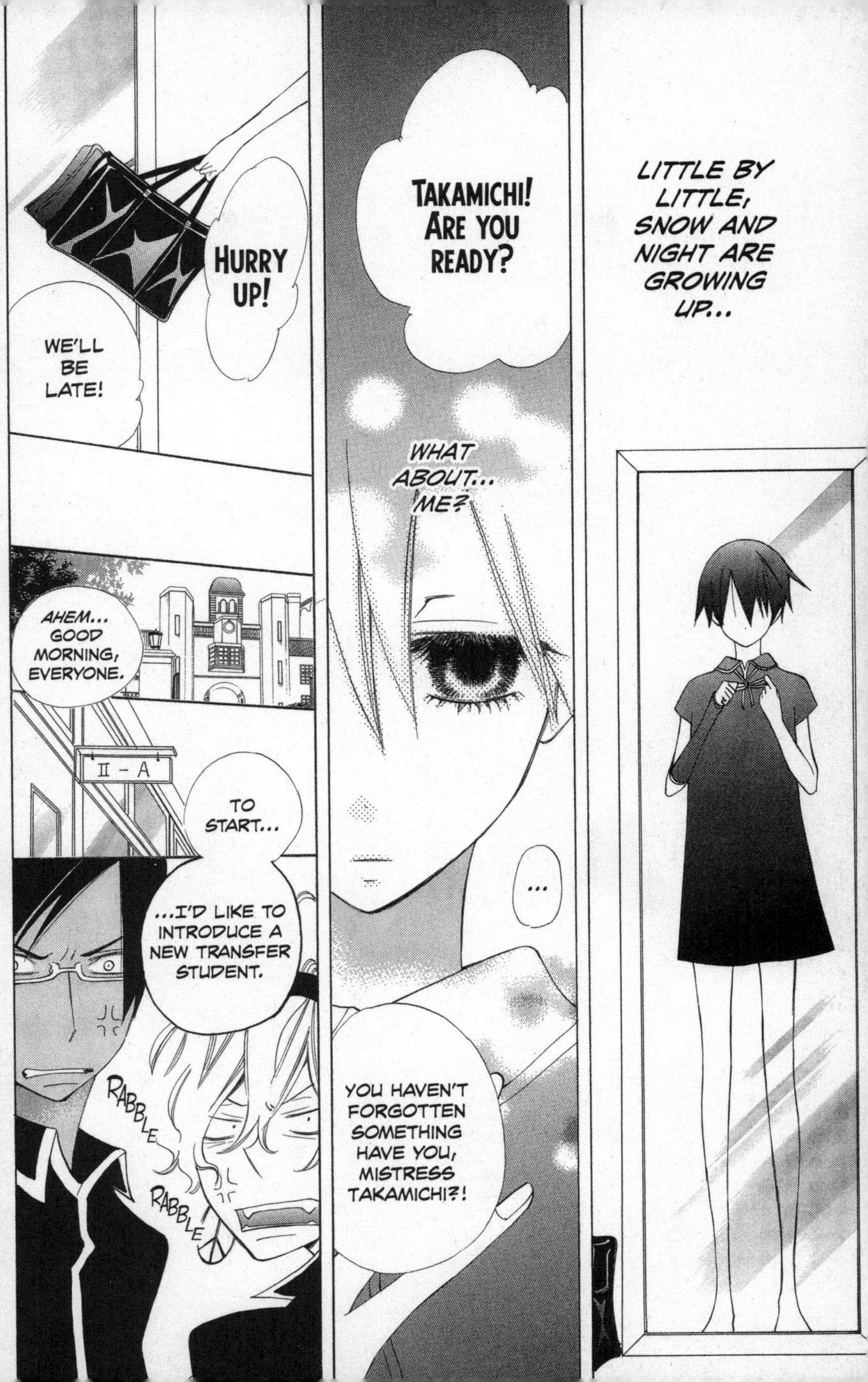
LITTLE BY LITTLE, SNOW AND NIGHT ARE GROWING UP...
TAKAMICHI! ARE YOU READY?
WHAT ABOUT... ME?
...
YOU HAVEN'T FORGOTTEN SOMETHING HAVE YOU, MISTRESS TAKAMICHI?!
HURRY UP!
WE'LL BE LATE!
AHEM... GOOD MORNING, EVERYONE.
II - A
TO START...
...I'D LIKE TO INTRODUCE A NEW TRANSFER STUDENT.
RABBLE
RABBLE

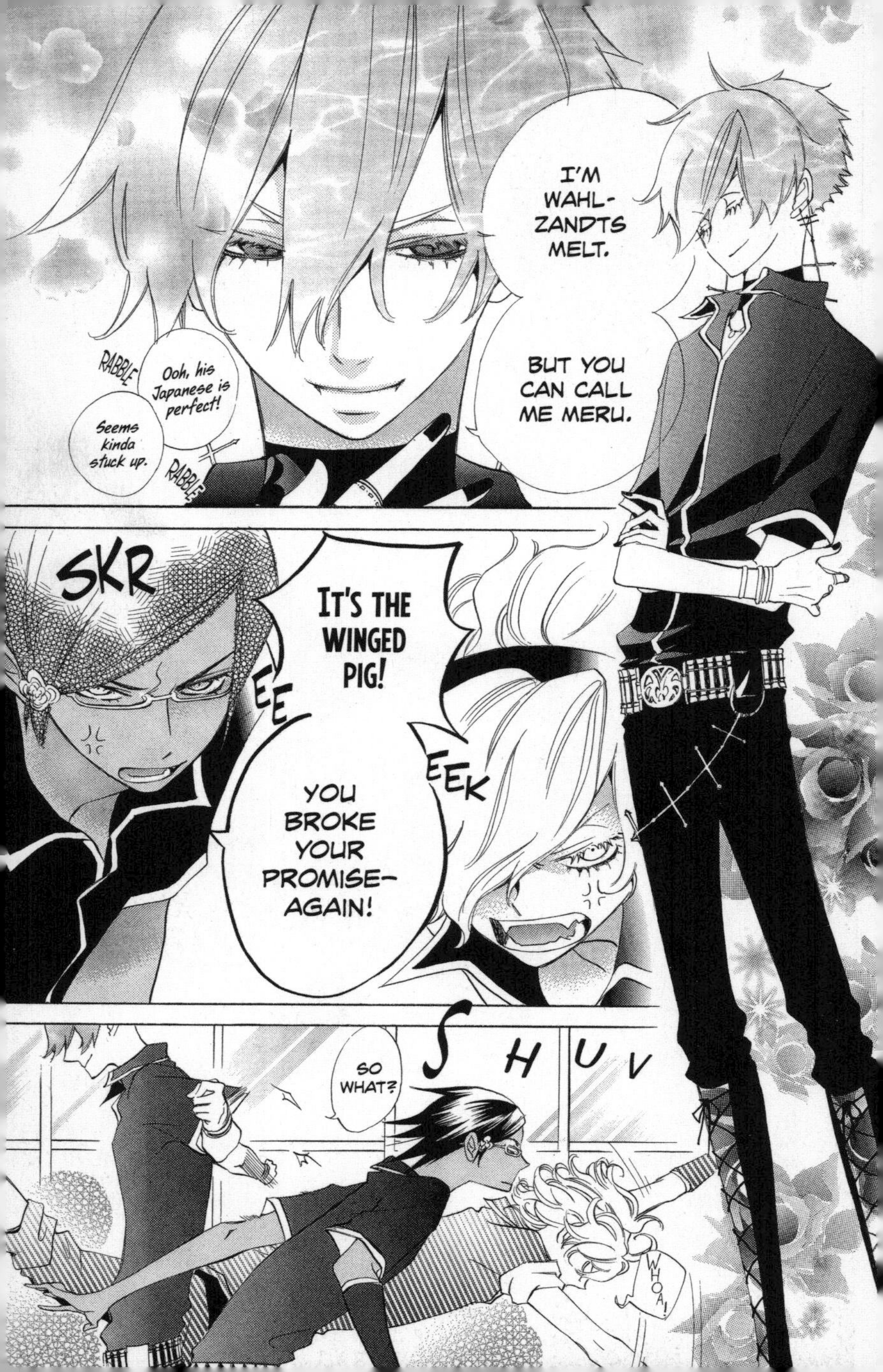
I'M WAHL-ZANDTS MELT.
BUT YOU CAN CALL ME MERU.
RABBLE
Ooh, his Japanese is perfect!
Seems kinda stuck up.
RABBLE
EEK
IT'S THE WINGED PIG!
SKR
EE
YOU BROKE YOUR PROMISE-AGAIN!
WHOA!
S H U V
SO WHAT?

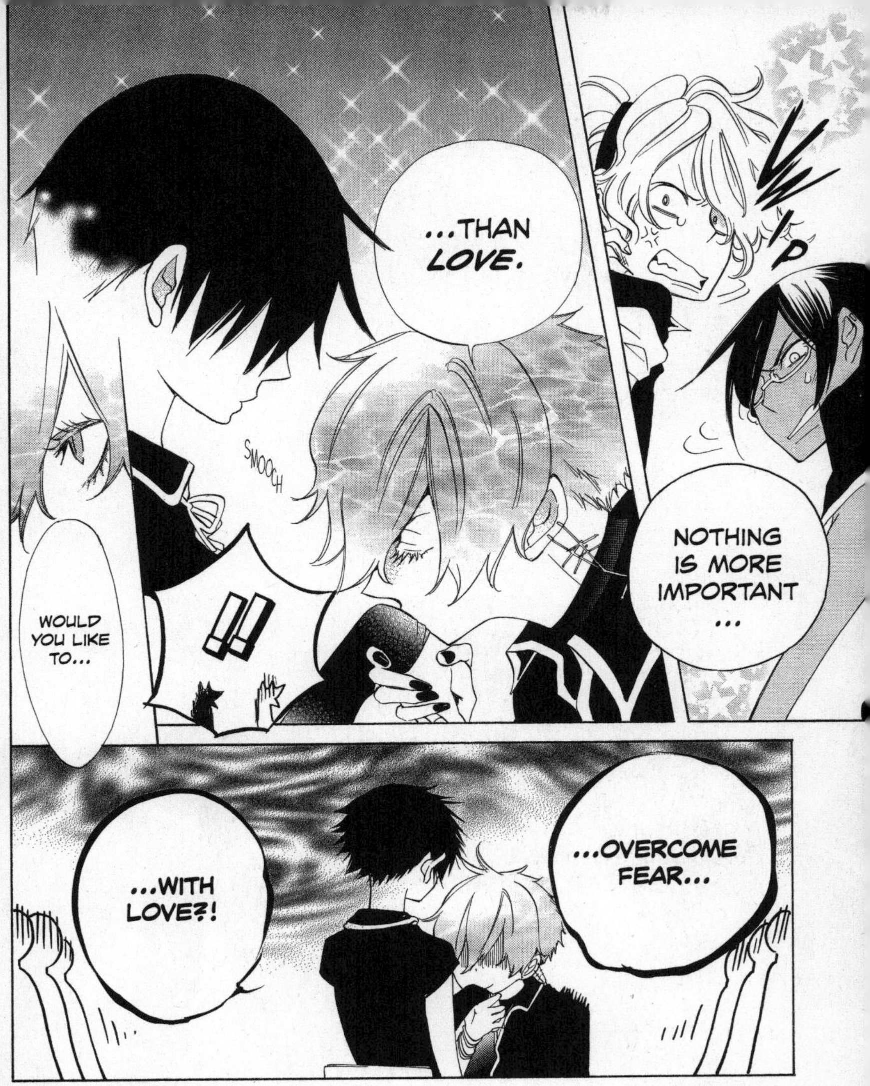
WHIP
NOTHING IS MORE IMPORTANT ...
...THAN *LOVE.*
SMOOCH
!!
WOULD YOU LIKE TO...
...OVERCOME FEAR...
...WITH LOVE?!
FOR THE REST OF THE DAY...
*We can't get close to her.*
...IT SEEMED THAT TAKAMICHI WOULD HAPPILY SLAY ANYONE WHO GOT NEAR HER...

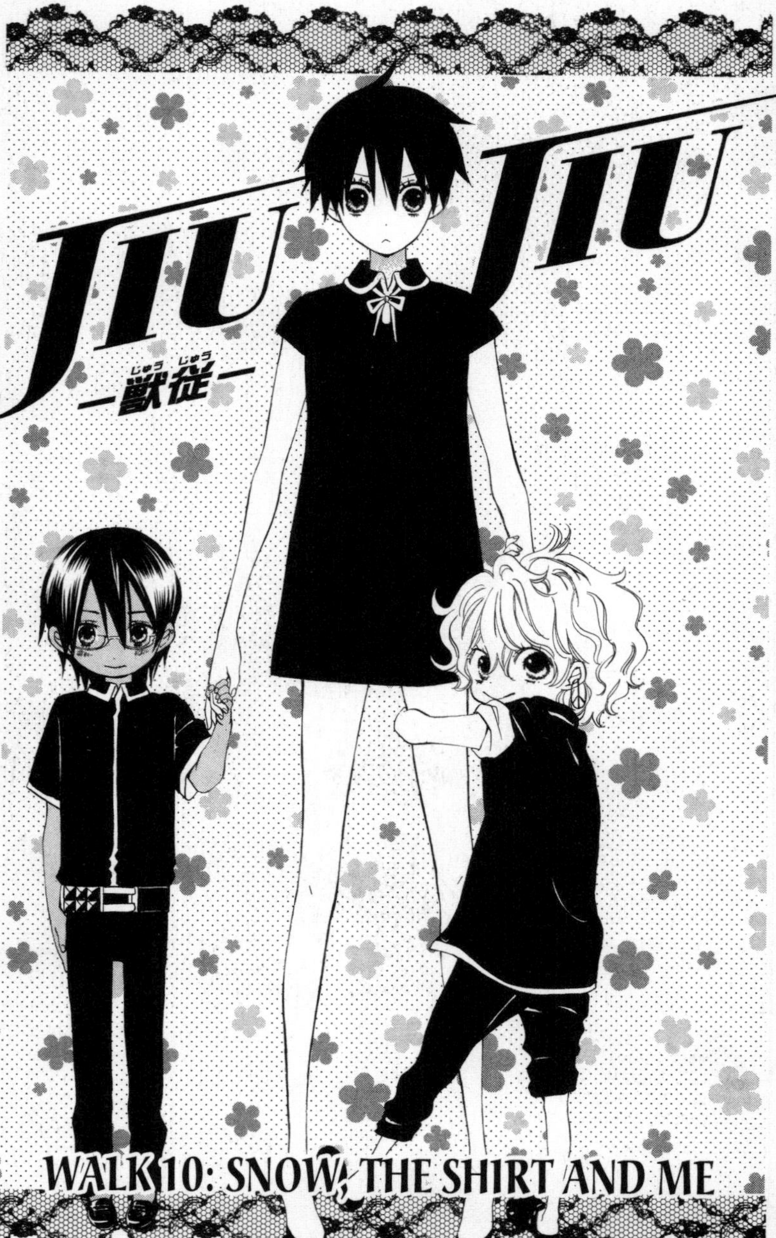
JIU JIU
じゅう じゅう
—獣従—
WALK 10: SNOW, THE SHIRT AND ME

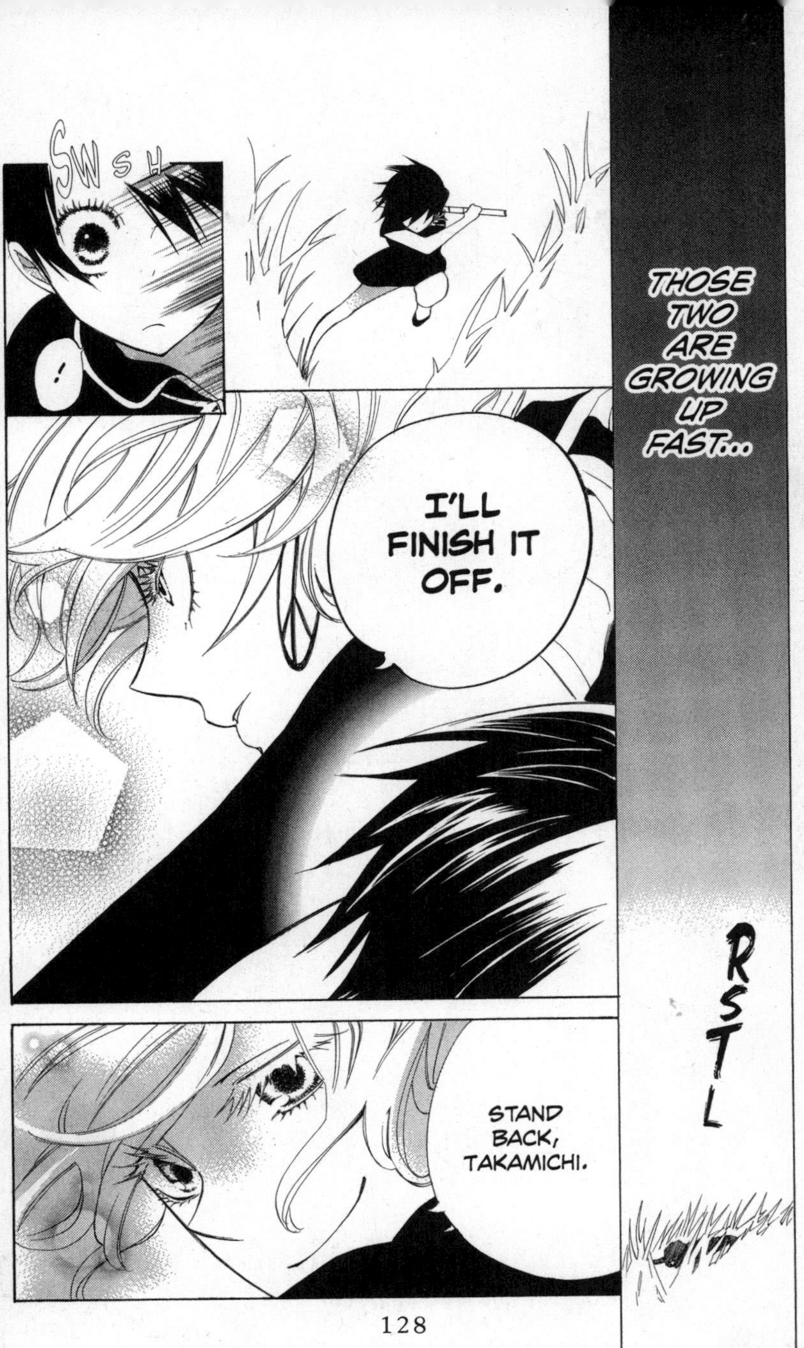
THOSE TWO ARE GROWING UP FAST...
RSTL
SWSH
!
I'LL FINISH IT OFF.
STAND BACK, TAKAMICHI.

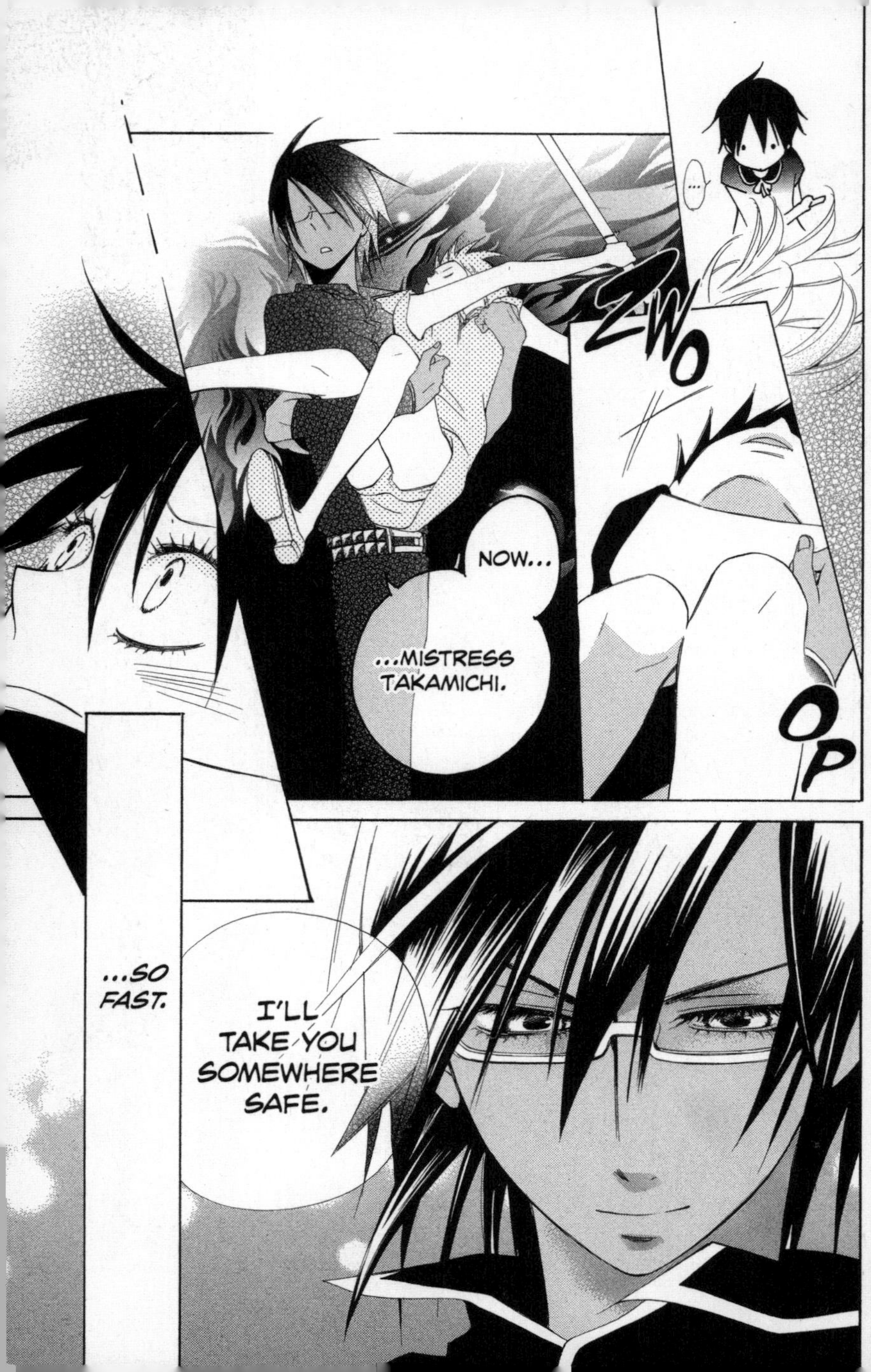
...
...
ZWOOP
NOW...
...MISTRESS TAKAMICHI.
I'LL TAKE YOU SOMEWHERE SAFE.
...SO FAST.

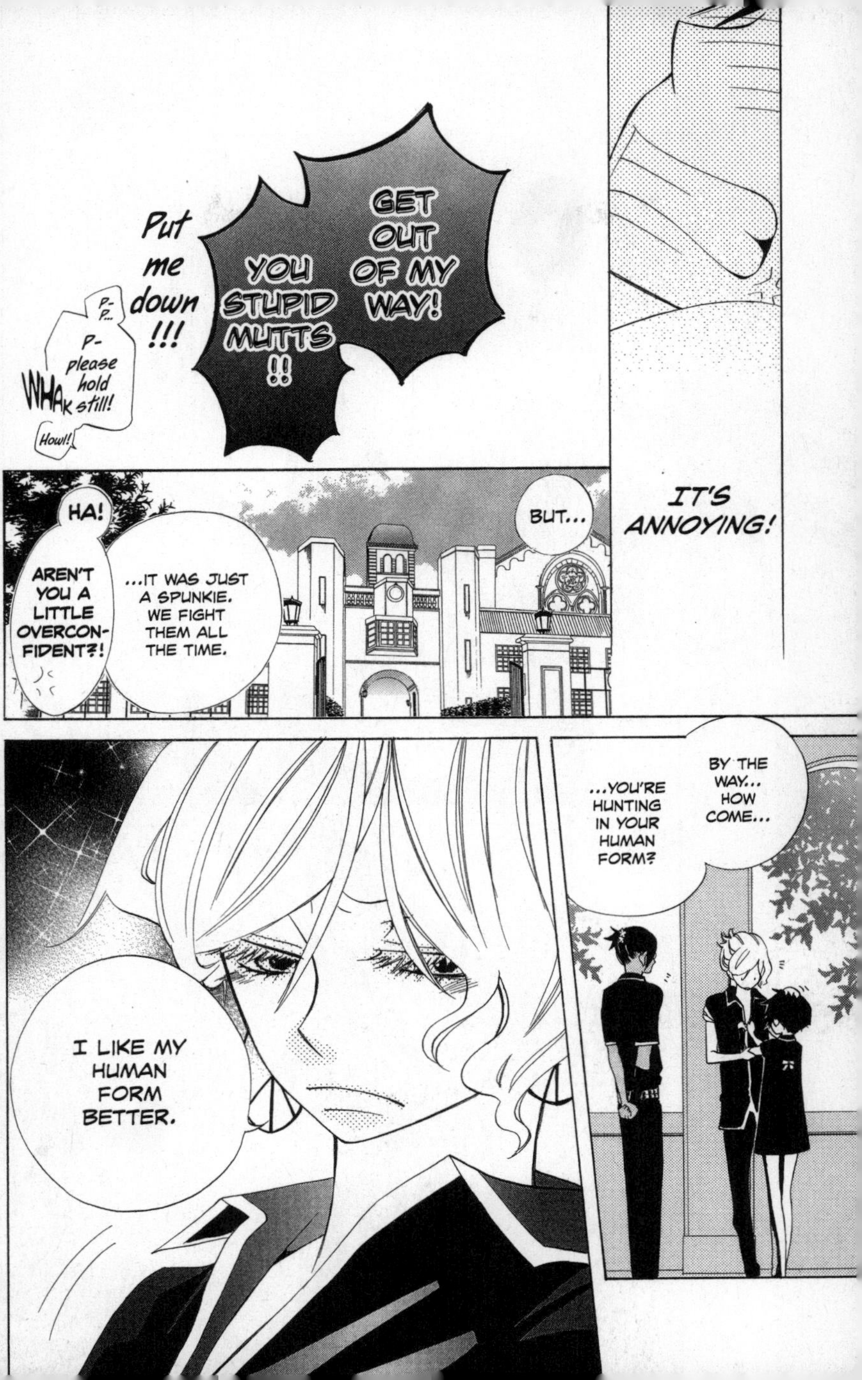
IT'S ANNOYING!
GET OUT OF MY WAY! YOU STUPID MUTTS!!
Put me down!!!
P-P... P-please hold still!
WHAK
Howl!
BUT...
...IT WAS JUST A SPUNKIE. WE FIGHT THEM ALL THE TIME.
HA!
AREN'T YOU A LITTLE OVERCON-FIDENT?!
BY THE WAY... HOW COME...
...YOU'RE HUNTING IN YOUR HUMAN FORM?
I LIKE MY HUMAN FORM BETTER.

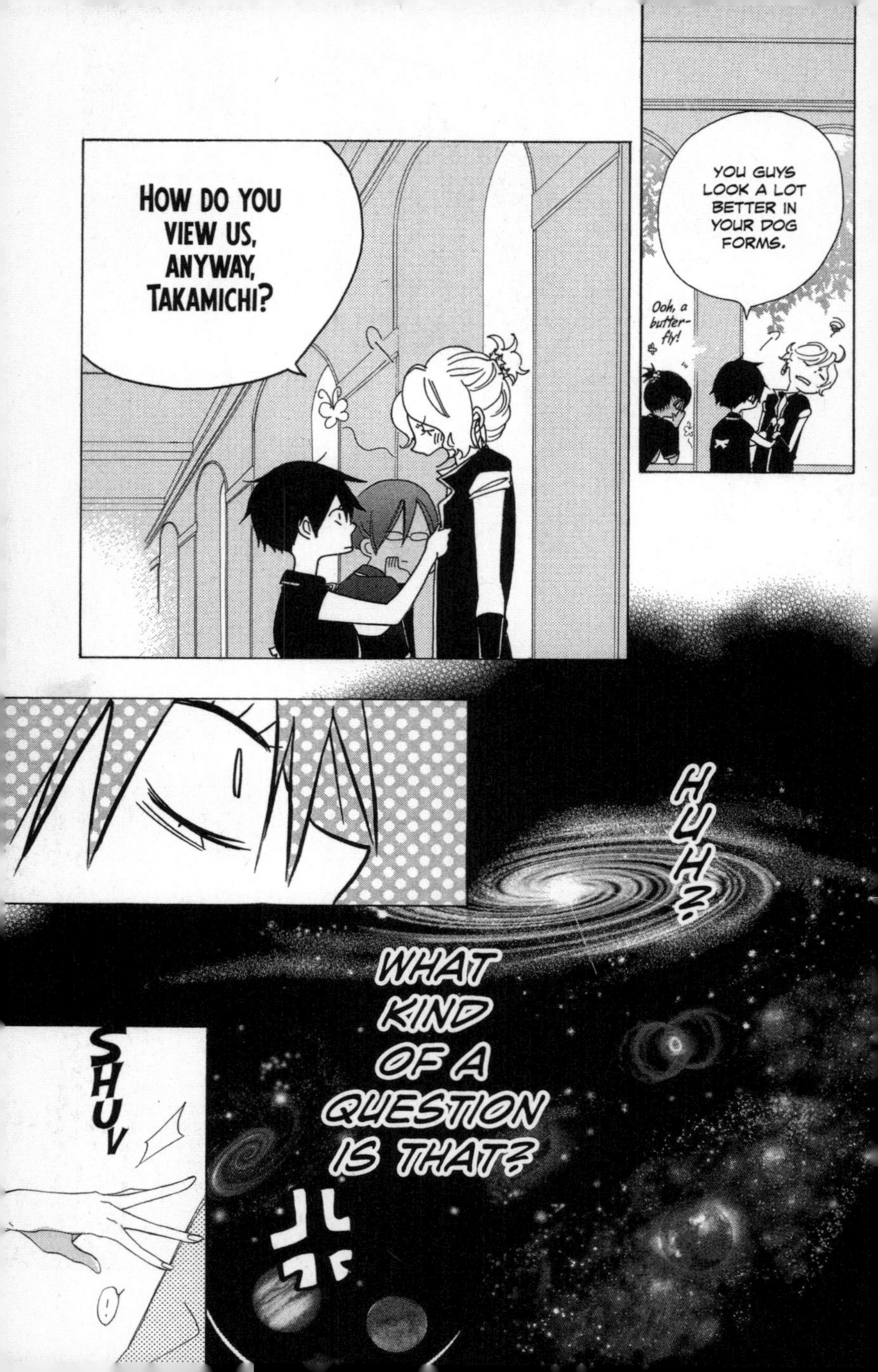
YOU GUYS LOOK A LOT BETTER IN YOUR DOG FORMS.
Ooh, a butter-fly!
HOW DO YOU VIEW US, ANYWAY, TAKAMICHI?
HUH?
WHAT KIND OF A QUESTION IS THAT?
SHUV

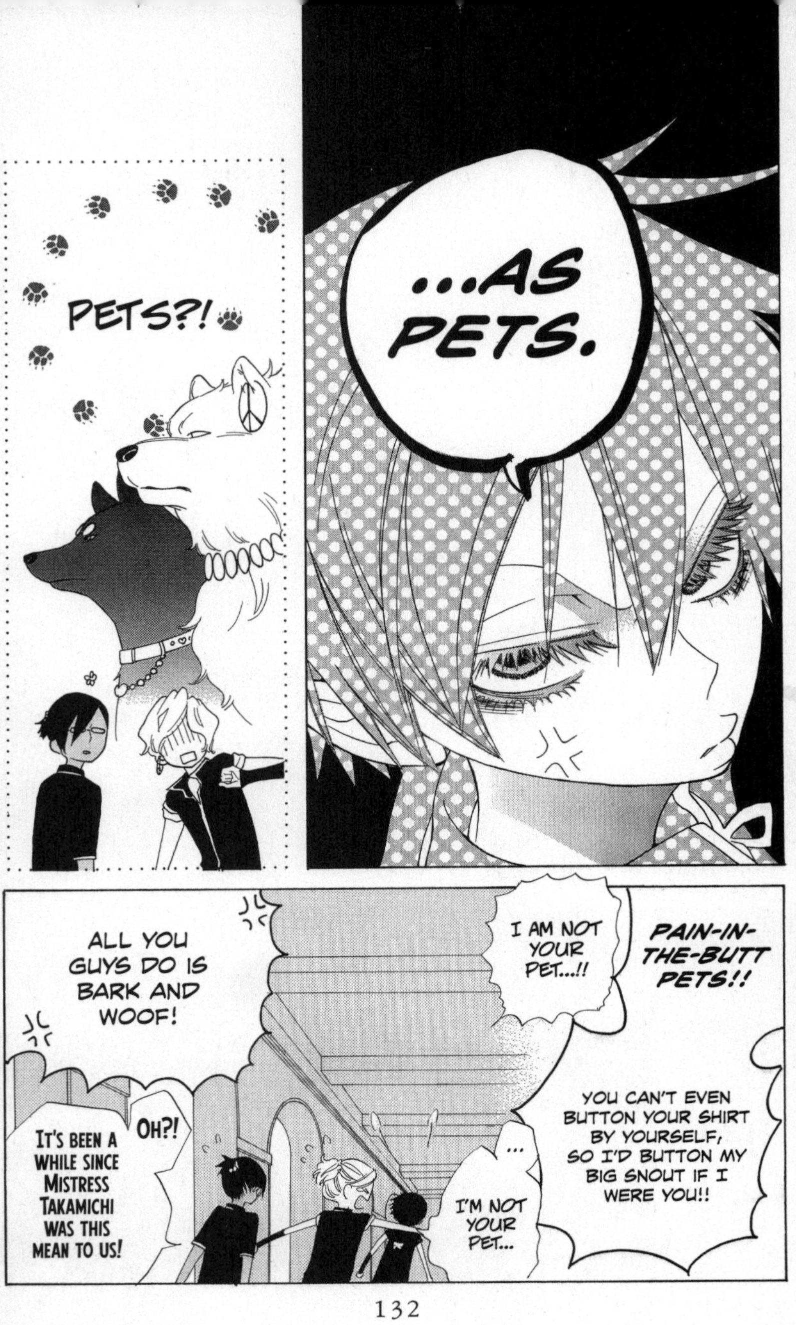
...AS PETS.
PETS?!
PAIN-IN-THE-BUTT PETS!!
I AM NOT YOUR PET...!!
ALL YOU GUYS DO IS BARK AND WOOF!
YOU CAN'T EVEN BUTTON YOUR SHIRT BY YOURSELF, SO I'D BUTTON MY BIG SNOUT IF I WERE YOU!!
...
I'M NOT YOUR PET...
OH?!
IT'S BEEN A WHILE SINCE MISTRESS TAKAMICHI WAS THIS MEAN TO US!

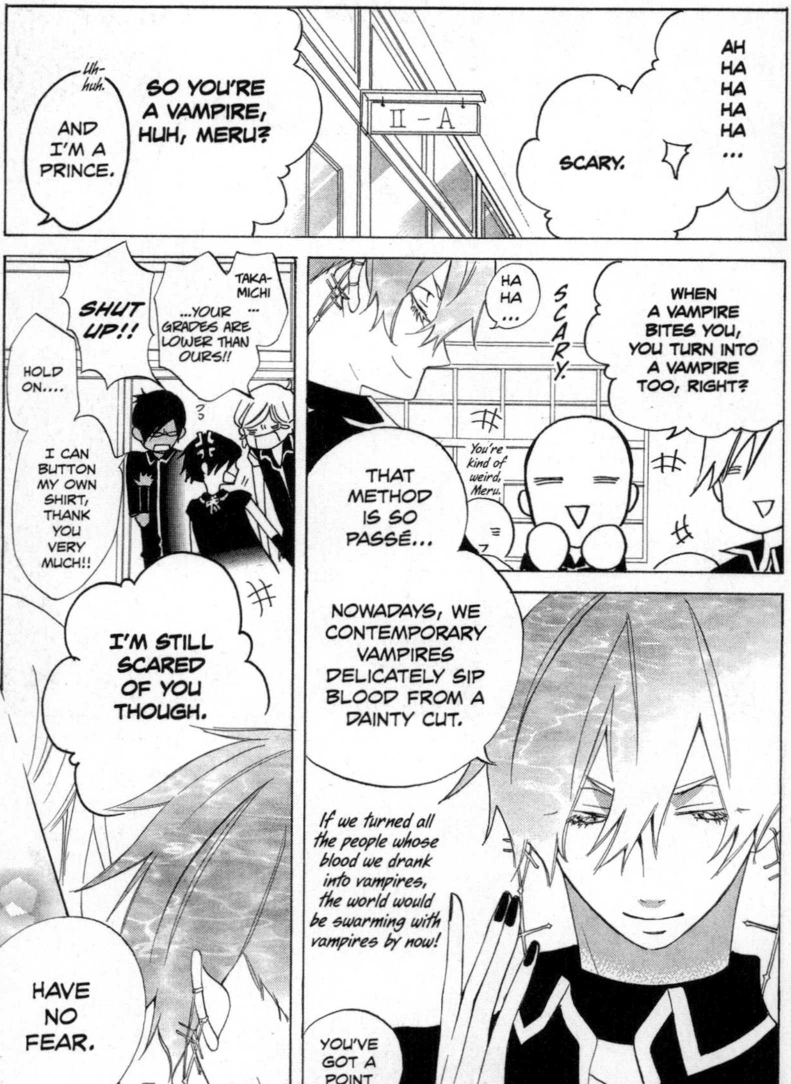
AH HA HA HA HA ...
SCARY.
SO YOU'RE A VAMPIRE, HUH, MERU?
Uh-huh.
AND I'M A PRINCE.
WHEN A VAMPIRE BITES YOU, YOU TURN INTO A VAMPIRE TOO, RIGHT?
SCARY.
HA HA ...
You're kind of weird, Meru.
THAT METHOD IS SO PASSÉ...
TAKAMICHI ...
...YOUR GRADES ARE LOWER THAN OURS!!
SHUT UP!!
HOLD ON....
I CAN BUTTON MY OWN SHIRT, THANK YOU VERY MUCH!!
NOWADAYS, WE CONTEMPORARY VAMPIRES DELICATELY SIP BLOOD FROM A DAINTY CUT.
If we turned all the people whose blood we drank into vampires, the world would be swarming with vampires by now!
YOU'VE GOT A POINT THERE...
I'M STILL SCARED OF YOU THOUGH.
HAVE NO FEAR.

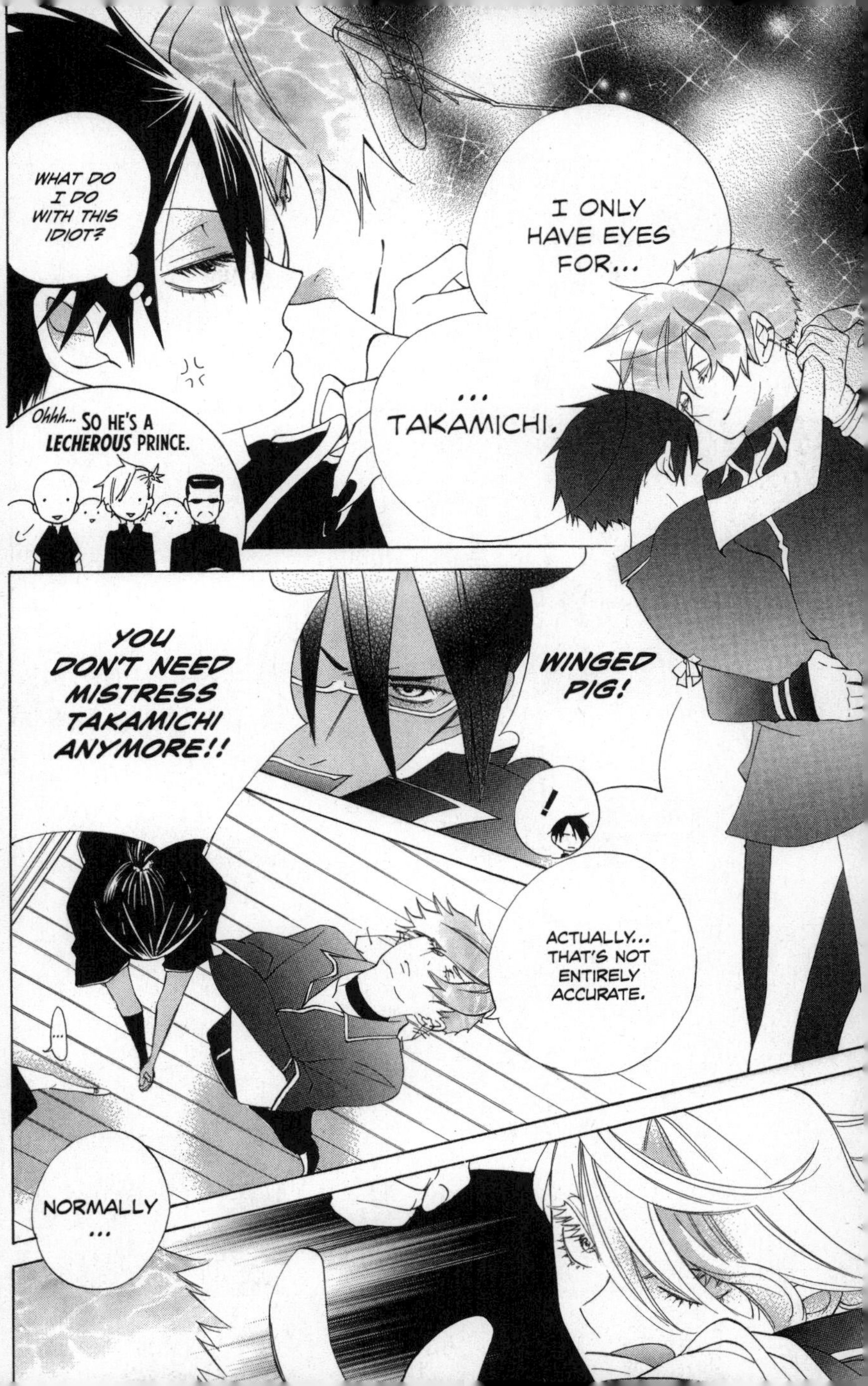
I ONLY HAVE EYES FOR...
... TAKAMICHI.
WHAT DO I DO WITH THIS IDIOT?
Ohhh... SO HE'S A LECHEROUS PRINCE.
WINGED PIG!
YOU DON'T NEED MISTRESS TAKAMICHI ANYMORE!!
!
ACTUALLY... THAT'S NOT ENTIRELY ACCURATE.
...
NORMALLY ...

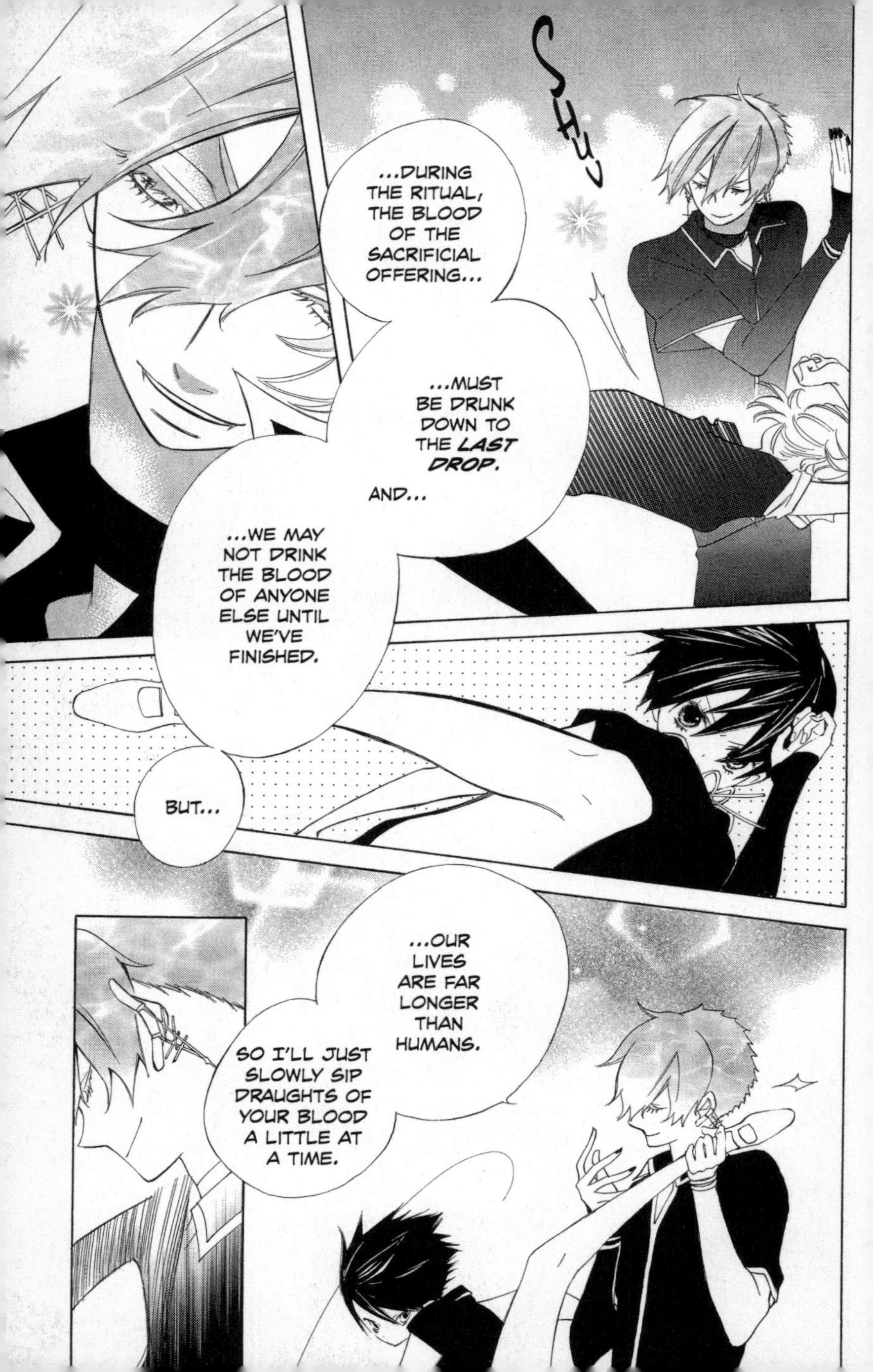
SHUU
...DURING THE RITUAL, THE BLOOD OF THE SACRIFICIAL OFFERING...
...MUST BE DRUNK DOWN TO THE *LAST DROP*.
AND...
...WE MAY NOT DRINK THE BLOOD OF ANYONE ELSE UNTIL WE'VE FINISHED.
BUT...
...OUR LIVES ARE FAR LONGER THAN HUMANS.
SO I'LL JUST SLOWLY SIP DRAUGHTS OF YOUR BLOOD A LITTLE AT A TIME.

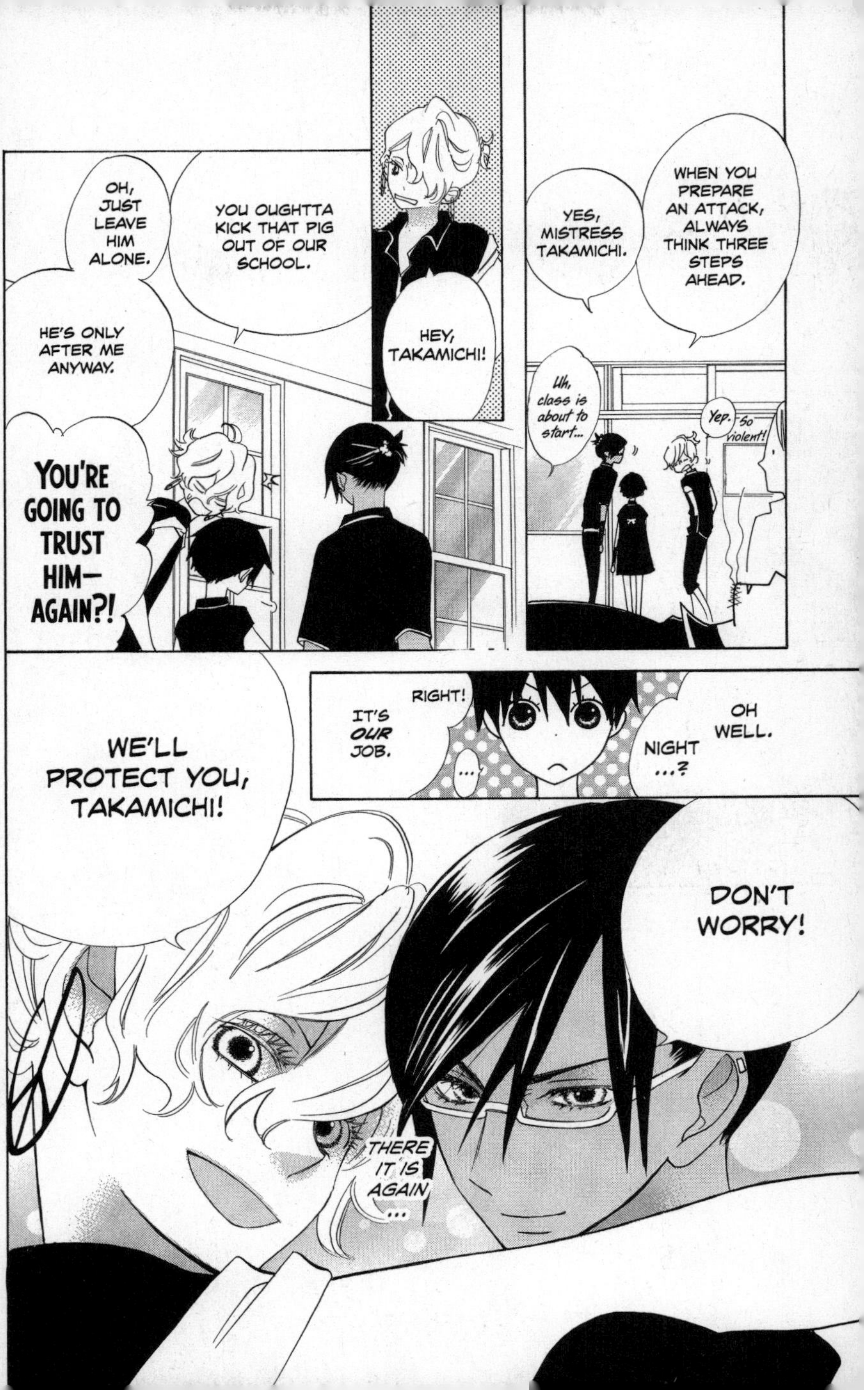
WHEN YOU PREPARE AN ATTACK, ALWAYS THINK THREE STEPS AHEAD.
YES, MISTRESS TAKAMICHI.
Yep.
So violent!
Uh, class is about to start...
HEY, TAKAMICHI!
YOU OUGHTTA KICK THAT PIG OUT OF OUR SCHOOL.
OH, JUST LEAVE HIM ALONE.
HE'S ONLY AFTER ME ANYWAY.
YOU'RE GOING TO TRUST HIM—AGAIN?!
OH WELL.
NIGHT ...?
RIGHT!
IT'S *OUR* JOB.
...
DON'T WORRY!
WE'LL PROTECT YOU, TAKAMICHI!
THERE IT IS AGAIN ...

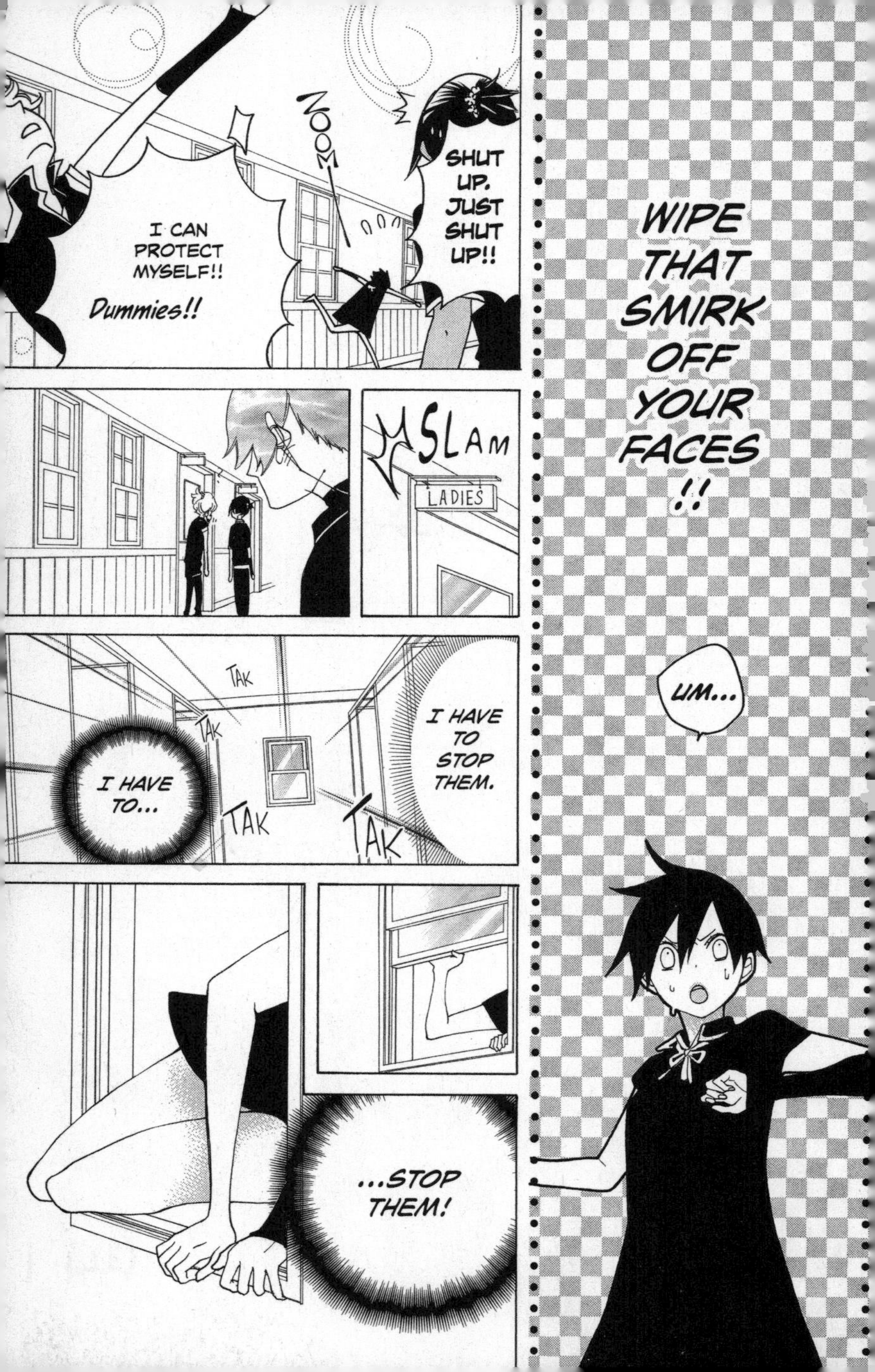
WIPE THAT SMIRK OFF YOUR FACES!!
UM...
SHUT UP. JUST SHUT UP!!
ZOOM
I CAN PROTECT MYSELF!!
Dummies!!
SLAM
LADIES
I HAVE TO STOP THEM.
TAK
TAK
TAK
TAK
I HAVE TO...
...STOP THEM!

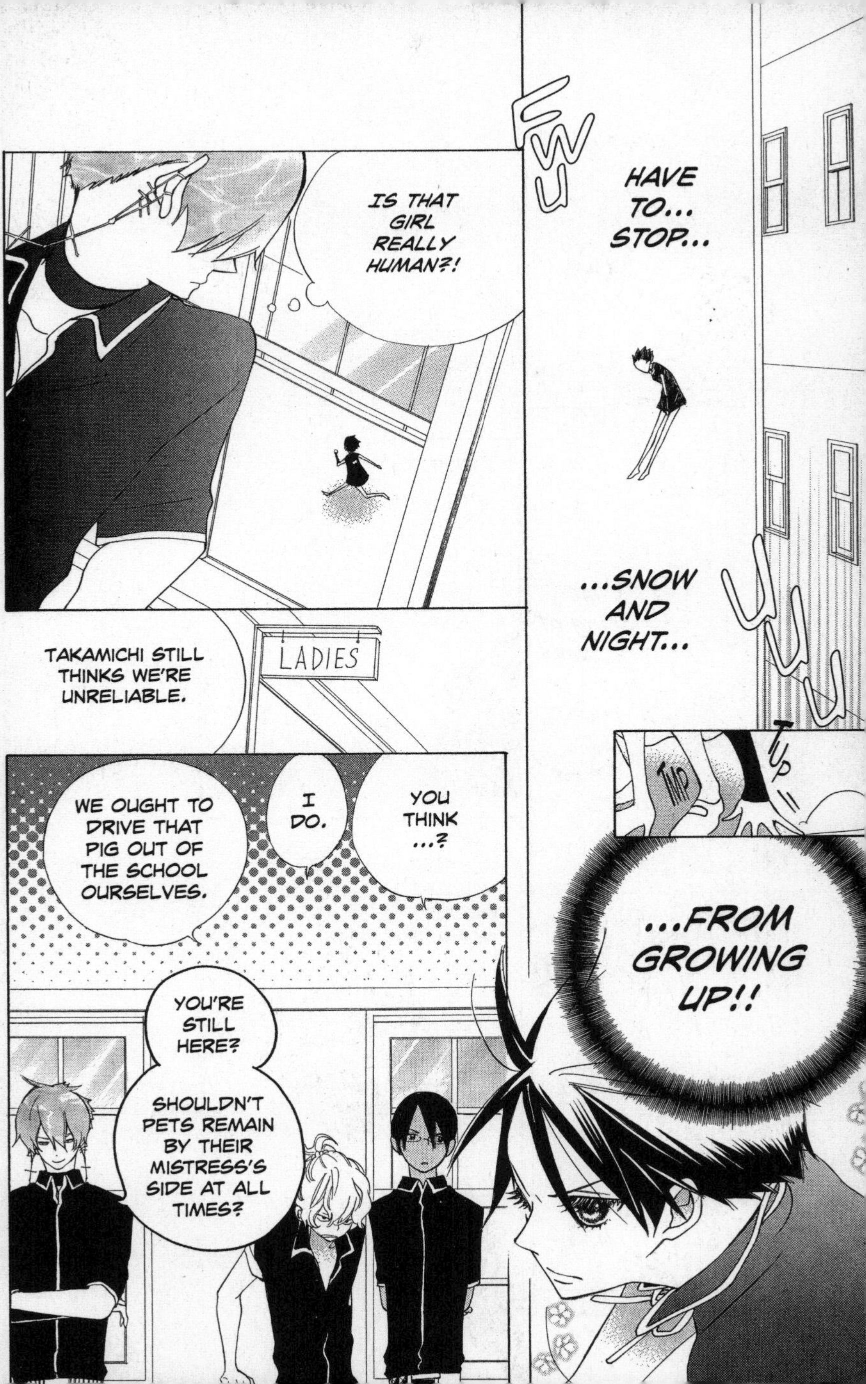
FWU
HAVE TO... STOP...
...SNOW AND NIGHT...
UUUU
TMP
TUP
...FROM GROWING UP!!
IS THAT GIRL REALLY HUMAN?!
LADIES
TAKAMICHI STILL THINKS WE'RE UNRELIABLE.
YOU THINK ...?
I DO.
WE OUGHT TO DRIVE THAT PIG OUT OF THE SCHOOL OURSELVES.
YOU'RE STILL HERE?
SHOULDN'T PETS REMAIN BY THEIR MISTRESS'S SIDE AT ALL TIMES?

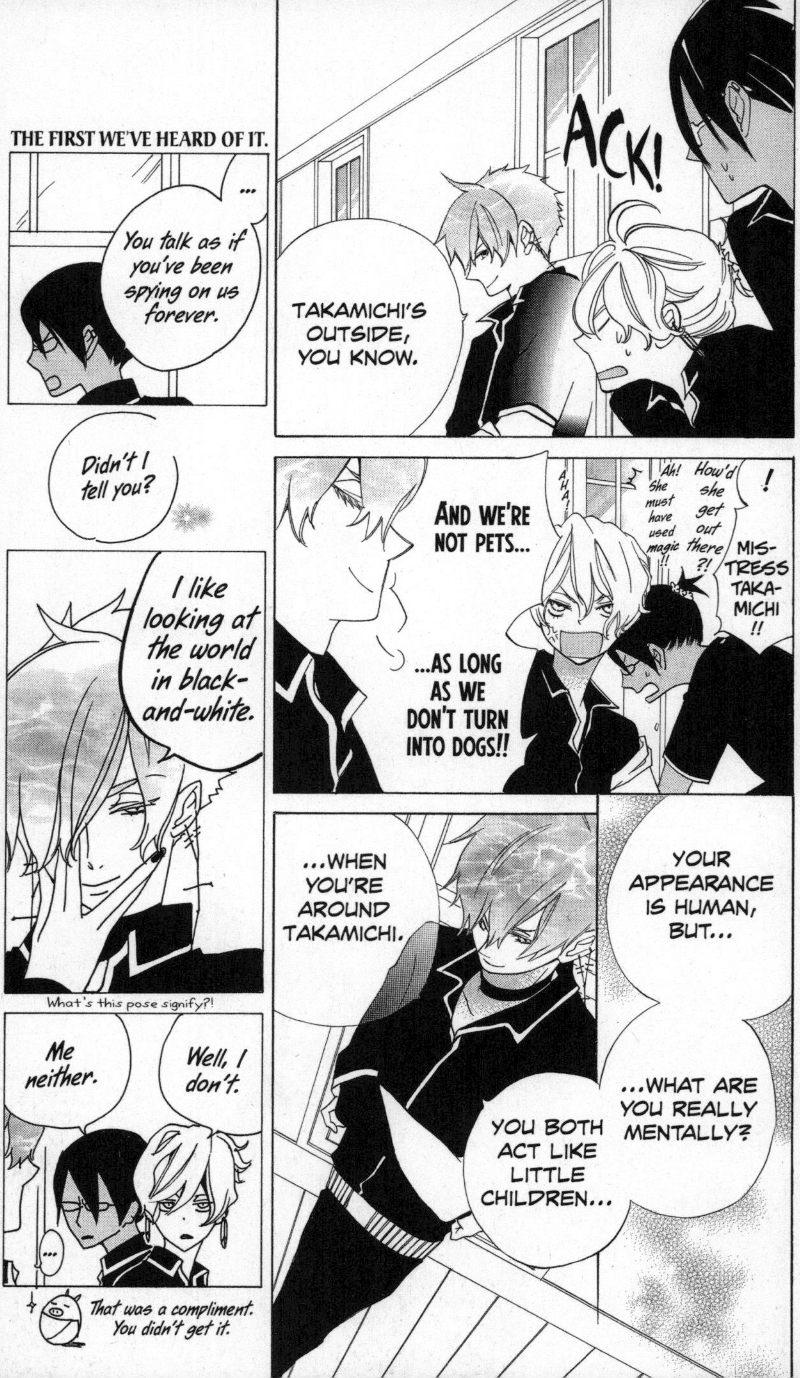
ACK!
TAKAMICHI'S OUTSIDE, YOU KNOW.
THE FIRST WE'VE HEARD OF IT.
...
You talk as if you've been spying on us forever.
Didn't I tell you?
!
MISTRESS TAKAMICHI!!
How'd she get out there?!
Ah! She must have used magic!!
AHA!
AND WE'RE NOT PETS...
...AS LONG AS WE DON'T TURN INTO DOGS!!
YOUR APPEARANCE IS HUMAN, BUT...
...WHAT ARE YOU REALLY MENTALLY?
...WHEN YOU'RE AROUND TAKAMICHI.
YOU BOTH ACT LIKE LITTLE CHILDREN...
I like looking at the world in black-and-white.
What's this pose signify?!
Well, I don't.
Me neither.
...
That was a compliment. You didn't get it.

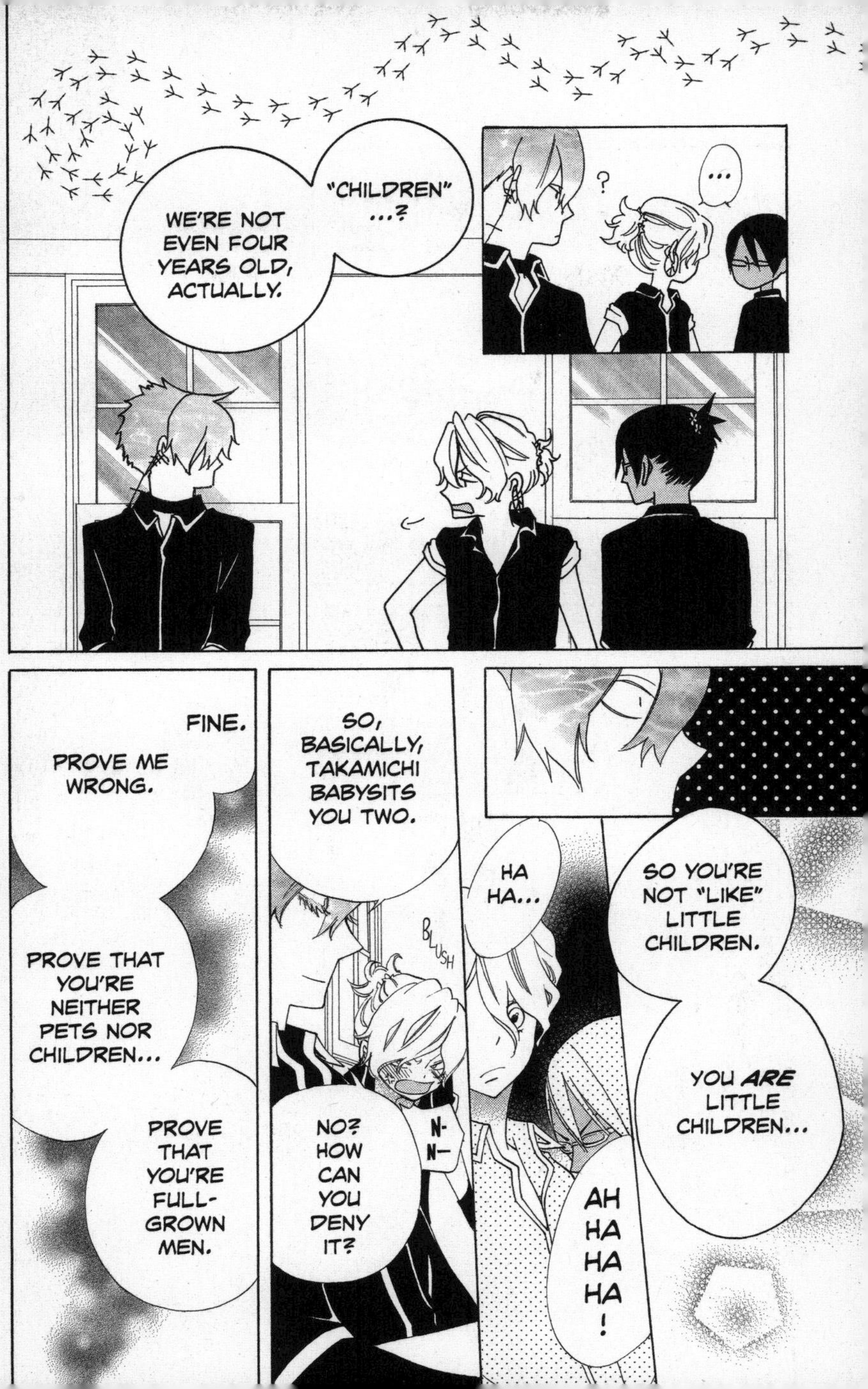
?
…
"CHILDREN"...?
WE'RE NOT EVEN FOUR YEARS OLD, ACTUALLY.
SO YOU'RE NOT "LIKE" LITTLE CHILDREN.
YOU *ARE* LITTLE CHILDREN...
HA HA...
AH HA HA HA!
SO, BASICALLY, TAKAMICHI BABYSITS YOU TWO.
BLUSH
N- N–
NO? HOW CAN YOU DENY IT?
FINE.
PROVE ME WRONG.
PROVE THAT YOU'RE NEITHER PETS NOR CHILDREN...
PROVE THAT YOU'RE FULL-GROWN MEN.

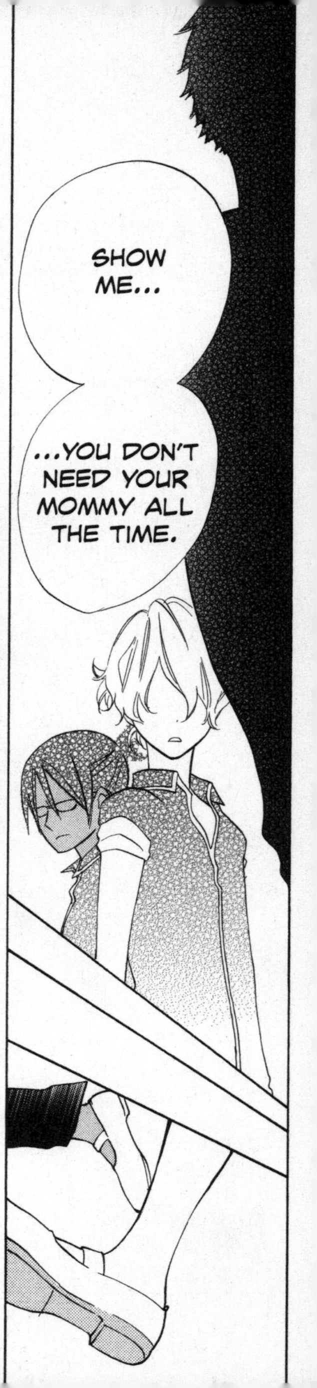
SHOW ME...
...YOU DON'T NEED YOUR MOMMY ALL THE TIME.
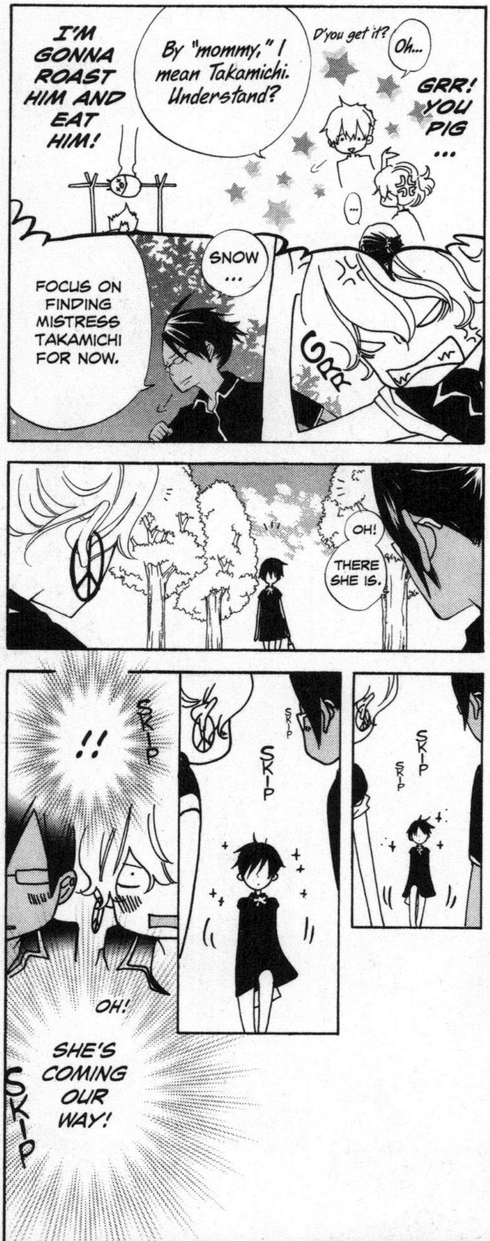
Oh...
D'you get it?
GRR! YOU PIG...
By "mommy," I mean Takamichi. Understand?
I'M GONNA ROAST HIM AND EAT HIM!
...
SNOW...
GRRR
FOCUS ON FINDING MISTRESS TAKAMICHI FOR NOW.
OH!
THERE SHE IS.
SKIP
SKIP
SKIP
SKIP
SKIP
!!
SKIP
OH!
SHE'S COMING OUR WAY!
SKIP

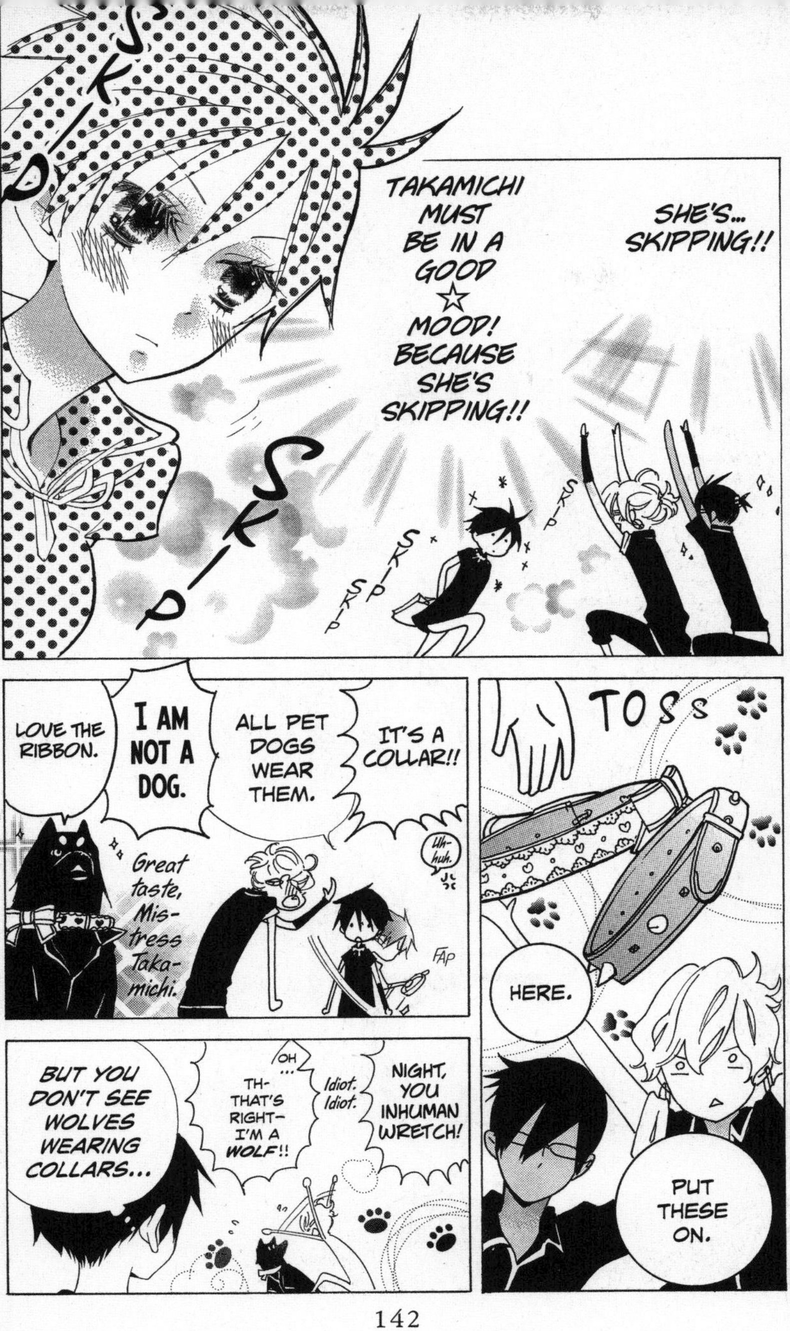

SHE'S... SKIPPING!!
TAKAMICHI MUST BE IN A GOOD ☆ MOOD! BECAUSE SHE'S SKIPPING!!
SKIP
SKIP
SKIP
SKIP
SKIP
TOSS
HERE.
PUT THESE ON.
IT'S A COLLAR!!
ALL PET DOGS WEAR THEM.
I AM NOT A DOG.
LOVE THE RIBBON.
Uh-huh.
Great taste, Mistress Takamichi.
FAP
NIGHT, YOU INHUMAN WRETCH!
Idiot. Idiot.
OH ...
TH-THAT'S RIGHT— I'M A WOLF!!
BUT YOU DON'T SEE WOLVES WEARING COLLARS...

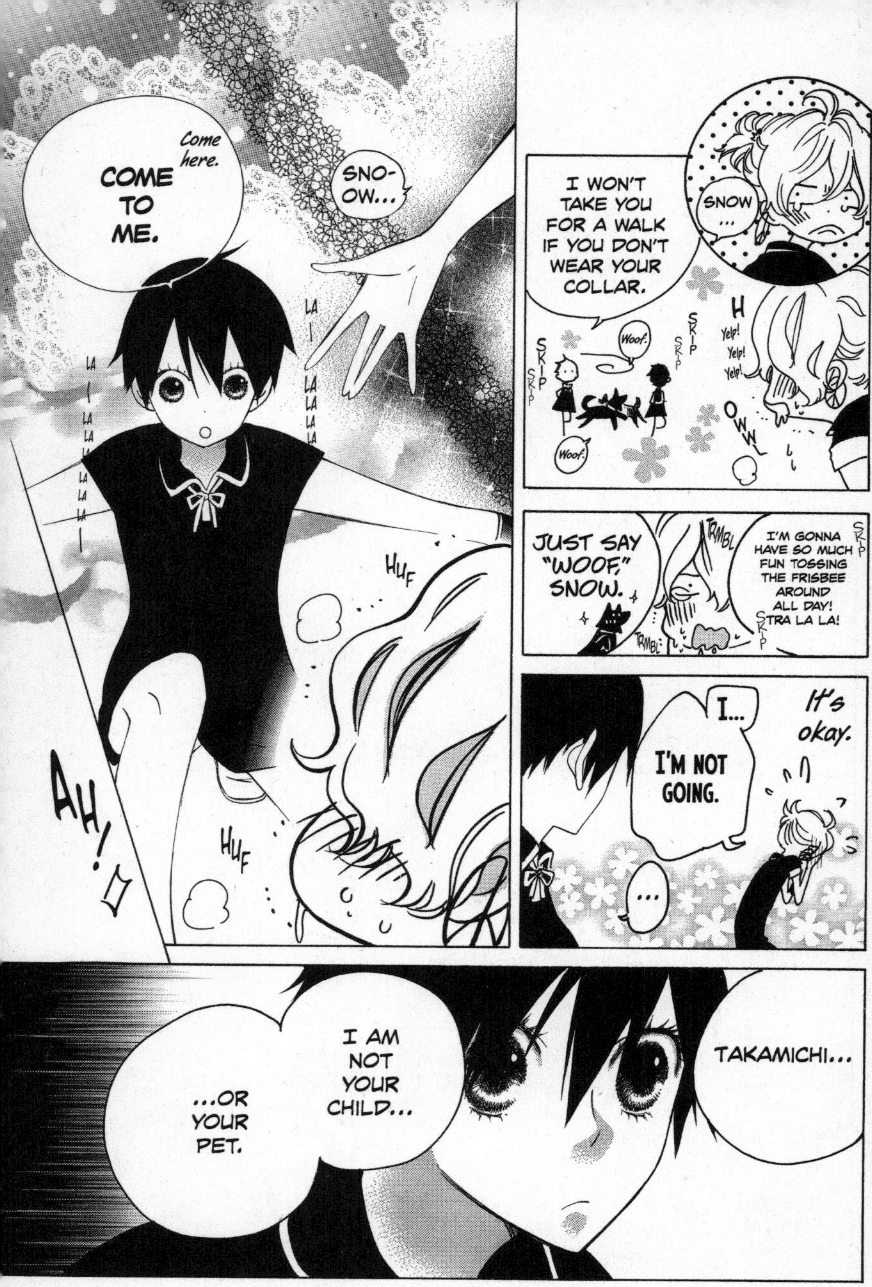
SNOW ...
I WON'T TAKE YOU FOR A WALK IF YOU DON'T WEAR YOUR COLLAR.
Yelp! Yelp! Yelp!
H
OWWL
SKIP SKIP
SKIP SKIP
Woof.
Woof.
I'M GONNA HAVE SO MUCH FUN TOSSING THE FRISBEE AROUND ALL DAY! STRA LA LA!
SKIP SKIP
TRMBL
TRMBL
JUST SAY "WOOF," SNOW.
It's okay.
I... I'M NOT GOING.
...
SNO-OW...
Come here.
COME TO ME.
LA LA LA LA LA LA LA
LA LA LA LA LA LA LA LA
HUF
HUF
AH!
TAKAMICHI...
I AM NOT YOUR CHILD...
...OR YOUR PET.

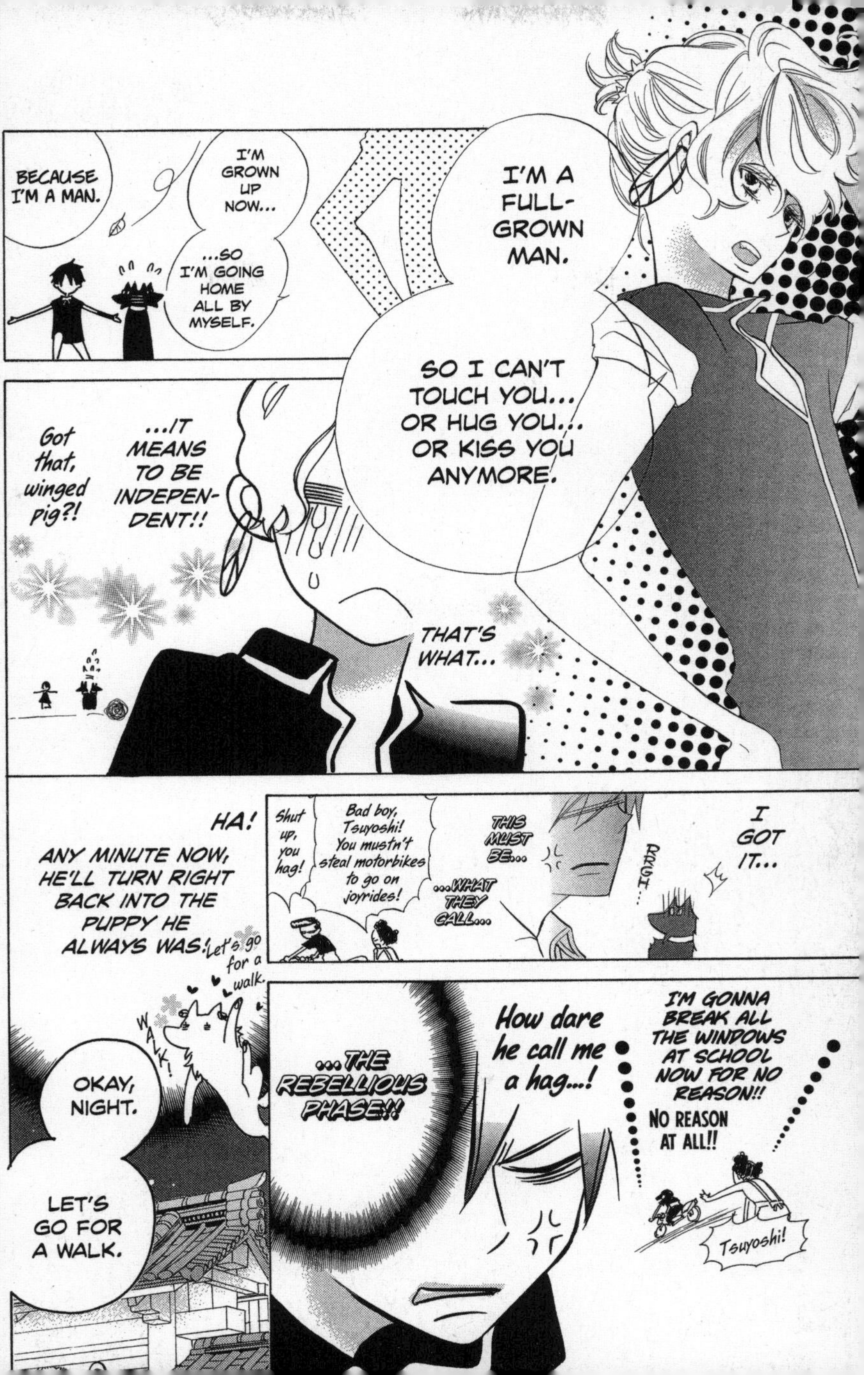
I'M A FULL-GROWN MAN.
I'M GROWN UP NOW...
...SO I'M GOING HOME ALL BY MYSELF.
BECAUSE I'M A MAN.
SO I CAN'T TOUCH YOU... OR HUG YOU... OR KISS YOU ANYMORE.
THAT'S WHAT...
...IT MEANS TO BE INDEPENDENT!!
Got that, winged pig?!
I GOT IT...
RRGH...
THIS MUST BE...
...WHAT THEY CALL...
Bad boy, Tsuyoshi! You mustn't steal motorbikes to go on joyrides!
Shut up, you hag!
HA!
ANY MINUTE NOW, HE'LL TURN RIGHT BACK INTO THE PUPPY HE ALWAYS WAS!
I'M GONNA BREAK ALL THE WINDOWS AT SCHOOL NOW FOR NO REASON!!
NO REASON AT ALL!!
Tsuyoshi!
How dare he call me a hag...!
...THE REBELLIOUS PHASE!!
Let's go for a walk.
WALK!
OKAY, NIGHT.
LET'S GO FOR A WALK.

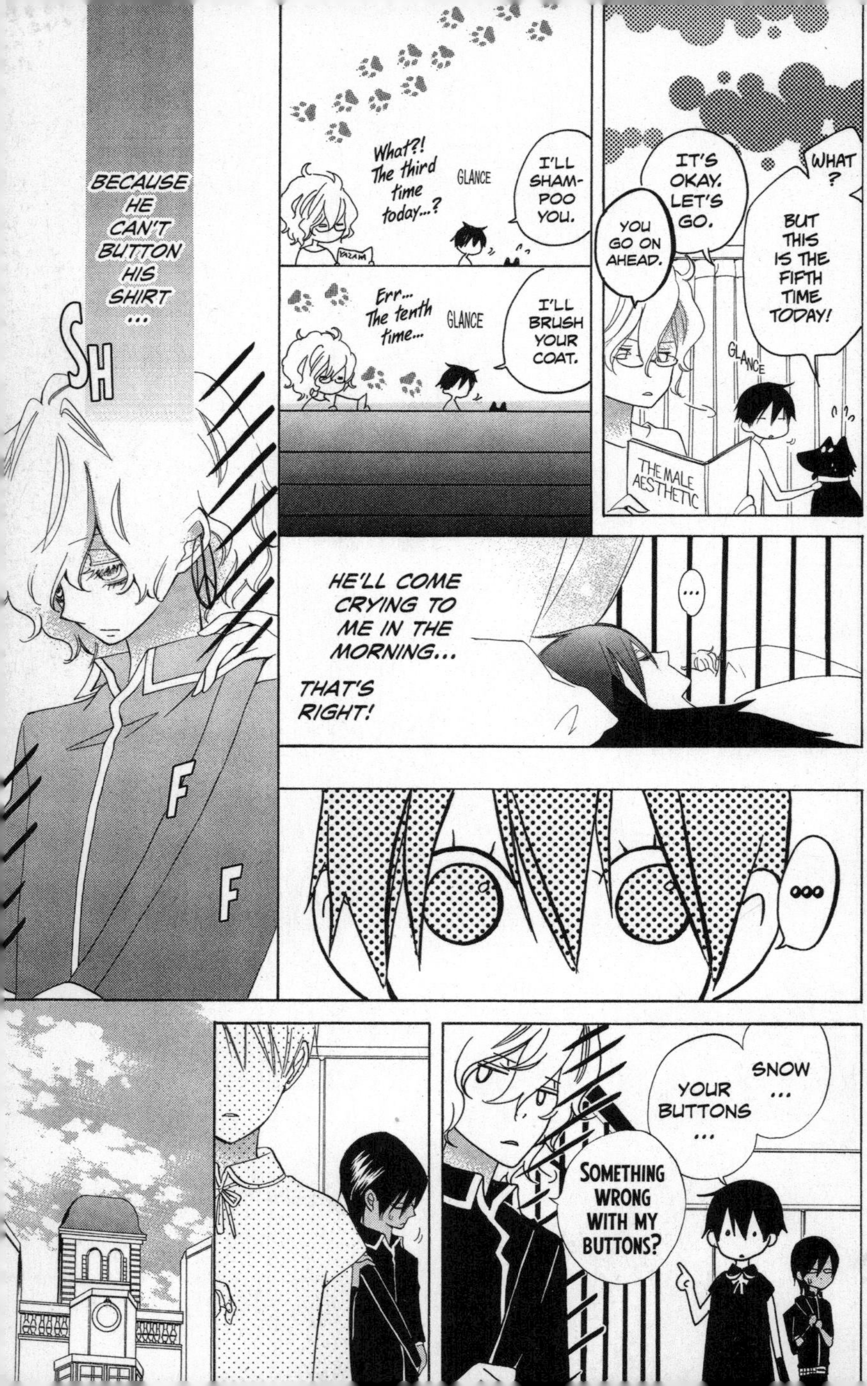
WHAT?
BUT THIS IS THE FIFTH TIME TODAY!
IT'S OKAY. LET'S GO.
YOU GO ON AHEAD.
GLANCE
THE MALE AESTHETIC
I'LL SHAM-POO YOU.
GLANCE
What?! The third time today...?
I'LL BRUSH YOUR COAT.
GLANCE
Err... The tenth time...
...
HE'LL COME CRYING TO ME IN THE MORNING...
THAT'S RIGHT!
...
BECAUSE HE CAN'T BUTTON HIS SHIRT...
SH
F
F
SNOW... YOUR BUTTONS...
SOMETHING WRONG WITH MY BUTTONS?

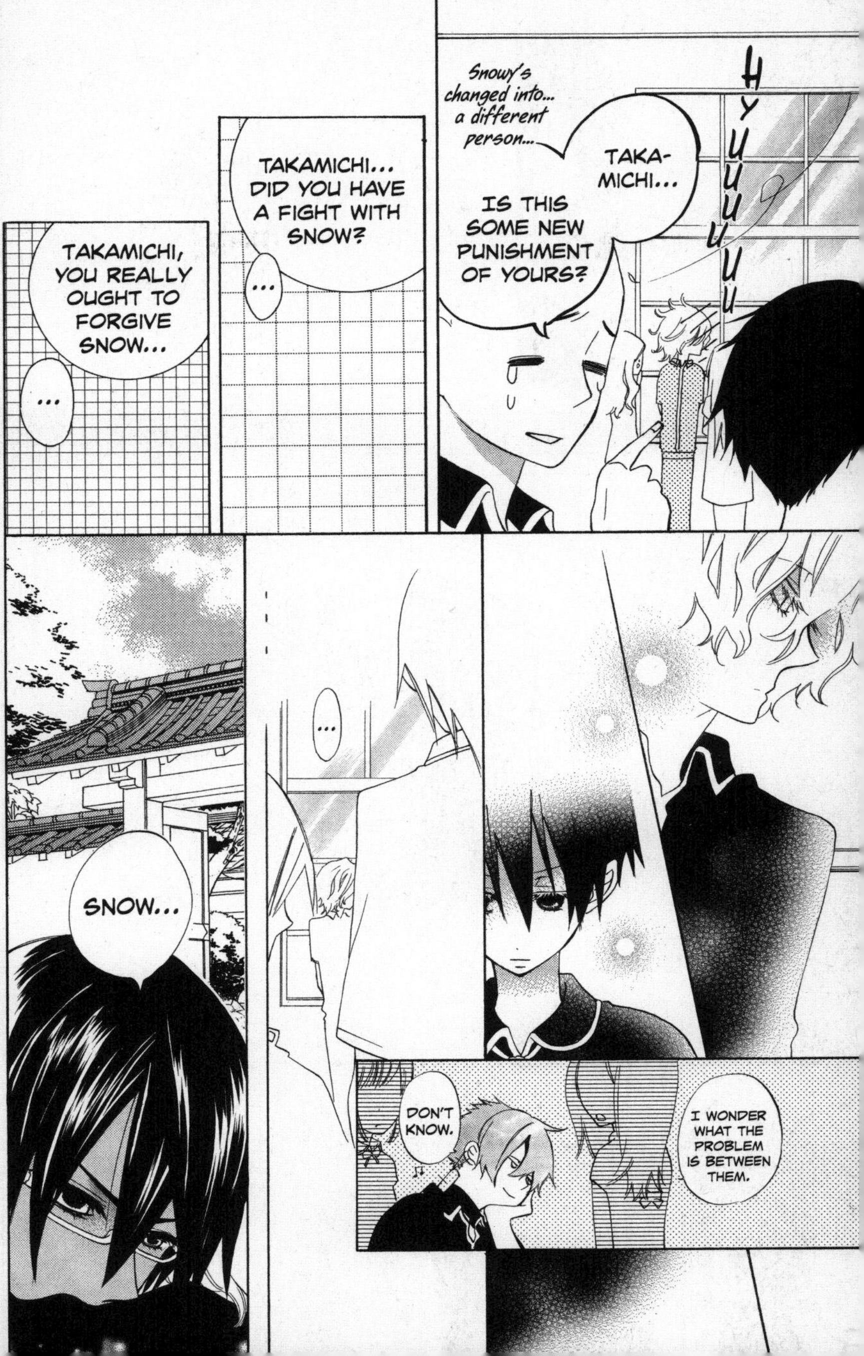
HYUUUUUU
TAKA-MICHI... IS THIS SOME NEW PUNISHMENT OF YOURS?
Snowy's changed into... a different person...
TAKAMICHI... DID YOU HAVE A FIGHT WITH SNOW?
...
TAKAMICHI, YOU REALLY OUGHT TO FORGIVE SNOW...
...
...
I WONDER WHAT THE PROBLEM IS BETWEEN THEM.
DON'T KNOW.
SNOW...

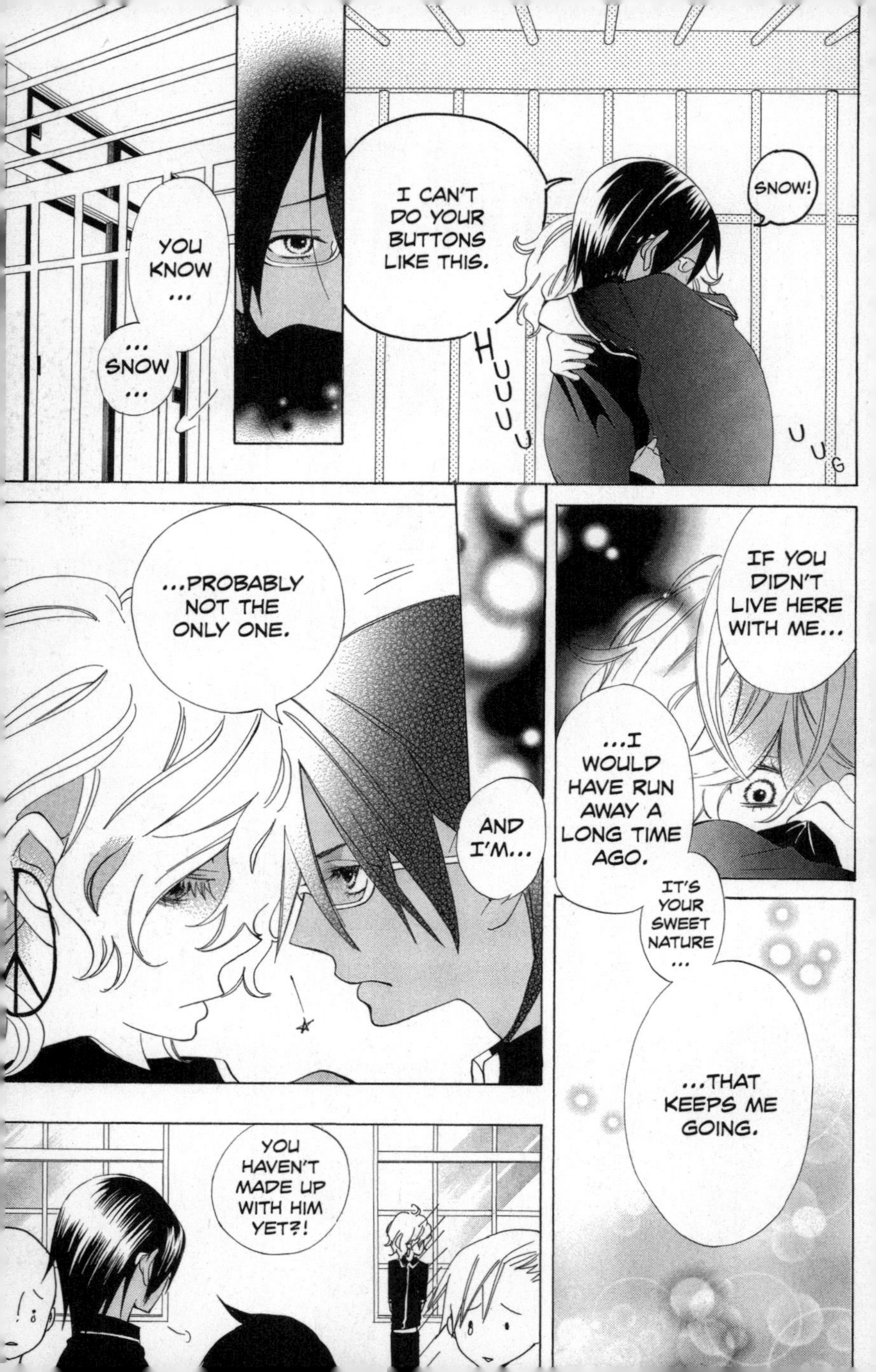
SNOW!
HUUUU
UUG
I CAN'T DO YOUR BUTTONS LIKE THIS.
YOU KNOW...
...SNOW...
IF YOU DIDN'T LIVE HERE WITH ME...
...I WOULD HAVE RUN AWAY A LONG TIME AGO.
IT'S YOUR SWEET NATURE...
...THAT KEEPS ME GOING.
AND I'M...
...PROBABLY NOT THE ONLY ONE.
YOU HAVEN'T MADE UP WITH HIM YET?!

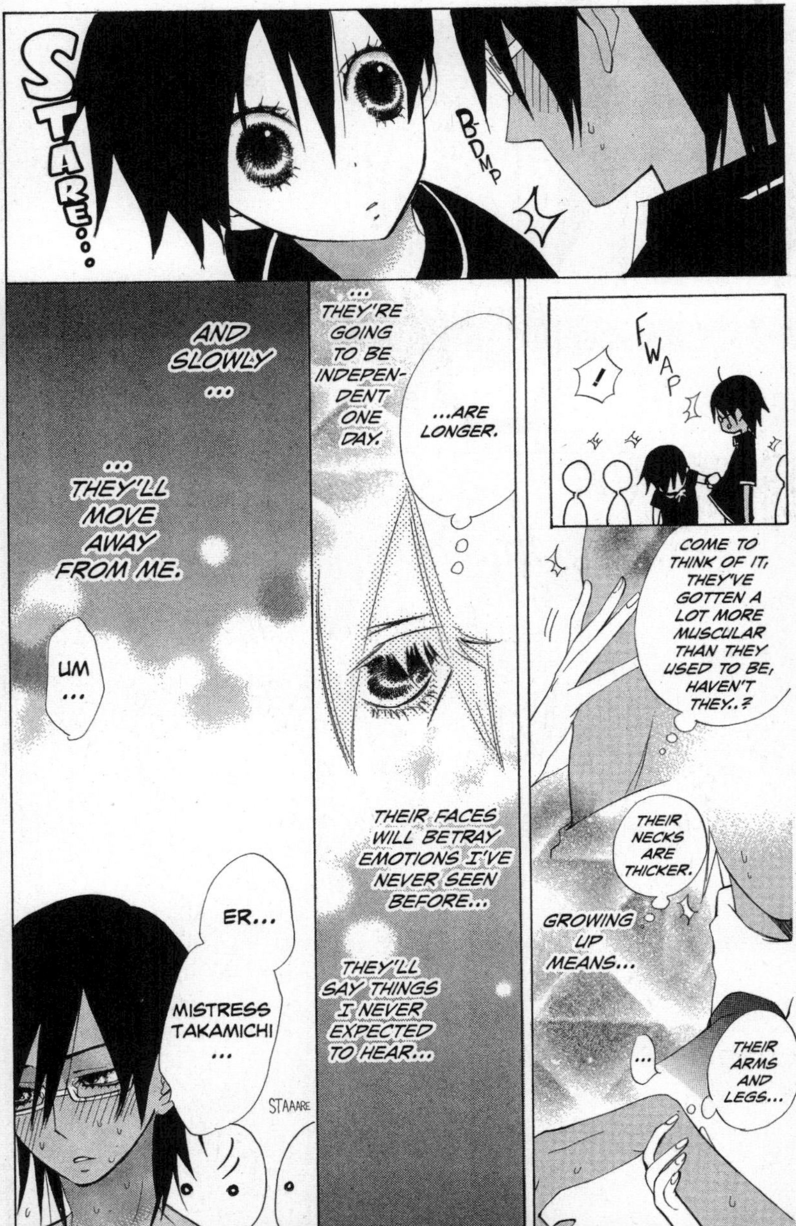
B-DMP
STARE...
FWAP
!
COME TO THINK OF IT, THEY'VE GOTTEN A LOT MORE MUSCULAR THAN THEY USED TO BE, HAVEN'T THEY..?
THEIR NECKS ARE THICKER.
GROWING UP MEANS...
THEIR ARMS AND LEGS...
...
... THEY'RE GOING TO BE INDEPENDENT ONE DAY.
...ARE LONGER.
THEIR FACES WILL BETRAY EMOTIONS I'VE NEVER SEEN BEFORE...
THEY'LL SAY THINGS I NEVER EXPECTED TO HEAR...
AND SLOWLY...
... THEY'LL MOVE AWAY FROM ME.
UM...
ER...
MISTRESS TAKAMICHI...
STAAARE

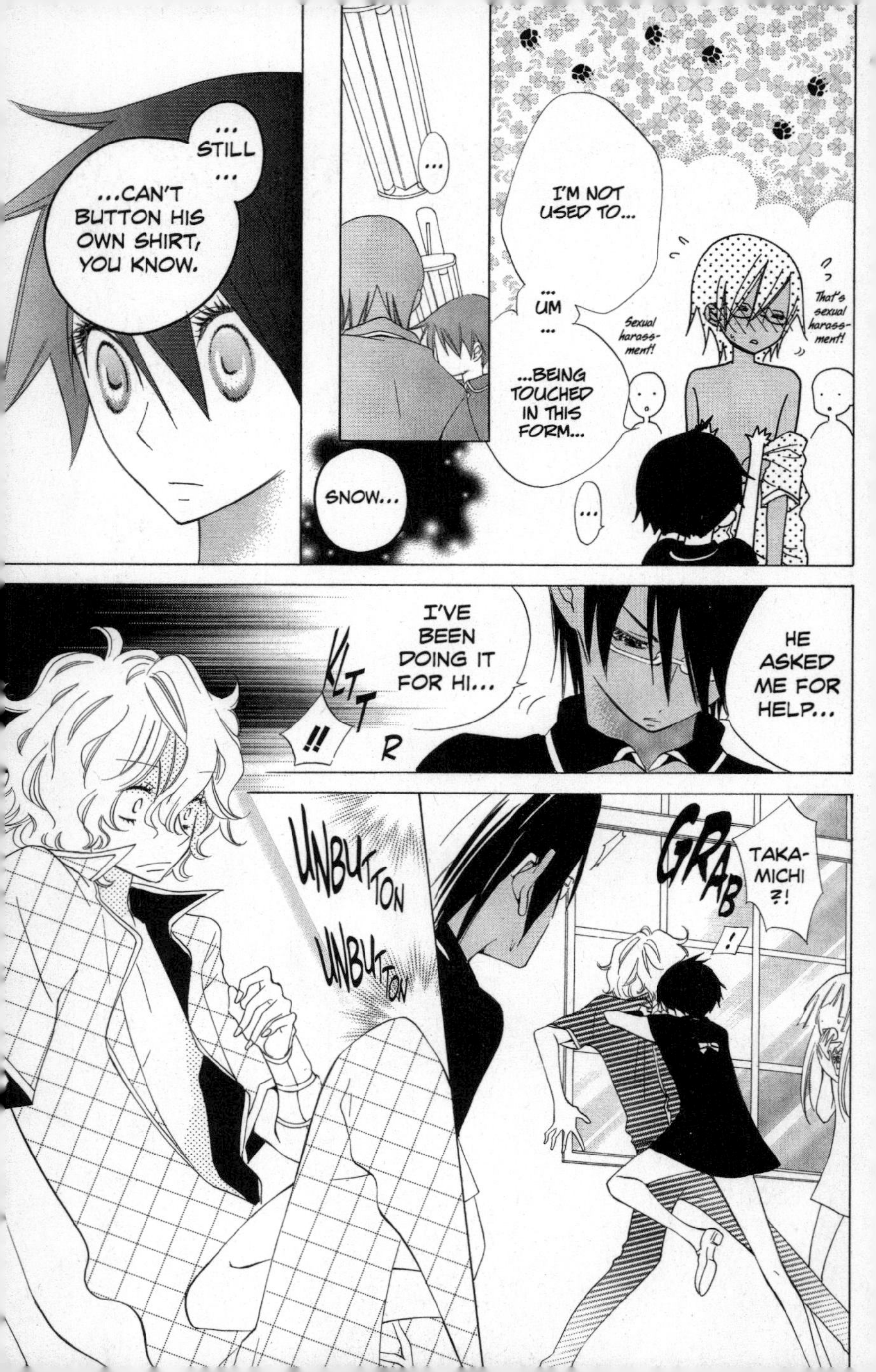
I'M NOT USED TO...
... UM ...
...BEING TOUCHED IN THIS FORM...
That's sexual harassment!
Sexual harassment!
...
SNOW...
...
... STILL ...
...CAN'T BUTTON HIS OWN SHIRT, YOU KNOW.
HE ASKED ME FOR HELP...
I'VE BEEN DOING IT FOR HI...
KLTTR
!!
TAKAMICHI?!
GRAB
!
UNBUTTON
UNBUTTON

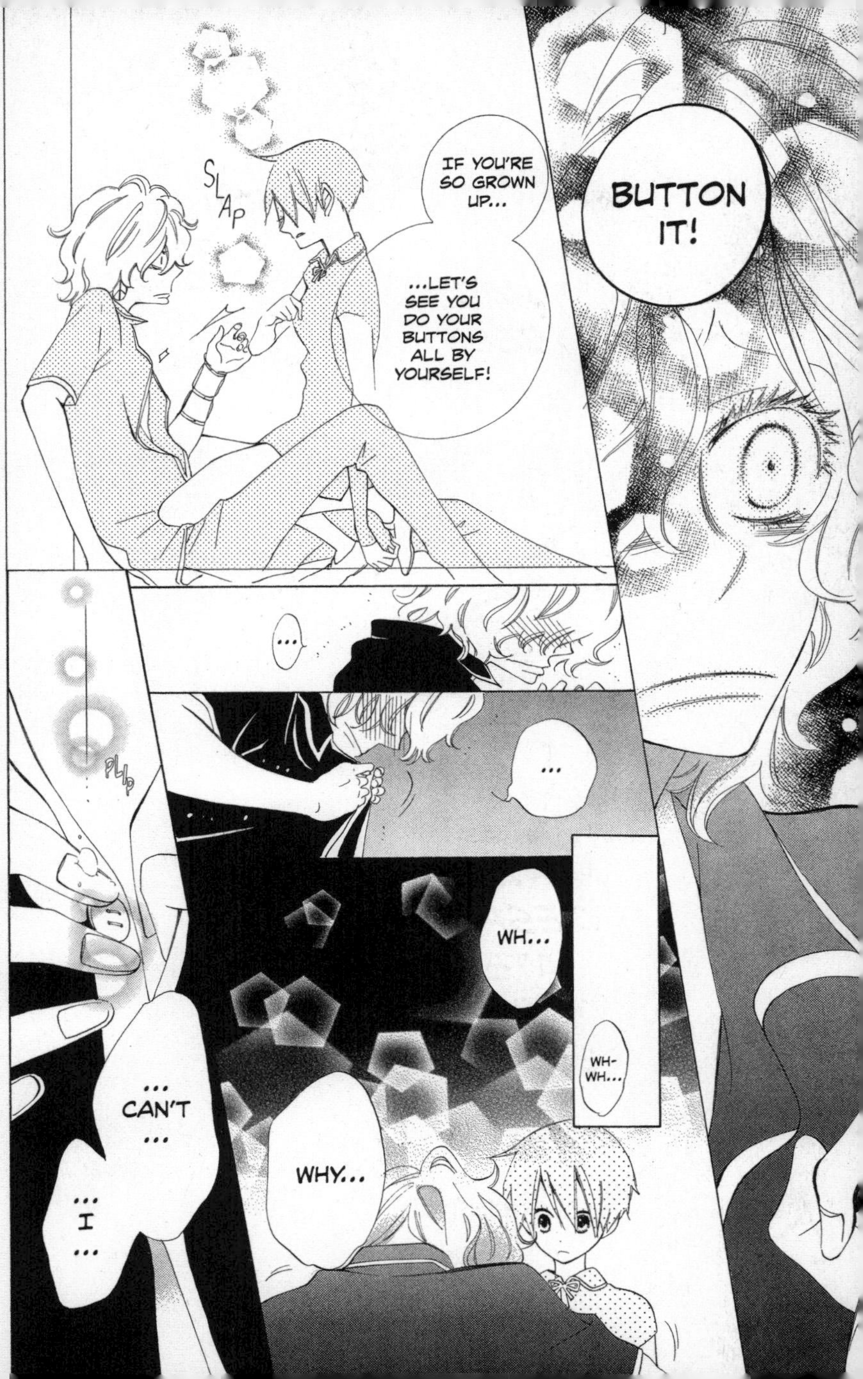
BUTTON IT!
IF YOU'RE SO GROWN UP...
...LET'S SEE YOU DO YOUR BUTTONS ALL BY YOURSELF!
SLAP
...
...
PLIP
WH...
WH-WH...
WHY...
... CAN'T ...
... I ...

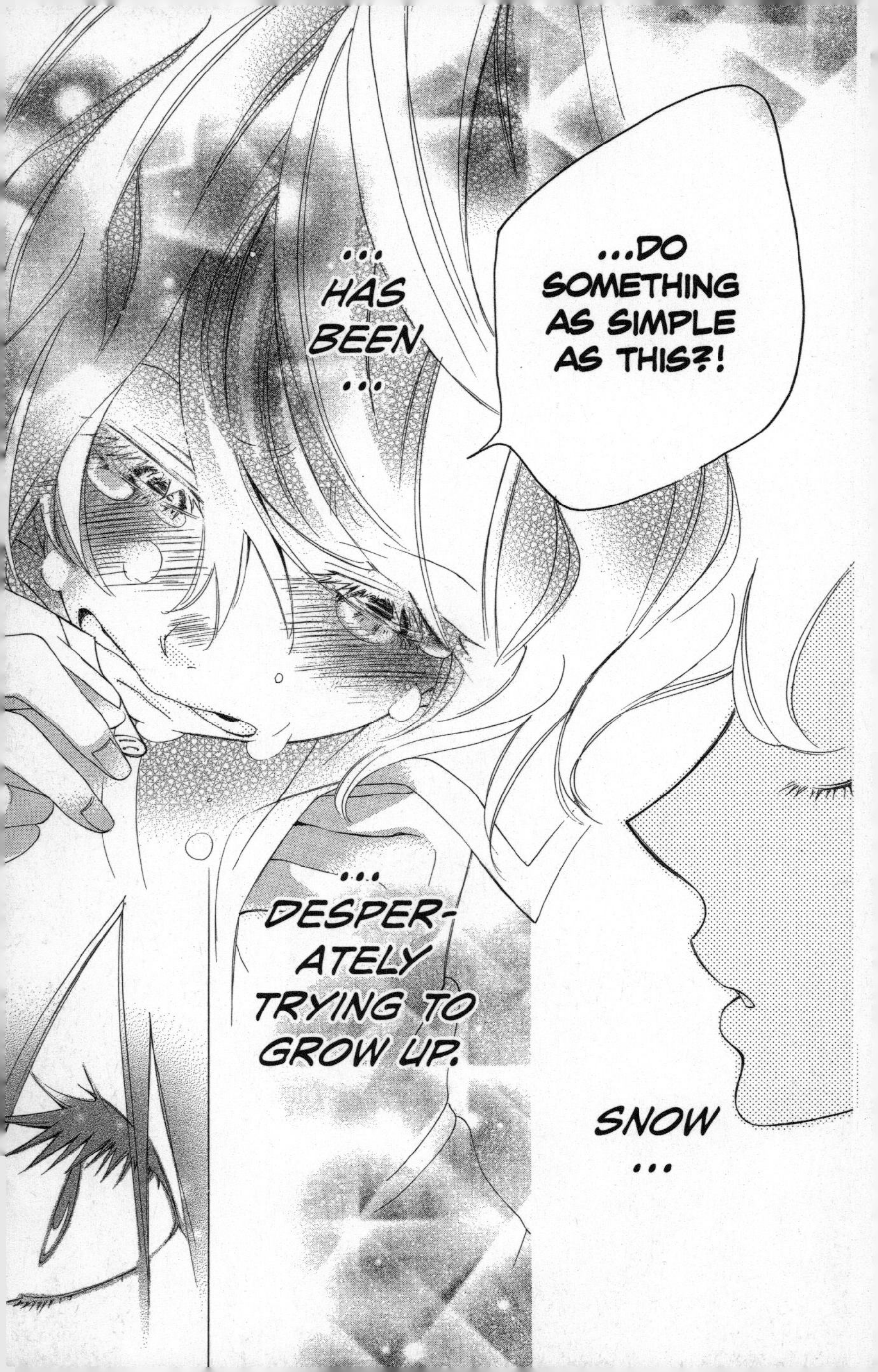
...DO SOMETHING AS SIMPLE AS THIS?!
... HAS BEEN ...
SNOW ...
... DESPER-ATELY TRYING TO GROW UP.

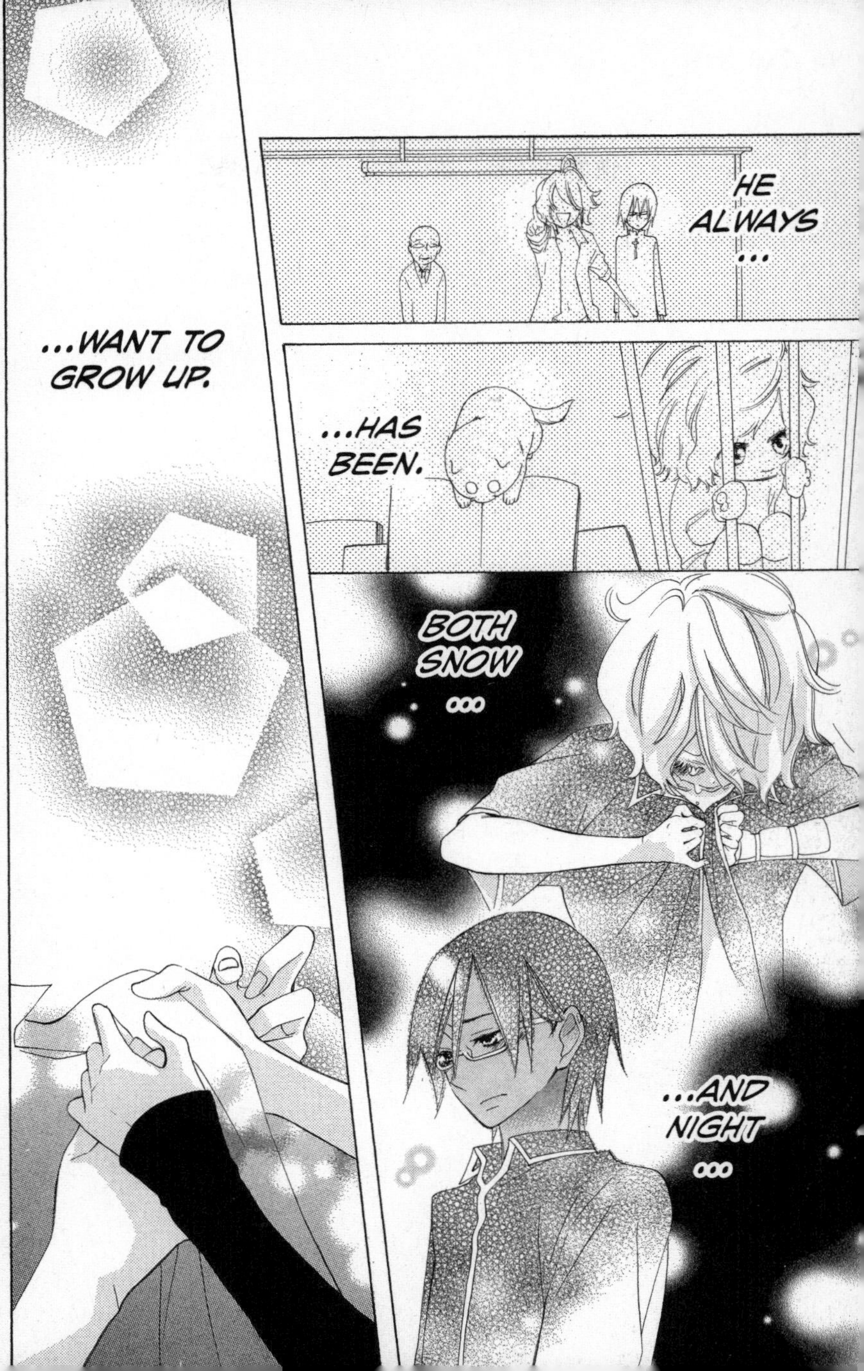
HE ALWAYS...
...HAS BEEN.
BOTH SNOW...
...AND NIGHT...
...WANT TO GROW UP.

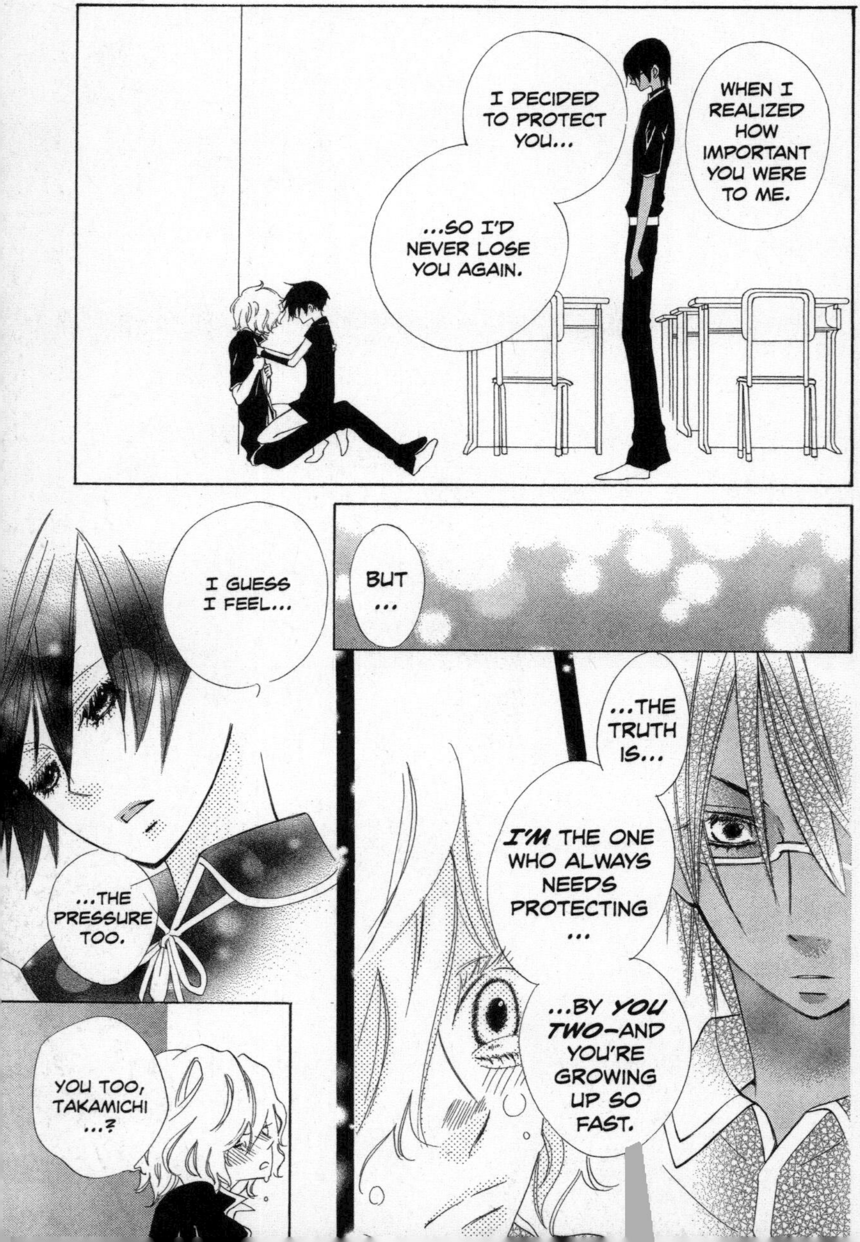
WHEN I REALIZED HOW IMPORTANT YOU WERE TO ME.
I DECIDED TO PROTECT YOU...
...SO I'D NEVER LOSE YOU AGAIN.
BUT ...
I GUESS I FEEL...
...THE PRESSURE TOO.
YOU TOO, TAKAMICHI ...?
...THE TRUTH IS...
I'M THE ONE WHO ALWAYS NEEDS PROTECTING ...
...BY YOU TWO—AND YOU'RE GROWING UP SO FAST.

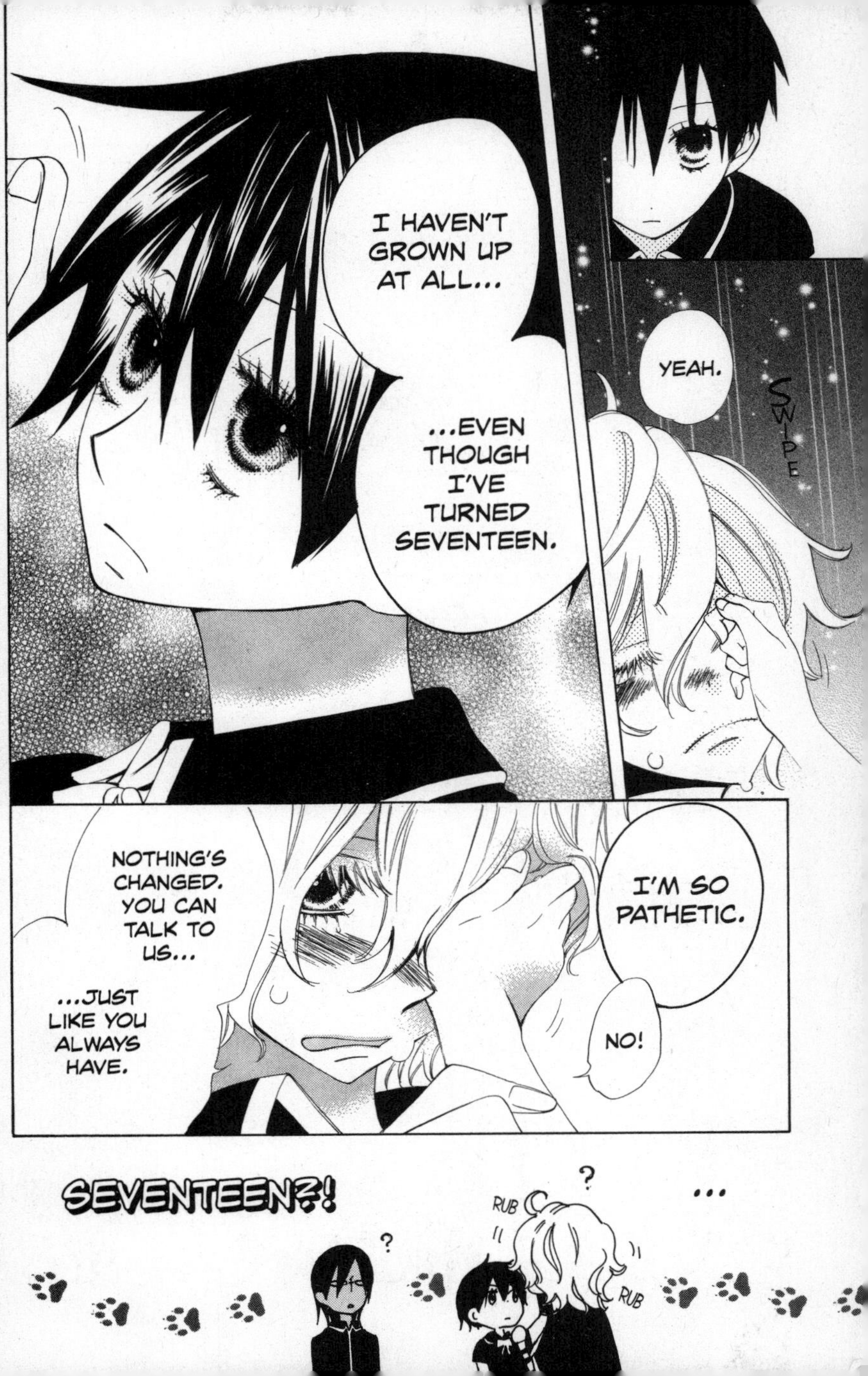
YEAH.
SWIPE
I HAVEN'T GROWN UP AT ALL...
...EVEN THOUGH I'VE TURNED SEVENTEEN.
I'M SO PATHETIC.
NO!
NOTHING'S CHANGED. YOU CAN TALK TO US...
...JUST LIKE YOU ALWAYS HAVE.
...
?
RUB
RUB
?
SEVENTEEN?!

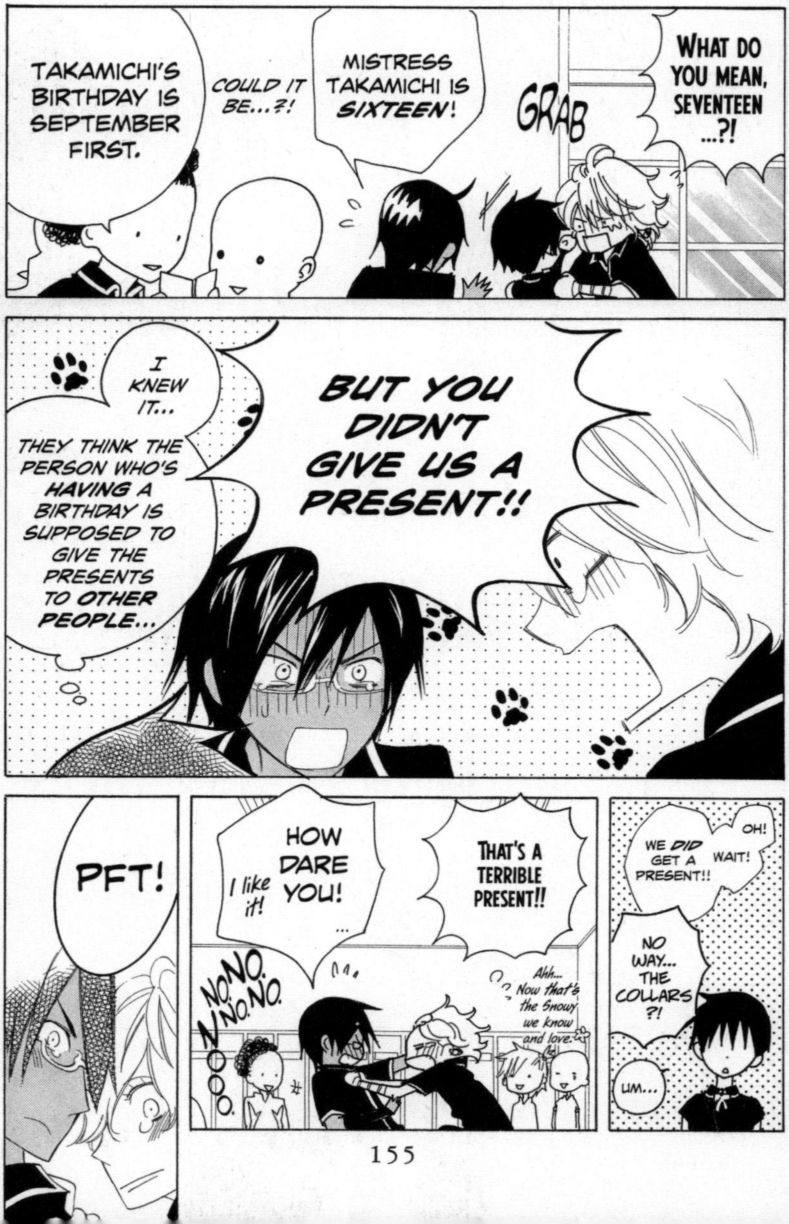
WHAT DO YOU MEAN, SEVENTEEN ...?!
GRAB
MISTRESS TAKAMICHI IS SIXTEEN!
COULD IT BE...?!
TAKAMICHI'S BIRTHDAY IS SEPTEMBER FIRST.
BUT YOU DIDN'T GIVE US A PRESENT!!
I KNEW IT...
THEY THINK THE PERSON WHO'S HAVING A BIRTHDAY IS SUPPOSED TO GIVE THE PRESENTS TO OTHER PEOPLE...
OH! WAIT!
WE DID GET A PRESENT!!
NO WAY... THE COLLARS?!
UM...
THAT'S A TERRIBLE PRESENT!!
HOW DARE YOU! I like it! ...
NO.NO. NO.NO. NOOOO.
Ahh... Now that's the Snowy we know and love.
PFT!

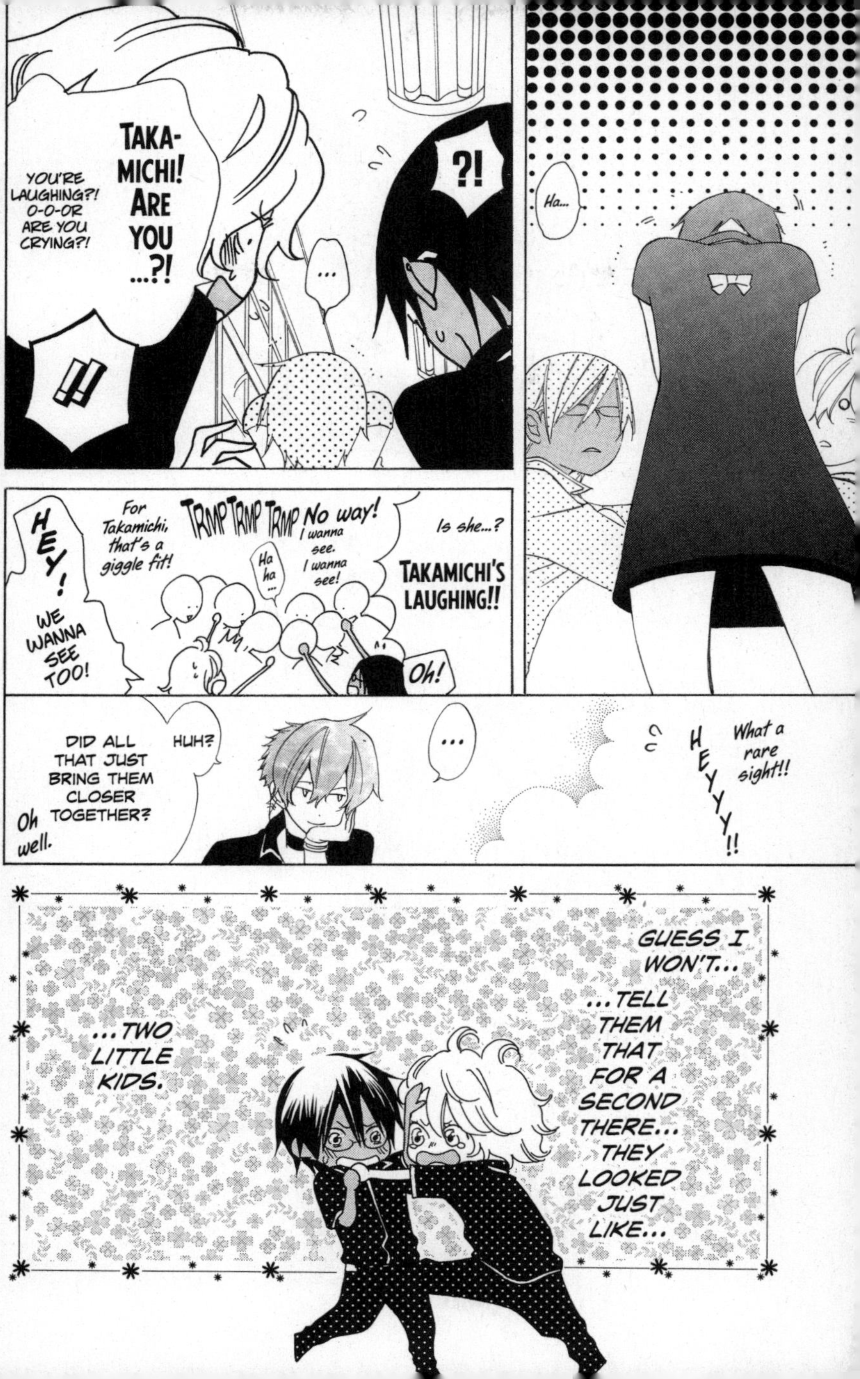
Ha...
?!
...
TAKA-MICHI! ARE YOU ...?!
YOU'RE LAUGHING?! O-O-OR ARE YOU CRYING?!
!!
Is she...?
TAKAMICHI'S LAUGHING!!
No way! I wanna see. I wanna see!
Ha ha ...
Oh!
TRMP TRMP TRMP
For Takamichi, that's a giggle fit!
HEY! WE WANNA SEE TOO!
What a rare sight!!
HEYYY!!
...
HUH?
DID ALL THAT JUST BRING THEM CLOSER TOGETHER?
Oh well.
GUESS I WON'T...
...TELL THEM THAT FOR A SECOND THERE... THEY LOOKED JUST LIKE...
...TWO LITTLE KIDS.

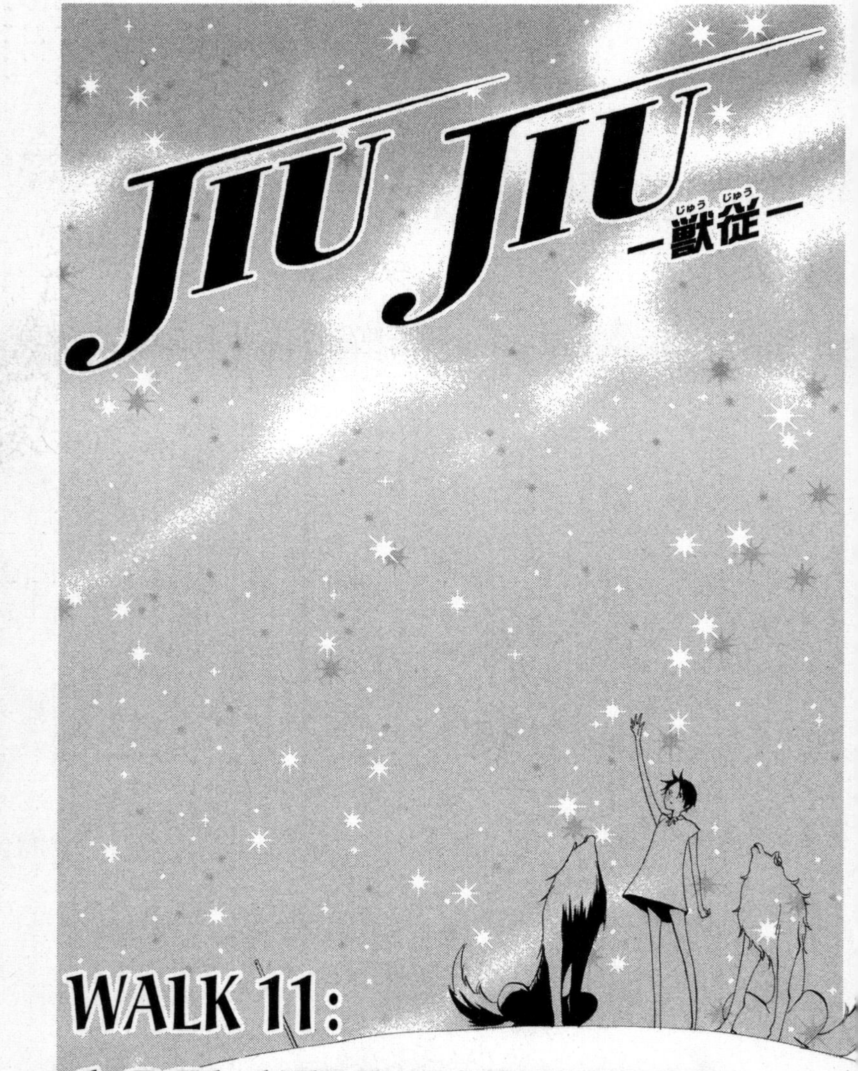
JIU JIU
じゅう じゅう
—獣従—
WALK 11:
A BELATED BIRTHDAY

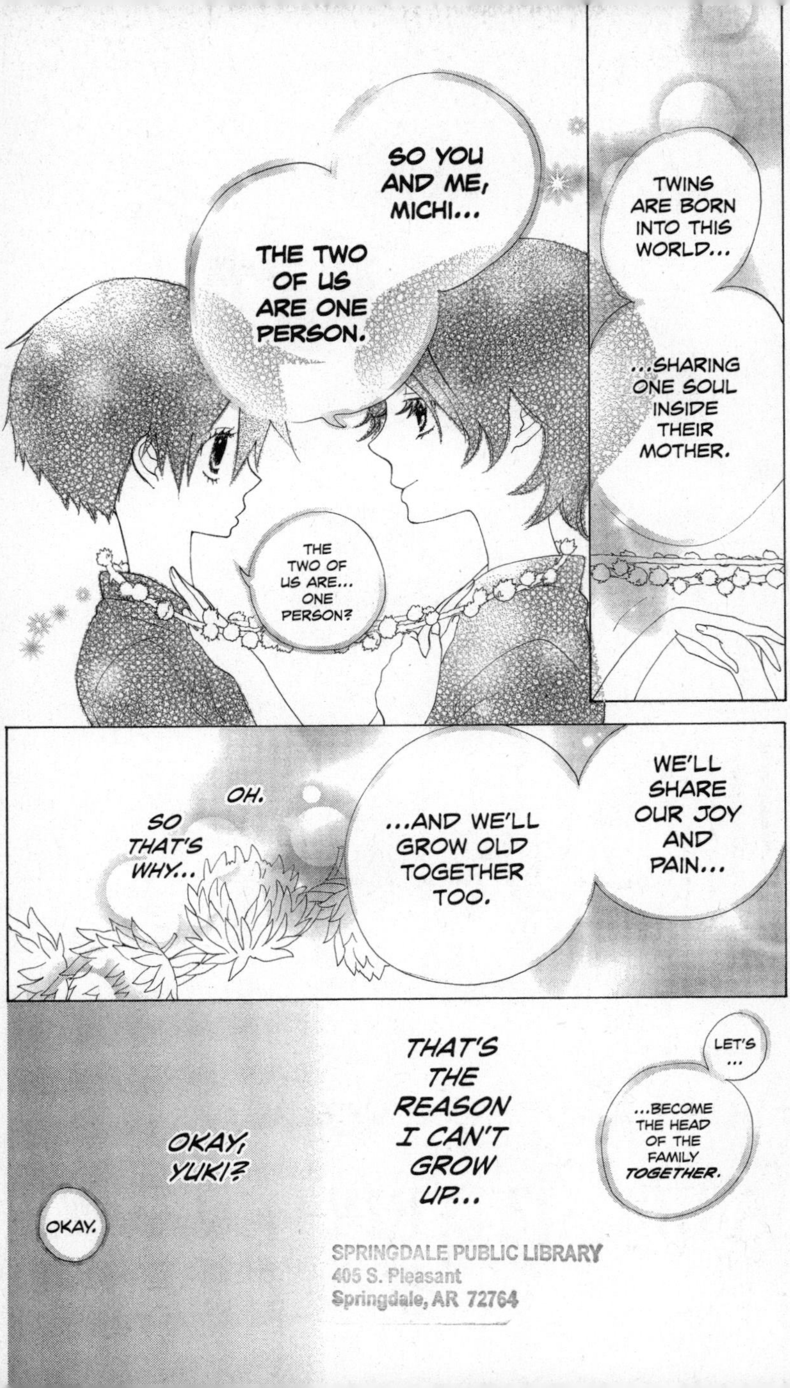
TWINS ARE BORN INTO THIS WORLD...
...SHARING ONE SOUL INSIDE THEIR MOTHER.
SO YOU AND ME, MICHI...
THE TWO OF US ARE ONE PERSON.
THE TWO OF US ARE... ONE PERSON?
WE'LL SHARE OUR JOY AND PAIN...
...AND WE'LL GROW OLD TOGETHER TOO.
OH.
SO THAT'S WHY...
LET'S...
...BECOME THE HEAD OF THE FAMILY TOGETHER.
THAT'S THE REASON I CAN'T GROW UP...
OKAY, YUKI?
OKAY.

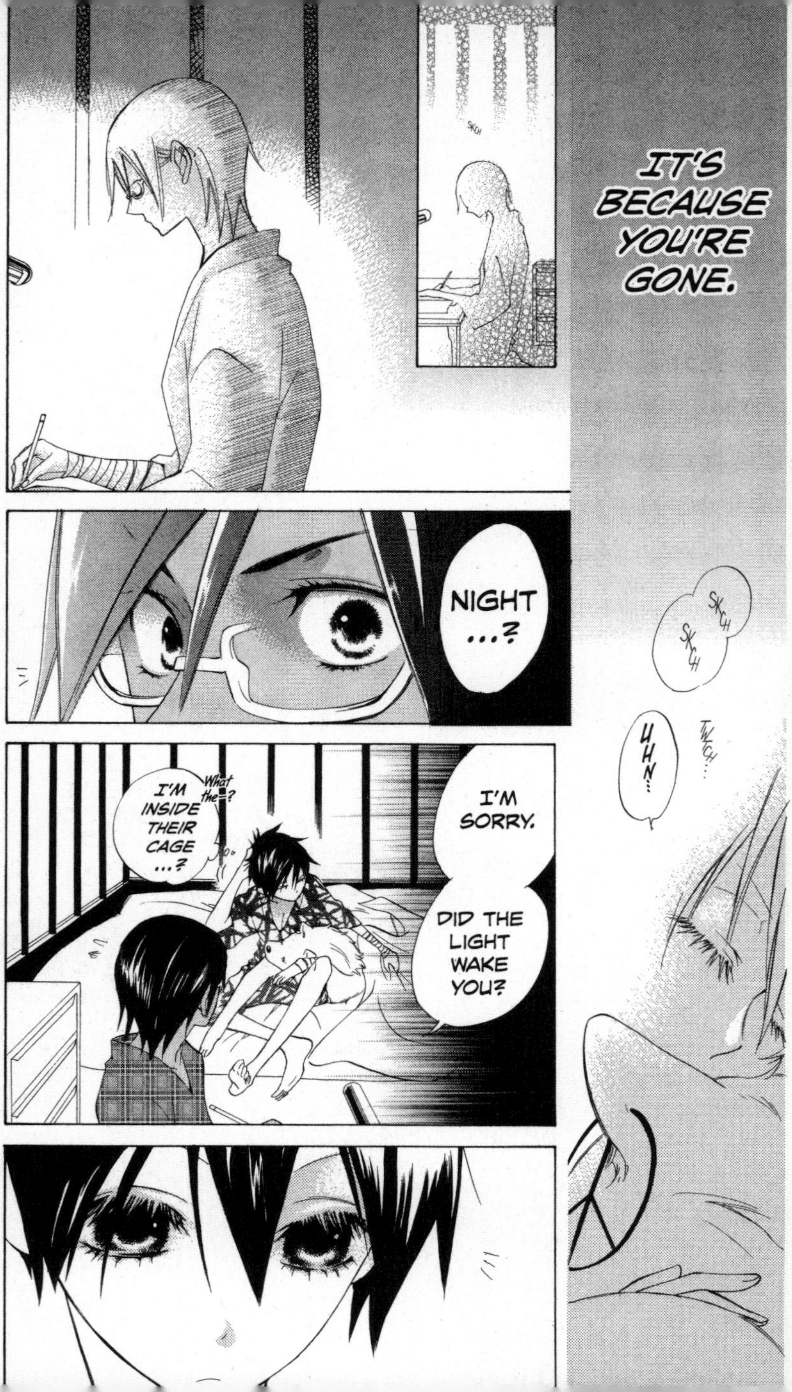
IT'S BECAUSE YOU'RE GONE.
SKCH
SKCH
UHN...
TWITCH...
SKCH
NIGHT ...?
I'M SORRY.
DID THE LIGHT WAKE YOU?
What the—?
I'M INSIDE THEIR CAGE ...?

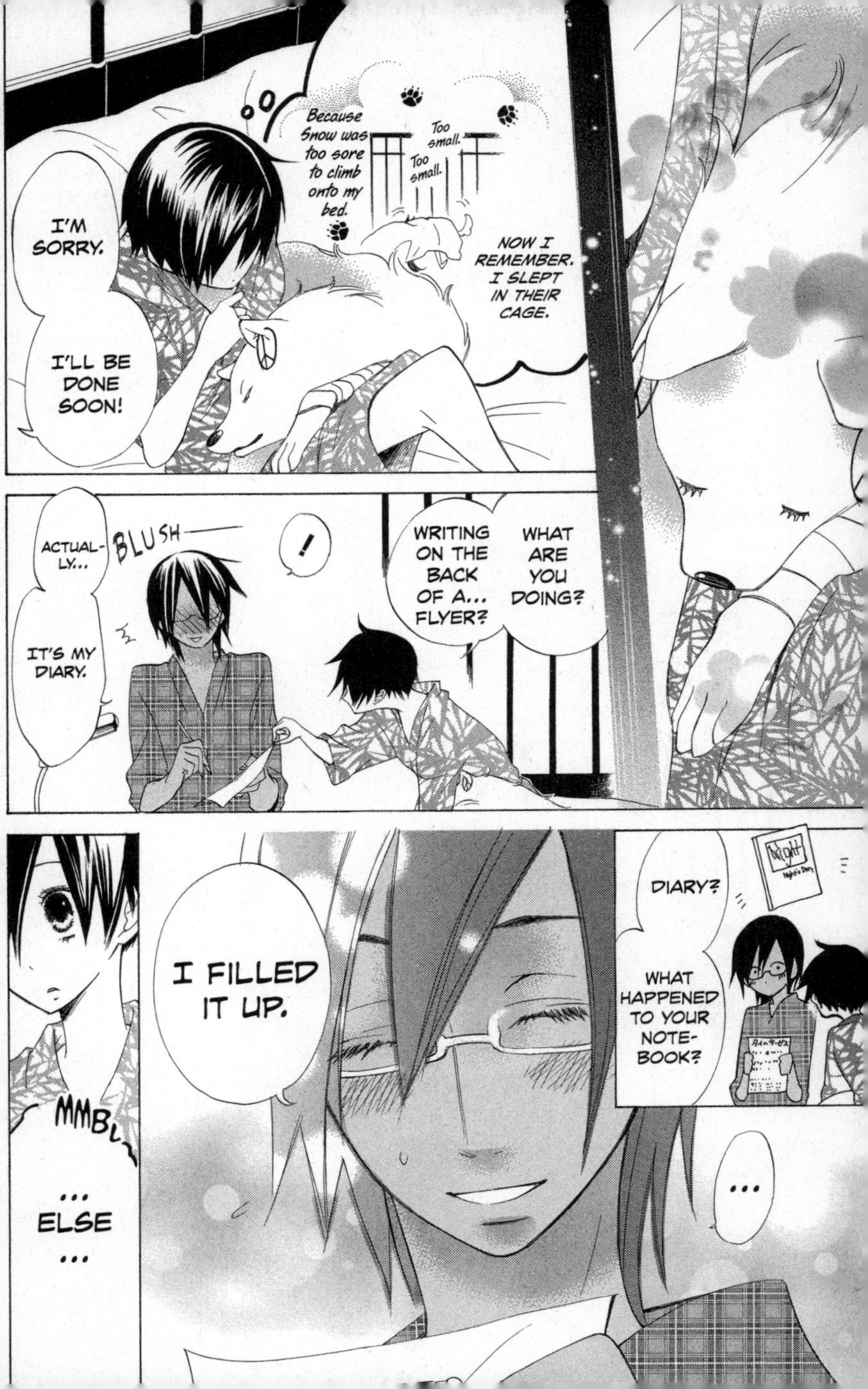
NOW I REMEMBER. I SLEPT IN THEIR CAGE.
Because Snow was too sore to climb onto my bed.
Too small.
Too small.
I'M SORRY.
I'LL BE DONE SOON!
WHAT ARE YOU DOING?
WRITING ON THE BACK OF A... FLYER?
!
BLUSH
ACTUAL-LY...
IT'S MY DIARY.
DIARY?
WHAT HAPPENED TO YOUR NOTE-BOOK?
...
I FILLED IT UP.
MMBL
... ELSE ...

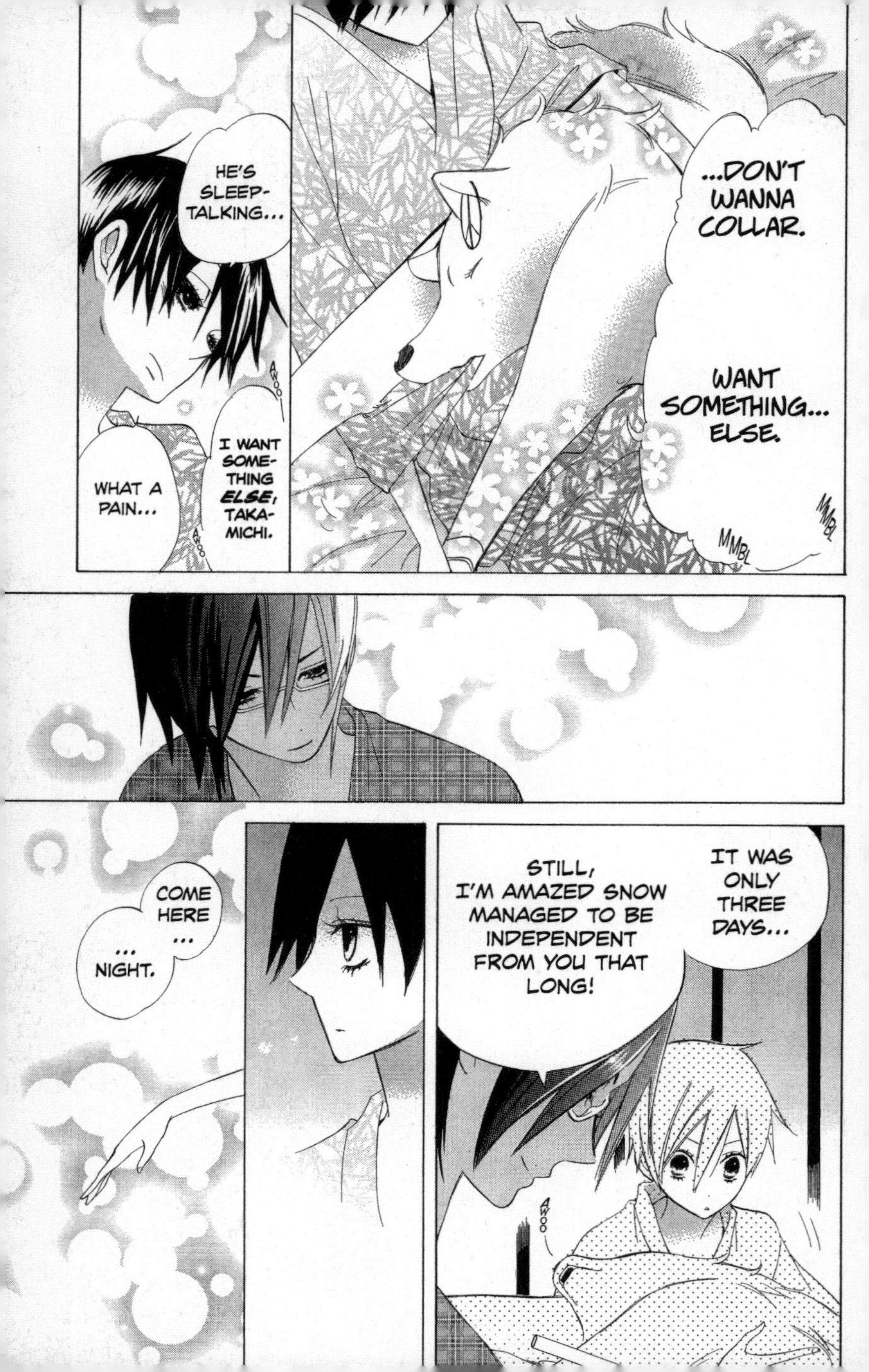
...DON'T WANNA COLLAR.
WANT SOMETHING... ELSE.
MMBL
MMBL
HE'S SLEEP-TALKING...
I WANT SOMETHING *ELSE*, TAKAMICHI.
AWOO
AWOO
WHAT A PAIN...
IT WAS ONLY THREE DAYS...
STILL, I'M AMAZED SNOW MANAGED TO BE INDEPENDENT FROM YOU THAT LONG!
AWOO
COME HERE ... ... NIGHT.

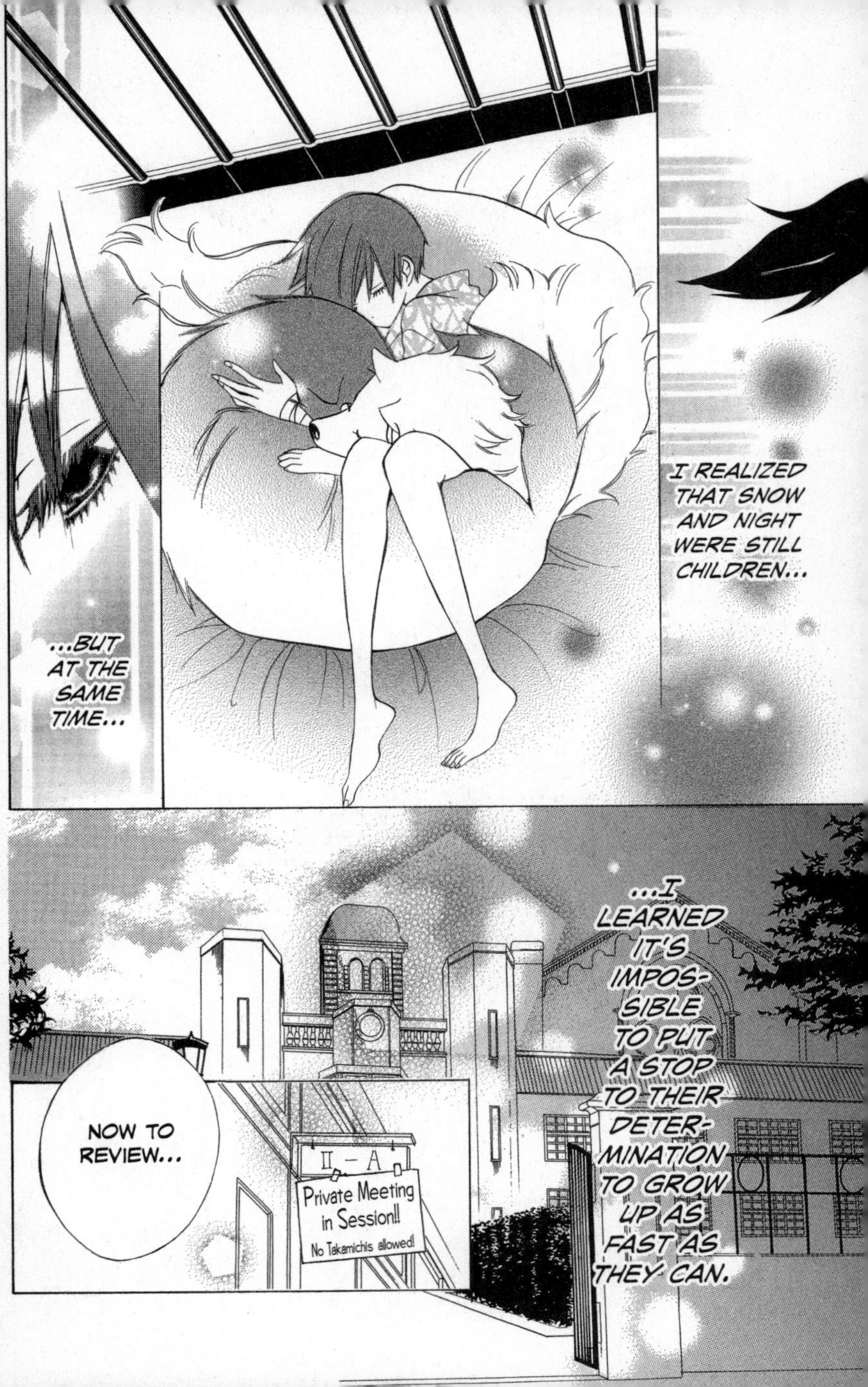
I REALIZED THAT SNOW AND NIGHT WERE STILL CHILDREN...
...BUT AT THE SAME TIME...
...I LEARNED IT'S IMPOSSIBLE TO PUT A STOP TO THEIR DETERMINATION TO GROW UP AS FAST AS THEY CAN.
II-A
Private Meeting in Session!!
No Takamichis allowed!
NOW TO REVIEW...

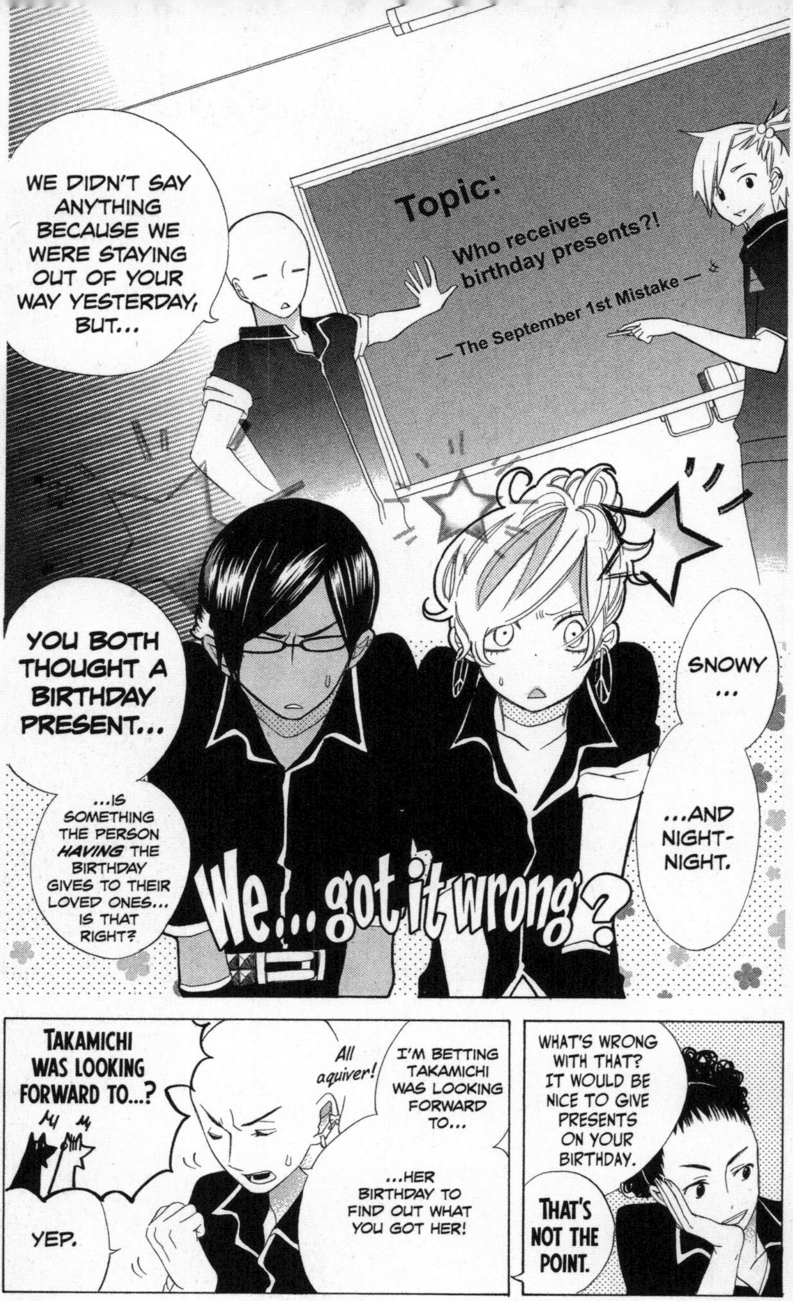
Topic:
Who receives birthday presents?!
— The September 1st Mistake —
WE DIDN'T SAY ANYTHING BECAUSE WE WERE STAYING OUT OF YOUR WAY YESTERDAY, BUT...
YOU BOTH THOUGHT A BIRTHDAY PRESENT...
...IS SOMETHING THE PERSON *HAVING* THE BIRTHDAY GIVES TO THEIR LOVED ONES... IS THAT RIGHT?
SNOWY ...
...AND NIGHT-NIGHT.
We... got it wrong?
WHAT'S WRONG WITH THAT? IT WOULD BE NICE TO GIVE PRESENTS ON YOUR BIRTHDAY.
THAT'S NOT THE POINT.
I'M BETTING TAKAMICHI WAS LOOKING FORWARD TO...
All aquiver!
...HER BIRTHDAY TO FIND OUT WHAT YOU GOT HER!
TAKAMICHI WAS LOOKING FORWARD TO...?
YEP.

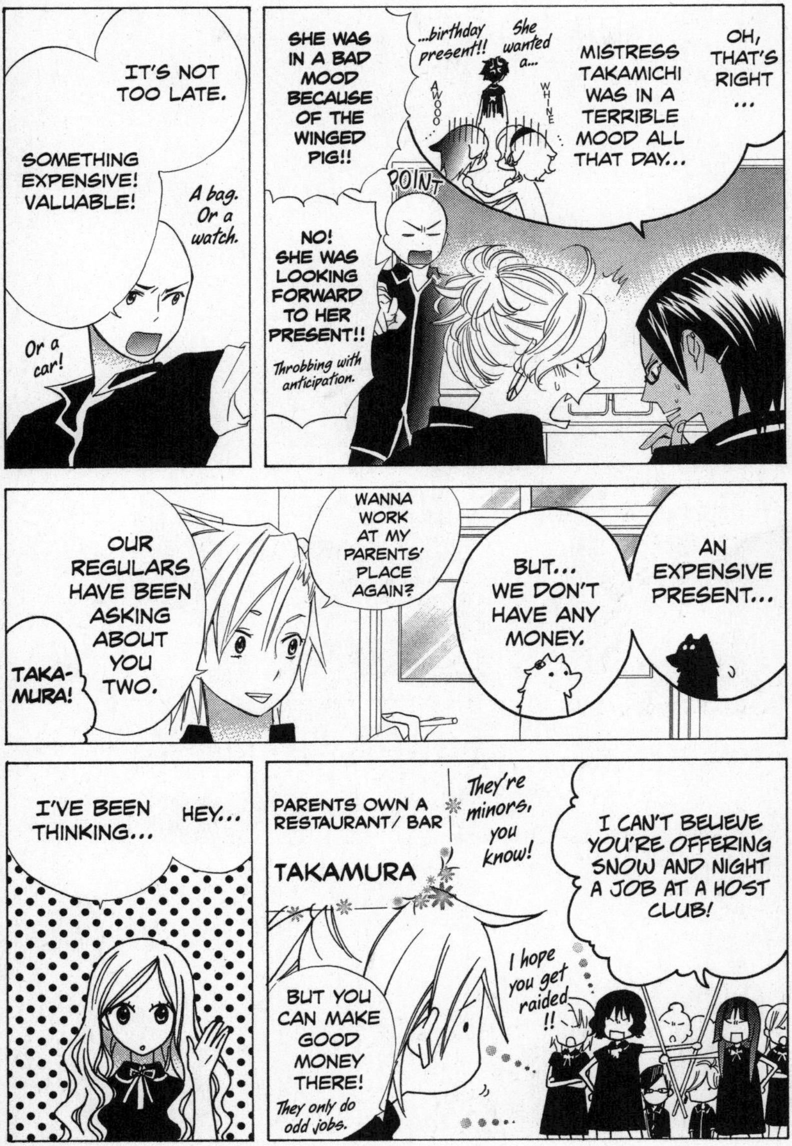
OH, THAT'S RIGHT ...
MISTRESS TAKAMICHI WAS IN A TERRIBLE MOOD ALL THAT DAY...
She wanted a...
...birthday present!!
AWOOO
WHINE
SHE WAS IN A BAD MOOD BECAUSE OF THE WINGED PIG!!
POINT
NO! SHE WAS LOOKING FORWARD TO HER PRESENT!!
Throbbing with anticipation.
IT'S NOT TOO LATE.
SOMETHING EXPENSIVE! VALUABLE!
A bag. Or a watch.
Or a car!
AN EXPENSIVE PRESENT...
BUT... WE DON'T HAVE ANY MONEY.
WANNA WORK AT MY PARENTS' PLACE AGAIN?
OUR REGULARS HAVE BEEN ASKING ABOUT YOU TWO.
TAKAMURA!
I CAN'T BELIEVE YOU'RE OFFERING SNOW AND NIGHT A JOB AT A HOST CLUB!
They're minors, you know!
PARENTS OWN A RESTAURANT/ BAR
TAKAMURA
I hope you get raided!!
BUT YOU CAN MAKE GOOD MONEY THERE!
They only do odd jobs.
HEY...
I'VE BEEN THINKING...

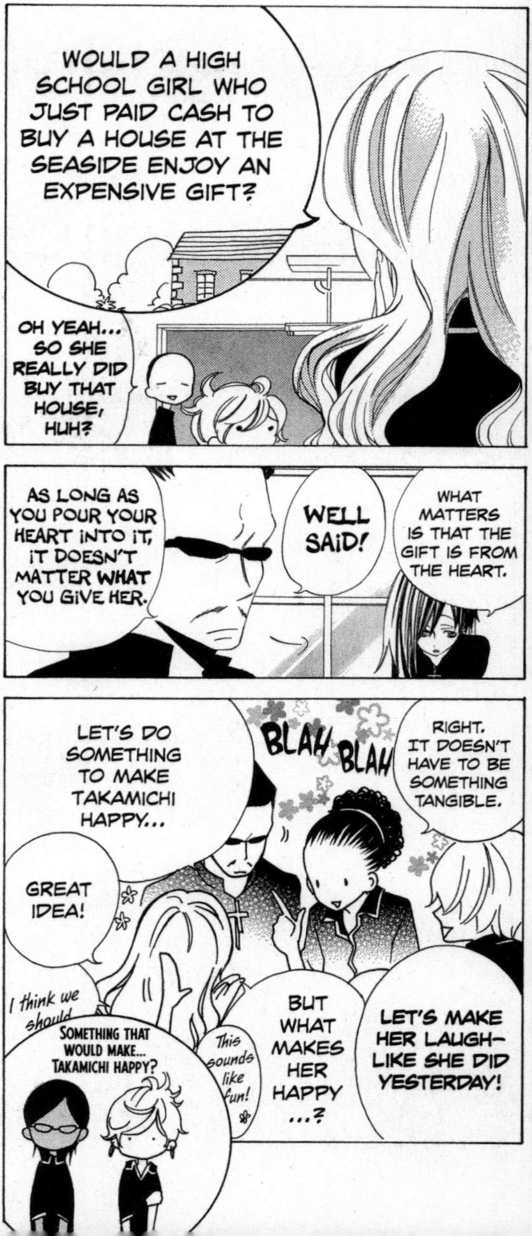
WOULD A HIGH SCHOOL GIRL WHO JUST PAID CASH TO BUY A HOUSE AT THE SEASIDE ENJOY AN EXPENSIVE GIFT?
OH YEAH... SO SHE REALLY DID BUY THAT HOUSE, HUH?
WHAT MATTERS IS THAT THE GIFT IS FROM THE HEART.
WELL SAID!
AS LONG AS YOU POUR YOUR HEART INTO IT, IT DOESN'T MATTER WHAT YOU GIVE HER.
RIGHT. IT DOESN'T HAVE TO BE SOMETHING TANGIBLE.
BLAH BLAH
LET'S DO SOMETHING TO MAKE TAKAMICHI HAPPY...
GREAT IDEA!
LET'S MAKE HER LAUGH—LIKE SHE DID YESTERDAY!
BUT WHAT MAKES HER HAPPY ...?
This sounds like fun!
I think we should
SOMETHING THAT WOULD MAKE... TAKAMICHI HAPPY?

Also in vol. 3...

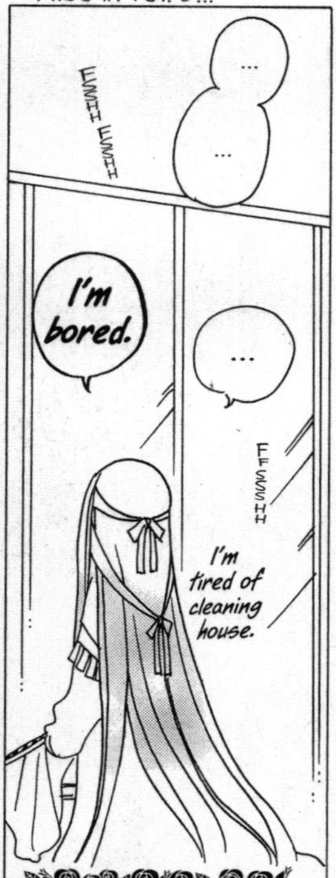
...
...
FSSH FSSH
...
FFSSSH
I'm bored.
I'm tired of cleaning house.

I just want to be loved..♡
So if you wouldn't mind writing love letters to this lonely bewildered soul, please send them to the following address...

**Lily Selkie, c/o Jiu Jiu Fan Mail**
**VIZ Media,**
**P.O. Box 77064**
**San Francisco, CA 94107**

Advance apologies for any delayed replies!!

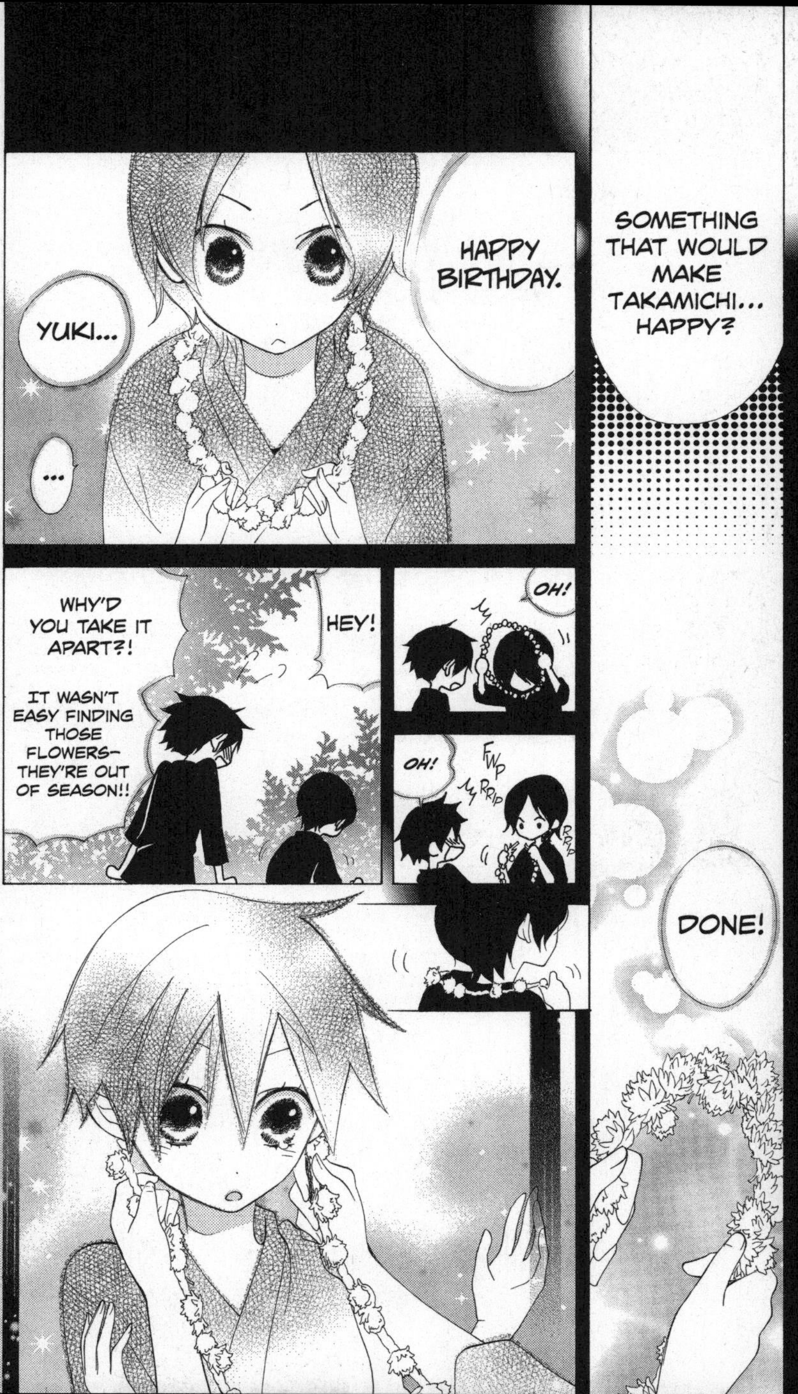
SOMETHING THAT WOULD MAKE TAKAMICHI... HAPPY?
HAPPY BIRTHDAY.
YUKI...
...
OH!
OH!
FWP
RRIP
HEY!
WHY'D YOU TAKE IT APART?!
IT WASN'T EASY FINDING THOSE FLOWERS— THEY'RE OUT OF SEASON!!
DONE!

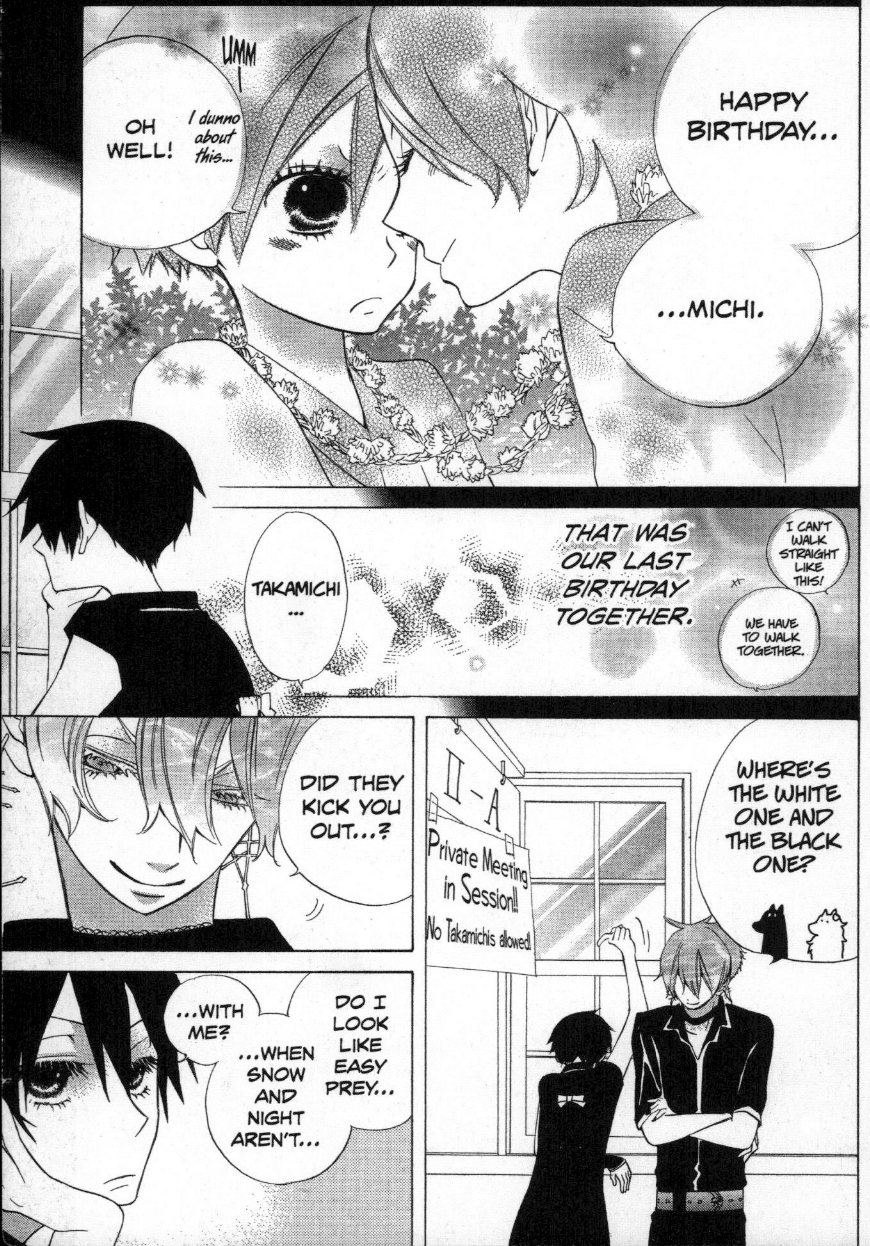
HAPPY BIRTHDAY...
...MICHI.
UMM
I dunno about this...
OH WELL!
I CAN'T WALK STRAIGHT LIKE THIS!
WE HAVE TO WALK TOGETHER.
THAT WAS OUR LAST BIRTHDAY TOGETHER.
TAKAMICHI...
WHERE'S THE WHITE ONE AND THE BLACK ONE?
II-A
Private Meeting in Session!!
No Takamichis allowed!
DID THEY KICK YOU OUT...?
DO I LOOK LIKE EASY PREY...
...WHEN SNOW AND NIGHT AREN'T...
...WITH ME?

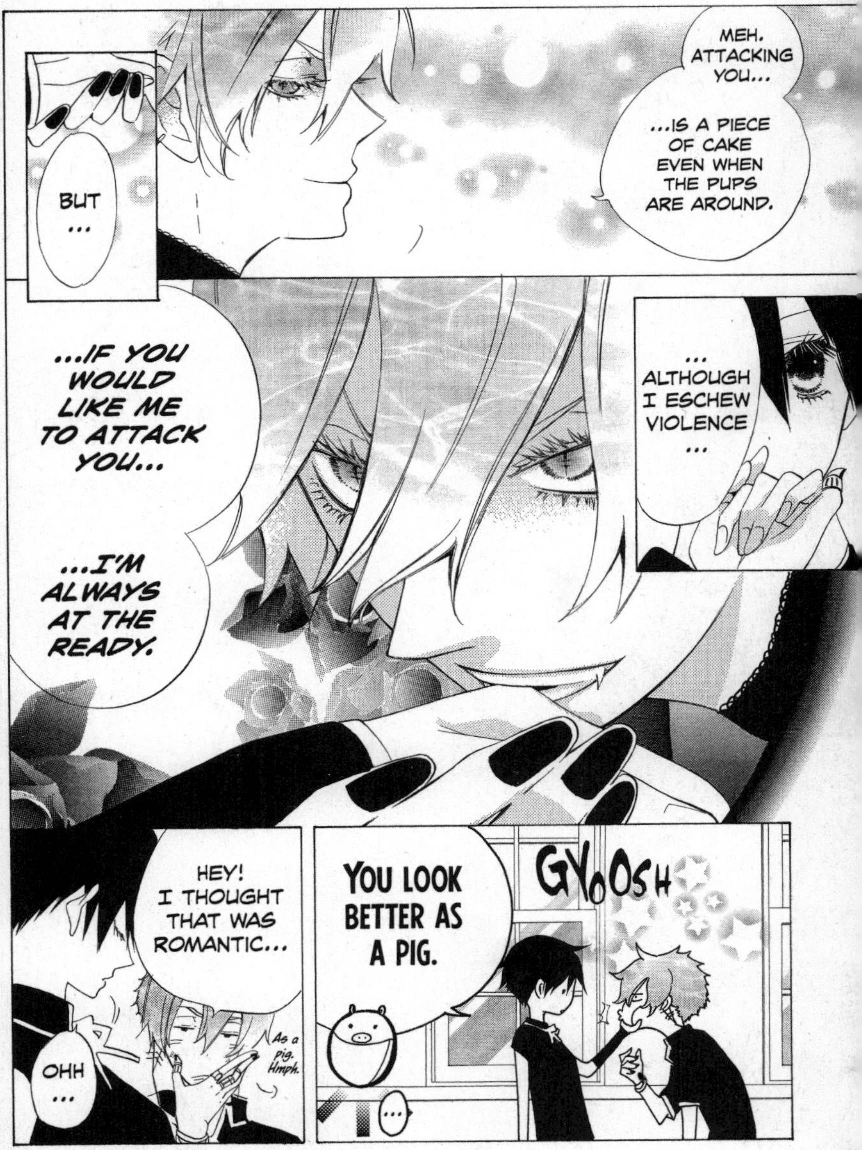
MEH. ATTACKING YOU...
...IS A PIECE OF CAKE EVEN WHEN THE PUPS ARE AROUND.
BUT ...
... ALTHOUGH I ESCHEW VIOLENCE ...
...IF YOU WOULD LIKE ME TO ATTACK YOU...
...I'M ALWAYS AT THE READY.
GYOOSH
YOU LOOK BETTER AS A PIG.
...
HEY! I THOUGHT THAT WAS ROMANTIC...
As a pig. Hmph.
OHH ...

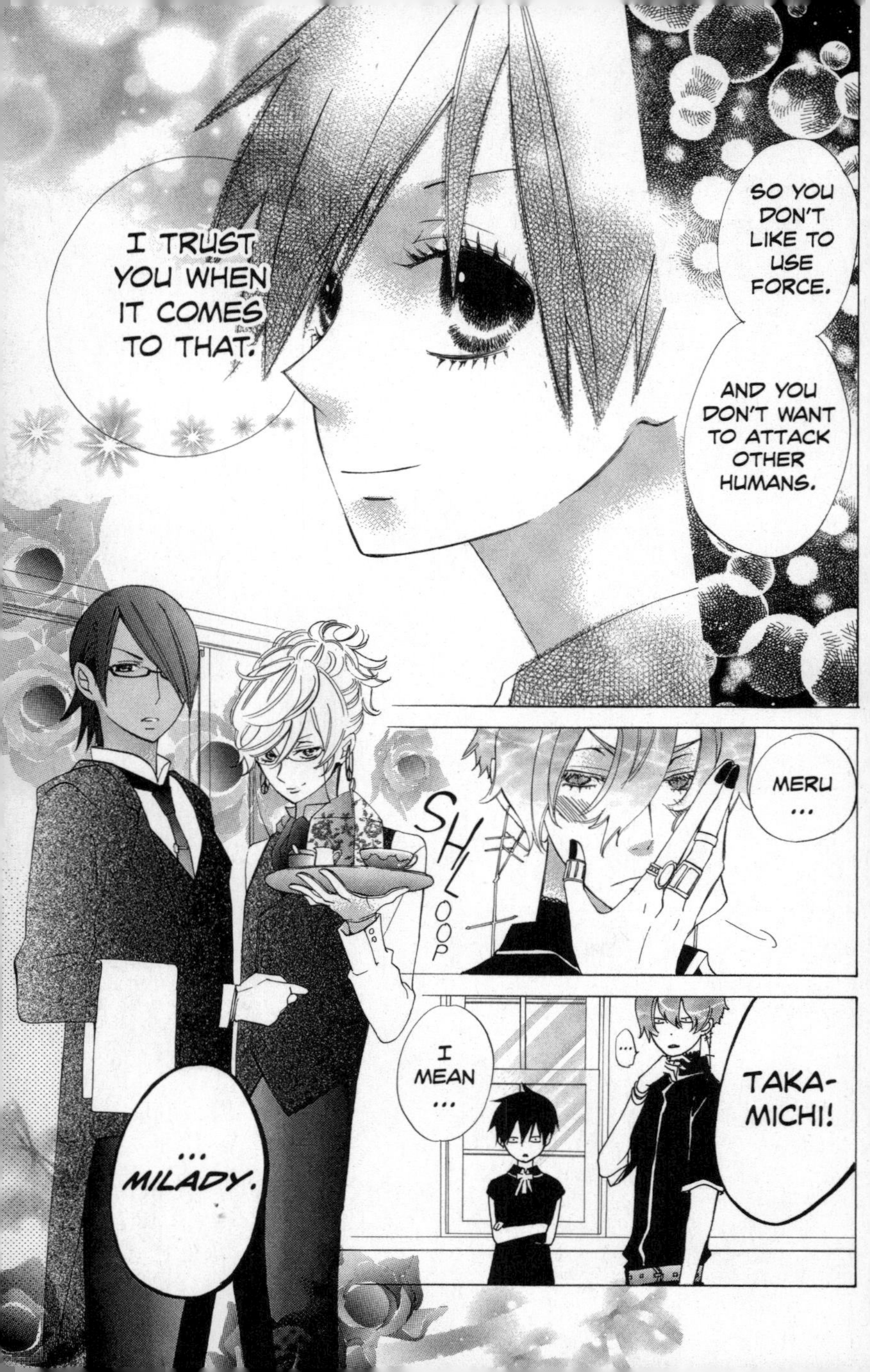
SO YOU DON'T LIKE TO USE FORCE.
AND YOU DON'T WANT TO ATTACK OTHER HUMANS.
I TRUST YOU WHEN IT COMES TO THAT.
MERU ...
SHLOOP
TAKA-MICHI!
...
I MEAN ...
... MILADY.

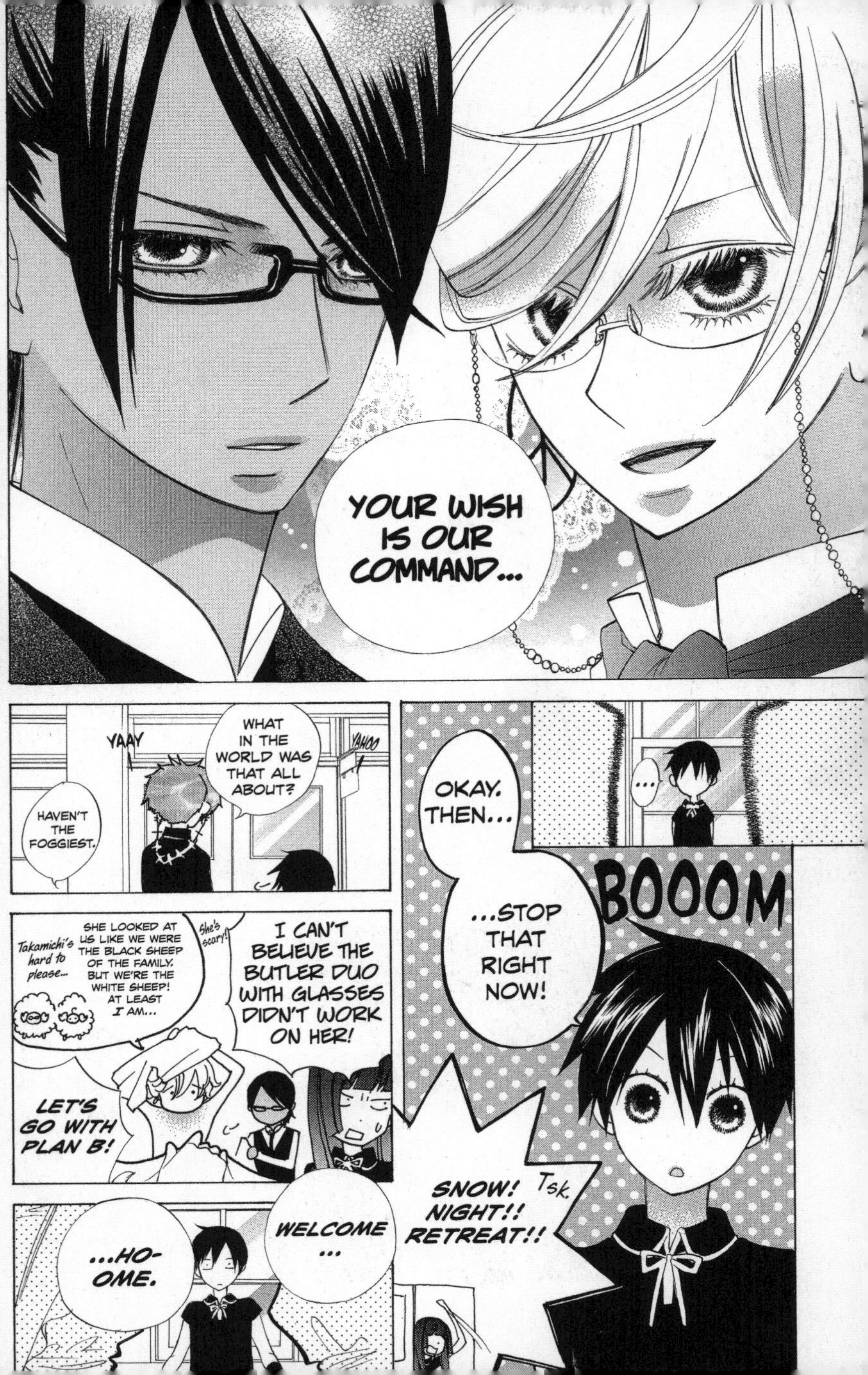
YOUR WISH IS OUR COMMAND...
...
OKAY. THEN...
...STOP THAT RIGHT NOW!
BOOOM
Tsk.
SNOW! NIGHT!! RETREAT!!
YAHOO
WHAT IN THE WORLD WAS THAT ALL ABOUT?
YAAY
HAVEN'T THE FOGGIEST.
I CAN'T BELIEVE THE BUTLER DUO WITH GLASSES DIDN'T WORK ON HER!
She's scary!
SHE LOOKED AT US LIKE WE WERE THE BLACK SHEEP OF THE FAMILY. BUT WE'RE THE WHITE SHEEP! AT LEAST I AM...
Takamichi's hard to please...
LET'S GO WITH PLAN B!
WELCOME...
...HO-OME.

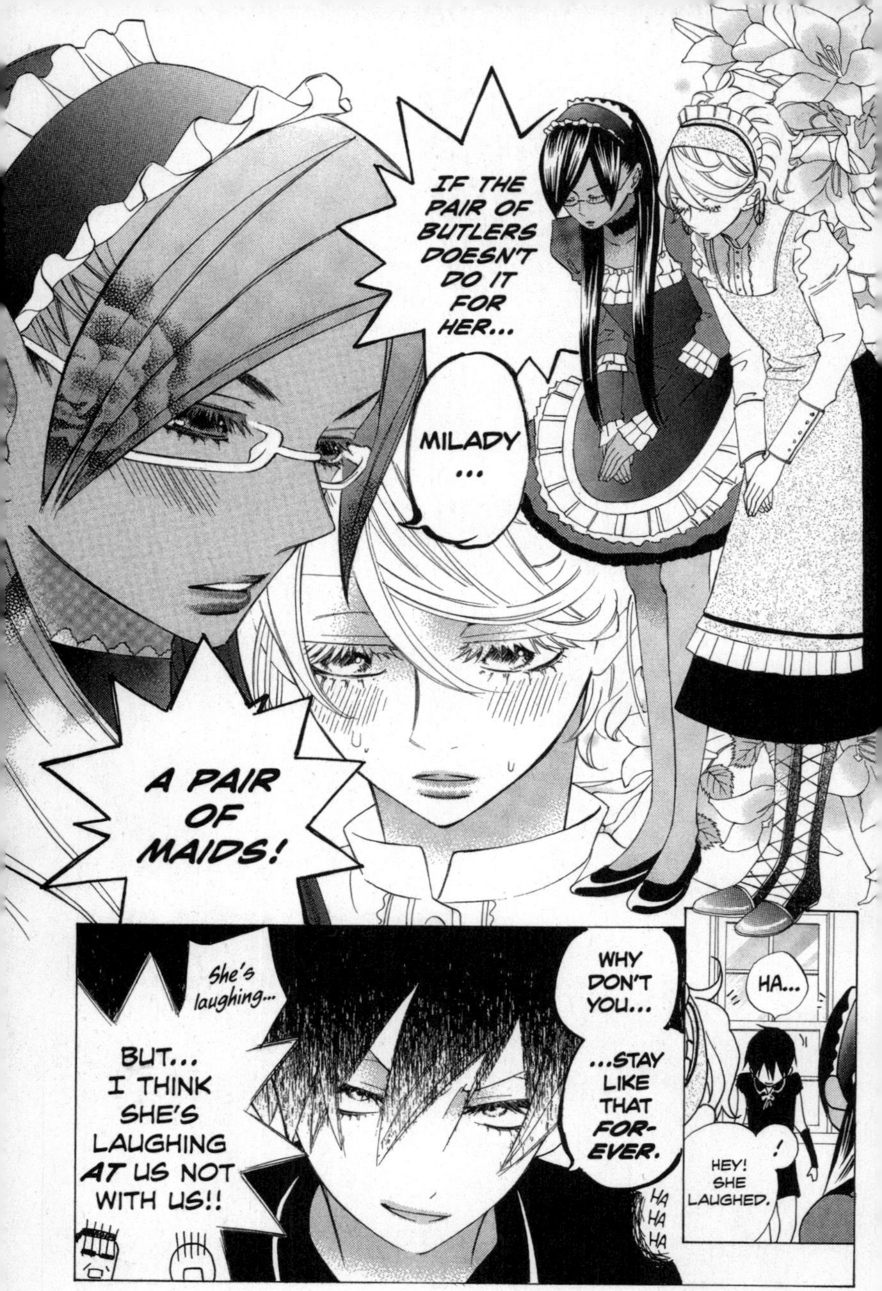
IF THE PAIR OF BUTLERS DOESN'T DO IT FOR HER...
MILADY ...
A PAIR OF MAIDS!
HA...
HEY! SHE LAUGHED.
WHY DON'T YOU...
...STAY LIKE THAT FOR-EVER.
HA HA HA HA
She's laughing...
BUT... I THINK SHE'S LAUGHING AT US NOT WITH US!!

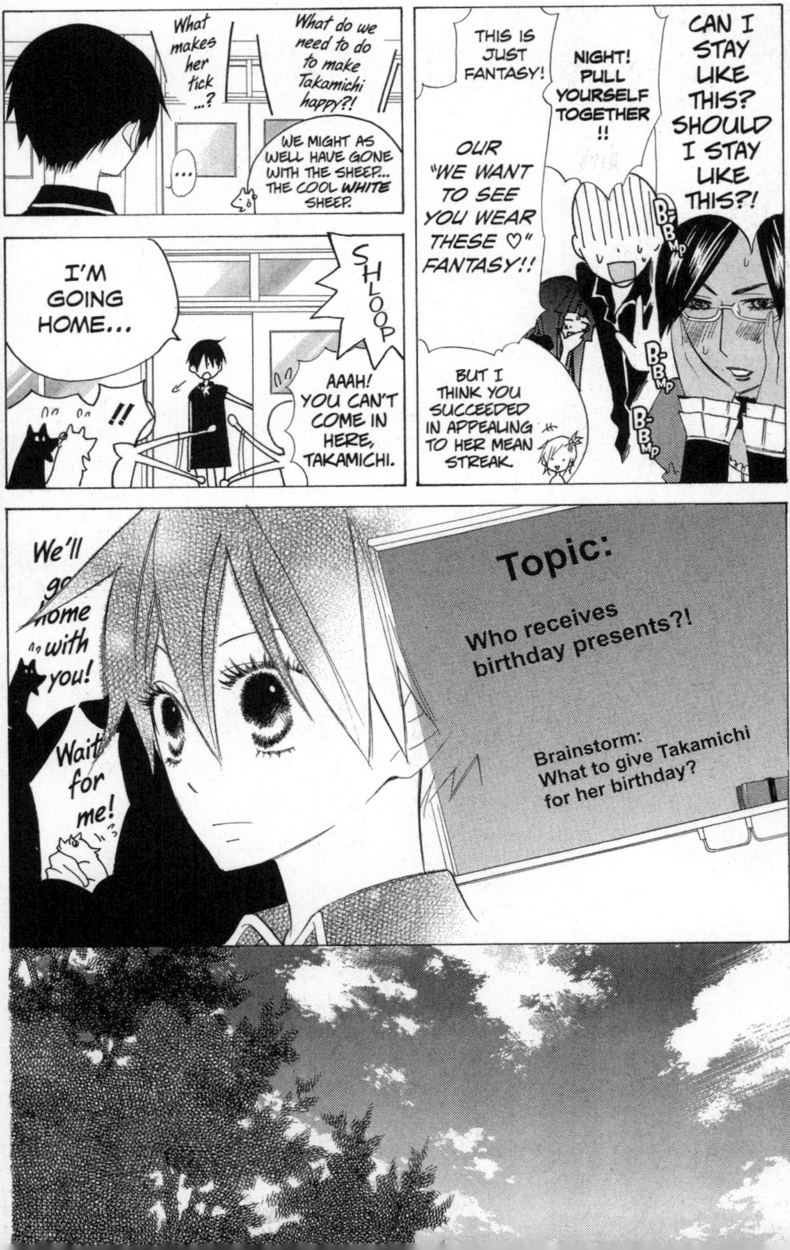
CAN I STAY LIKE THIS? SHOULD I STAY LIKE THIS?!
B-BMP
NIGHT! PULL YOURSELF TOGETHER !!
THIS IS JUST FANTASY!
OUR "WE WANT TO SEE YOU WEAR THESE ♡" FANTASY!!
B-BMP
B-BMP
BUT I THINK YOU SUCCEEDED IN APPEALING TO HER MEAN STREAK.
What do we need to do to make Takamichi happy?!
What makes her tick ...?
WE MIGHT AS WELL HAVE GONE WITH THE SHEEP... THE COOL WHITE SHEEP.
...
SHLOOP
AAAH! YOU CAN'T COME IN HERE, TAKAMICHI.
!!
I'M GOING HOME...
Topic:
Who receives birthday presents?!
Brainstorm:
What to give Takamichi for her birthday?
We'll go home with you!
Wait for me!

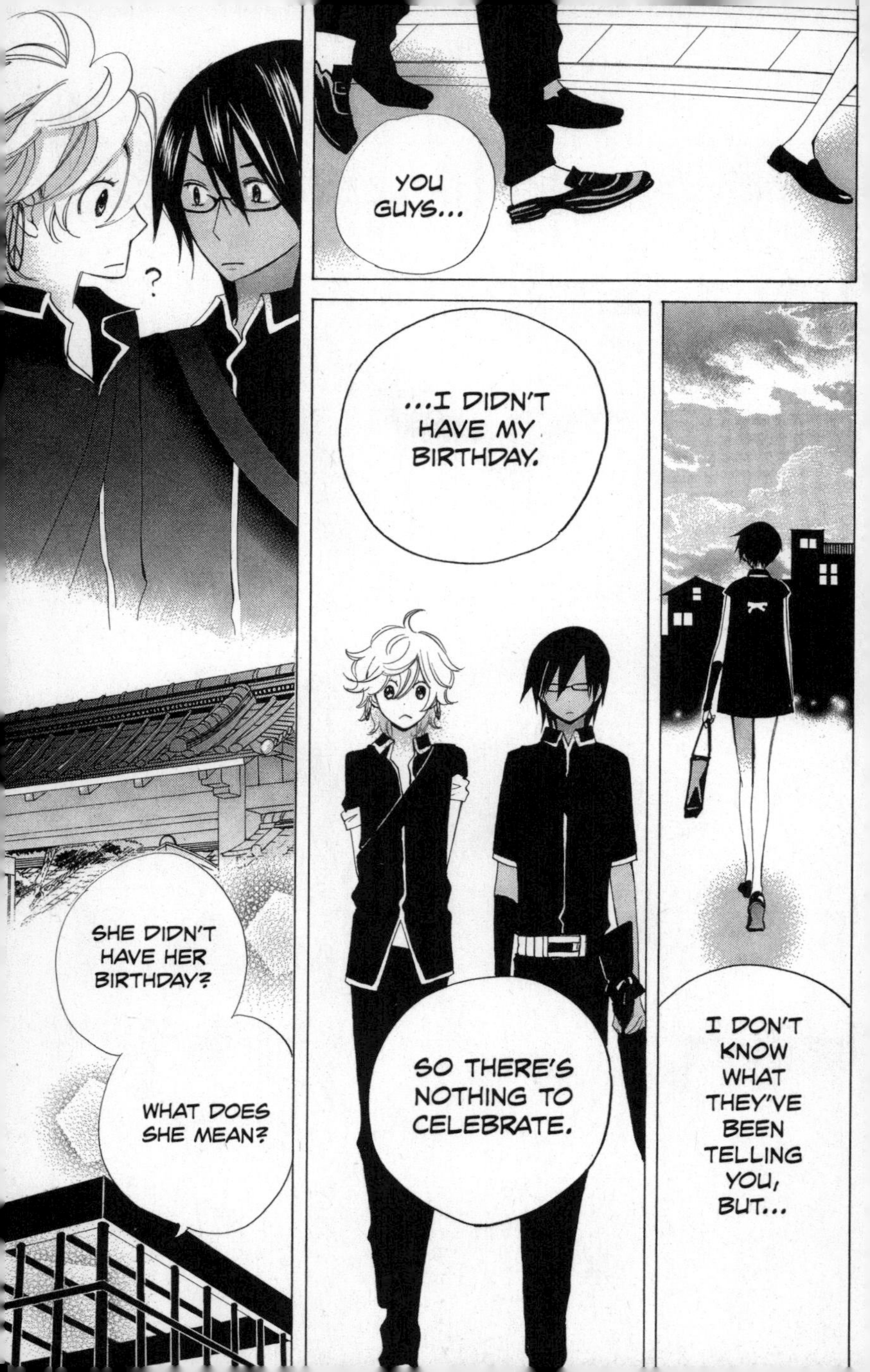
YOU GUYS...
I DON'T KNOW WHAT THEY'VE BEEN TELLING YOU, BUT...
...I DIDN'T HAVE MY BIRTHDAY.
SO THERE'S NOTHING TO CELEBRATE.
?
SHE DIDN'T HAVE HER BIRTHDAY?
WHAT DOES SHE MEAN?

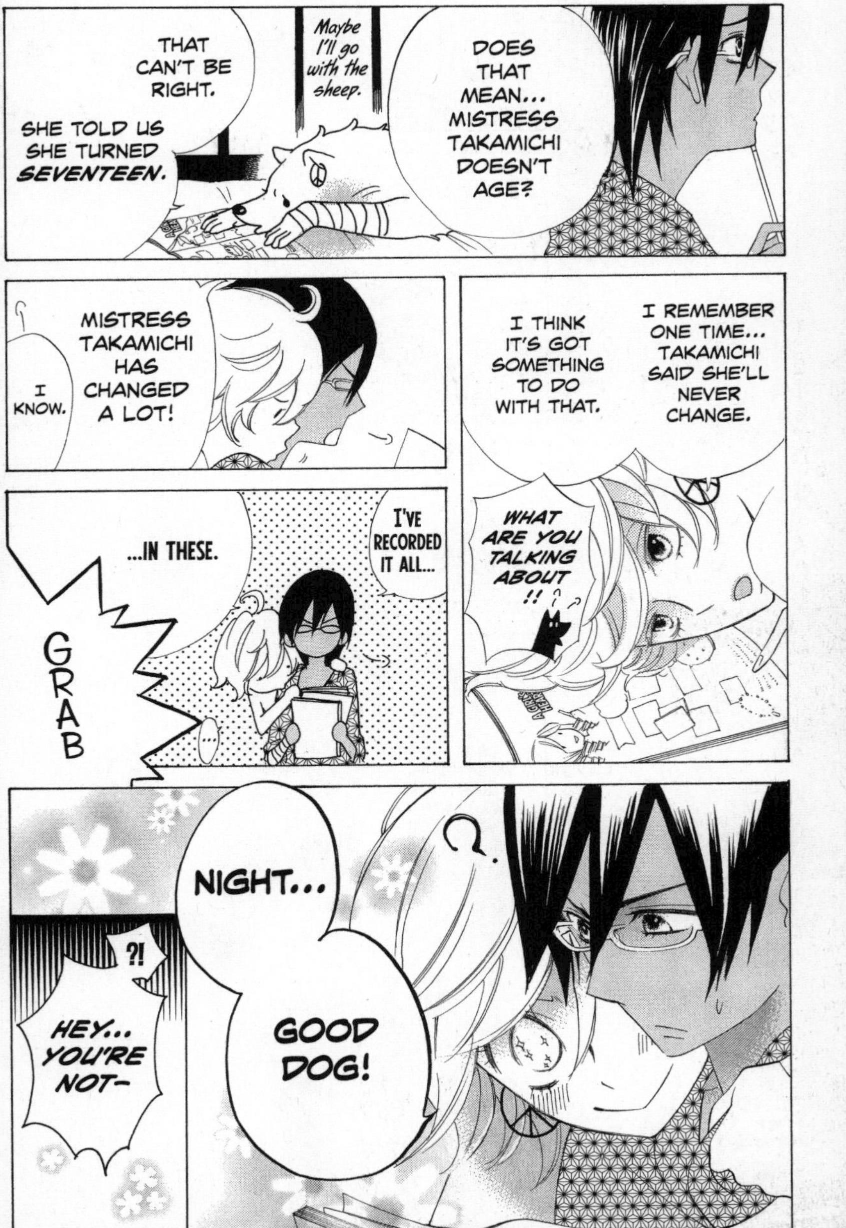
DOES THAT MEAN... MISTRESS TAKAMICHI DOESN'T AGE?
Maybe I'll go with the sheep.
THAT CAN'T BE RIGHT.
SHE TOLD US SHE TURNED *SEVENTEEN*.
I REMEMBER ONE TIME... TAKAMICHI SAID SHE'LL NEVER CHANGE.
I THINK IT'S GOT SOMETHING TO DO WITH THAT.
*WHAT ARE YOU TALKING ABOUT!!*
MISTRESS TAKAMICHI HAS CHANGED A LOT!
I KNOW.
I'VE RECORDED IT ALL...
...IN THESE.
GRAB
...
NIGHT...
GOOD DOG!
?!
*HEY... YOU'RE NOT-*

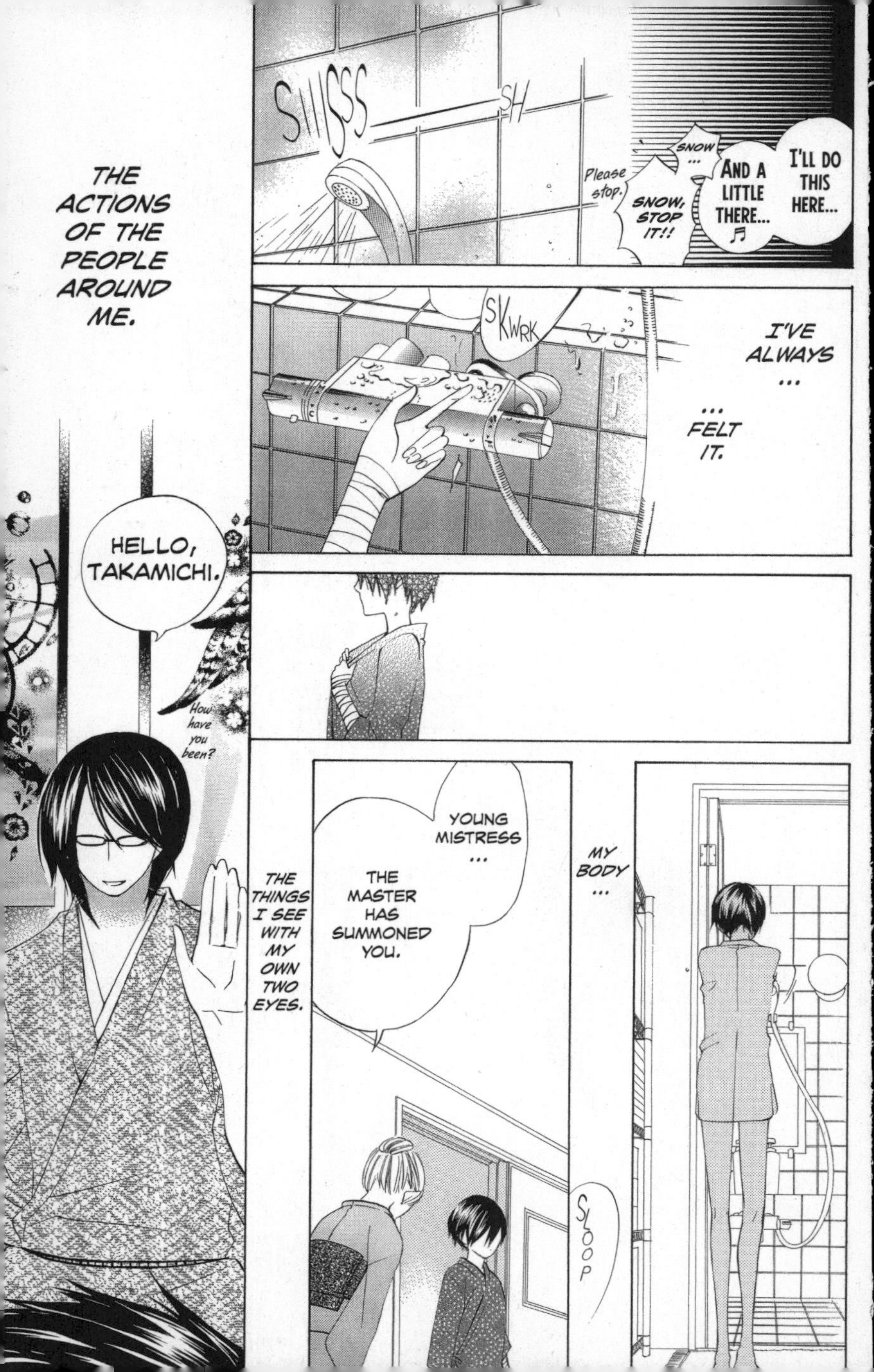
SHHSSS
SH
I'LL DO THIS HERE...
AND A LITTLE THERE... ♬
SNOW...
SNOW, STOP IT!!
Please stop.
SKWRK
I'VE ALWAYS...
...FELT IT.
MY BODY...
YOUNG MISTRESS...
THE MASTER HAS SUMMONED YOU.
THE THINGS I SEE WITH MY OWN TWO EYES.
SLOOP
THE ACTIONS OF THE PEOPLE AROUND ME.
HELLO, TAKAMICHI.
How have you been?

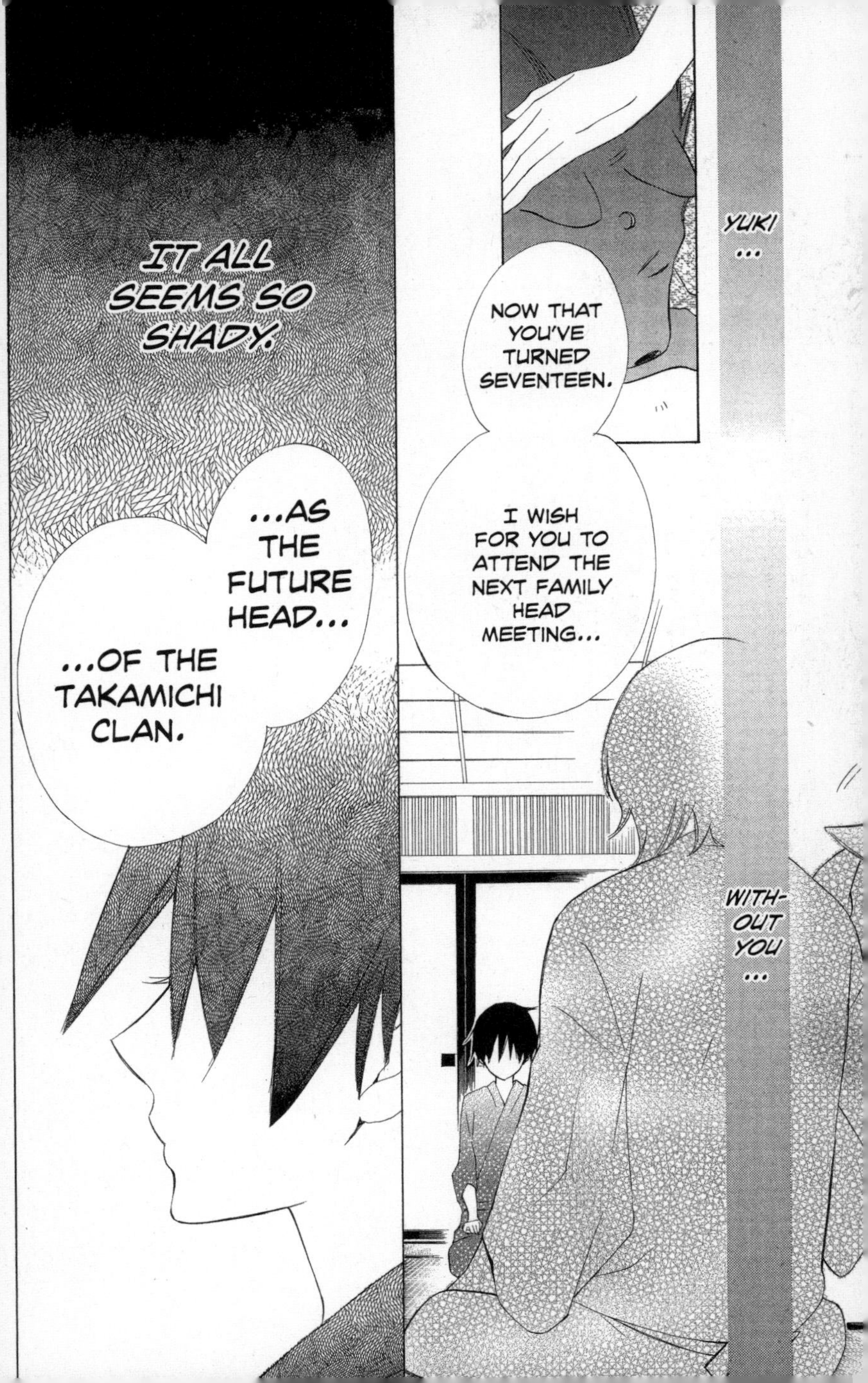
YUKI...
NOW THAT YOU'VE TURNED SEVENTEEN.
I WISH FOR YOU TO ATTEND THE NEXT FAMILY HEAD MEETING...
WITH-OUT YOU...
IT ALL SEEMS SO SHADY.
...AS THE FUTURE HEAD...
...OF THE TAKAMICHI CLAN.

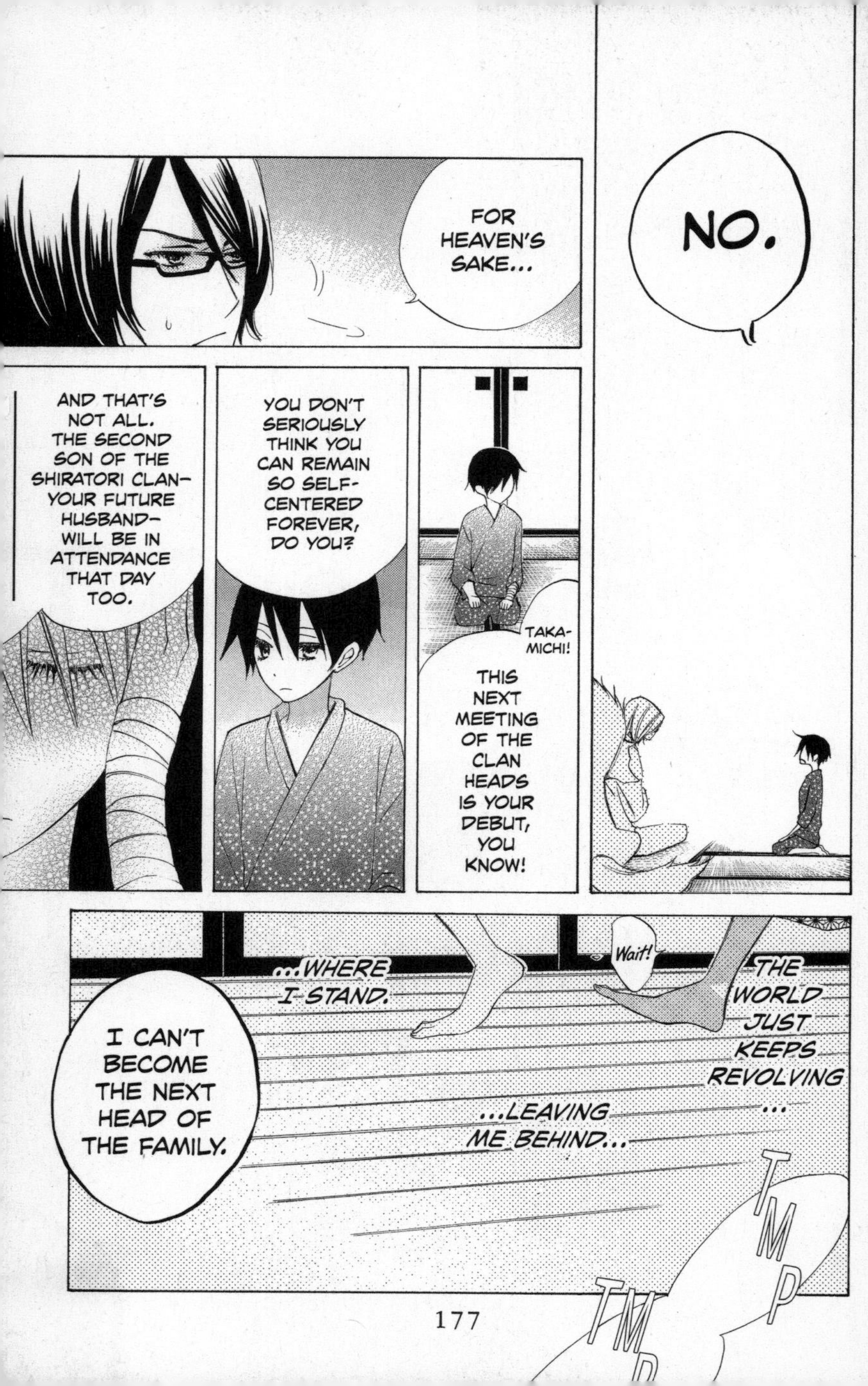
NO.
FOR HEAVEN'S SAKE...
TAKA-MICHI!
THIS NEXT MEETING OF THE CLAN HEADS IS YOUR DEBUT, YOU KNOW!
YOU DON'T SERIOUSLY THINK YOU CAN REMAIN SO SELF-CENTERED FOREVER, DO YOU?
AND THAT'S NOT ALL. THE SECOND SON OF THE SHIRATORI CLAN—YOUR FUTURE HUSBAND—WILL BE IN ATTENDANCE THAT DAY TOO.
THE WORLD JUST KEEPS REVOLVING...
Wait!
...WHERE I STAND.
...LEAVING ME BEHIND...
I CAN'T BECOME THE NEXT HEAD OF THE FAMILY.
TMP
TMP

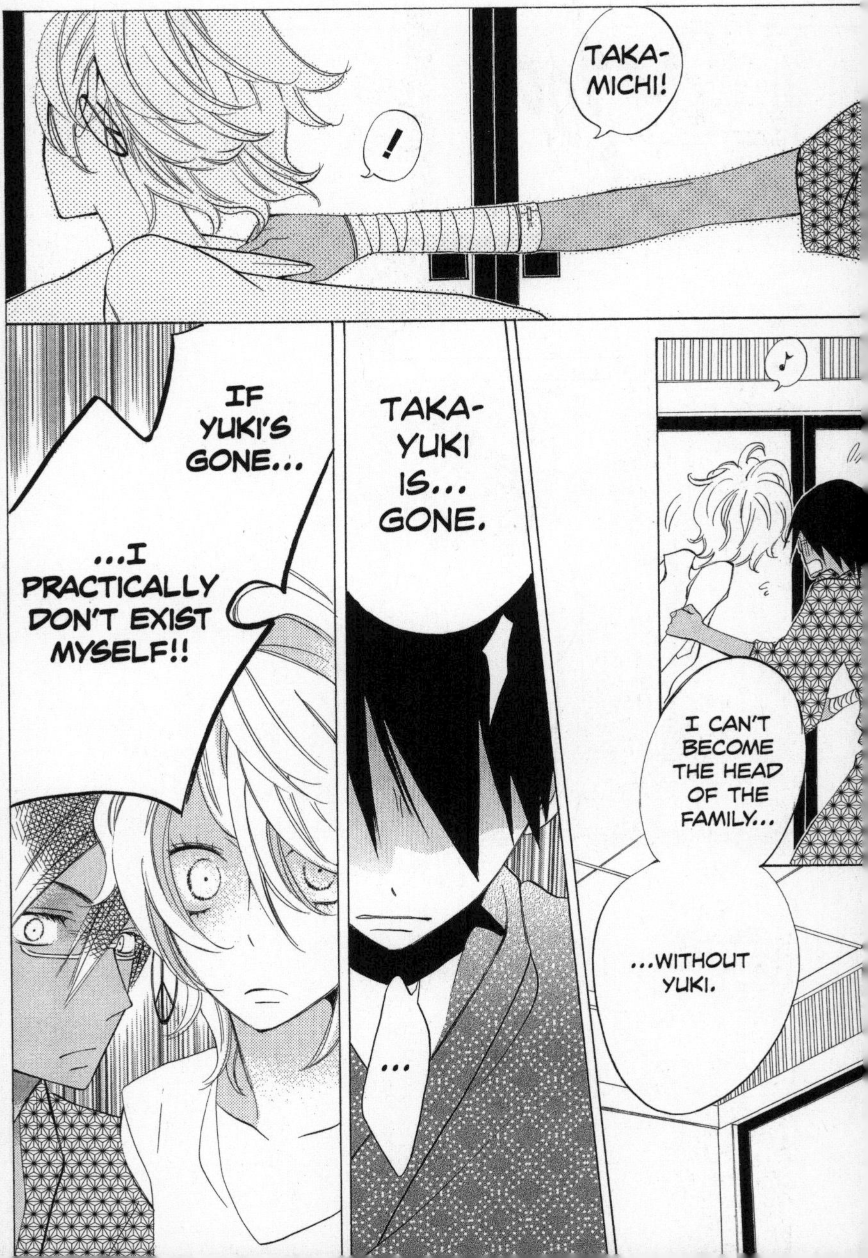
TAKA-MICHI!
!
I CAN'T BECOME THE HEAD OF THE FAMILY...
...WITHOUT YUKI.
TAKA-YUKI IS... GONE.
...
IF YUKI'S GONE...
...I PRACTICALLY DON'T EXIST MYSELF!!

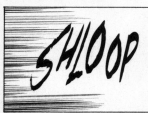

SHLOOP

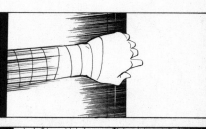

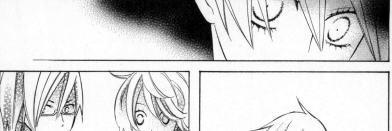

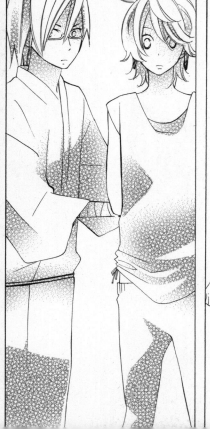

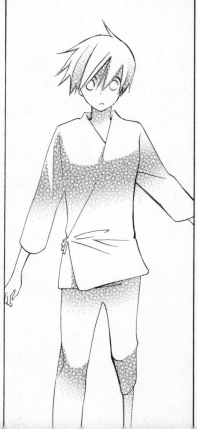

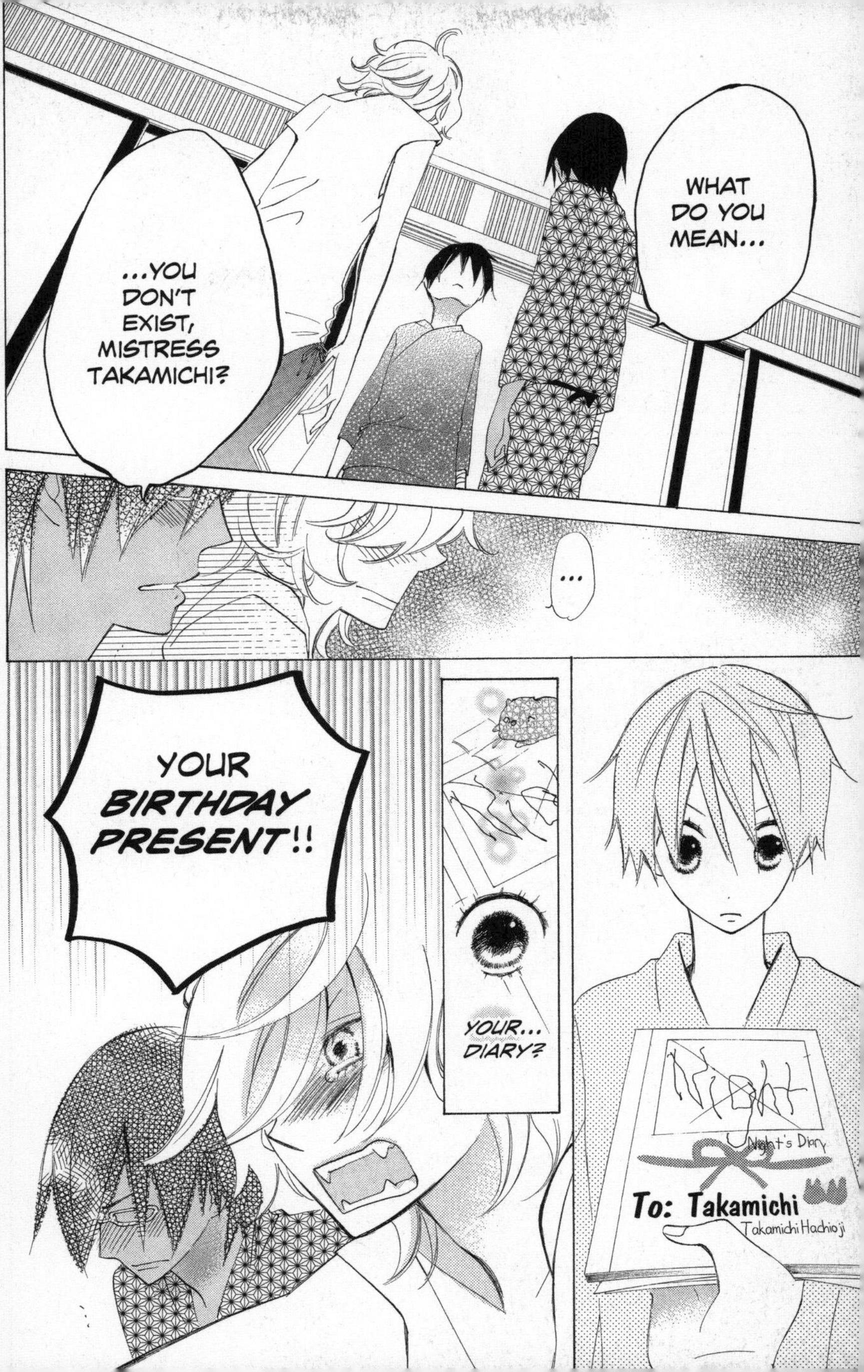
WHAT DO YOU MEAN...
...YOU DON'T EXIST, MISTRESS TAKAMICHI?
...
Night's Diary
To: Takamichi
Takamichi Hachioji
YOUR... DIARY?
YOUR *BIRTHDAY PRESENT*!!

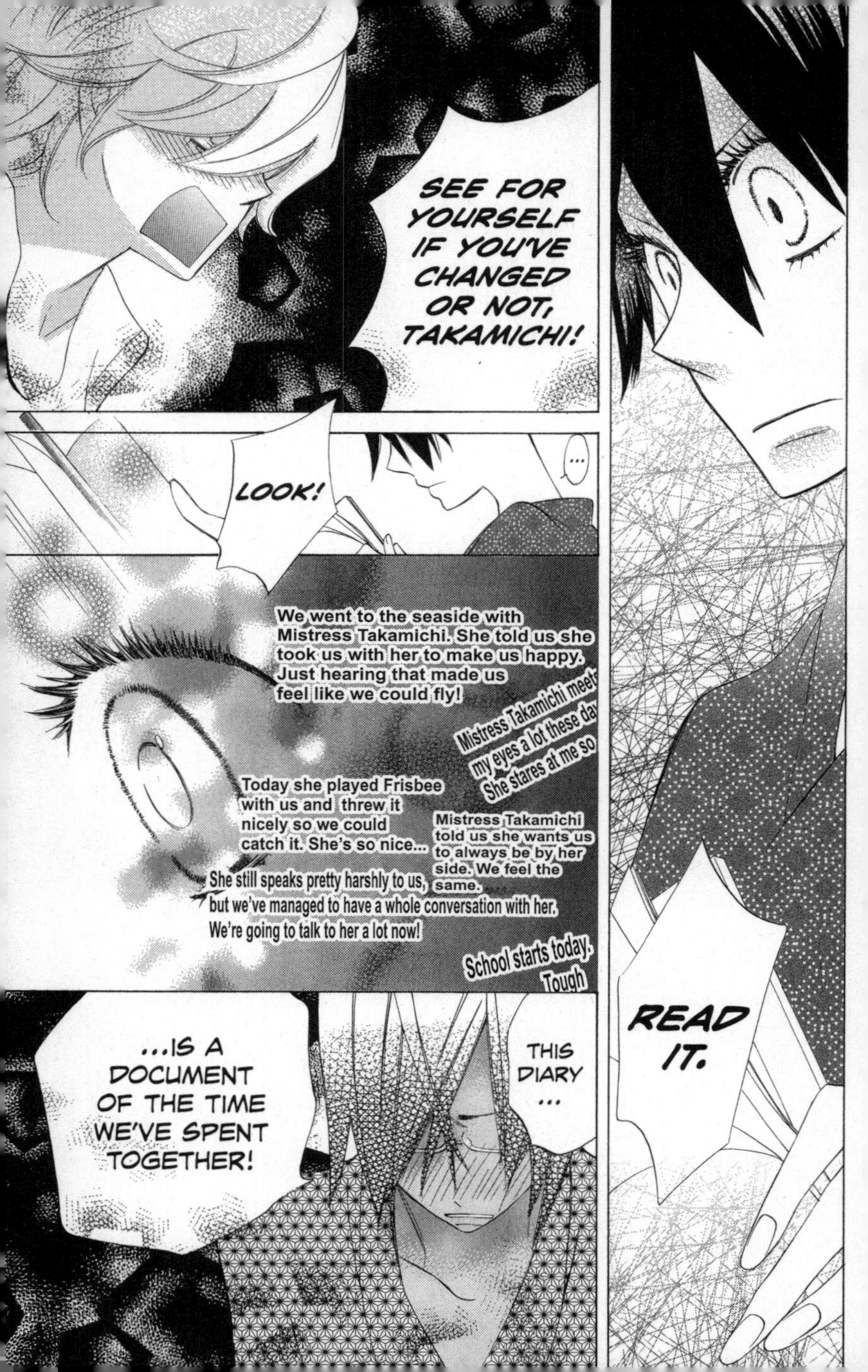
READ IT.
SEE FOR YOURSELF IF YOU'VE CHANGED OR NOT, TAKAMICHI!
...
LOOK!
Mistress Takamichi meets my eyes a lot these day
She stares at me so
We went to the seaside with Mistress Takamichi. She told us she took us with her to make us happy. Just hearing that made us feel like we could fly!
Mistress Takamichi told us she wants us to always be by her side. We feel the same.
Today she played Frisbee with us and threw it nicely so we could catch it. She's so nice...
School starts today. Tough
She still speaks pretty harshly to us, but we've managed to have a whole conversation with her. We're going to talk to her a lot now!
THIS DIARY ...
...IS A DOCUMENT OF THE TIME WE'VE SPENT TOGETHER!

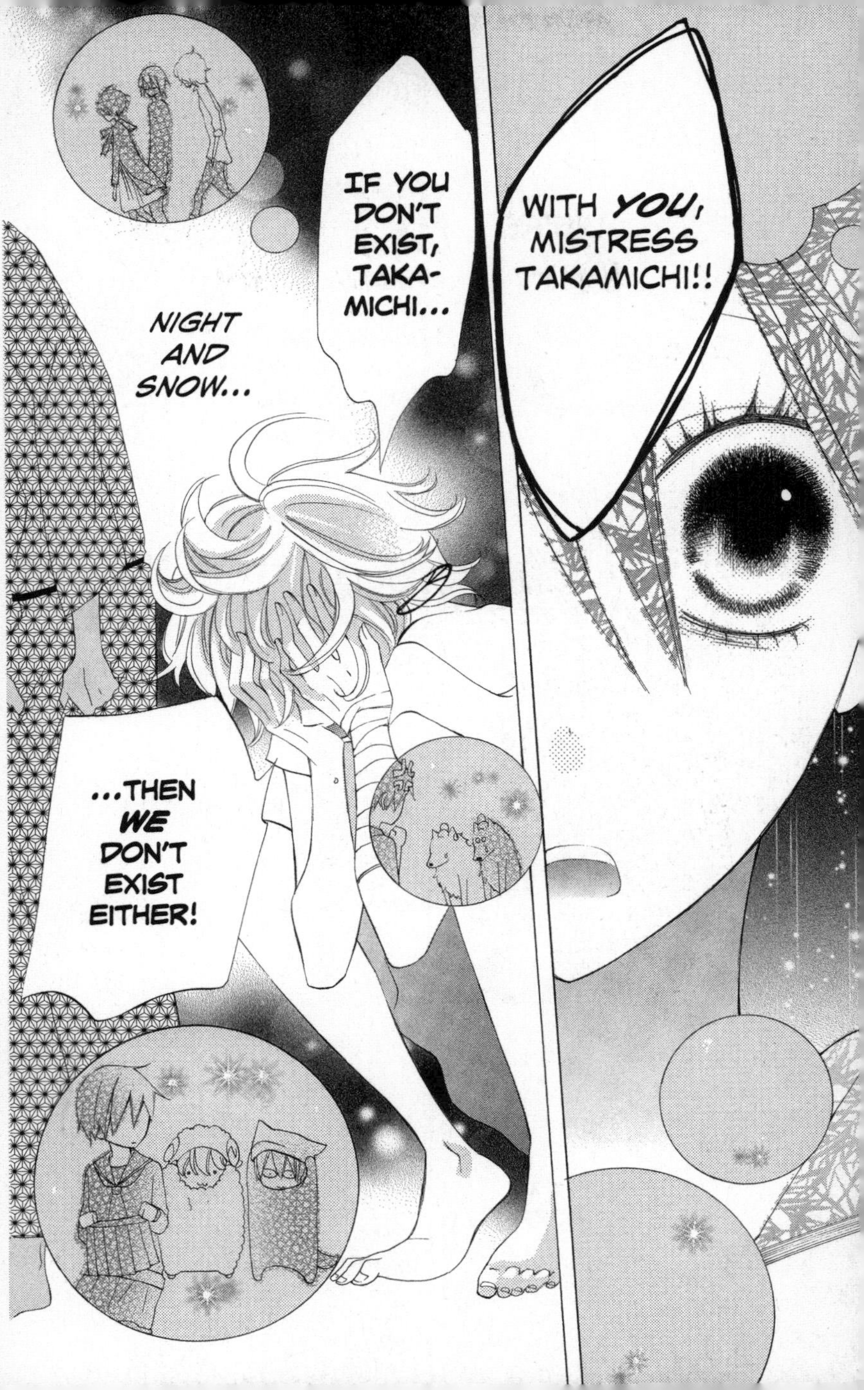
IF YOU DON'T EXIST, TAKA-MICHI...
NIGHT AND SNOW...
...THEN *WE* DON'T EXIST EITHER!
WITH *YOU*, MISTRESS TAKAMICHI!!

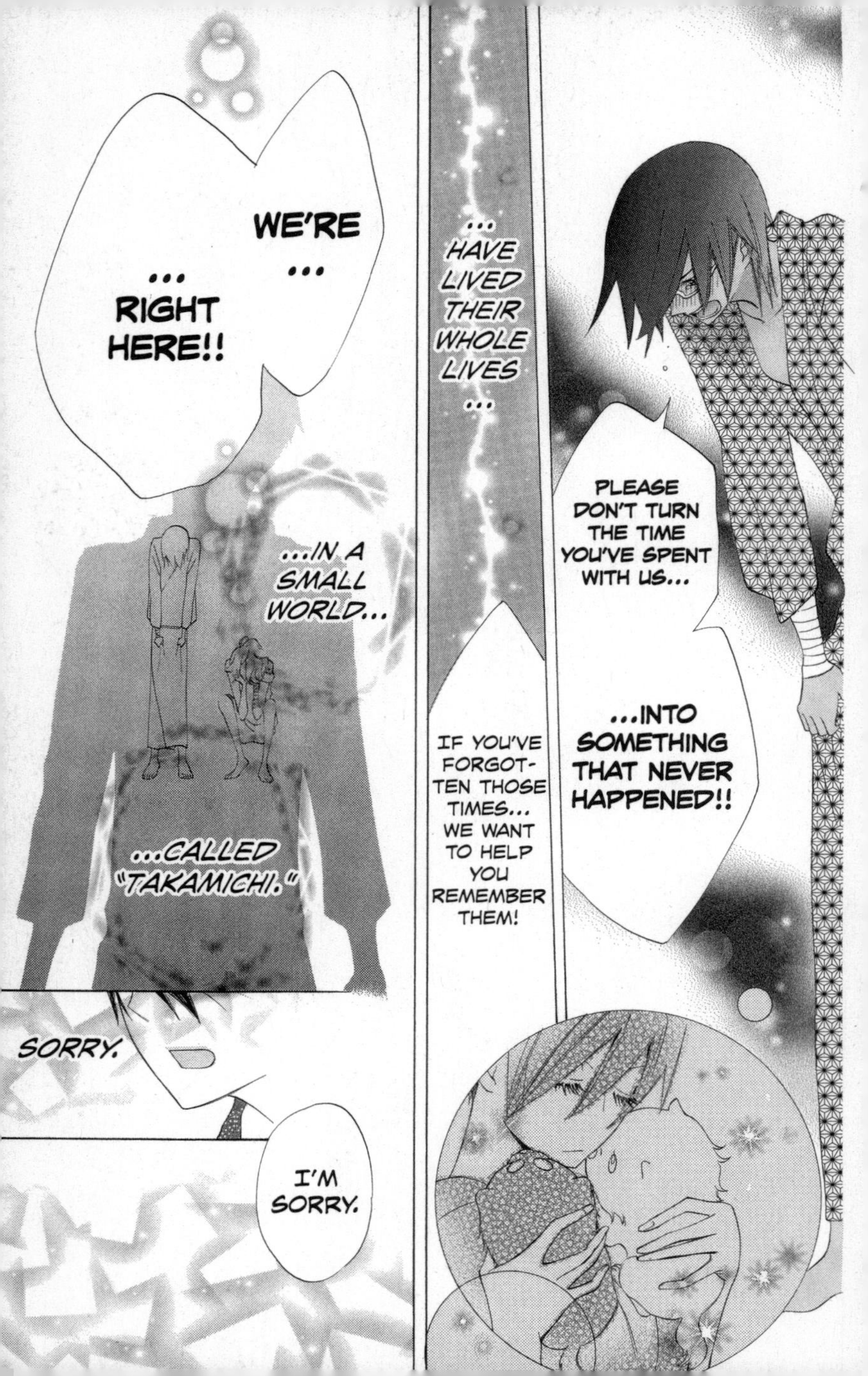
PLEASE DON'T TURN THE TIME YOU'VE SPENT WITH US...
...INTO SOMETHING THAT NEVER HAPPENED!!
IF YOU'VE FORGOT-TEN THOSE TIMES... WE WANT TO HELP YOU REMEMBER THEM!
...HAVE LIVED THEIR WHOLE LIVES...
WE'RE...
...RIGHT HERE!!
...IN A SMALL WORLD...
...CALLED "TAKAMICHI."
SORRY.
I'M SORRY.

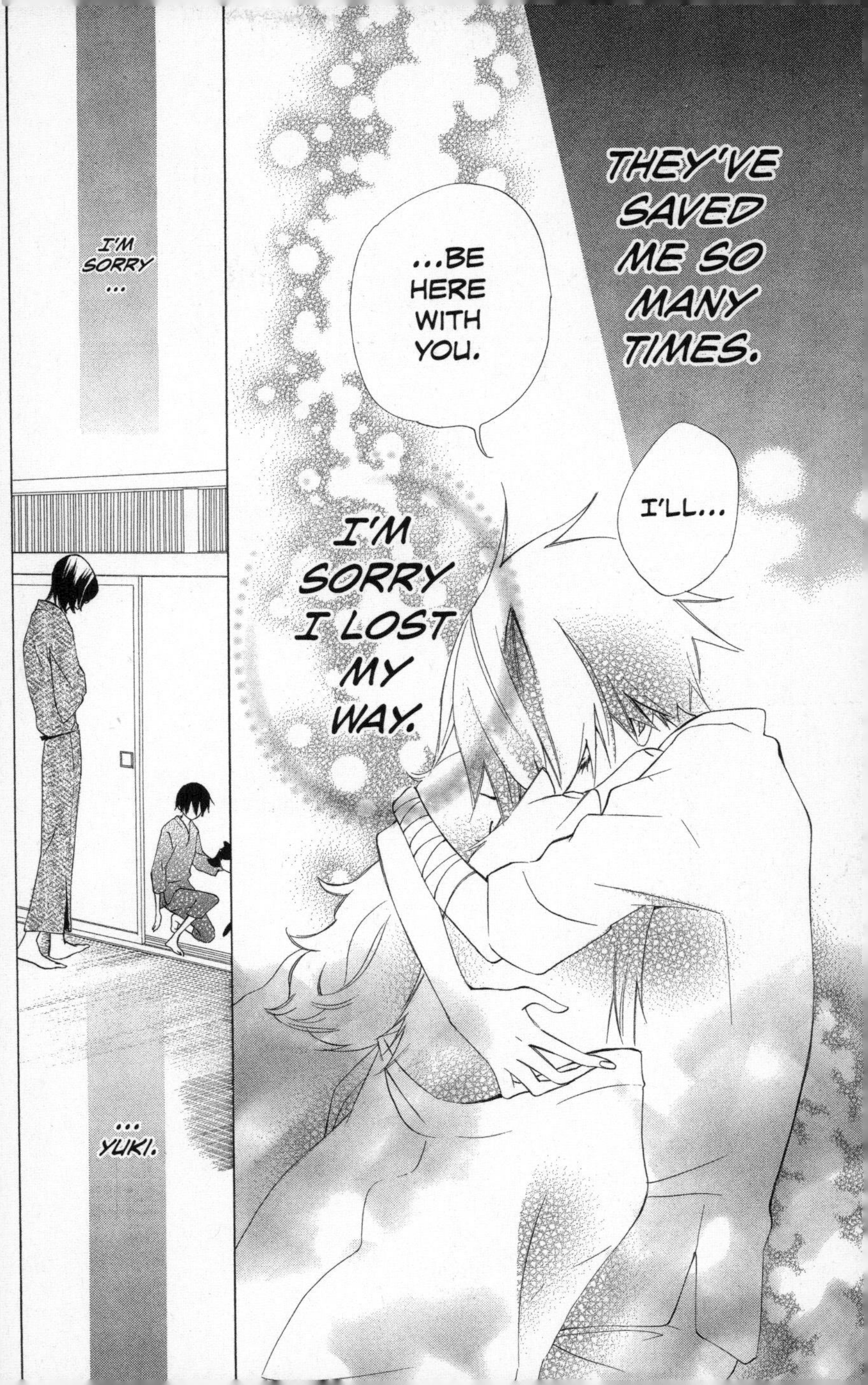
THEY'VE SAVED ME SO MANY TIMES.
I'LL...
...BE HERE WITH YOU.
I'M SORRY I LOST MY WAY.
I'M SORRY...
...YUKI.

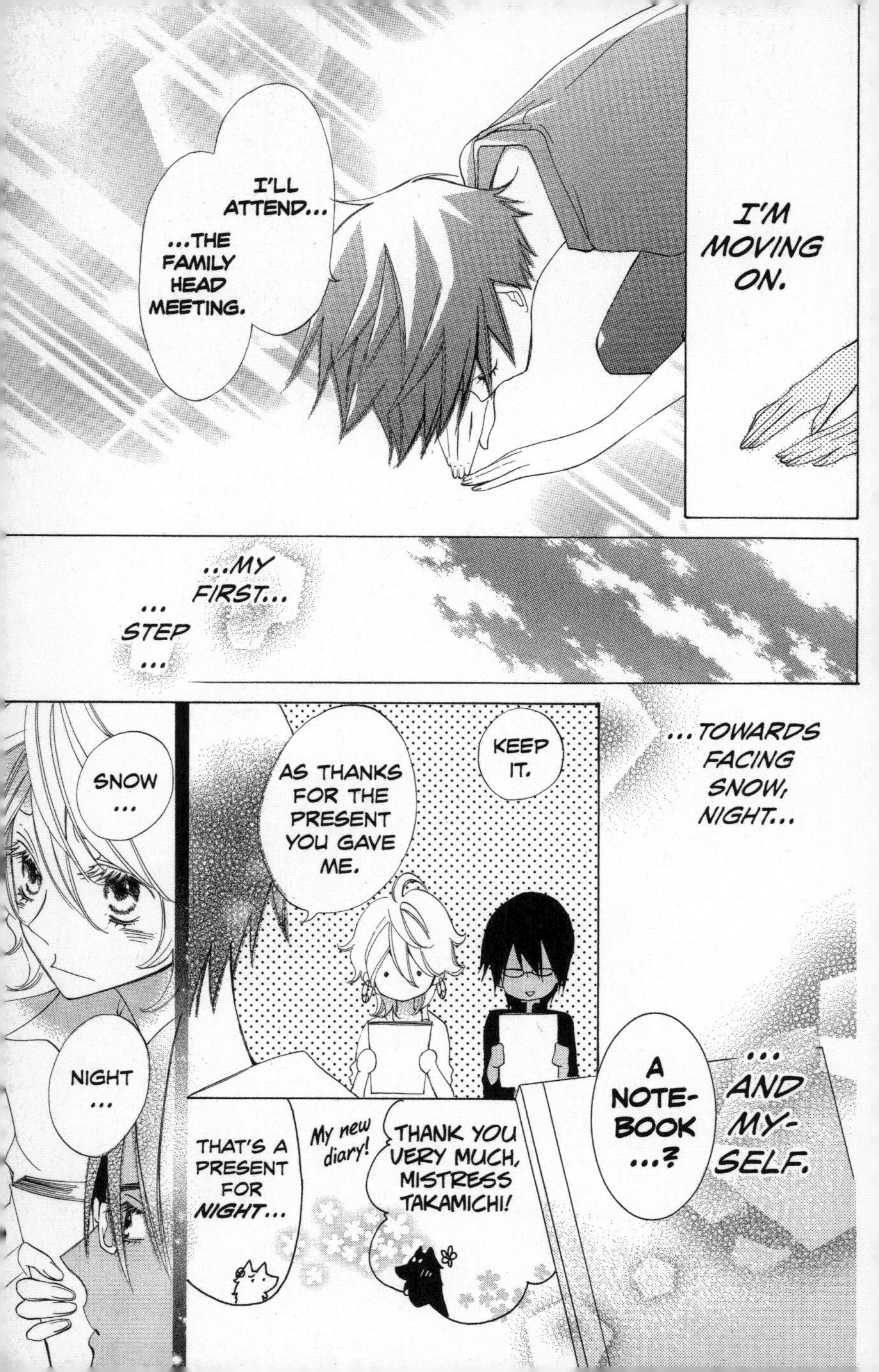
I'M MOVING ON.
I'LL ATTEND... ...THE FAMILY HEAD MEETING.
...MY FIRST... ...STEP...
...TOWARDS FACING SNOW, NIGHT...
...AND MYSELF.
A NOTE-BOOK...?
KEEP IT.
AS THANKS FOR THE PRESENT YOU GAVE ME.
THANK YOU VERY MUCH, MISTRESS TAKAMICHI!
My new diary!
THAT'S A PRESENT FOR NIGHT...
SNOW...
NIGHT...

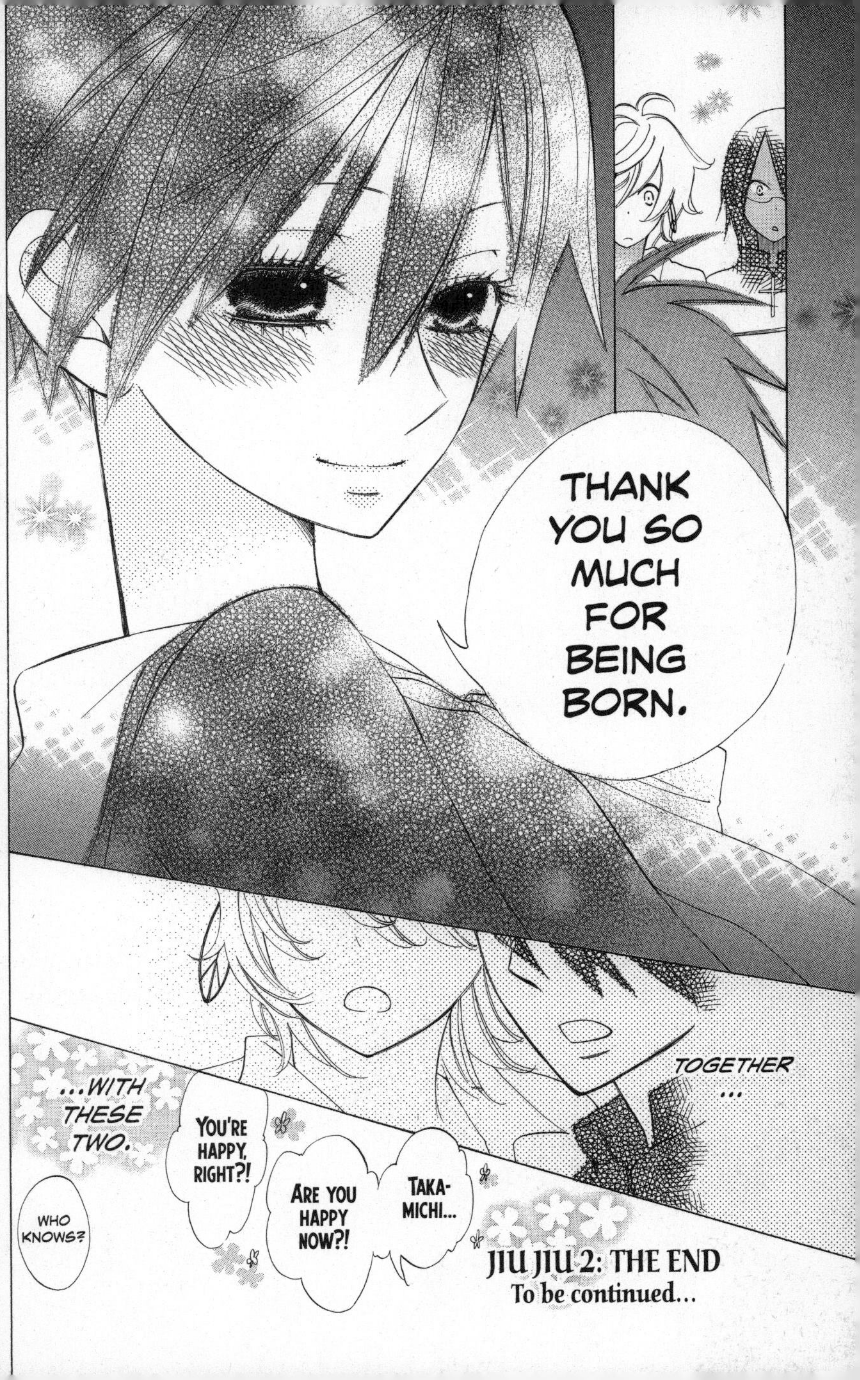
THANK YOU SO MUCH FOR BEING BORN.
TOGETHER ...
TAKA-MICHI...
ARE YOU HAPPY NOW?!
YOU'RE HAPPY, RIGHT?!
...WITH THESE TWO.
WHO KNOWS?
JIU JIU 2: THE END
To be continued...

Thank you very much for reading this volume! I'm looking forward to seeing you again. Tobina

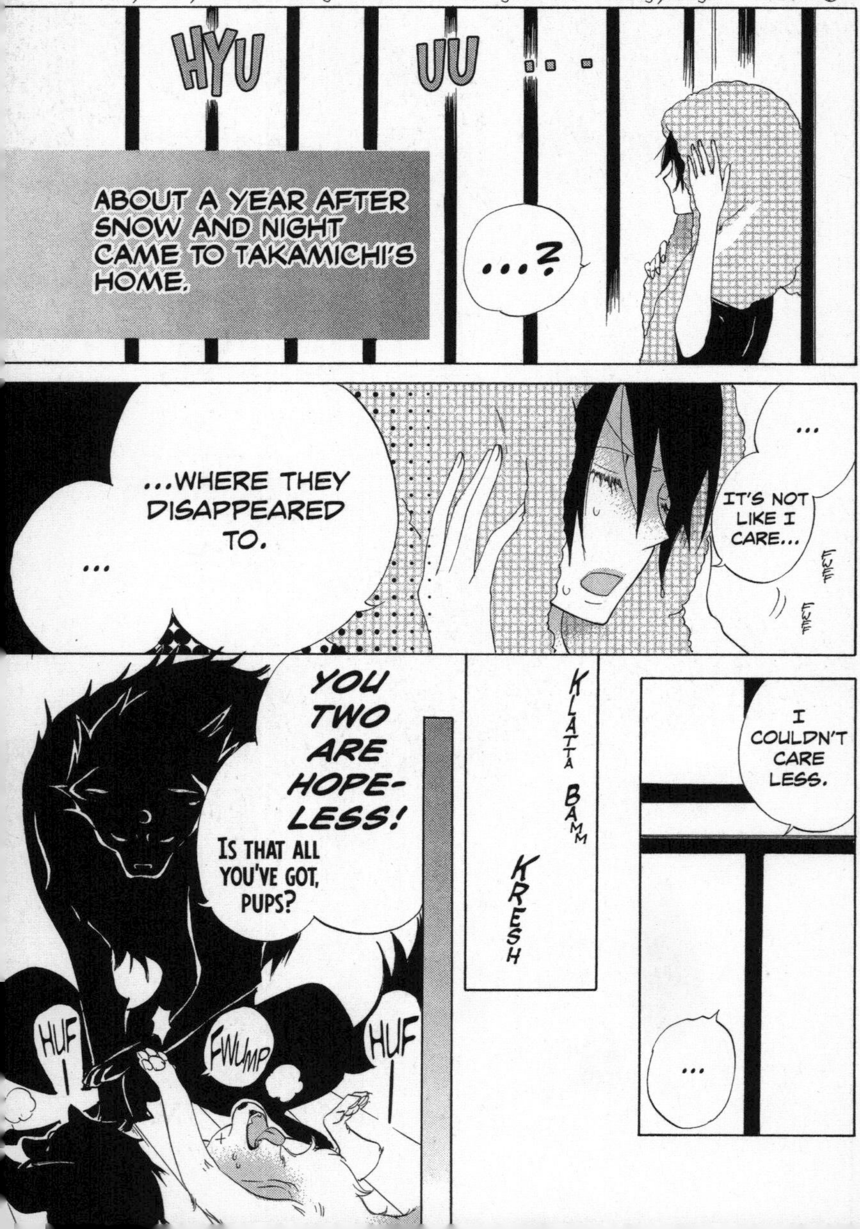
HYU
UU . . .
ABOUT A YEAR AFTER SNOW AND NIGHT CAME TO TAKAMICHI'S HOME.
...?
...
IT'S NOT LIKE I CARE...
...WHERE THEY DISAPPEARED TO.
...
I COULDN'T CARE LESS.
...
KLATTA BAMM
KRESH
YOU TWO ARE HOPE-LESS!
IS THAT ALL YOU'VE GOT, PUPS?
HUF
FWUMP
HUF

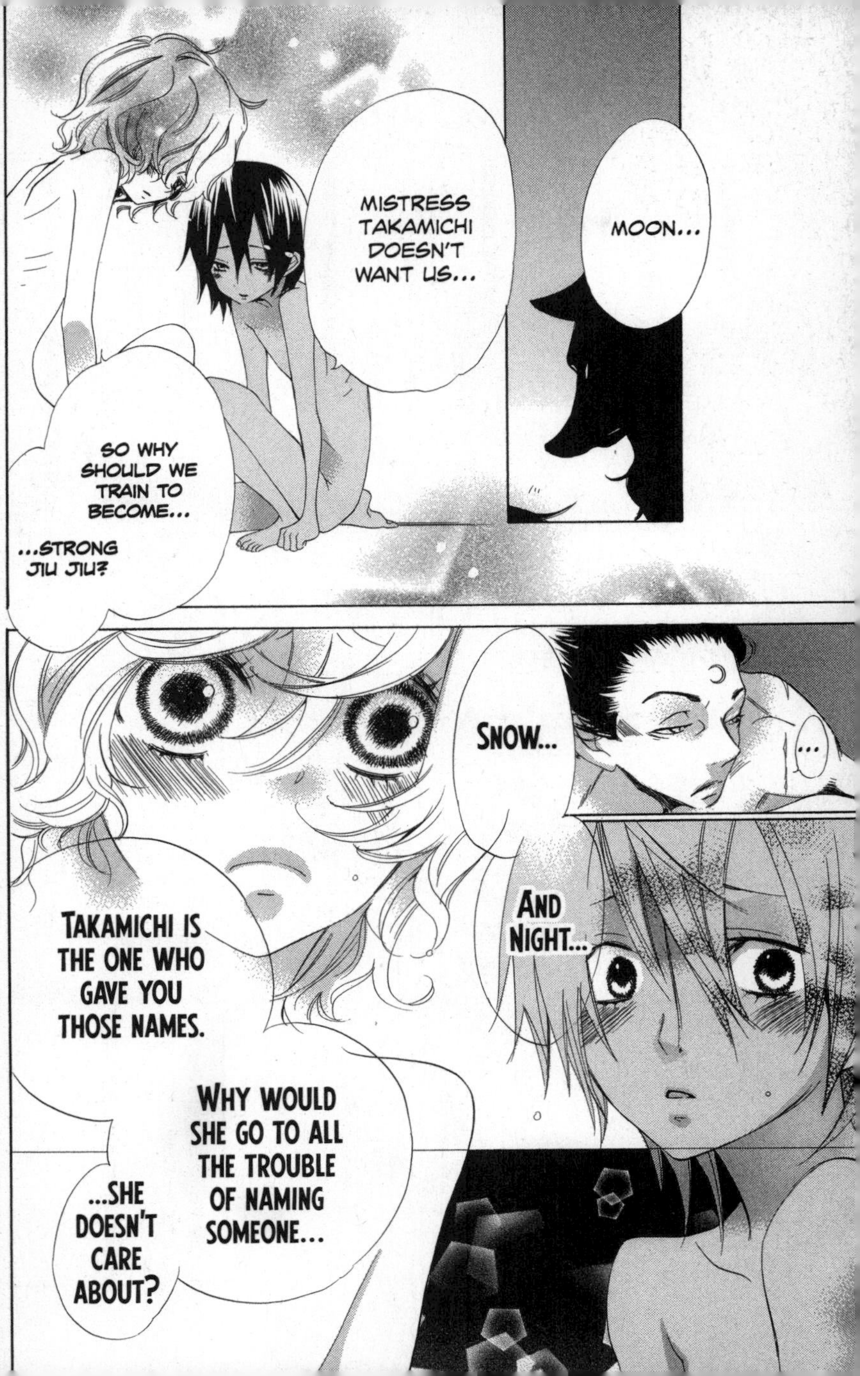
MOON...
MISTRESS TAKAMICHI DOESN'T WANT US...
SO WHY SHOULD WE TRAIN TO BECOME...
...STRONG JIU JIU?
...
SNOW...
AND NIGHT...
TAKAMICHI IS THE ONE WHO GAVE YOU THOSE NAMES.
WHY WOULD SHE GO TO ALL THE TROUBLE OF NAMING SOMEONE...
...SHE DOESN'T CARE ABOUT?

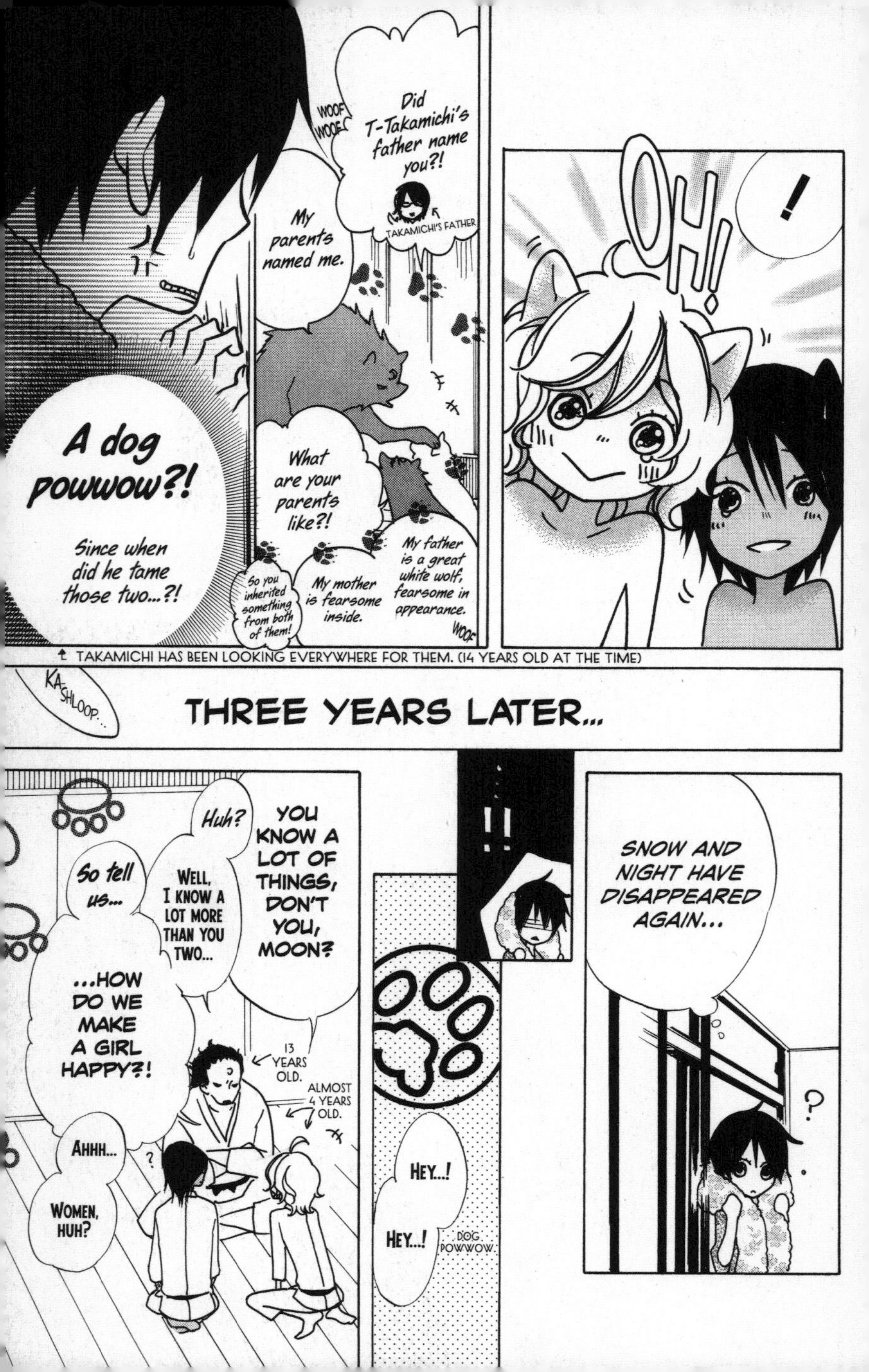
OH!
!
WOOF WOOF
Did T-Takamichi's father name you?!
TAKAMICHI'S FATHER
My parents named me.
What are your parents like?!
My father is a great white wolf, fearsome in appearance.
My mother is fearsome inside.
So you inherited something from both of them!
WOOF
A dog powwow?!
Since when did he tame those two...?!
TAKAMICHI HAS BEEN LOOKING EVERYWHERE FOR THEM. (14 YEARS OLD AT THE TIME)
THREE YEARS LATER...
KA-SHLOOP...
SNOW AND NIGHT HAVE DISAPPEARED AGAIN...
?
!!
HEY...!
HEY...!
DOG POWWOW.
YOU KNOW A LOT OF THINGS, DON'T YOU, MOON?
Huh?
WELL, I KNOW A LOT MORE THAN YOU TWO...
So tell us...
...HOW DO WE MAKE A GIRL HAPPY?!
13 YEARS OLD.
ALMOST 4 YEARS OLD.
AHHH...
?
WOMEN, HUH?

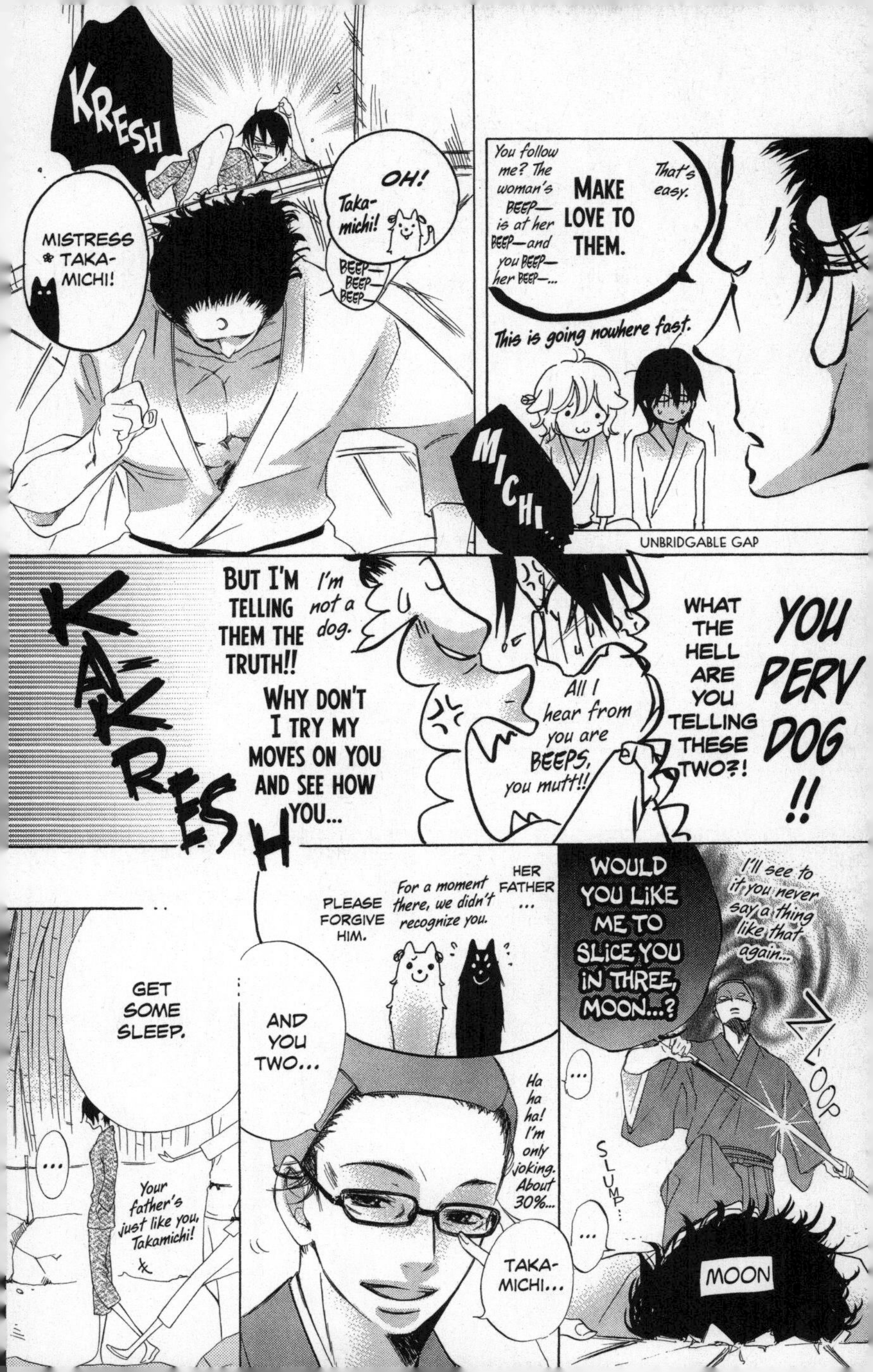
That's easy.
MAKE LOVE TO THEM.
You follow me? The woman's BEEP— is at her BEEP—and you BEEP— her BEEP—...
This is going nowhere fast.
MICHI...
UNBRIDGABLE GAP
KRESH
OH! Takamichi!
BEEP— BEEP— BEEP—
MISTRESS TAKAMICHI!
YOU PERV DOG!!
WHAT THE HELL ARE YOU TELLING THESE TWO?!
All I hear from you are BEEPS, you mutt!!
I'm not a dog.
BUT I'M TELLING THEM THE TRUTH!!
WHY DON'T I TRY MY MOVES ON YOU AND SEE HOW YOU...
KA-KRESH
I'll see to it you never say a thing like that again...
WOULD YOU LIKE ME TO SLICE YOU IN THREE, MOON...?
ZLOOP
...
SLUMP...
...
MOON
HER FATHER...
For a moment there, we didn't recognize you.
PLEASE FORGIVE HIM.
AND YOU TWO...
Ha ha ha! I'm only joking. About 30%...
TAKAMICHI...
......
GET SOME SLEEP.
...
Your father's just like you, Takamichi!

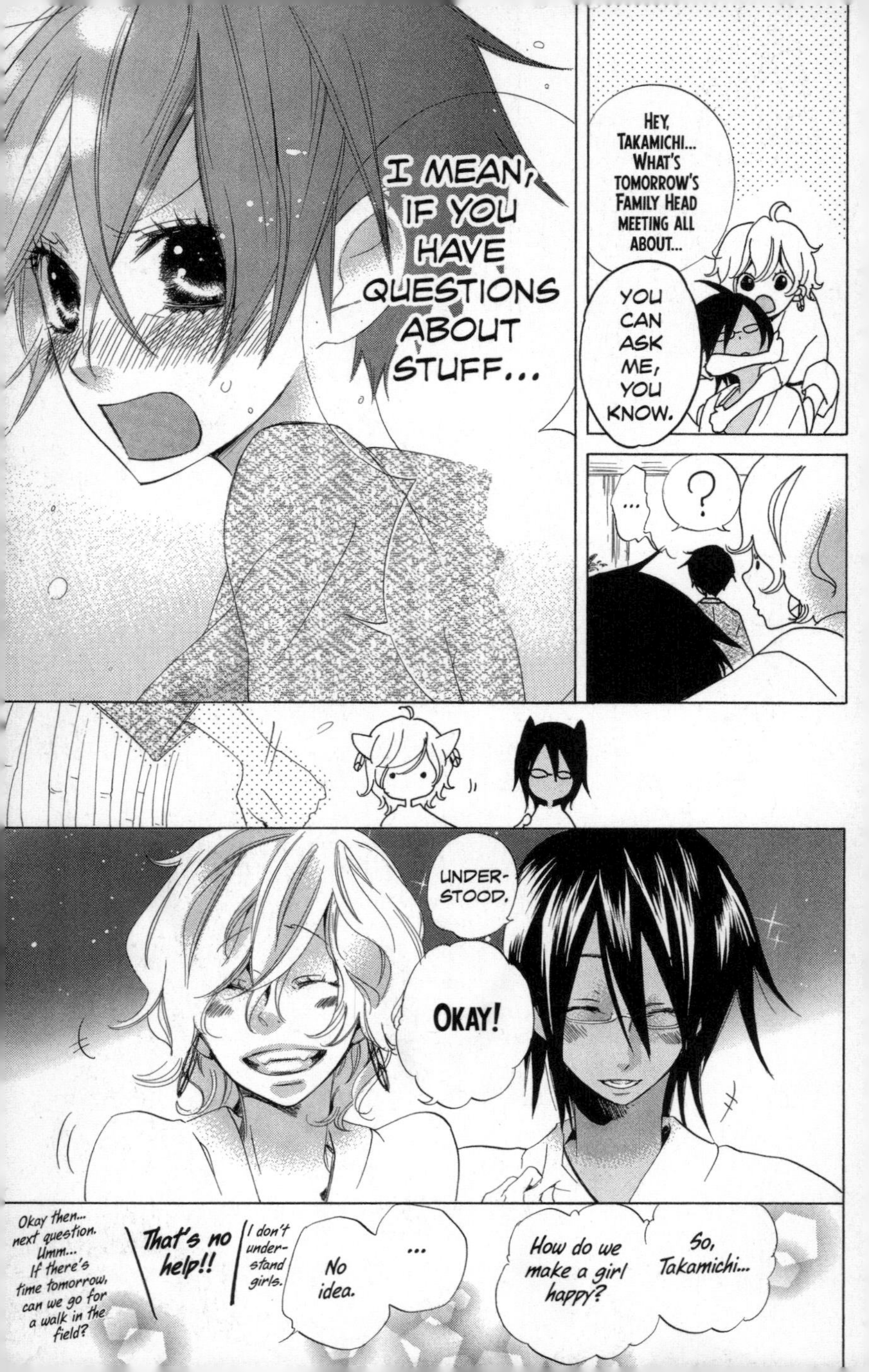
HEY, TAKAMICHI... WHAT'S TOMORROW'S FAMILY HEAD MEETING ALL ABOUT...
YOU CAN ASK ME, YOU KNOW.
...
?
I MEAN, IF YOU HAVE QUESTIONS ABOUT STUFF...
UNDER-STOOD.
OKAY!
So, Takamichi...
How do we make a girl happy?
...
No idea.
I don't under-stand girls.
That's no help!!
Okay then... next question. Umm... If there's time tomorrow, can we go for a walk in the field?

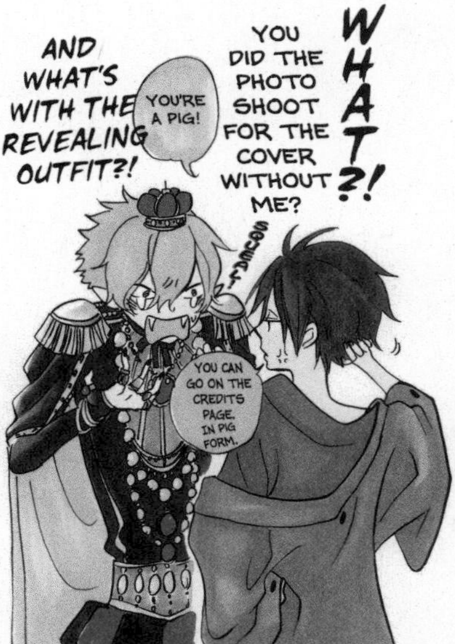
WHAT?!
YOU DID THE PHOTO SHOOT FOR THE COVER WITHOUT ME?
YOU'RE A PIG!
AND WHAT'S WITH THE REVEALING OUTFIT?!
SQUEEZE!
YOU CAN GO ON THE CREDITS PAGE. IN PIG FORM.

**Touya Tobina is from Tokyo. Her birthday is May 23 and her blood type is O. In 2005, her series *Keppeki Shonen Kanzen Soubi* (*Clean Freak Fully Equipped*) won the grand prize in the 30th Hakusensha Athena Shinjin Taisho (Hakusensha Athena Newcomers Awards).**

# JIU JIU
## VOL. 2
### Shojo Beat Edition

## STORY AND ART BY
# Touya Tobina

English Translation/Tetsuichiro Miyaki
English Adaptation/Annette Roman
Touch-up Art & Lettering/James Gaubatz
Design/Yukiko Whitley
Editor/Annette Roman

JIUJIU by Touya Tobina
© Touya Tobina 2010
All rights reserved.
First published in Japan in 2010 by HAKUSENSHA, Inc., Tokyo.
English language translation rights arranged with HAKUSENSHA, Inc., Tokyo.

Printed in the U.S.A.

Published by VIZ Media, LLC
P.O. Box 77010
San Francisco, CA 94107

10 9 8 7 6 5 4 3 2 1
First printing, October 2012

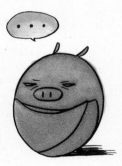

www.viz.com

www.shojobeat.com

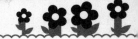
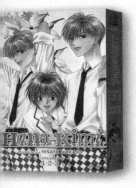 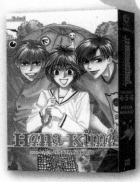 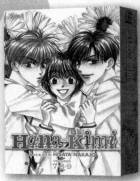

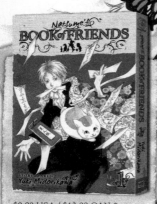

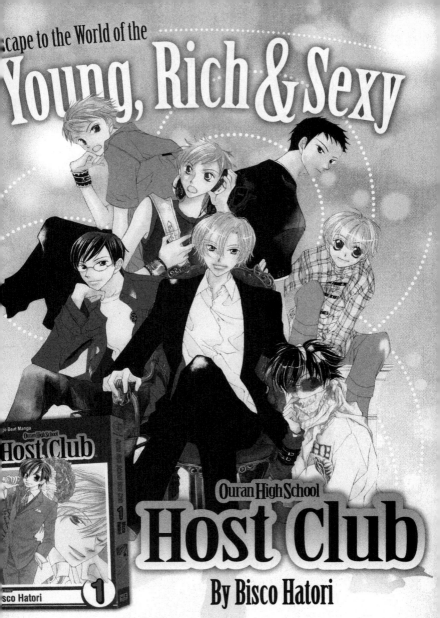

...cape to the World of the

# Young, Rich & Sexy

*Ouran High School*

# Host Club

## By Bisco Hatori

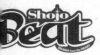

RATED
TEEN
ratings.viz.com

VIZ
media
www.viz.com

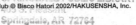

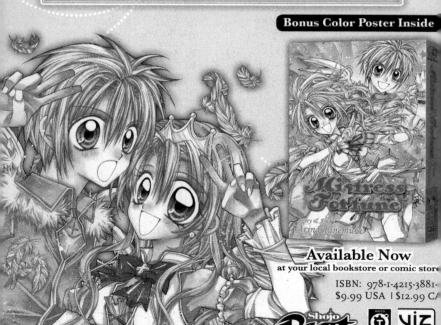

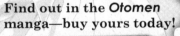
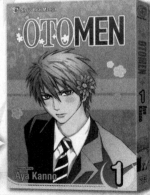
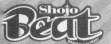

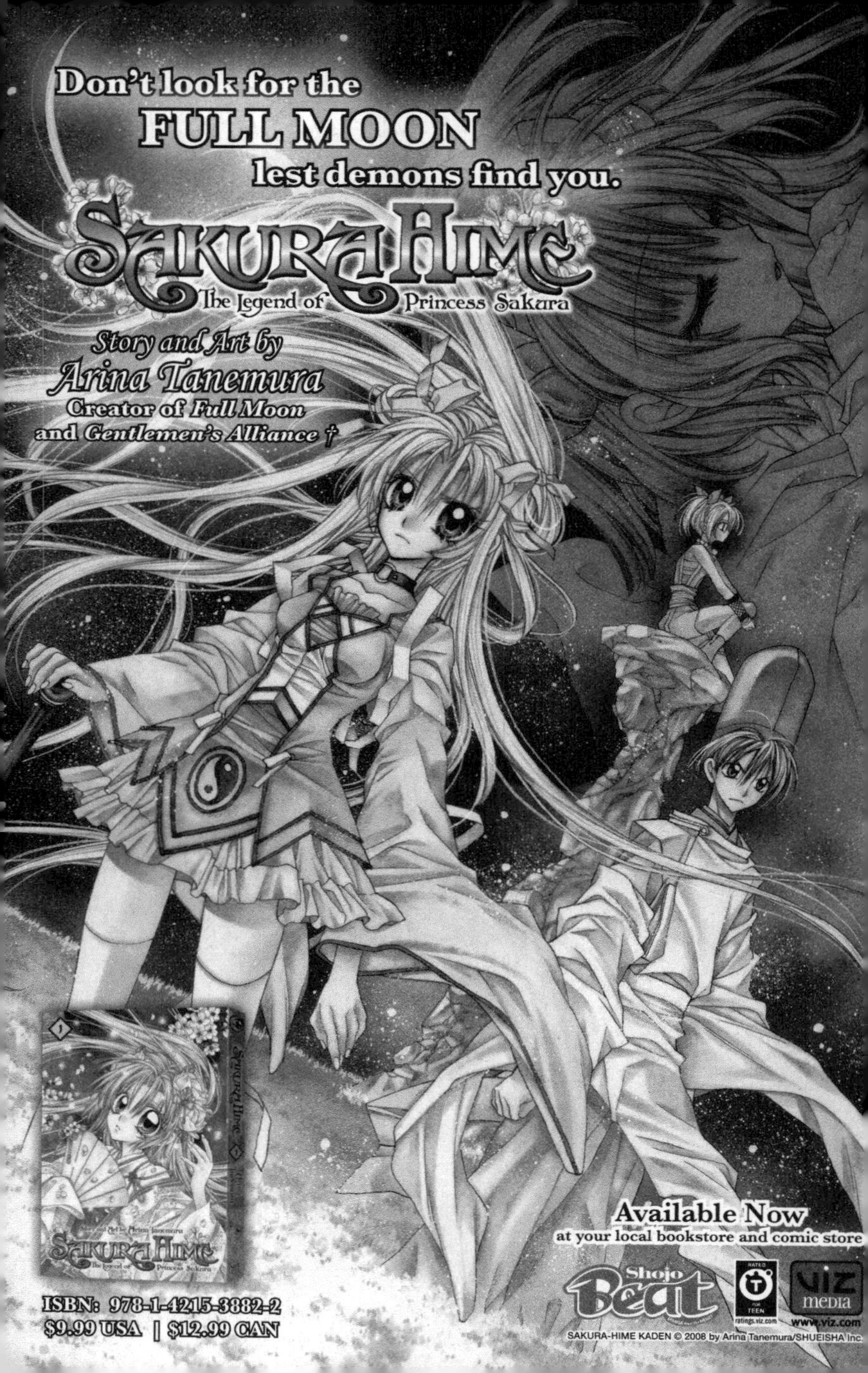
Don't look for the
FULL MOON
lest demons find you.
SAKURA HIME
The Legend of Princess Sakura
Story and Art by
Arina Tanemura
Creator of Full Moon
and Gentlemen's Alliance †
Available Now
at your local bookstore and comic store
ISBN: 978-1-4215-3882-2
$9.99 USA | $12.99 CAN
Shojo Beat
RATED T FOR TEEN
ratings.viz.com
VIZ media
www.viz.com
SAKURA-HIME KADEN © 2008 by Arina Tanemura/SHUEISHA Inc.

# This is the last page.

In keeping with the original Japanese comic format, this book reads from right to left—so action, sound effects, and word balloons are completely reversed. This preserves the orientation of the original artwork—plus, it's fun! Check out the diagram shown here to get the hang of things, and then turn to the other side of the book to get started!

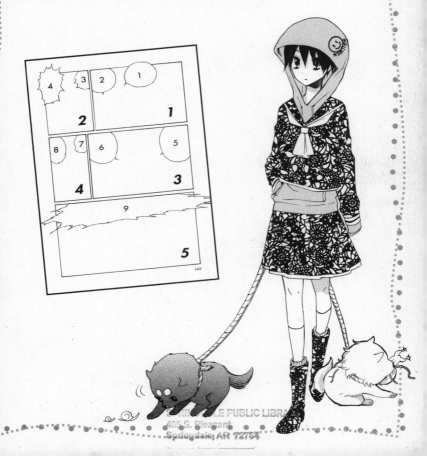